The Emotional Experience of Adoption

Adoption is an extremely complex and emotionally demanding process for all those involved. This book explores the emotional experience of adoption from a psychoanalytic perspective, and demonstrates how psychoanalytic understanding and treatment can contribute to thinking about and working with adopted children and their families.

Drawing on psychoanalytic, attachment and child development theory, and detailed in-depth clinical case discussion, *The Emotional Experience of Adoption* explores issues such as:

- the emotional experience of children placed for adoption, and how this both shapes and is shaped by unconscious processes in the child's inner world
- how psychoanalytic child psychotherapy can help as a distinctive source of understanding and as a treatment for children who are either in the process of being adopted or already adopted
- how such understanding can inform planning and decision making amongst professionals and carers.

The Emotional Experience of Adoption explains and accounts for the emotional and psychological complexities involved for the children, parents and professionals in adoption. It will be of interest and relevance to anyone involved at a personal level in the adoption process or professionals working in the fields of adoption, social work, child mental health, foster care and family support.

Debbie Hindle is Head of the Clinical Training in Child and Adolescent Psychotherapy at the Scottish Institute of Human Relations, and also works in the Looked After and Accommodated Child and Adolescent Mental Health Service in Glasgow.

Graham Shulman is a consultant child and adolescent psychotherapist who currently works in NHS Lanarkshire. He was until recently Senior Tutor for the Clinical Training in Child and Adolescent Psychotherapy and Organising Tutor for the Therapeutic Skills with Children and Young People Course at the Scottish Institute of Human Relations. He is Joint Editor of the *Journal of Child Psychotherapy*.

The Emotional Experience of Adoption

A psychoanalytic perspective

**Edited by Debbie Hindle
and Graham Shulman**

Routledge
Taylor & Francis Group

LONDON AND NEW YORK

First published 2008
by Routledge
2 Park Square, Milton Park, Abingdon, Oxon OX14 4RN

Simultaneously published in the USA and Canada
by Routledge
270 Madison Ave, New York, NY 10016

*Routledge is an imprint of the Taylor & Francis Group, an informa
business*

© 2008 Debbie Hindle and Graham Shulman, selection and editorial
matter; individual chapters, the contributors

Typeset in Times New Roman by
HWA Text and Data Management, Tunbridge Wells
Printed and bound in Great Britain by
Antony Rowe Ltd, Chippenham, Wiltshire

British Library Cataloguing in Publication Data
A catalogue record for this book is available from the British Library

Library of Congress Cataloging-in-Publication Data
A catalog record for this book has been requested

ISBN10: 0–415–37275–5 (hbk)
ISBN10: 0–415–37276–3 (pbk)
ISBN10: 0–203–92936–5 (ebk)

ISBN13: 978–0–415–37275–6 (hbk)
ISBN13: 978–0–415–37276–3 (pbk)
ISBN13: 978–0–203–92936–0 (ebk)

Contents

Notes on editors and contributors

Pamela Bartram trained at the Tavistock Clinic and is a consultant child and adolescent psychotherapist, working in the NHS. Originally a music therapist, she retains a particular interest in the non-verbal aspects of therapeutic communication and has developed further interests in the curative factors in psychoanalytic interventions and the development of attachment relationships complicated by adoption and by disability. Her publications include a chapter in *Autism and Personality* (edited by A. Alvarez and S. Reid, Routledge, 1999), and *Understanding Your Young Child with Special Needs*, one of a series of books from the Tavistock Clinic, published by Jessica Kingsley.

Kate Cairns is a social worker and teacher. With her partner Brian and their three birth children she shared in providing permanence to twelve other children. She is now Training Director for Akamas, a company producing and providing online accredited qualifications for the children's services workforce.

Francesca Calvocoressi had a career in art history and publishing before qualifying as a child and adolescent psychotherapist. She works in the NHS in Scotland and at the Scottish Institute of Human Relations where she trained. Her particular interests are early infant–parent relationships and fostered and adopted children. She is an active campaigner for the wider recognition of child psychotherapy in Scotland.

Caroline Case trained at the Scottish Institute of Human Relations, Edinburgh. She is a child and adolescent psychotherapist at the Knowle Clinic, Bristol and an Analytical Art Therapist in private practice. She has published widely. Her most recent publications are: *Imagining Animals: Art, Psychotherapy and Primitive States of Mind* (Routledge, 2005); *The Handbook of Art Therapy*, 2nd edition (Routledge, 2006), co-written with Tessa Dalley; *Supervision of Art Psychotherapy: A Theoretical and Practical Handbook* (Routledge, 2007), co-edited with Joy Schaverien and *Art Therapy with Children: From Infancy to Adolescence* (Routledge, 2007), co-edited with Tessa Dalley.

Tessa Dalley is a child and adolescent psychotherapist working at the Northgate Clinic, London and the Parent–Infant Project at the Anna Freud Centre, London. She also has a small private practice. She is a qualified art therapist and has published a number of books, reviews and articles on art therapy and child psychotherapy. Her most recent publications are *The Handbook of Art Therapy*, 2nd edition (Routledge, 2006), co-written with Caroline Case and *Art Therapy with Children: From Infancy to Adolescence* (Routledge, 2007), co-edited with Caroline Case.

Judith Edwards is a consultant child and adolescent psychotherapist working and teaching on various courses at the Tavistock Clinic, London, where she is the Organizing Tutor of the MA in Psychoanalytic Studies. A previous editor of the *Journal of Child Psychotherapy*, she also edited *Being Alive: Building on the Work of Anne Alvarez* (Routledge, 2002). Other recent publications, apart from those in academic journals, include chapters in *Autism and Personality* (edited by A. Alvarez and S. Reid, Routledge, 1999), *Personality Development: A Psychoanalytic Perspective* (edited by D. Hindle and M. Vaciago Smith, Routledge, 1999) and a chapter on the poetry of Yeats, 'The elusive pursuit of insight', in *Acquainted with the Night* (edited by H. Canham and C. Satyamurti, Karnac Books, 2003).

Debbie Hindle is a child and adolescent psychotherapist, trained at the Tavistock Clinic, London. She is currently the Organizing Tutor for the Clinical Training in Child Psychotherapy at the Scottish Institute of Human Relations and works clinically in the Looked After and Accommodated Child and Adolescent Mental Health Service in Glasgow. She has published numerous papers in the *Journal of Child Psychotherapy* and other professional journals, and with M. Vaciago Smith has co-edited *Personality Development: A Psychoanalytic Perspective* (Routledge, 1999). She received her Doctorate in Psychoanalytic Psychotherapy from the Tavistock Clinic/UEL in 2000 for her work on assessing siblings in foster care.

Valli Kohon is a child and adolescent psychotherapist, trained at the Tavistock Clinic. She is also a psychoanalyst, a Fellow of the British Psychoanalytical Society. With her husband, Gregorio Kohon, she co-founded the Brisbane Centre for Psychoanalytic Studies, where she developed theoretical, observational and clinical courses for therapists working with children. Her extensive teaching experience has included workshops, lectures and seminars in a number of different countries, such as Peru, Cuba, Spain, Sweden, Australia and New Zealand. For several years she was a Toddler Group Leader at the Anna Freud Centre, where she has also taught on the child psychotherapy training course. She currently works as a consultant child and adolescent psychotherapist at the Portman Clinic and in private practice.

Monica Lanyado is a training supervisor and seminar leader on the Child and Adolescent Psychotherapy training at the British Association of Psycho-therapists (BAP). She helped to found the Child and Adolescent Psychotherapy training at the Scottish Institute of Human Relations and was the first Organising Tutor of the course. She is joint editor with Didier Houzel of the European Federation of Psychoanalytic Psychotherapy (EFPP) Book Series, and joint editor with Ann Horne of the Independent Psychoanalytic Approaches with Children and Adolescents Series, the first book of which, *A Question of Technique*, co-edited with Ann Horne, was published in 2006 by Routledge. She is co-editor – again with Ann Horne – of *The Handbook of Child and Adolescent Psychotherapy* (Routledge, 1999) and author of *The Presence of the Therapist: Treating Childhood Trauma*, published in 2004 by Routledge.

Molly Ludlam, is a psychoanalytic psychotherapist with individuals, couples and parents in private practice and with clinical teams at the Scottish Institute of Human Relations. An Associated Member of the Society for Couple Psychoanalytic Psychotherapists, her interest in couple, family and parent–child relationships stems from experience as a secondary schoolteacher and a social worker in an NHS Child and Family Mental Health Team. Her recent publications are 'The parental couple: Issues for psychotherapeutic practice', in *Sexual and Relationship Therapy* (vol. 20 (3), 2005) and 'Psychotherapy for the parents as a couple', in D. Scharff & J. Savege Scharff (eds) *New Paradigms for Treating Relationships* (Jason Aranson, 2006) and she is co-editor, with Viveka Nyberg of *Couple Attachments: Theoretical and Clinical Studies* (Karnac, 2007).

Lisa Miller has recently retired from the Child and Family Department of the Tavistock Clinic, where she worked for many years as a consultant child and adolescent psychotherapist and latterly was head of the department. She had been heavily involved with training child psychotherapists and with the development of child psychotherapy as a profession. She has published a number of papers and contributed to a number of books. She is a former editor of the *Journal of Child Psychotherapy* and the current editor of the *International Journal of Infant Observation and its Applications*.

Margaret Rustin is a consultant child and adolescent psychotherapist and Head of Child Psychotherapy at the Tavistock and Portman NHS Foundation Trust. She has had a long-term involvement in work with adopted children and their parents, and is a Professional Advisor to the Adoption team at Coram Family. Her publications include *Assessment in Child Psychotherapy* (edited jointly with Emanuela Quagliata, Tavistock/Karnac Series, new edition 2004); *Closely Observed Infants* (joint editor and contributor with Lisa Miller, Michael Rustin and Judy Shuttleworth, Duckworth, 1989); *Psychotic States in Children* (joint editor and contributor with Alex and Helene Dubinsky and Maria Rhode, Duckworth, 1997); and the chapter 'Where do I belong? Dilemmas for children and adolescents who have been adopted or brought up in long-term foster care', in *Creating New Families: Therapeutic Approaches to Fostering, Adoption and Kinship Care* (edited by Jenny Kenrick, Caroline Lindsey and Lorraine Tollemache, London: Karnac, 2006).

Graham Shulman is a consultant child and adolescent psychotherapist who trained at the Tavistock Clinic and currently works in NHS Lanarkshire. He was until recently Senior Tutor on the Child Psychotherapy Training and

Organising Tutor for the Therapeutic Skills with Children and Young People Course at the Scottish Institute of Human Relations. He is also joint editor of the *Journal of Child Psychotherapy*. He is the father of an adopted child.

John Simmonds is Director of Policy, Research and Development at the British Association for Adoption and Fostering. He is a social worker and has worked as consultant to children's homes and adolescent units. He has been involved in a wide range of development projects in both the statutory and voluntary sectors. He was editor of the *Journal of Social Work Practice* and has written widely on children's issues. Before his current post, he was Senior Lecturer and Programme Coordinator at Goldsmith's College, University of London. He is the father of two adopted children.

Sheila Spensley trained in clinical psychology and in child psychotherapy at the Tavistock Clinic and has a BAP training in adult psychotherapy. Now semi-retired, she was formerly an NHS consultant clinical psychologist specialising in psychoanalytic psychotherapy. She has had many years' experience of working psychoanalytically with psychotic and borderline adults and children, including hospital in-patients. She has also been closely involved in the training of child psychotherapists in Scotland. She is currently researching mother–child attachment in relation to learning deficit in children and is a Fellow of the IPA Research Group. Publications include *Frances Tustin* (Routledge, 1995) and papers and chapters focusing on the interface of autistic and psychotic pathology.

Jenny Sprince is an Organisational Consultant and a consultant child and adolescent psychotherapist, specialising in work with looked after children and their carers. She has worked extensively with children, teachers and care staff in EBD (Educational Behavioural Difficulties) schools, children's homes and other residential settings, as well as social service departments and private fostering agencies. She is consultant psychotherapist to Thornby Hall Therapeutic Community (part of Childhood First) and a director of Placement Support, a company providing psychodynamic consultation and therapeutic services to looked after children and their carers in various settings.

Sally Wassell is an independent social worker who has 25 years' experience as a practitioner in adoption. She is currently instructed on a frequent basis by courts in Scotland, England and Northern Ireland for care proceedings. Her particular interests are the application of attachment and attribution theories and the value of a resilience-based approach within the re-parenting of vulnerable children and young people. Sally co-authored, with Brigid Daniel, *Child Development for Child Care and Protection Workers* (Jessica Kingsley, 1999) and *Assessing and Promoting Resilience in Vulnerable children* (3 volume set: *The Early Years, The School Years, Adolescence*, Jessica Kingsley, 2002).

Foreword

Adoption is a theme of both universal interest and profound and unusual particularity. In this book, Hans Christian Andersen's tale of *Thumbelina* and the story of Heathcliff in Emily Brontë's *Wuthering Heights*, which appear in the first and final chapters, attest to the former. In between, we are offered a series of rich, moving, and often very painful stories arising from therapeutic engagements with adopted children and their families by some of the most experienced and thoughtful practitioners working in this field.

Recent developments in UK government policy with respect to adoption and children in public care embody the difficulty, or perhaps the impossibility, of ever properly bridging the gap between these polarities of the universal and the particular when it comes to adoption. Policies advocating the removal of barriers to opportunity for children in care or placed for adoption are laudable in their intentions, but tend to be silent on the complex and unique emotional realities facing these children and young people, and their carers. This book is a courageous and important contribution to redressing this balance.

The emotional realities of abuse, neglect and abandonment experienced by so many of the children who are placed for adoption are almost unthinkably painful. Yet the task of trying to live lives as 'ordinary' as possible in the face of such experiences, and of helping adoptive families integrate this 'unthinkability' is *the* crucial contribution that therapists and social workers can make in this field. The need to link understanding of inner and outer world experience in this work requires therapists who can move creatively 'beyond the consulting room', and social workers who can engage with the emotional complexity of inner worlds. One of the great strengths of this book is that it shows these two professions working together at their best to support what John Simmonds calls an 'environmental therapy' – adoption.

The state of mind that is quietly but insistently advocated here is a kind of unflinching capacity to bear emotional pain. As Lisa Miller writes in her chapter, 'We have no wish to believe it. Our minds shy away from thoughts of a harmless baby's pain … Social workers and adoption workers do their best in most cases to prepare prospective parents for the potential difficult times as they receive a small child into their family. Yet it remains hard to remember that the years before adoption do not go away and that the problems may not be temporary'. Because we 'have no wish to believe it' adoption practice and policy is often subtly undermined by the need to believe the opposite – that a clean slate, a new start, a happy ending can be magically produced. The structure of fantasy that pervades adoption work is therefore a recurring theme in these pages. Grasping the power of such fantasies is part of the 'self-knowledge' we need, but it is also what makes sense of the universality that is inscribed in each unique and particular story of adoption.

I am privileged to have been asked to write the foreword to this book. Although replete with the accumulated experience and wisdom of the authors, it is also highly accessible. Everyone who takes the time to read it will learn much, and their appreciation of the demands and rewards of adoption and the supporting work of professionals in the field will be considerably deepened.

Andrew Cooper
Professor of Social Work, the Tavistock Clinic and
University of East London

Preamble

Debbie Hindle

> Lives and stories are enmeshed in a complex interweaving of disparate elements which can never be summed up as a totality but only ever grasped in partial and transitory ways.
>
> (Phil Cohen 1995: 3)

'Are you adopted?' asked a 9-year-old girl. After a brief pause, she added that she was. She said she had three families and named each one in turn – her birth family, her foster family and her adoptive family. She went on to tell me what being adopted meant – that she would stay with her adoptive family – 'it's a forever family, no matter what'.

All this took place in the first few minutes of our meeting to think about whether ongoing psychotherapy could be helpful to this young girl. I took up her question to me, wondering if she thought that *only* if I too had been adopted would I know what it was like for her. Her description of her three families encompasses so many of the issues that arise for children who have been adopted – likeness and difference, discontinuity, transitions and loss, as well as the hope of something sustaining and enduring. But in spite of her explanation and apparent understanding, I was left with a question about what it meant to her to be adopted and whether she and I together could begin to apprehend the emotional complexity of her experience.

This vignette was one of many starting points for the inception of this book. Not long before this, Graham Shulman and I had begun working together as Senior Tutor and Organising Tutor for the clinical training in child psychotherapy at the Scottish Institute of Human Relations. Students on the training came from Scotland, Northern England and Northern Ireland and in their respective work settings, undertook a range of clinical work, under supervision, with children, young people and their parents. During this time, in our teaching and training and in our own clinical work, we were struck by the number of primarily late-placed adopted children who had been referred to child and adolescent mental health services and other agencies where consultation, family work or psychotherapy was being offered. This led to many hours of reading and reflection as we thought about and tried to understand the very particular issues and dilemmas that arose for these children and their adoptive parents.

Two books were influential in the genesis of this book. The first was *After Adoption: Working with Adoptive Families*, edited by Rena Phillips and Emma McWilliam and published by the British Agencies for Adoption and Fostering in 1996. Taken together, this wide-ranging selection of papers promoted the importance of and need for comprehensive post-adoption services that would be sensitive and responsive to the needs of adopted children and their families. They advocated the importance of listening to the views and experiences of adoptive families, the need for access to a range of different approaches to meet different circumstances, perhaps at different times, and what they described as the 'twin imperatives' – continuity of service and a co-ordinated approach to service provision. In her chapter on 'Psychotherapy', Mary Boston raised a question that we found resonated with our ongoing thinking: 'Why is it that good parenting and loving care are not always enough to make up for these early deprivations, and why do some adopted children appear to be doing their best to repeat the pattern of their lives and to cause further disruption of placement?' But how this question is addressed in relation to the provision of therapeutic post-adoption services varies. Our aim in bringing together the chapters in this book has been not to promote a particular treatment modality, but to understand what can be learned from clinical work about the complexity of an adopted child's inner world and how this may impact on and reverberate with the inner worlds of their adoptive parents.

The second book that has most closely fitted with our proposed theme is *The Dynamics of Adoption: Social and Personal Perspective*, edited by A. Treacher and I. Katz and published by Jessica Kingsley in 2000. This book arose from the work of the Centre for Adoption and Identity Studies at the University of East London and the Tavistock Clinic. It is informed by psychoanalytic theory and highlights the complexity of the adoption experience for all those involved in the adoption process – the birth parents, the adoptee, the adoptive parents and the professional networks involved. Throughout this book, several themes emerge and re-emerge – the importance of a sense of personal narrative, the capacity to find meaning in the context of relationships, and the necessity of apprehending, however intangible, a sense of truth. While the book covers a wide range of issues and combines moving personal accounts with chapters from professionals, no direct work with children or young people is described.

These two books prompted us to consider whether there were aspects of clinical work with children, adolescents and their families, already published in different journals which could be brought together with newly written material and could extend and inform what has previously been written. It is our view that a psychoanalytic perspective provides a distinctive source of understanding. We believe that the detailed clinical work described in this book reflects the emotional and psychological complexities – for the child, parents and professionals – involved in becoming an adoptive family, and the need to take such complexities into account.

There are many issues that are not touched on or addressed in this book – open and kinship adoption, trans-racial and inter-country adoption, among others. Sadly, space has prevented us from exploring the importance of sibling relationships to children who have been separated from their families of origin and the many different ramifications of this. However, we are firmly of the view that a psychoanalytic perspective has a useful contribution to make in the field of adoption. As Brodzinsky *et al.* (1998: 13) write: 'Despite the absence of strong empirical support for many of the psychodynamic assumptions regarding adoption, the theory continues to inform clinical and casework practice with adoptees, adoptive parents and birth parents in very meaningful ways.'

References

Brodzinsky, D., Smith, D. and Brodzinsky, A. (1998) *Children's Adjustment to Adoption: Developmental and Clinical Issues*, London: Sage Publications.
Cohen, P. (1995) *Frameworks for a Study of Adoptive Identities*, Working Paper no. 1, London: University of East London and Centre for Adoption and Identity Studies.

Acknowledgements

We would like to thank Kirsty Smy for taking us through the process of editing this book and the editor Grace McInnes for her additional support. The Scottish Institute of Human Relations provided a 'home' in which we could begin to think about and develop our thoughts about this book. We are also grateful to NHS Lanarkshire for allowing study leave for Graham Shulman to work on the book and to NHS Greater Glasgow for similarly allowing time for Debbie Hindle to dedicate time to this project.

Two contributors have asked that special thanks be given to two individuals who provided clinical material which was included in their chapters. Margaret Rustin drew on material gathered in the course of clinical research undertaken by Debbie Hindle, and Sheila Spensley was very appreciative of the work by Sue Davies, which she supervised and included in her chapter.

We are particularly grateful to Robert Fleming, Martin Lyon and Marta Vaciago Smith for the time they gave to reading and commenting on various drafts of chapters. Their responses were supportive and also challenging and helped to keep us focused and to task.

Special thanks must be given to John Simmonds, who encouraged us to continue at the very points when we felt most uncertain and reminded us of the importance of drawing on psychoanalytic thinking in seeking meaning and in grappling with difficult or uncomfortable insights. We are also appreciative of the time that Andrew Cooper gave to reading the text and writing the foreword to this book.

None of this could have been undertaken without the support of our partners, Moira Shulman and Ken Ross. Ken spent many hours formatting, proofreading, cross-referencing, keeping track of e-mails, various versions of the papers sent and generally keeping the whole project in order. Without his help in the preparation of the manuscript, it would have been impossible for us to have managed all the organisation that editing a book like this requires.

Finally, it would have been impossible for this book to have been written if it had not been for the courage and commitment of the adoptive children and their families, who have engaged in the challenging struggle to understand and make sense of their lives and relationships.

Permissions

We are grateful for permission from Taylor and Francis Ltd. (http://www.informaworld.com) to publish revised versions of the following papers originally published in the *Journal of Child Psychotherapy*:

Bartram, P. (2003) 'Some Oedipal problems in work with adopted children and their parents', *Journal of Child Psychotherapy*, 29 (1): 21–36.

Case, C. (2005) 'The mermaid: moving towards reality after trauma', *Journal of Child Psychotherapy*, 31 (3): 335–51.

Edwards, J. (2000) 'On being dropped and picked up: adopted children and their internal objects', *Journal of Child Psychotherapy*, 26 (3): 349–67.

We would also like to thank the publishers of the *Journal of Social Work Practice* (http://www.tandf.co.uk) for allowing us to re-publish:

Hindle, D. (1998) 'Loss and recovery in adoption: a child's perspective', *Journal of Social Work Practice*, 12 (1): 17–26.

And finally, we are grateful to Sage Publications for permission to publish a revised version:

Rustin, M. (1999) 'Multiple families in mind', *Clinical Child Psychology and Psychiatry*, 4 (1): 51–62.

Note on confidentiality

Throughout the book, all names of persons referred to have been changed and every effort has been made to disguise their identity, but not in ways that change the meaning of the clinical material.

Note on terminology

The spelling of fantasy with 'f' and phantasy with 'ph' have been used to distinguish between those which are conscious and those which are unconscious.

Introduction

Debbie Hindle and Graham Shulman

> ... the unseen forces which shape our emotional responses through life, are ... the patterns of emotional experience with other people, most powerfully set up in infancy. These patterns are not immutable but ... once established are hard to break.
>
> (Gerhardt 2004)

Adoption is profoundly complex. It encompasses issues of identity and sense of self, the question of origins and the sense of belonging, the experience of loss and the capacity to form new attachment relationships. These are in turn intimately linked with attachment relationships and emotional life and development from infancy. Adoption offers the possibility of a new beginning and of regeneration, but it also contains the potential for disappointment, destruction and at its worst psychological disaster; psychologically, adoption is therefore a highly charged – one might say 'supercharged' – process. It is a field in which diverse realms of individual experience and society interact. It spans the inner and outer worlds in particularly complicated ways. It involves the internal worlds of the birth family and adoptive child and family; the themes of parental sexuality, procreation or infertility; the professional networks around looked after children and around adoption and adoptive families; the law and the legal system; social and cultural values and beliefs; ideology; and even myth. As a psychological field, adoption thus involves *a distinctive constellation of emotional forces*.

Our aim in this book is to consider the emotional complexities of adoption, and how these affect the experience and dynamics of adoption for the child, adoptive parents and professional system. We believe that a psychoanalytic perspective – with its focus on the inner world, and on emotional and unconscious processes – can contribute to the thinking, planning and practice of all those involved in adoption. It goes without saying that this is one perspective amongst many, and we hope that readers will find their own applications and ways of making meaningful links according to their experience and place in the adoption process. We also believe the book has implications for policy makers, in terms of highlighting the need for post-adoption therapeutic services.

Changes in patterns of adoption

Triseliotis *et al.* (1997) outlined five periods of adoption in the Western tradition from ancient to modern times. Only in the second period, in the latter part of the nineteenth century (in the United States) and the early part of the twentieth century (in the United Kingdom) was adoption legalised as we know it today. Since the Second World War, there have been significant changes in the patterns of adoption coinciding with medical advances, social changes and changing societal attitudes. These include: the availability of contraception and the legalisation of abortion, the changes in the composition and types of family structures, and changing attitudes towards illegitimacy. Adoption has become one of many different ways of being a family and of raising children.

The third period of adoption came to be known as the era of the 'perfect baby' for the 'perfect couple' (Triseliotis *et al.*, 1997: 7) and was characterised by the matching of 'healthy' infants (under one year of age) with families seeking to raise a child as their own. From the late 1960s and early 1970s (the fourth period) fewer infants were 'relinquished' for adoption, while simultaneously, more children were received into care, many from backgrounds of abuse and neglect. Along with these children, placed in foster or residential care, there were also an increasing number of children with special needs, children with mental or physical disabilities, children from different race or ethnic backgrounds or groups of siblings who were 'hard to place'. An increasing number of children were living a life in care that was too unstable and uncertain and did not provide them with the security and sense of belonging to a family that could meet their lifelong needs. In this period in the evolution of adoption, there was a trend towards a more child-centred approach where the primary objective is the long-term welfare of the children placed for adoption.

A fifth period, however, emerged in the latter part of the twentieth century with the increase in inter-country adoption and acceptance of a wider range of parents and families available to adopt children (including single parents, same sex parents, re-constituted families, as well as extended family members). These latter two trends have taken adoption into an often turbulent public debate and have highlighted the at times competing needs of adults seeking to adopt a child and the needs of children. Throughout all these phases, there has also been a growing awareness of the importance of knowing one's origins and heritage. Now embedded in good adoption practice, there is an increasing openness about adoption and an understanding of the significance of this with regard to a sense of identity.

Many of the children being adopted from care will have been cared for and have relationships with their birth parents, know other members of their birth families and may have formed close relationships with previous foster parents and their extended families. For these children, being adopted needs to be set against a recognition that the child is bringing with them experience, memories and relationships that have been formative and developmentally significant. Watson (1994) in Triseliotis *et al.* (1997: 2) provides a definition of adoption that captures the continuing role of the child's biological family in the context of a child's adoptive family:

> Adoption is a means of meeting the developmental needs of a child by legally transferring ongoing parental responsibility from birth parents to adoptive parents, recognising that in the process we have created a new kinship network that forever links these two families together through the child who is shared by them both. This kinship network may also include significant other families, both formal and informal, that have been part of the child's experience.

In England, the Prime Minister's Review of Adoption (PIU, 2000) provided an impetus to this new landscape of adoption by modernising the legal, policy and practice framework and increasing the number of children placed for adoption. To this end, local authorities are encouraged to include adoption as a permanency planning option and to ensure that where it is in the child's best interests adoption is pursued. Along with the increased numbers of children from a wider age range and varied circumstances, there has also been a recognition of the need for the provision of adoption support services. The complexity of children's needs, the lifelong implications of adoption and the three parties to adoption – child, birth parents and adoptive families – together with the evidence from research have all highlighted the fact that family making through adoption is a complex and challenging process. It is recognised that some families need to access adoption sensitive services at different points in the adoption process and family life cycle. Local authorities are required to set in place a range of services, to work in partnership with universal services, such as health or education or to commission services from specialist providers. While the provision of services post-adoption are not comprehensive, the framework and principles supporting the importance of ongoing services for all those affected by adoption is formally acknowledged.

This book is not an attempt to address systematically the whole range of issues in relation to adoption, or to produce a comprehensive account of psychoanalytic writings about and approaches to adoption. Our aim is a more modest one: to promote interest in, and curiosity about, the potential applications of a psychoanalytic perspective to the adoption process, and its relevance to the experience of adoption, amongst a wider audience than those who might access articles in professional journals. Although a number of articles on adoption using a psychoanalytic framework have been published in journals, and some chapters in books, these are scattered and some are not easily accessible. We wished to gather together a selection of these for publication in book form, combined with a number of contributions that we have invited for the book.

We should stress from the outset that the central theme of this book is not the question of what type of therapeutic help or support adoptive children and families need or should be given, though consideration of the emotional complexities of adoption certainly has implications for this question, and we do aim to convey what psychoanalytic child psychotherapy in particular can offer. However, it is not our purpose to advocate a single approach to supportive or clinical interventions for adoptive children and their families, and indeed we would be wary of any approach presented as 'the' appropriate model of intervention. In our experience, as in all areas, the therapeutic or supportive input suited to a given child or family depends on many complicated factors, and an approach that is helpful for one child or family may not be for another. In short, we aim to promote not a particular way of working but *a way of thinking*.

The emotional complexities of adoption

The emotional tasks and challenges for the adopted child are formidable. Equally, so are the emotional tasks and challenges for adoptive parents. We feel this cannot be overstated. Indeed, one of the points we wish to highlight is the way in which failure to sufficiently acknowledge or understand the former can lead at times to failure to adequately recognise the latter. When this occurs, at best it may result in unanticipated or misconstrued problems – problems which an adoptive family might be able to overcome either within their existing supportive framework or with additional input; at worst it may have psychologically disastrous consequences for all involved, with either the breakdown of an adoptive placement – sometimes within days or weeks – or a chronic or cyclical situation of severe difficulties and stresses within the family.

There has been an increasing awareness of the impact of early experience on later development and relationships. At the same time, the way in which complex emotional difficulties are manifested can sometimes be hard to identify or make sense of (see Chapter 17). The curious fact is that while there is widespread professional and public recognition of the general nature and scale of the emotional challenges for adoptive child and parents, we regularly continue to hear of cases where there have been significant difficulties for those involved in giving adequate attention and thought to the *specific* nature and severity of the emotional challenges for a given child and family. It is not realistic or possible to avoid or bypass difficulties, and this is not the aim; however, we believe a process which is mindful of, and attentive to, the nature and scale of emotional challenges and complexities for an individual baby or child and their adoptive family, is both possible and desirable.

The emotional complexity for the adopted child of forming attachments to new parents while *simultaneously* being faced with the task of mourning the loss in relation to birth parents (and often other carers) is well recognised and has been extensively written about. This is also true for the parallel, though not identical, situation for adoptive parents who have the task of forming a new relationship with, and becoming new parents for their adopted child, while simultaneously being faced with or reminded of (consciously or otherwise) their own losses, whether in relation to having children or other past losses.

The adopted child experiences multiple losses, though the exact combination will naturally depend on the child's individual history and the circumstances of the adoption: these include the loss of the birth mother or primary attachment figure; the loss of the birth parents as carers; the loss of the birth family (however bad the actual circumstances might have been); the loss of foster carers or other family carers; the loss in relation to the discontinuity of the child's 'personal narrative' – the lack of the ordinary experience of a child's early history and development being known directly and held in mind by their primary attachment figures; the loss that may be involved in the painful recognition of what the child has missed in their early experience; and the loss associated with the reality that the adoptive parents may be less than the ideal parents the child might have hoped for or expected.

In addition, the adopted child will have in mind a version – more or less conscious – of what their birth mother and father felt about the loss of their child; this may be the product of imaginative conjecture, or what the child has been told, or a combination of the two. However it is arrived at, it is likely to have a significant influence on the adopted child's sense of self and self-image; that is, whether the child imagines the birth mother and father felt sadness at the loss of their child, or relief, or indifference, or – worst of all – felt glad to be rid of them. This question clearly links with – though it is not the sole determinant of – the adopted child's inner sense of worth and of being valued.

An individual child's inner capacity to process and bear disturbing and sometimes overwhelming feelings and anxieties connected with loss will always depend on the one hand on the capacity of the supportive environment and network around them to provide containment of these, and on the other hand on the child's inner resources, the balance of strengths and vulnerabilities of the child, and the child's temperament and capacity to make use of the support and help that are available. Particular problems arise when patterns of emotional response and interaction that have been laid down from infancy and the earliest years *seriously impair a child's ability to form and make use of relationships with new attachment figures and other adults.*

When this happens in the circumstances of an adopted child in an adoptive family, adoptive parents often find themselves in the perplexing and hurtful situation where their adopted child seems unable to respond to and make use of the ordinary parental love and care they have to offer. This can lead to a situation where adoptive parents feel hurt, rejected, incompetent, powerless, helpless and even guilty either because they feel their parenting is not ameliorating the child's underlying difficulties or disturbance, or because they feel responsible for the child's inability to form the kind of attachment to them that they had hoped for. A powerful sense of failure may ensue, though aspects of this may not be entirely conscious. *Molly Ludlam* has written about this issue in her chapter 'The longing to become a family: support for the parental couple'.

A further level of complexity involves the question of when losses are actually *felt* or recognised by the adopted child, and how they are experienced and worked through at different developmental stages and transitions. The already considerable challenges of different developmental stages – and transitions between these – are heightened for the adopted child by the additional issues in relation to adoption; at the same time, these developmental stages in turn revive or intensify issues of adoption. An obvious example is that of adolescence and puberty: for instance, the ordinary challenges of puberty and emergent sexuality may for an adopted child be considerably more difficult to negotiate because they touch on painful issues such as the child's conception, their birth parents' relationship and so on, as well as the possible issue of infertility in adoptive parents. Developmental stages and transitions may present opportunities for adoption issues to be further worked through, but equally they may reveal a child's underlying profound lack of internal resources to manage these. Trying to disentangle how far an adopted child is struggling with developmental issues and how far they are struggling with adoption issues – for example, ordinary separation anxiety as against out-of-the-ordinary, catastrophic anxiety associated with the actual loss of the birth mother – and thus how to make sense of what the child is feeling, is an especially difficult task for child, parent and professional.

Key psychoanalytic concepts

Five key psychoanalytic concepts are central to the theme of this book. The first is the ***inner world***. This has a more specific meaning than the notion of the 'inner life' of a person; here we are drawing on Klein's (1940) formulation of the inner world as in effect an internal 'theatre of the mind', peopled by 'characters' with relationships, and made up of scenarios, actions, events and qualities. Klein suggested that a baby's primitive 'versions' or internal representations of its mother and others, and of experience, are built up from the very beginning of post-natal life. The 'characters' in the inner world are based on significant figures in an individual's life – mother, father, siblings, grandparents and others.

However, a young baby's understanding of, and capacity to represent, experience in the mind are at a rudimentary stage of development, and lack the coherence and organisation of a mature mind: consequently the 'inner world' of people and events – with its foundations in early *pre-verbal* experience – is thought to be coloured and shaped partly by emotions and fantasies (the earliest workings of the 'imagination'). Furthermore, the earliest contents of the inner world are thought to be embedded in the 'deepest' layers of the mind, and may be only partly, or not at all, available to waking consciousness. It may be difficult for some to conceive of the mental life of young babies in this kind of way, but recent research has found evidence that even foetuses in the womb dream (Hopson, 1998), as do babies from birth onward, and this seems to be suggestive of some form of primitive, pre-verbal 'representational' mental life even from before birth.

In this psychoanalytic model of the inner world, later versions and internal representations of people and experiences – from childhood, adolescence and adulthood – do not supersede or erase earlier ones but co-exist in the mind, though they may vary in the degree to which we are conscious of them or have conscious access to them. These different internal representations from different stages of development may also vary in the degree to which they influence our perceptions and experience of people and situations in the present, as well as our everyday moods and states of mind. Where the earliest of these continue to exert a significant or disproportionate influence on a person's mental life in later stages of development, this may have a serious and possibly profound effect on attachment and intimate relationships. It is for this reason that an awareness and understanding of an individual adopted child's inner world may be so important, particularly where trauma, abuse or neglect in infancy and early childhood have significantly influenced their earliest internal representations of people and experiences.

Freud (1914) ingeniously suggested that *what cannot be remembered gets repeated*. He argued that feelings and patterns of relating from infancy and very early childhood that are not accessible to conscious memory are repeated 'in action' in later relationships. Repetition in action, he suggests, is in effect a form of 'memory'. For Klein, this meant the enactment of 'internal scenarios' from the inner world of the past which may override living life in the present.

The second psychoanalytic concept central to this book is that of ***psychic pain*** (or 'mental pain'). Perhaps it would be more accurate to refer to this as a concept which psychoanalysis has formalised and elaborated, since literature and the arts through the ages contain many expressions of the idea of psychic pain, of which the following lines from Shakespeare are a superlative example:

> ... Better I were distract:
> So should my thoughts be sever'd from my griefs
> And woes by wrong imaginations lose
> The knowledge of themselves.
>
> (*King Lear*, IV.vi.: 278–81)

Psychoanalysis has in part been the systematic study of psychic pain, the ways in which the mind deals with psychic pain, and the impact of psychic pain on the development and growth of the mind, the personality and relationships. Meltzer and Harris (1976 [1994]), discussing mental pain in the context of families, raised the important and extremely useful question, 'Whose pain is this?' The answer to this question is not always clear or obvious when the emotional currents of two or more individuals converge. Meltzer and Harris (1976 [1994]: 389) thus suggest that, 'Study of mental pain requires not only definition of its quality and reference, but also of its distribution and source.'

We start from the assumption that psychic pain has a significant organising effect on the development of the mind and personality; that it may be partly or wholly unconscious; that the communication and containment of psychic pain is a primary – though by no means exclusive – function of relationships, beginning with the mother–infant relationship; and that psychic pain which is experienced as unbearable or overwhelming by an individual, family or wider system can have a disturbing or destructive effect on attachment and family relationships. This has obvious relevance to adopted children who have experienced severe neglect, trauma or abuse, and to the parenting of such children. It also has relevance to adoptive parents themselves, who often have their own painful and deep-seated issues of loss; here Meltzer's question 'Whose pain is this?' can be helpful in trying to sort out what feelings belong to whom and how the psychic pain of child and parents can significantly affect interactions in attachment relationships. This phenomenon is not specific to adoptive child–parent relationships, but we would suggest that typically there is *a distinctive interaction and intensity of psychic pain for adoptive child and parents*.

The third psychoanalytic concept is **ambivalence**: this refers to feeling both love and hate toward the same person. Although hate is part of human nature, it is inherently painful and anxiety-provoking to have feelings of hate toward the person you most love, and this gives rise to an inner state of conflict and tension. In infancy, the primary object of love and hate is the mother or primary attachment figure. When a very young baby feels cared for, understood and loved by the mother, it will evoke intense loving feelings toward the mother; in contrast, when a very young baby feels pain, frustration or distress it will evoke equally intense opposite feelings towards the mother. From earliest infancy therefore, these opposite currents of feeling co-exist in the baby and are in dynamic relation to one another. Because the 'constant *interaction* of love and hate' starts in the first weeks or months of life, Klein (1937) saw this as the most fundamental and archaic dimension of emotional life. The integration of love and hate, and the capacity to hold these opposing feelings towards the same person, is for this reason a primary emotional and developmental task, and remains a challenge in relationships throughout life.

The fourth psychoanalytic concept is **splitting**. The state of inner conflict and tension arising from the co-existence of love and hate felt toward the same person, may be experienced as overwhelming or threatening, and can lead to the fear that hate will outweigh or destroy love. This can in turn give rise to unbearable anxiety or psychic pain. One unconscious response to this is known as 'splitting'. This involves keeping very separate and far apart in the mind feelings of love and hate toward the same person; the function of this is partly to preserve the loving part of the self and to protect the object of love, and partly to avoid awareness of one's ambivalent feelings toward one person because the pain and anxiety of such awareness is felt to be intolerable. Splitting as a defence against the pain of 'love-and-hate' is a primitive form of intra-psychic mental functioning which has its origins in infancy and the relationship to the mother or primary attachment figure, but it can occur at any stage of development and mental life, and can extend to other areas of experience. Moreover, the concept has been extended in its application to include inter-psychic processes; thus, splitting can be seen to occur within families, groups, agencies, professional networks or society in general, wherever there is an unconscious need or desire to keep 'good' and 'bad' aspects of the same person, situation or experience separate and far apart because integration of them is felt to be profoundly painful, discomforting and disturbing.

The fifth key psychoanalytic concept is Bion's (1962) formulation about a type of knowledge (and learning) based on **truthfulness to emotional experience**. Bion conceptualised this in the context of relationships in terms of what he called the 'K link' between two people, where 'K' represents a particular kind of knowing based on emotional experience; in a relationship, 'K' involves 'getting to know' someone and 'getting to be known' by someone. These in turn involve being concerned with the truth about the other person; for Bion this means being open and truthful to the emotional experience of knowing that person and of being in a relationship with them.

Bion regarded this openness and truthfulness to the emotional experience of a relationship as essential to the development and growth of the mind. He saw the mother–infant relationship as the foundation and prototype for this process. Bion discusses some of the problems that arise, and the psychic consequences of these, when one person's emotional experience of another person is felt to be overwhelming or even unbearable. At its most extreme, emotional experience in a relationship can be 'unprocessable', and may be experienced as indigestible or even harmful to the self; in this situation either the emotional experience, or the other person, may come to be felt as hateful. Although Bion formulated these ideas in somewhat abstract terms as part of a wider scientific theoretical framework, they are readily applicable to any relationships and have a particular relevance to the adoption process, where being open to the emotional truth of knowing and getting to know someone can present profound challenges – especially when this involves a child with a seriously disturbed inner world, or for whom psychic pain is extreme.

In addition to these five concepts, individual chapters draw on or make reference to other psychoanalytic concepts and these are described by the authors of those chapters.

Multiple perspectives

Much of what follows is based on clinical work which illustrates ways of thinking from a psychoanalytic perspective. However, we feel there is a need for a wide theoretical base for understanding the complex emotional experiences of children, young people and their families where adoption is concerned. Developments in attachment theory, neurobiological research, and work on trauma have all greatly increased our understanding of the ways in which early relationships and experiences impact on the developing personality and mind, as elaborated on in *Sally Wassell's* chapter 'Why is early development important?' Family therapy and systems theory have contributed to an understanding of dynamics that can occur in families, between families and the professional network, and within the professional network. To this, we would add the importance of attending to the child or young person in context. For a child who has been adopted, this context will necessarily include their previous relationships and experiences, their developmental history and temperament, what sense the child has made of what has happened, their position in their new family and their *meaning* to their new parents, their new parents' own histories and the relationship between their parents, as well as the wider social, ethnic and cultural context.

For children who have suffered early adversity, the experience of family life has often been shattered. Lindsey and Barrett (2006: 14) poignantly describe the way in which 'the meaning of everyday concepts such as mother and father, daughter and son relationships' are changed and distorted by the experience of abuse and neglect. How these primary relationships are restored is the focus of much supportive and therapeutic work with adoptive families. But this work also must be seen in context – why have problems arisen at a particular point? How have the family tried to deal with their concerns? How do they formulate what is wrong? What help are they hoping to receive?

With complex situations, it seems to us that different treatment modalities may be needed, perhaps to address different aspects of presenting problems, as described by *Kate Cairns* in her chapter, 'Enabling effective support: secondary traumatic stress and adoptive families'. What seems important is that problems, should they arise, need to be sensitively and thoughtfully explored from a number of perspectives. When services and professionals are involved, they too are part of the wider context and need to find ways of not only of 'providing help', but also engaging *with* families in a way that makes sense to them and appreciates the reality of the many issues they may be facing. In this sense, we are very much in agreement with Brodzinsky *et al.* (1998: 89) who state that, 'In our opinion, no one treatment approach necessarily addresses the problems of adoptees better than others. What is more important than treatment modality or the therapists' theoretical orientation is a clear understanding of the adoption-related issues that are likely to emerge in the course of treatment and the availability of specific intervention strategies, incorporated into an overall treatment plan, that can help adoptees work through their unique life circumstances.'

A psychoanalytic perspective offers a window into the inner world of the adopted child through clinical encounters (Hart and Luckock, 2004). As Margaret Rustin (Chapter 4) eloquently expresses: 'Individual psychotherapeutic work can offer detailed descriptive accounts of adoptive experience from the perspective of internal reality, thus taking account of unconscious elements…' Single case studies give us in-depth and fine-grained narratives which elucidate these aspects of experience. While the clinical population of adopted children and their families is unlikely to represent a cross-section of adoptive families in general, it is our view that the kinds of emotional dynamics and processes seen in the clinical context reflect or throw light on particular features of the adoption process and experience – sometimes in heightened or accentuated form – and have broader applications. Much of what follows in this book is based on clinical work and it is of note that from Freud onwards, single case studies have contributed to the development of clinical practice and psychoanalytic theory. Yet the status of single case studies as a research modality and as a recognised source of new ideas has waxed and waned, although more recently this has been the subject of a lively and fruitful debate with the field of psychoanalysis (Midgley, 2006). It is our view that descriptive accounts of, and reflection on, clinical work capture something of the complexity of the human experience as it is felt and lived; and that they illuminate 'the complexity and multidimensionality of emotional and thinking processes as the essence of psychic structure and process' (Rustin, 2002: 127).

In relation to child psychotherapy, it is our experience that it is particularly when problems persist after the adoption, or have already persisted prior to the adoption, that individual work with a child may be considered in discussion with the adoptive parents. Establishing a therapeutic alliance with the adoptive parents and working with them in parallel with any ongoing work with the child is usual practice. However, there is no doubt that considering the possibility of individual psychoanalytic psychotherapy for an adopted child requires an additional level of sensitivity and thoughtfulness over and above the usual carefully considered approach to offering this particular form of therapeutic input. This is because, as mentioned earlier, adoption is an emotionally 'supercharged' field.

There are several dynamic issues related to this work with adopted children and their families that we think warrant consideration. From the adoptive parents' point of view, although the possibility of therapeutic work may raise hope that something can be done to help their child and their family, it can also give rise to feelings of exclusion, jealousy or even rivalry which may be experienced consciously or unconsciously. These feelings which are part of three-person relationships – from which feelings of jealousy and exclusion originate – are important and may need particular attention, as *Pamela Bartram's* chapter on 'Oedipal difficulties in the triangular relationship between the parents, the child and the child psychotherapist' clearly illustrates. Adoptive parents may need time to consider their own anxieties and uncertainties *as* adoptive parents in a way that feels helpful and beneficial to them.

From an adopted child's experience, establishing a therapeutic relationship inevitably revives and re-evokes often intense feelings and anxieties in relation to their adoption. The adopted child's one-to-one relationship with their therapist echoes and mirrors the dyadic experience of the one-to-one relationship of birth mother (or carer) and baby in infancy; simultaneously, it touches on the adopted child's feelings and anxieties in relation to his or her *new* primary attachment figure. Individual psychoanalytic psychotherapy, with its focus on and use of the relationship between child and therapist as a tool for understanding, therefore crystallises and brings into sharp relief the emotional experience of adoption.

Hopkins (2000: 346) in particular describes the way in which 'a therapist can provide a trial ground where new developments can be explored before they are taken home'. Conflicting or confusing feelings may need time to be 'gathered together', and anger or hurt – which may feel too dangerous to be exposed or expressed within the home – can be opened up in a therapeutic relationship. Hopkins (2000: 346) suggests that this is not because the child's relationship to the therapist is stronger, but the reverse, that these issues can be explored 'because there is much less at stake'. In addition, Hunter (2001), Kendrick (2000, 2006), as well as *Monica Lanyado* and *Francesca Calvocoressi* in their chapters in this book, have all written about working with children in 'transition' and the way in which a therapeutic relationship can help to 'bridge the gap' between previous relationships and their new family.

It is these complex issues and the way in which they may be either re-enacted or worked through in the context of a therapeutic relationship that require a further level of thinking and engagement for adopted children, their adoptive parents and their therapist and co-worker. We believe a psychoanalytic perspective provides such an additional level of thinking.

Adoptive family life cycle

Writing about adoption from a developmental perspective, Brodzinsky *et al.*
(1990, 1998) have provided an extensive analysis of virtually every aspect of this
process – from the birth mother's experience to the impact of family structure
on the adjustment of adopted children and the developmental changes that may
affect a child's understanding of adoption. Brodzinsky *et al.*'s work is not only
comprehensive, it has done much to change what had been 'held beliefs', replacing
these with well-researched findings. In particular, he and his colleagues have
developed the idea of 'the family life cycle' – the changes a family goes through
over time and the dynamic context of the family in relation to the broader socio-
cultural system (Carter and McGoldrick, 1989) – and have applied this to adoptive
families. They have identified and categorised what they describe as the unique
adoptive related tasks (which interact with the more universal tasks of family
life) between adoptive parents and adopted children, as these change during the
course of development. They summarise some of their findings in relation to being
an adoptive parent as follows: 'Among the many tasks experienced by parents
are those associated with coping with infertility and the transition to adoptive
parenthood, discussing adoption with their child, creating a family environment
that supports the child's exploration of adoption issues, helping their child cope
with loss, supporting a positive self-image and identity in their child in relation to
adoption, and in some cases, as the adoptee moves into adolescence and adulthood,
supporting their child's plans to search for birth family' (Brondzinsky *et al.*,
1998: 21–2). For children too, there are the tasks of understanding the meaning
of adoption, accommodating to the idea of having two families, integrating
adoption into their emerging identity, and in some cases, deciding to explore the
nature of their origins further. Brodzinsky *et al.* emphasise the uniqueness of
this experience for both parents and children and identify specific points where
developmental and cognitive shifts usher in increased understanding and an added
level of complexity.

Holding in mind a developmental frame within a family context fosters more
realistic expectations and may highlight where issues have become 'stuck' and
further help may be needed. But even where children have been adopted in
infancy, and more obviously for late-place adopted children, there are many
factors which may have already interfered with ordinary development. Separation,
loss, neglect, abuse or lack of emotional containment affect children in different
and cumulative ways, and may impact on their physical, cognitive, emotional,
social and personal development (see Chapter 2). These children may present as
regressed, developmentally delayed, precocious, pseudo-independent, worldly-
wise, yet immature – often in ways that can be hard to understand – and need
opportunities to negotiate earlier stages of development at a later stage.

Recent thinking about deprivation and abuse from a psychoanalytic perspective

This book falls into a 'tradition' of books with a psychoanalytic frame of reference focused on the emotional needs of children who have suffered early deprivation or abuse and who are in alternative care. Boston and Szur's (1983) ground breaking book on *Psychotherapy with Severely Deprived Children* describes the work of the Tavistock Fostering and Adoption Workshop – initially convened to offer consultation to social workers and residential staff – in which the importance of emotional understanding and provision of more intensive therapeutic help was explored and developed. In their book, the themes that emerged from this work, illustrated by individual case studies, provide a poignant testimony to the difficulties experienced by the children and by those endeavouring to help them. Since then, Hunter (2001) has written about her extensive experience of working with children in care whose lives had been severely disrupted. She repeatedly demonstrates a capacity not only to work with and to hold in mind the complex professional networks that surround each child (as well as the legal and placement issues so central to their stability and their future) but also to maintain a therapeutic stance which allows for in-depth understanding of the child's predicament.

More recently Kendrick *et al.* (2006) have edited a most comprehensive and helpful book, *Creating New Families: Therapeutic Approaches to Fostering, Adoption and Kinship Care*, also based on the work of the Fostering and Adoption Workshop and the Child and Family Department of the Tavistock Clinic. This represents the work of members of the multidisciplinary team who provide a variety of therapeutic interventions, including family work, work with parents or carers, with children and adolescents, and liaison and consultation work with professionals in different settings. They describe and illustrate the wide range of theoretical models they draw from, including systemic and psychodynamic thinking, attachment theory and research, neuroscientific research, as well as psychiatric, psychological and cognitive behavioural models of assessment and intervention.

In addition to these books there have been numerous papers describing various aspects of psychoanalytic understanding in a range of settings. While it would be impossible to do justice to all those who have contributed to this area of work, we wanted to highlight several contributions that have been particularly influential and have extended our understanding of children's responses to early experiences of deprivation and abuse and how we as clinicians might relate to and conceptualise our own responses. Henry [Williams] (1974) drew attention to deprivation deriving from internal processes, and psychological defensive structures which could leave a child 'doubly deprived' and unable to make use of more positive experiences or better circumstances. Symington (1985), although not strictly writing about deprived children, discussed the way in which omnipotence – described by Bick (1968) as a way of defending against fears of unintegration or disintegration – may have a 'survival function'. In this context, the need to be strong, invulnerable or all-powerful, she thought, needed to be acknowledged and addressed as an important and protective defensive structure. Emanuel (1984) described the idea of a preconception or an expectation of the experience of being known or understood, and a child's 'primary disappointment' and sense of deprivation when this has not taken place. Taken together, these clinicians have opened the door to important developments in our way of understanding and engaging with children therapeutically.

Alvarez (1992) has written extensively about her work with severely deprived children and has influenced clinical practice by pointing to the way in which deprivation may leave children with real developmental and emotional deficits. She describes the way in which children may need to be 'reclaimed' from withdrawn or empty states of mind, or the way in which a belief in goodness or the experience of containment may be underdeveloped, so that small overtures may need to be amplified. Her explorations into primitive states of mind and developmental processes have placed her in a good position to be what Altman (2001) describes as a 'border crosser': someone who can draw on and bring together different perspectives – from psychoanalysis, developmental psychology and findings from the burgeoning field of neurobiology.

The growth of research in developmental psychology has highlighted the importance of the concept of attunement between parents and infants (Stern, 1985; Trevarthen, 1979) which also has relevance for the relationship between therapist and child (Emde, 1999; Tronick, 2003). Lanyado (2004) describes the unique nature of this relationship, placing emphasis on the 'presence' of the therapist in the context of the therapeutic process. She helpfully delineates the various strands of the 'total therapeutic relationship' which intertwine in a way that may allow for the possibility of creativity and therapeutic change. These include: the transference relationship, in which aspects of relationships from the person's past are re-created and re-enacted in the present; the importance of the relationship with and qualities of the therapist; and the 'holding' of the therapy, which includes aspects of external support and management – especially important in work with children and young people (Lanyado, 2004: 10). To this she adds the particular difficulties of working with children and young people who have experienced trauma in terms of 'the intransigence and persistence of negative ways of relating, and of how enormously difficult it can be to let go of these entrenched patterns' (Lanyado, 2004: 12).

All these writers have opened the door to thinking differently about children who have experienced adversity, as well as having influenced clinical practice. Like the work of Terr (1991) and Gallagher *et al.* (1995), who extended what had been studied in relation to trauma to include a deeper understanding of its psychological impact on children, so too these writers have added an important dimension which includes an understanding of unconscious defensive structures; emotional, developmental and relational deficits; and the importance for any child of the psychic reality of their experience to be known and understood.

Psychoanalytic perspectives on adoption

The richness of the psychoanalytic view in relation to adoption has been well represented in the work of Brinich (1980, 1990). He explores the co-existence of feelings of both love and hate in parent–child relationships – the ordinary ambivalence of family emotional life – and the various ways in which this may be encountered in adoptive family relationships. He describes in detail the complex task for any adopted child – having to manage two sets of contradictory feelings in relation to two sets of parents. This unavoidable state of affairs creates a natural split and makes the developmental task of integrating feelings of love and hate towards the same person more difficult. Unwanted feelings such as hatred or rejection can be directed towards birth parents, thus preserving their love of adoptive parents. Conversely, or at a different stage in development, birth parents may be idealised, while adoptive parents are denigrated. When such splits occur, love and hate may be kept very far apart in the child's mind, thus making integration of these feelings more difficult to achieve. The ramifications of these different perspectives can be far reaching, not only in relation to the child's real and imagined parents, but also in relation to a sense of self. As Brinich (1980: 108) eloquently states, 'The adopted child must include two separate sets of parents within his representational world. He must also integrate into his representation of himself the fact that he was born to one set of parents but has been raised by another set of parents.'

Fleming (2005) suggests that this conceptual frame is even more complicated in the current practice of adoption, which may include many more placements other than infant adoption. There may be relationships with foster carers or extended family members who have cared for the child and developed attachments after the child's removal from birth parents, but before adoption – not to mention the possibility of repeated attempts at rehabilitation with birth parents, perhaps involving a series of different placements. It is clear that these children would not fall into a simple triangular set of relationships; rather the range of significant people and carers may form a complex geometric shape with many more aspects than the two sets of parents that Brinich describes. This issue, of having multiple prior experiences of families and how this may impact on the internal worlds of adopted children is elaborated on by *Margaret Rustin* in her chapter, 'Multiple families in mind'.

Adoptive parents too may find it hard to integrate their feelings of love and hate, and may split these – consciously or unconsciously – between their adopted child and a fantasised or wished-for biological or adopted child. Brinich (1990) describes this complicated matrix of feelings, in which aspects of their child may be 'disowned' or are felt to be 'not a part of them', in contrast with the feelings they may harbour towards an 'unknown', imagined child they did not have. Given this context, it may be harder for adoptive parents to accept *their* adopted child, with all their qualities – their faults as well as their gifts, their differences as well as their similarities – and to invest their hopes and feelings in them unreservedly. Recognising and reconciling what can be discrepant views and feelings may be an important step towards getting to know their child as the unique individual they are.

Gaining a perspective on a child's experience of adoption has been explored from a psychoanalytic perspective through research and clinical work. Of particular note is the work of the Anna Freud Centre research group on adopted children and the research and clinical work of Hodges (Hodges and Tizard, 1989a, 1989b; Tizard and Hodges, 1978; Hodges, 1984, 1990). Their early studies and clinical discussions set the scene for more recent research, which has had a significant impact on our understanding of how late-adopted children adapt to their new families and what qualities in their adoptive parents may facilitate this. Whilst it would not be possible in this introduction to do justice to all that emerged in their thoughtful and detailed work, there are several themes which are relevant to the chapters that follow.

Hodges (1990) discusses the 'inner world' in which both conscious and unconscious fantasies contribute to the way in which reality is apprehended and to a child's unique sense of self and others. Many of the children and young people described in the following chapters will have experienced some form of abuse, neglect or early trauma, which will have shaped or distorted their expectations of others and their ways of relating. A psychoanalytic perspective highlights the serious consequences for young children of having their instinctual impulses – including their sexual phantasies – stimulated or enacted in reality (as in the case of sexual abuse), or their aggressive impulses met with aggression, rather than mediated in the context of more loving relationships.

Hodges (1984) suggests that an adopted child's fantasies about their adoption are comparable to a birth child's earliest fantasies about the nature of the relationship between their parents and their resultant conception. How to reconcile fantasies with the reality of life and of their own particular experiences is an ongoing task. Hodges (1984: 48) goes on to state that 'the two fundamental questions which adopted children have to confront in their development [are]: "Who were my first parents, what were they like?" and "Why did they give me up?"' To these questions, for children who knew and may have loved their parents but experienced abuse or trauma with them, we would add a further question: 'What happened and why?' The way in which these questions are encountered and explored is linked to a child's age, and cognitive and emotional development, but may also be mediated through fantasy.

Members of the Anna Freud Centre research group on adopted children found that there were certain similarities and recurring themes that emerged in the material of adopted children. Fantasies of 'not being wanted', of having been stolen or kidnapped or of having a dead or ill biological mother resonated with a particular internal representation of a parent, the self and the nature of the interaction between them. Part of any adopted child's environment is their parents' own fantasies about the adoption and their child's birth parents (Hodges, 1990: 64). But for late-placed adopted children, the questions about being given up may be expressed in different ways and may be repeatedly tested out in their new homes: put succinctly by Salo (1990: 85) 'Will they want to keep me? Am

I wantable?' This may be the basis for much of the provocation, confusion of identity and enactments that adoptive parents often have to endure and which can erode their love and undermine their confidence.

Salo (1990: 86) discusses the difficult and regressed behaviour that adopted parents may be faced with, sometimes for long periods of time. Yet this is at odds with what is hoped for: 'the parents wish that family life which they provide should be sufficient in itself to compensate the child for the effects of any past deprivations, and that it should speedily result in a child whose development is as adequate as any (idealised) child born to them' (Hodges *et al.*, 1985).

More recently, Rustin (2006) poignantly identifies a fundamental question for children who are fostered or adopted – 'where do I belong?'. Rustin (2006: 107) points out that '[t]he idea of belonging somewhere is an ordinary and fundamental building block of personal identity'. She discusses the emotional 'challenges of development' for looked after and adopted children whose sense of belonging and therefore personal identity has not been securely established due to early experiences of abuse, neglect or trauma. She draws particular attention to the group of children who show 'inhibition and delayed development', and to the fact that often these children are less likely to be a focus of concern because they do not cause trouble to parents and other adults, though they may be showing signs that therapeutic help is needed. Rustin (2006: 125) emphasises the importance, when working therapeutically with such emotionally scarred and vulnerable children, of '"tiptoeing" up to the child's pain alongside a clear-sighted focus on the nature of the distress and its underlying sources'.

The complex interplay of forces in the inner world of the adopted child

The fact that these issues so readily arise and the way in which they might linger long after childhood takes us full circle to the heart of psychoanalytic thinking – interest in and curiosity about the basic questions of life and of who we are. Focusing on the inner world of the child, however, touches on painful issues – particularly in relation to separation and loss. For children placed in an adoptive home from birth or early infancy, there is the loss of parents they cannot remember or never knew. But for late-adopted children, as discussed previously, there may be multiple losses. In addition to the loss of the continuity of their lives, many of these children have not had the early experience of attunement and thoughtful emotional interactions that would help them develop the inner resources they would need to make sense of all that had happened. For these children, their experiences may be so fragmented and disorganised that it is difficult for them to gather a sufficient sense of who or what has been lost even to grieve.

Fahlberg (1991) regards the capacity to grieve previous losses as crucial to the establishment of new relationships and describes the way in which unresolved losses may interfere with this process. Yet many of the children who come into care have also been traumatised, either by the impact of a single event that had precipitated their reception into care, or more often in a cumulative way over time. Trauma is characterised by being overwhelmed and not being able to think symbolically (Garland, 1991). The word 'trauma', from its Greek derivation, means 'wound' and implies either a physical or an emotional shock, experienced also as a psychic shock. In contrast, the work of mourning is the gradual letting go of lost relationships through separation or death, of lost fantasies, or even aspects of the self. This process involves relinquishing what has been lost, internalising aspects of this in the self and embracing reality in a different and important way (Freud, 1917).

Eth and Pynoos (1985) describe the interplay of these two processes – grief and trauma resolution – and the way in which this causes a 'psychological dysynchrony': that is, the difficulty in negotiating these two processes simultaneously. Pynoos (1992) states that 'children seem particularly vulnerable to the dual demands of trauma mastery and grief work', as trauma interferes with the working-through of childhood bereavement and vice versa.

In therapeutic work, issues related to trauma may obscure or overshadow more complex feelings of loss or mourning, perhaps for long periods. In the chapters that follow, there are many examples of this. What then happens to the fantasies related to adoption, described earlier, which may require a further level of thought and psychological adjustment? As Falhberg (1991: 150) says, 'For children who have at one time had an attachment to their birth parents, even if the relationship was not a psychologically healthy one, mourning their loss is a life task.' Issues connected with adoption may not arise until later in therapy, or as a child develops and begins to formulate their own questions about their origins and why they came to be adopted. This is beautifully illustrated in *Debbie Hindle's* chapter, 'Loss, recovery and adoption: a child's perspective', where a young girl begins to develop her own adoption story, in which the compassion and tears of the adoptive mother bring the child – dead and abandoned in hospital – to life. This story has all the hallmarks of a myth, in terms of its powerful symbolic meaning, which goes far deeper than knowledge about actual events. In our experience, these three themes – trauma, loss and mourning, and fantasies about adoption – weave in and out of clinical work with adopted children, as these shifting perspectives take the foreground, or fade into the background.

What follows was never intended to be, nor ever could be, a comprehensive account of adoption issues, but through clinical work, we are able to access some of the complexities of the emotional experience of adoption.

The structure of the book

Deciding upon a suitable structure for the book proved to be a challenging task. The emotional complexities of adoption span different levels and stages of development and experience. How to organise the various emotional themes of adoption into a meaningful structure? How to combine disparate and dispersed elements into some form of coherence? For instance, ought we to arrange the book in terms of the different emotional tasks of adoption, or different developmental stages of infancy, childhood and adolescence, or different stages of the adoption process? Perhaps this challenge that we faced in organising the material for the book mirrors that of the emotional task of adoption itself in having to bring together, make sense of and give some order to the disparate aspects of emotional experience dispersed across different stages and phases of life. The issue of structure is of course fundamental to adoption in terms of creating and providing a new family structure for the adopted child.

The final structure we decided on is one that begins by addressing a number of overarching issues and questions relevant to the book as a whole. It then moves on to a more specific consideration of the particular nature and type of emotional states and processes that are central to the theme of the book. Next, we focus on three key emotional dimensions of the adoption process or experience, before returning at the end to a further exploration of the more primitive emotional states and processes so typically at play in adoption, and finally some concluding thoughts.

Part I contains three introductory chapters that seek to place in context the clinical material to be discussed in subsequent chapters: the relevance of psycho-analytic thinking to current policy and practice in adoption; recent research in neurobiology and attachment theory; and a discussion of how psychoanalytic child psychotherapy works and how it can help adopted children and families. Part II considers the importance of understanding unconscious emotional dynamics and processes that can occur in the internal world of the individual child, or in the professional network around adoption, or within adoptive families. In Part III the focus shifts to clinical encounters: the detailed clinical case discussions in this section illustrate how unconscious primitive states of mind, if they are not contained, can impact on relationships in damaging and destructive ways, and the relevance of this to adopted children in their lives. Parts IV, V and VI focus on the emotional tasks and complexities of three key aspects of the adoption experience: first, joining and becoming part of a family, with the associated theme of belonging; second, being part of a family, with specific reference to emotional issues and dynamics linked to dyadic and triadic relationships; and third, the developmental stage of adolescence, with particular reference to primitive emotional issues linked to the core adolescent tasks of establishing a mature identity and separation from the family.

In the Endpiece, the primitive emotional issues of adoption are explored from a different angle, through a work of literature; this comprises a close reading of Emily Brontë's classic novel *Wuthering Heights* which is considered as a cautionary tale of adoption. Lastly, in Final Thoughts the editors draw together some ideas and reflections that have emerged from the book.

References

Altman, N. (2001) 'Bridging the Atlantic for psychoanalysis: an appreciation of the contribution of Anne Alvarez', in J. Edwards (ed.) *Being Alive: Building on the Work of Anne Alvarez*, London: Brunner-Routledge.
Alvarez, A. (1992) *Live Company*, London: Routledge.

Bick, E. (1968) 'The experience of the skin in early object relations', *International Journal of Psychoanalysis*, 49: 484–6.

Bion, W.R. (1962) *Learning from Experience*, London: Marefield Reprints.

Boston, M. and Szur, R. (1983) *Psychotherapy with Severely Deprived Children*, London: Routledge and Kegan Paul.

Brinich, P. (1980) 'Some potential effects of adoption on self and object representations', *Psychoanalytic Study of the Child*, 35: 107–33.

Brinich, P. (1990) 'Adoption, ambivalence and mourning: Clinical and theoretical inter-relationships', *Adoption and Fostering*, 14 (1): 6–17.

Brodzinsky, D.W. and Schechter, M.D. (eds) (1990) *The Psychology of Adoption*, New York: Oxford University Press.

Brodzinsky, D.W., Smith, D.W. and Brodzinsky, A.B. (1998) *Children's Adjustment to Adoption: Developmental and Clinical Issues*, London: Sage Publications.

Carter, B. and McGoldrick, M. (1989) 'Overview: the changing family life cycle. A framework for family therapy', in B. Carter and M. McGoldrick (eds) *The Changing Family Life Cycle*, London: Allyn and Bacon.

Emanuel, R. (1984) 'Primary disappointment', *Journal of Child Psychotherapy*, 10 (1): 71–87.

Emde, R. (1999) 'Moving ahead: integrating influences of affective processes for development and for psychoanalysis', *International Journal of Psychoanalysis*, 80 (3): 317–39.

Eth, S. and Pynoos, R. (1985) 'Interaction of trauma and grief in childhood', in S. Eth and R. Pynoos (eds) *Post-Traumatic Stress Disorder in Children*, Washington, DC: American Psychiatric Press.

Falhberg, V. (1991) *A Child's Journey Through Placement*, London: British Association for Adoption and Fostering.

Fleming, R. (2005) 'Psychoanalytic thinking about adoption', unpublished paper.

Freud, S. (1914) 'Remembering, repeating and working through', *S.E.* XII.

Freud, S. (1917) 'Mourning and melancholia', *S.E.* XIV.

Gallagher, M., Leavitt, K. and Kimmel, H. (1995) 'Mental health treatment of cumulatively/ repeatedly traumatized children', *Smith College Studies in Social Work*, 65 (3): 205–37.

Garland, C. (1991) 'External distress and the internal world: an approach to psychotherapeutic understanding of survivors', in J. Holmes (ed.) *Handbook of Psychotherapy for Psychiatrists*, Edinburgh: Churchill Livingstone.

Gerhardt, S. (2004) *Why Love Matters: How Affection Shapes a Baby's Brain*, London and New York: Routledge.

Hart, A. and Luckock, B. (2004) *Developing Adoption Support and Therapy: New Approaches for Practice*, London: Jessica Kingsley.

Henry, G. [Williams] (1974) 'Doubly deprived', *Journal of Child Psychotherapy*, 3 (4): 15–28.

Hodges, J. (1984) 'Two crucial questions – adopted children in psychoanalytic treatment', *Journal of Child Psychotherapy*, 10 (1): 47–56.

Hodges, J. (1990) 'The representation of self and objects in early maternal deprivation and adoption', *Journal of Child Psychotherapy*, 16 (1): 53–73.

Hodges, J. and Tizard, B. (1989a) 'IQ and behavioural adjustment of ex-institutional adolescents', *Journal of Child Psychology and Psychiatry*, 30 (1): 53–75.

Hodges, J. and Tizard, B. (1989b) 'Social and family relationships of ex-institutional adolescents', *Journal of Child Psychology and Psychiatry*, 30 (1): 77–97.

Hodges, J., Bolletti, R., Salo, F. and Oldeschulte, R. (1985) 'Remembering is so much harder', *Bulletin Anna Freud Centre*, 18: 169–79.

Hopkins, J. (2000) 'Overcoming a child's resistance to a late adoption: how one new attachment can facilitate another', *Journal of Child Psychotherapy*, 26 (3): 335–47.

Hopson, J.L. (1998) 'Fetal psychology', *Psychology Today*, September/October: 44–8.

Hunter, M. (2001) *Psychotherapy with Young People in Care: Lost and Found*, Hove: Brunner-Routledge.

Kendrick, J. (2000) 'Be a kid: the traumatic impact of repeated separations on children who are fostered and adopted', *Journal of Child Psychotherapy*, 26 (3): 393–412.

Kendrick, J. (2006) 'Work with children in transition', in J. Kendrick, C. Lindsey and L. Tollemach (eds) *Creating New Families: Therapeutic Approaches to Fostering, Adoption and Kinship Care*, London: Karnac.

Kendrick, J., Lindsey, C. and Tollemach, L. (eds) (2006) *Creating New Families: Therapeutic Approaches to Fostering, Adoption and Kinship Care*, London: Karnac.

Klein, M. (1937) 'Love, guilt and reparation', in *Love, Guilt and Reparation*, London: Hogarth, 1975. Reprinted by London: Virago, 1988.

Klein, M. (1940) 'Mourning and its relation to manic-depressive states', in *Love, Guilt and Reparation*, London: Hogarth, 1975. Reprinted by London: Virago, 1988.

Lanyado, M. (2004) *The Presence of the Therapist: Treating Childhood Trauma*, Hove: Brunner-Routledge.

Lindsey, C. and Barrett, S. (2006) 'A systemic conceptual framework', in J. Kendrick, C. Lindsey, and L. Tollemach (eds) *Creating New Families: Therapeutic Approaches to Fostering, Adoption and Kinship Care*, London: Karnac.

Meltzer, D. and Harris, M. (1976) 'A psychoanalytic model of the child-in-the-family-in-the-community', in A. Hahn (ed.) *Sincerity and Other Works: Collected Papers of Donald Meltzer*, London: Karnac, 1994.

Midgley, N. (2006) 'The "inseparable bond between cure and research": clinical case study as a method of psychoanalytic inquiry', *Journal of Child Psychotherapy*, 32 (2): 122–47.

Performance and Innovation Unit (PIU) (2000) *Prime Minister's Review of Adoption*, London: Cabinet Office

Pynoos, R. (1992) 'Grief and trauma in children and adolescents', *Bereavement Care*, 11 (1): 2–10.

Rustin, M. (2006) 'Where do I belong? Dilemmas for children and adolescents who have been adopted or brought up in long-term foster care', in J. Kendrick, C. Lindsey and L. Tollemach (eds) *Creating New Families: Therapeutic Approaches to Fostering, Adoption and Kinship Care*, London: Karnac.

Rustin, M. J. (2002) ' Looking in the right place: complexity theory, psychoanalysis and infant observation', *International Journal of Infant Observation and its Applications*, 5 (1): 122–44.

Salo, F. (1990) 'Well, I couldn't say no, could I? Difficulties in the path of late adoption', *Journal of Child Psychotherapy*, 16 (1): 75–91.

Stern, D. (1985) *The Interpersonal World of the Infant*, New York: Basic Books.

Symington, I. (1985) 'The survival function of primitive omnipotence', *International Journal of Psychoanalysis*, 66: 486.

Terr, L. (1991) 'Childhood trauma: An outline and overview', *American Journal of Psychiatry*, 148, 1: 10–20.

Tizard, B. and Hodges, J. (1978) 'The effect of early institutional rearing on the development of eight-year-old children', *Journal of Child Psychology and Psychiatry*, 19 (2): 99–118.

Trevarthen, C. (1979) 'Communication and cooperation in early infancy: a description of primary intersubjectivity', in M. Bullowa (ed.) *Before Speech*, Cambridge: Cambridge University Press.

Triseliotis, J., Shireman, J. and Hundleby, M. (1997) *Adoption: Theory, Policy and Practice*, London: Cassell.

Tronick, E.Z. (2003) 'Of course all relationships are unique: how co-creative processes generate mother–infant and parent–therapist relationships and change other relationships', *Psychoanalytic Inquiry*, 23 (3): 473–91.

Watson, K. (1994) 'The history of adoption', Keynote address, North American Council on Adoptable Children. Reprinted in *Family Matters (Oregon's Special Needs Adoption Newsletter)*, 7 February: 1–2, 7.

Part I
Setting the scene

Introduction

Graham Shulman

The three chapters in this first section set the scene in different ways and provide a context for those that follow. They lay out the broad conceptual foundations of the book and introduce readers to the characteristics and approach of a psychoanalytic perspective.

In the opening chapter, 'Developing a curiosity about adoption: a psychoanalytic perspective', *John Simmonds* describes the distinctive contribution that a psychoanalytic perspective can make to thinking about adoption. Simmonds argues that psychoanalysis has a 'unique position in the human sciences', and that a psychoanalytic approach goes to the emotional heart of human relationships with its focus on how feelings and unconscious fantasies shape relationships and interactions. He stresses the explanatory power of psychoanalytic understanding, with its emphasis on underlying meaning rather than merely on external behaviour or 'symptoms' and their management or treatment. This is in turn linked to the way in which a psychoanalytic therapeutic approach functions as a medium of change. Simmonds also gives a historical outline of the changing views about, and attitudes to, adoption within a social and professional context and suggests that a psychoanalytic perspective converges with current thinking in the field of adoption. Finally, through a reading of the fairy tale *Thumbelina*, Simmonds illustrates the emotional drama of curiosity about the past and the predicament of adopted children.

In the second chapter, 'Why is early development important?', *Sally Wassell* discusses some of the findings and theoretical developments in related fields which lend weight to the psychoanalytic focus on the significance and relevance of experience in infancy. The meaning and importance of experience in infancy has been a fundamental premise of psychoanalytic thinking from its beginning. Wassell's discussion of attachment theory, research into the attachment patterns of adoptive parents, and neuroscience research on brain development explores the relevance of infancy to emotional, psychological and cognitive development and in turn to adoption. Wassell considers the implications for adoption practice of the findings in these fields. She argues that these findings highlight the critical importance of early intervention in relation to children who have experienced abuse, neglect or trauma. The chapter also stresses the importance of 'the development of a wide range of therapeutic and support services for the adoptive child'.

The third chapter, 'Understanding an adopted child: a child psychotherapist's perspective' by *Lisa Miller*, focuses on individual psychoanalytic psychotherapy as a therapeutic option for adopted children and adolescents experiencing serious emotional difficulties. Miller describes the nature of psychoanalytic psychotherapy, how it works, and the type of damage or disturbance at pre-verbal or non-verbal levels that it is well suited to address. She illustrates these points with detailed and vivid extracts from clinical material which bring to life those aspects of the inner world and of unconscious processes that can find expression and can be engaged within the therapeutic frame. The chapter reflects the way in which psychoanalytic psychotherapy serves not only as a therapeutic modality but also as a distinctive lens through which to see and understand those problems of emotional and mental life that have their roots in infancy and early development.

1 Developing a curiosity about adoption

A psychoanalytic perspective

John Simmonds

Psychoanalytic understanding has a distinctive contribution to make to our understanding about individual, group and social processes. Over the course of its development, its intense focus on the depth and richness of the human psyche has given it a unique position in the human sciences. In part this results from many of its ideas coming principally from clinical work with patients and in part from the fact that it has never avoided confronting some of the darker, more disturbing and even sinister aspects of human emotion and behaviour. But maybe above all, it has almost exclusively relied in its approach to providing therapy on the essence of what it is to be human – people communicating with each other through on-going relationships that have meaning, are structured, provide consistency and are relatively long lasting. In particular, it has developed a powerful perspective on the impact that people have on each other, often unknowingly, through the concept of transference and countertransference. Its focus on the importance of understanding through reflective consideration of the emotional content of what is inside the therapist and what is inside the child or adolescent in interaction makes it distinct. This explanatory and relational perspective is central to bringing about change and drives the power of its therapeutic endeavour. However, many of these principles, indeed the psychoanalytic approach to therapeutic interventions, do not sit easily in the modern world's demand for quick – if not instant – solutions to human problems. With the demand for evidence-based, low-cost and low-skill interventions, psychoanalytic psychotherapy sits uneasily in the modern world of child and adolescent mental health. However, whatever challenges it faces, it has never been static and recent explorations of some of the links between its fundamental concepts of the structure of emotional processes, attachment theory and neuroscience (Fonagy, 2001; Fonagy *et al.*, 2002; Siegel, 1999) have been re-affirming and continue to deepen its knowledge base.

One issue that has driven psychoanalytic approaches to therapy is its radical intent. While the relief of symptoms may be a part of its intended outcome, the psychoanalytic therapist is also concerned with a deeper understanding about the meaning of symptoms – emotional and behavioural – and their place in the greater architecture of the individual psyche. The focus of therapy is not therefore just to relieve the person's symptoms but to understand and explore their meaning with the object of re-integrating them within the psyche. The symptom is not therefore regarded as a foreign object inside the person, to be ejected in the process of therapy, but a source of learning about something that is important about the individual. It is important not to misunderstand this, because for the most part the removal of symptoms is probably what drives the individual – or in the case of children and adolescents, their parents – to seek therapy in the first place. Therapists cannot ignore this, as symptoms do have very real consequences and cause great misery and pain. However, the significance of the psychoanalytic approach is that it has taken a perspective that symptoms are a route into an individual's history and story – they tell us something about people that needs to be paid attention to and understood. This is not some romanticisation of the 'symptom' but a recognition of the part that uncomfortable and painful thoughts, feelings and behaviour play in the relational and social basis of human beings and the individual drive to create and have a sense of both meaning and belonging. Symptoms may threaten this sense of meaning and belonging but exploring and understanding them may be the pathway through which people can relate to both themselves and others. In this sense, the curiosity of psychoanalysis is one of the great humanising influences in mental health.

Adoption as an intervention: ordinary or extraordinary parenting?

Adoption is also one of the most radical interventions that can be made in the life of a child. Adoption changes everything. Whatever the child brings into their adoptive home – their genetic inheritance, their personality, their pre-birth and pre-placement experiences, their class, ethnicity, language, culture and family history – it will be changed by the people, circumstances and opportunities that make up their new world. And the adoptive home – the people, circumstances and opportunities – will also be changed by the child and what they bring to the placement. It is a therapeutic intervention of the most monumental kind and like all interventions, it is intended to change things for the better. What is striking about it as a therapeutic intervention of course is that the primary therapeutic agent is the loving and caring of ordinary but really quite exceptional adults as adoptive parents.

In recent years, there has been increasing concern about the nature of this 'ordinariness' in adoptive parents and the extent to which the 'exceptional' is really a requirement – whatever the exact definition of the 'exceptional' might actually be. What once had been considered to be the primary therapeutic agent – the placement itself – has given way to a debate about whether, as a necessary condition, it requires a skill and knowledge base to provide what can be called therapeutic parenting. There are however, some difficulties with this. The adoption of young children is a highly emotive subject. The image of an abandoned, unwanted or unloved child is both a disturbing and also an appealing image, to which most people will respond immediately and instinctively. The Tsunami disaster in 2005 brought thousands of requests from people wanting to know how to adopt orphaned children. National Adoption Week 2006 in the UK produced 3500 telephone calls after children needing adoptive homes were shown on GMTV and several thousand information packs were requested by people interested in applying to adopt. Adoption draws on the powerful desire in adults to provide something that children need – lifelong, loving parents and a home they can call their own and which lasts through childhood and beyond. It also draws on the need that adults have to be parents. This powerful combination is the basis of successful adopter recruitment campaigns.

However, as instinctive as this response might be, it is often negated by the fear of individuals or couples that they will not meet the strict standards that agencies set to become an adopter, or that the process will take too long (Performance and Innovation Unit, 2000). Addressing misconceptions about the process to create a more open, welcoming and realistic picture of the adopter approval process, as well as creating greater consistency and transparency, has been an important policy and practice objective for some time (Secretary of State for Health, 2000; Dept. of Health, 2001). However, this has also created a dilemma – for while campaigns that encourage people to come forward to meet the demand for adoptive homes are important, the children who need adoptive homes often have complex special needs. These may result from abuse and neglect but other factors like genetic vulnerability, mother's drug use/diet/health in pregnancy, premature birth and perinatal complications may be significant. The placement of sibling groups, children with a black or a mixed race heritage and the need to consider contact with birth parents and other relatives will complicate the process. Experiences in care, the length of time in care or the number of placements in care will add to this.

While the number of children adopted from care increased steadily to 2005[1] (Dept. for Education and Skills, 2006), there is still a significant mismatch between children needing homes and those approved to take them. This has resulted in a sizable proportion of children who have had a 'best interest decision' made that they should be placed for adoption, never in fact being placed. In one study (Selwyn *et al.*, 2006) of 130 children who had a best interest decision that they should be placed for adoption, 104 were matched, although 15 of these disrupted during introductions. Ninety-six children (74 per cent) were actually placed in families and at follow up after, on average, 7 years, 80 (61 per cent) were still there. It is also important to note that in this sample, while many of the children had severe and persistent problems at placement, only 7 per cent received therapeutic help from Child and Adolescent Mental Health Services. However, this increased to 55 per cent on follow up, although only 16 per cent received more than an initial consultation.

If the appeal to ordinary people to come forward to adopt is to be helpful, it should be modified by simultaneously making it clear that adopters have the capacity to manage the complex needs of children who are to be adopted – that which makes up the extra-ordinary. Children who have been abused or neglected and who have experienced disrupted early-caring relationships and uncertain plans have exceptional needs, because their developmental pathways have been so distorted. Changing the material, emotional, and social circumstances and opportunities for the better may be necessary for children who have had such a poor start in life. Not to do so is very likely to result in the continuation of that trajectory, with many of the poor child development outcomes that are known to be the result – and for some this may include death. However, the most significant questions that needs to be addressed are: Is such a profound change in the child's circumstances and opportunities through adoption actually sufficient in itself to turn this trajectory around? Is what starts out as a major piece of environmental therapy enough?

The answer to these questions for many adoptive children is 'No'. In the course of their developmental pathway something, although it is probably no one thing, seems to have become locked inside them that prevents them from fully making use of their new relationships, circumstances and opportunities. Why is it that ordinary, but what in many circumstances is really quite exceptional, loving and caring does not seem to be enough to unlock this? One likely explanation is that children who have lived their early lives in circumstances of overwhelming fear and anxiety have found ways of surviving threats to their physical, psychological and social being; what they learnt was adaptive in those circumstances of great threat, but in their new more ordinary circumstances (in their adoptive homes) this learning is maladaptive. Psychoanalysis has shown the ways in which such psychological coping mechanisms or defences can become engrained in the personality in the form of unconscious patterns of feeling, thought and action from infancy onwards.

More generally, anybody involved in mental health work with children and adolescents will be confronted with the question – what has locked them into the emotional, cognitive and behavioural traps they find themselves in? How much then do proposed interventions need to focus on what is going on inside the child, what is happening in the relationships the child has with significant adults and/or peers or what is missing from the child's external world of opportunities that needs to be improved or changed? It is the familiar territory of the distinction between the internal psychological world of the individual, relationships and the environment in which the individual lives and then, the important connections between them. Adoption might therefore be an extreme form of environmental therapy but it is intended to have an impact on what goes on inside the child, in the child's relationships with others and in their increasing engagement with education, leisure and recreation and – in time – employment, politics and the wider social world.

The development of adoption as an intervention: what is it a symptom of?

Adoption literature has frequently debated whether the fact of adoption is a risk factor for those children adopted (Brodzinsky *et al.*, 1998; Brodzinsky and Palacios, 2005). One important distinction that has been identified in this is the difference between adoption as an intervention for maltreated children from the care system in the UK and adoption as a solution to the (largely historical) problem of unwanted pregnancy, social stigma and shame. These are somewhat different problem types. Adoption historically focused on the problems of social order, with the baby a very passive victim of the birth mother's (and father's) transgression of the rules of 'accepted' social behaviour. Currently, the child in need of placement is the primary concern because of the actual or potential risks to them that result from their birth parents' behaviour. In this sense the child is an active victim and their development – and even survival – a matter of direct concern involving the legal intervention of the State. The psychology of adoption in these two different contexts is somewhat different. With 'relinquished' infants, adoption psychology has developed out of a fairly lengthy period where the placement was itself considered to be sufficient to set the child on a normal developmental pathway. The child's past – their genetic, family and social inheritance and any pre-placement experience, as well as the fact of adoption – was largely considered to be a matter of irrelevance and in many cases was actively thought to be best locked away as a secret. Such extremes gradually gave way to a recognition of the existence of the child's curiosity about origins, the importance of knowledge about the reasons for 'being given up' to adoption and eventually indirect and even direct contact with birth mothers and others. This has been paralleled by concerns about the significance of separation and loss on the child, even when the placement was made in the first few weeks after birth. Other concerns have centred on the impact on family dynamics of the adoption story or secret, or anxiety about rejection and belonging. Denial, anxiety, loss and separation, family dynamics and birth family issues including an adoption identity have been the focus of discussion and concern for mental health professionals in relation to adoption of this type.

Is it right then to regard adoption as symptomatic? Is it a problem to be solved? In this sense, are the manifestations of some of the emotional and behavioural problems associated with it in need of diagnosis, treatment and eventually elimination? A psychoanalytic view would, as I suggested earlier, identify any symptoms as indicative of a story that has meaning and in that sense needs to be understood. The symptoms may cause real pain and distress, and the primary wish may be to just get rid of them, but the risk is that in the process something about the person or the situation may get lost or denied – and in fact the likelihood is that the 'symptom' will re-appear in some form, because the story has not gone away. Adoption practice started out with a view that it was better denied and not treated as something that signifies anything at all – and some people in their later years are still discovering that they were in fact adopted 50 or 60 years earlier. But the existence of such massive denial does suggest of course that, rather than being insignificant, it is so significant that, if it was known and thought about, it would create so much anxiety and raise so many questions that it would be intolerable and destructive. So what might be revealed – the couple's infertility, the child's social origins and illegitimate beginning, the means by which the child was acquired, the child rejecting their adoptive parents in favour of their birth parents? Adoption and the adopted child may therefore generally be regarded as symptomatic of things that are embedded in the history of the family but which cannot be thought or talked about. The adoption 'symptom' in such situations is therefore the route into important parts of the individual and family story. It inevitably has meaning to the individual and has potential to be the means by which they are more meaningfully connected to and a part of their social group. But curiosity and knowledge about it were thought to be better avoided because of the dangerous story that they might tell.

The importance of curiosity

Adoption has in many respects moved on from this. A more up-to-date view is that curiosity is important for all children in order to learn about the world and that they should be able to ask questions and engage adults in a discussion, whatever anxiety this may stir up. Openness – the structural arrangements put in place to maintain some form of contact between the adopted child and their birth family – and 'communicative openness' – the state of mind of the adopter, child and birth family to adoption (Brodzinsky and Pinderhughes, 2002) – is the modern approach in adoption. What has become symptomatic has shifted to a somewhat different domain, although the anxiety and difficulties associated with the adoption story have not gone away. Much of this now centres around the issues outlined above – the child's emotional and behavioural problems that impact directly on their well-being and development and their relationship with their adoptive parent/s. So what has become symptomatic can mainly be attributed to a combination of direct maltreatment and the consequences of a poor start in life, which results in the intervention of child protection services. In a significant number of families (Rushton *et al.*, 2003), these emotional and behavioural problems cause great consternation and acute unhappiness and for some, threaten the on-going integrity of the family. Although this issue is well known, finding helpful ways of addressing it has not proved to be easy. Attachment theory and more particularly attachment disorder have come to dominate the discourse – but as powerful as attachment disorder is as an explanatory concept, it has not readily translated into a set of interventions that solve the problem. Adopted children and their families are often directly faced with these perplexing and serious issues which do not easily lend themselves to explanation or intervention. Curiosity in these circumstances takes on a different meaning and this needs to be unpicked.

Explanation and intervention in modern adoption

The relationship between explanation and intervention is a significant issue in many situations involving children, not just adoption. Making sense of a child or adolescent's feelings or behaviour is important to parents and to mental health professionals. It is core to being human and to human relationships, and to being able to carry out the tasks of daily living: if a parent comes to understand that Dave is hungry, tired, cold, or isn't feeling well, then they can put a course of action into effect to address this. At another level, explaining is also core to the tasks of the mental health professional: Dave is feeling anxious because he is worried that his mother will leave him; or Dave is behaving like this because he is angry that he was left so long. Explanations – whether routine daily explanations, or complex multi-dimensional assessments – are central to being able to take action, whether it is the provision of a routine meal or a therapeutic intervention.

However, commonplace as they are, coming up with an explanation is not necessarily straightforward. They are usually approximations of what a parent or professional has seen, heard or felt and are often not so much science as 'best guesses'. They also usually have qualities of contingency: 'let's try this and see if I was right and if it works'. Of course, carers and professionals usually develop a repertoire of explanations that results in them not having to treat every situation as unique. Experience will play an important part in this and over the course of time they will develop general concepts, frameworks and models which organise the data of new experience and give it predictive meaning and power. However, there are occasions when, for instance, a child gives a series of clues suggesting that they are hungry but providing them with food doesn't seem to make them feel any better. The carer may try other explanations and interventions based on what they know and find that nothing seems to work as expected. There does not appear to be a coherent explanation that makes sense of the child's state so that the intervention changes that state. It is often not clear in such situations whether it is the explanation that is wrong or the intervention designed to address the problem.

This probably lies at the heart of many issues facing adopters today – what they anticipated was that the problems the child brought with them would be turned around by their ordinary loving and caring. But the child does not and cannot respond to this and this creates an emotional atmosphere that is profoundly disturbing. It impacts on their sense of well-being, in the feelings they have about their competence and with couples, their feelings about each other, in their connection to their social world and most significantly about the child. They become immersed in a dark and what often feels unremitting story of powerful feelings and unbearable thoughts.

In such situations, adopters will most likely try to understand their predicament by referring to the child's past. In reality, they haven't shared or shaped the child's earlier experience, so that coming up with explanations about feeling or emotion can be a bit of a hit-or-miss affair. Of course, everybody would expect there to be a period of 'getting to know you' and of adjustment. But most adopters would expect that pretty soon they will come to understand and have a reasonably coherent picture of the child, across a span of daily routines, as well as – eventually – some understanding of the deeper issues about the child's personality. It is a reasonable assumption, based on the adaptability of human beings to each other in new relationships and of the process of necessary adjustment that this requires. It is this that makes up the importance of the ordinariness in adoption – that parents and children can grow to understand and love one another when the basic conditions are in place that enable and promote this.

However, when understanding does not develop, explanation may then seem inadequate as a basis for action. In such circumstances, the overarching explanation may be that something in the child's past is getting in the way – perhaps they have an attachment disorder which needs to be identified and dealt with. It is probably also inevitable that at some level, the adoptive parent will come to feel that it is something about them that is wrong – they do not have the patience or the skills or can't find sufficient love. Whether the answer lies with the child or the adopter, there is growing disillusion about the possibility of developing a relationship that is meaningful and resembles something of what is anticipated and expected from child/parent relationships.

There can be real problems in such situations of constructing explanations and interventions that do justice to these powerful feelings of disillusionment, with real fears of rejection and breakdown. While professional explanations can be detailed and rigorous, they are often devoid of very much meaning to the lay person or the child. Everyday explanations may be more meaningful but they often lack the richness or depth that fully captures the narrative of experience, the connections between events and their forward momentum and how these can change over time.

Curiosity and the problem of the woman in a fairytale

The importance of curiosity, explanation and understanding is powerfully set out in the fairy tale *Thumbelina* (Andersen, 1984). It is a story of almost unimaginable terror about two characters, a woman who wishes for a child and the child herself – Thumbelina. On the surface, the relationship between them is that of mother and child. However, there is something odd about the woman's predicament, because although she wants a child, she does not know 'where she might get one'. This woman's problem arises not through her inability to conceive a child (as is so often the case with adopters and infertility) but in not knowing how to get one. This is something like the kinds of questions that young children have about how babies are made and the kinds of stories that parents make up to avoid giving young children sexual information that they can't understand, because it is unimaginable, anxiety provoking or maybe rather ugly. But this is not a child trying to imagine how babies are made, but a woman. The reader is invited to be curious about what might have happened to this woman, so that in her mind she is unable to conceive of the process by which babies are made: that getting pregnant requires a sexual relationship between two people. What experiences might she have had that have so completely blocked this out? Individuals do not usually find themselves in such a strange emotional state, so that one of the fundamentals of human life is unimaginable. Is this what in modern day thinking is a response to trauma? In desperation, the woman turns to an old witch – much as an adopter might turn to an adoption agency – and pleads, '*I'd so much like to have a little child! Won't you please tell me where I can get one from?*' Even this question suggests that she sees the growth of a child as something that happens outside of her, rather than something that happens inside her (as a pregnancy), or between her and somebody else, as a conception. It adds to the rather bleak and worrying picture about the state of this woman's mind and again invites curiosity about what might have happened to her before the story begins. In a few sentences, we have been invited to think about a troubling and sterile world – very different to the ordinary human world, where babies result from the coming together of two adults and growth through pregnancy happens inside the woman. The witch is more directly responsive to the woman's request than would be allowed in most adoption agencies, maybe enticed by the payment of a shilling, and gives her a grain of barley. Although what results seems more like growth during pregnancy, the witch tells the woman that this grain of barely is different, '*it's not the kind that grows in the farmer's field or that hen's eat*'. Consistent with the woman's plight, the child does not grow inside her, but rather by some magical process. And this continues, for '*in the middle of a flower, on a green stool, sat a tiny little girl, delicate and lovely: she was not above an inch tall, and so she was called Thumbelina*'. However, even this is odd, because Thumbelina arrives as a '*tiny little* girl', not a baby.

The whole narrative has a dreamlike quality. It is a familiar world but, in reality, events do not happen in the way that they are described. The woman is identifiable – even believable – but she is living in a world that works to different rules. This is the world of dreams.

What happens next is terrifying and the worst of all possible nightmares. However, it may also give us some insight into what could have happened to the woman to bring her to the frozen emotional state just described. As such, the emotional state between the woman and Thumbelina is not so much that of mother and child but rather a picture of her internalised, traumatised state of mind. *Thumbelina* is therefore a story about what happened to a woman that created her frozen state.

Andersen has created a narrative in *Thumbelina* that explicitly records the unfolding of traumatic events in much the same way as a dream captures experience, thought and feeling. By using the medium of a fairy story, he has been able to capture the powerlessness of the victim role in traumatic circumstances and the unfolding of the inevitable tragedy. The opening few paragraphs might be thought of as describing, in a very condensed form, the problem of a woman in a precarious emotional state, almost psychotic. The middle and bulk of the story explains why and what happened to her that brought this about and the end describes the emotional resolution.

As perfect as Thumbelina's conception and arrival is, it is quickly overshadowed by the wicked nature of all-too-human intention and behaviour, in the form of an '*old toad who comes hopping in through the window, where there was a broken pane of glass*'. Thumbelina is stolen and immediately thrust from the innocence of childhood to the premature confrontation with adult sexuality and desire, '*She'd make a nice wife for my son!*' There are dark and overpowering associations: '*The toad looked very big and wet and ugly and lived at the bottom of the garden in ground that was marshy and muddy.*' Thumbelina is imprisoned on a water lily in the middle of a lake and cries bitterly at the separation from her mother. She is then confronted by the toad and her son swimming out '*to fetch her pretty bed which they wanted to have ready in the bride's bedroom*'. How would Thumbelina reconcile the toad's wish for her to have '*a very nice place to live*' when this was '*down below in the mud*' and then what would she have made of her future husband, when all he could say was 'Croak, croak, croak'? This is truly shocking.

Andersen gives us some insight into the experiences of a child who has been confronted by an adult (represented by the toad) whose own needs and desires have overwhelmed those of the child. It is a scenario that many adoptive parents have to face. Whatever preparation and training they have received and whatever messages are conveyed about the complex backgrounds and traumatic experiences of children placed for adoption, being confronted and forced to think about the child's prior experience can be overwhelming. However, it is not that the child describes their experiences directly; they very often cannot do this. The trauma is acted out in emotions and behaviour that only hint at what lies underneath. Any child who has been identified by a mother as a partner – and particularly a sexual partner – for their son would need to develop defences that enabled them to survive such dangerous and abusive intent. This might include an instinctive survival response that shuts down the sense of having an internal world of thought and feeling. Rather than an internal world that is meaningful and coherent and gives a strong sense of self and identity, it is a world that threatens to overwhelm with images and feelings that are terrifying and to be avoided. These primitive defences may come to completely block out the idea of relationships (and eventually sexual relationships) and leave an adult woman feeling perplexed or terrified by the idea of what happens when two people come together. The problem with these kinds of traumatic narratives, once established in a child's mind, is that they are very difficult to articulate: because doing so – telling the story – means re-living the very thing that needs to be avoided.

Is Andersen giving us a clue to the question as to why the woman didn't know how she could get a child? Was it that she had been so abused that she had come to block out any idea of having an inner world, block out a world of relationships that are sinister and ugly, or block out ideas about a dangerous sexuality? This is not a story about what will happen to Thumbelina but a story about what has happened.

If this woman lives in a frozen world where nothing can be imagined because it is too terrifying, what would we think if we tried to get to know her? How would we respond and judge what is likely to be her strange presentation and strange behaviour? Would we be able to explain – or even begin to be able to get to know – what horrors she has been through? Could we begin to make a relationship with her and could we begin to like her? And what if she were a child placed for adoption – what might her behaviour signify; what explains her frozen or maybe aggressive state? Can we begin to make a relationship with her as a child and can we begin to understand her?

Andersen suggests that this distressing message can be heard by those ready to listen, as Thumbelina is eventually heard by the '*little fishes, swimming down below* '. They were upset by the plans that were being made for her and so gnawed through the lily's stalk until it '*floated away down the stream … far away down the stream … far away where the toad could not reach her.*' This rescue may be something like the actions of social workers exercising their child protection responsibilities and they are joined by numerous other professionals that usually take part in this in the form of little birds sitting in the bushes who sing '*What a charming little maiden.*' Of course, being set free from the evil intentions of the toad results in a less sinister atmosphere but this is a far from satisfactory place for Thumbelina to be. The fish and the birds may see 'the goodness' in Thumbelina, but it is admiration from the outside – not a relationship with her which she experiences on the inside as safe and meaningful. There is also no acknowledgement in these admiring looks of the terrifying ordeal that she has been through. However, a butterfly takes a liking to Thumbelina and makes more meaningful contact with her. This changes her feelings for the moment and '*she is happy that the toad could no longer reach her and that the sun is shining on the water*'. She reaches out and tries to establish a firmer link with the butterfly, by tying her sash first to the butterfly and then to the leaf she is on. For a moment she feels more securely linked in a safe place to somebody that likes her and wants to be with her – as children can feel with foster carers. But this proves to be short lived – as many children in care discover – as a great cockchafer flies by and '*in a flash fastens his claws about her slender waist and flies up into the tree with her*'. Tragically, the leaf floats away with the butterfly tied to it and consequently leads to its death. One more good experience has died in Thumbelina's mind but '*the cockchafer cares nothing for that*'.

What are the consequences of this further loss for Thumbelina? Is this experience going to reinforce a belief that relationships never last: that just at the point that you start to feel safe with somebody, then something outside of your control snatches it away and that this feels like one more death? Andersen is continuing to remind us of the serious consequences for children when they do not have a secure, loving and lasting relationship with a caring adult. In Andersen's world, children are objects for the gratification of adults, or at best something to be admired from the outside. This message continues to be reinforced, for while the cockchafer is kind to her in giving her honeydew from the flowers to eat – and indeed tells her that she is very pretty – this is no protection from the cruel comments of other cockchafers in the family: '*But she's only got two legs – what a pitiful-looking thing she is!*' '*She hasn't any feelers!*' '*Her waist is so thin – pooh, she looks just like a human! How ugly she is!*' This cruel attack on Thumbelina comes also to infect the cockchafer's view of her and he flies her down from the tree where '*she wept because she was so ugly ... yet she was the loveliest little thing you could imagine.*' Small children are not in a position to defend themselves from the views of others and the cockchafer's perception of her as ugly comes to dominate the view that she has of herself. This is the beginning of a period of desperate bleakness for Thumbelina. The external world that she now comes to live in symbolises the combined impact of being separated from her mother, the toad's plans for her, the death of the butterfly and the cruel cockchafers. But this is not something that she just experiences in the external world – it has come to dominate the view that she has of herself. So we see her living alone and she cares for herself as best she can but eventually a long cold winter descends, the birds fly away, the trees and flowers wither and even the '*large dock-leaf she had lived under curled up and nothing was left of it but a shrivelled yellow stalk. She was dreadfully cold ... and might have frozen to death.'*

Thumbelina eventually arrives in a pitiful state at the home of a field-mouse, who takes pity on her and welcomes her into her warm house. But despite the welcoming overtures, the relationship is still compromised by the field-mouse's insistence on what Thumbelina can do for her: *'You're welcome to stay with me for the winter, but you must keep my room nice and clean, and tell me stories, for I'm very fond of stories.'* In fact, this failure to appreciate Thumbelina's own needs only deepens as the field-mouse, perhaps out of some interest in securing Thumbelina's future, identifies a wealthy and scholarly mole as a potential husband. However, he is blind – presumably to both who Thumbelina is and what she needs. But as desperately unhappy and as trapped as she feels into agreeing to marry the mole, he nevertheless provides her with a route out of the tragedy of her impoverished and traumatised emotional and social circumstances. He had *'recently dug himself a long passage through the earth'*. In the passage is a dead bird, a swallow, but Thumbelina is told not to be afraid of it, as it died quite recently. This dead swallow encapsulates Thumbelina's traumatic experience and the desperate, near-death state she found herself in after being ejected from the cockchafer's tree. The mole makes a hole through which light shines into the passage from the outside world above and Thumbelina sees the dead bird and feels *'so sorry for it'*. Possibly for the first time she is seeing herself for what has happened to her. The mole can't stand this expression of sorrow and kicks the swallow, saying *'That's one that won't whistle any more.'* It is a cruel and contemptuous act and one that the field-mouse also shares in. However, Thumbelina persists in her care of the dead bird, *'she bent down, gently moved aside its feathers that lay over its head, and kissed its closed eyes.'* And while doing so, a memory is stirred of happier times: *'Perhaps this is the one that sang so beautifully for me during the summer.'* These are powerfully emotional stirrings and later in the night Thumbelina returns to care for the bird, after plaiting a rug of hay and putting cotton-wool around its body. These tender and caring thoughts and actions are reminiscent of what all small children need – but especially when they are frozen through fear. Thumbelina then *'lays her head on the bird's breast, but as she did so, she was quite startled, for it felt just as if something were knocking inside. It was the bird's heart.'* This is the beginning of the swallow coming back to life, and Thumbelina continues to show her tender care and concern, something which the swallow acknowledges: *'Thank you, thank you, pretty little child! ... I'm so nice and warm now, I shall soon get my strength back and be able to fly out again into the warm sunshine!'*

This is a scene of extraordinary therapeutic power and it determines the unfolding of the rest of the story. The swallow indeed recovers its health and eventually leaves Thumbelina. Although the swallow offers to take her, Thumbelina does not want to make the field-mouse sad – a telling reminder of the perverse bonds that children can find themselves trapped in with abusive adults. The consequence of this is that the plans for her marriage to the mole are finalised, despite her deep unhappiness. It is only on the day of the wedding itself, and in the process of saying goodbye to the world that she knows but cannot reach, that the swallow returns to rescue her. Their relationship proves to be the enduring link and the route to a life where Thumbelina eventually feels secure and happy.

Thumbelina is a story about the qualities in relationships that promote emotional health. While not strictly an adoption story, it is the story of a sequence of relationships that in some ways does parallel the modern-day equivalent of children's experiences of abuse and then placements with different people who have different intentions and different qualities. Some of these intentions are cruel and abusive and mark out the preoccupations of adults who see children for what they can get. These are the kinds of relationships that can threaten and destroy emotional growth. The depth of the story, while configured through a traditional victim–persecutor–rescuer dynamic, conveys the complexity of the emotional state of the woman at the beginning of the story and helps us to understand how these experiences have become internalised.

While the story is based on a narrative of what happens between individuals and of their cruelty or kindness to each other, these individuals also represent a constellation of internal figures that continue to tell and re-tell the story in the woman's mind. They are what lock her into her precarious emotional state, even if the environment radically changes around her. Children may start out as victims to be rescued by child protection services from persecuting, dangerous parents. Adopters may become rescuers of victim children from unsatisfactory state care systems. But it is a profound shock when children turn out to be persecutors of victim parents – angry, ungrateful, dismissive and disturbing. What Andersen helps us to do is develop some insight into the processes by which this can happen and then keep repeating itself. He also gives a profound insight into the process by which emotional growth becomes unlocked and moves forward.

It is not the purpose of this chapter to suggest that adoption is the equivalent of a symptom of great disturbance. It is not. Adopted children and adoptive families are a rich and varied group. But I have tried to move the debate about modern adoption into a more humanising framework, not by romanticising about it in the way that it can appear in recruitment campaigns or the media but by rooting it in what psychoanalytic thinking has taught us about the nature of human psyche and relationships. Of course, Thumbelina's predicament is the predicament of some adopted children – indeed for some it is an unnervingly accurate portrayal. For many it is not, but it is does suggest that curiosity and knowledge about the past and its impact on the present will always be important. But while curiosity and knowledge are fundamental to growth, they also create anxiety and fear. This highlights the importance of a place and most particularly relationships where children can explore their anxious and unnerving thoughts and feelings for their significance and meaning. For many, their adoptive parents will through ordinary but extraordinary love provide this. For others, it will take the insight, commitment and expertise of psychotherapy to achieve this.

The richness of psychoanalytic understanding is that it pays significant attention to the content of people's minds, to the connections or lack of connections between different experiences in the mind and then to what happens on the outside through relationships. It might be thought of as 'par excellence' – a story-telling medium that comes closer to conveying the richness of experience than any other. It has also paid considerable attention to disturbed and disturbing experience, to narratives about the unthinkable and the unimaginable, including not being able to think at all. It is a framework therefore that explores and explains but accepts that, as unbearable as it is, the inexplicable is particularly worth paying attention to.

There is nothing mysterious in this. The increasing recognition of the importance of trauma and terror resulting from real events in children's lives is important. One of the features of trauma is powerlessness, with the individual not being able to anticipate or predict life threatening events, control the way that they unfold or manage the impact or consequences that they have on the individual. Trauma and terror create an internal world adjusted to such experience and have the power to continue to re-create that world, however destructive that it might be for the individual or those around them. Exploring and explaining the underlying traumatic narratives and the full force and impact of them on the child, the adopters and mental health professionals is very difficult. It is something that can happen in the detail of an analytic session, or over the course of treatment – but in the absence of that some fairy stories are extraordinary renditions of the impact of trauma and the terror that is a part of it.

Note

1   The rate has recently dropped off again in England and Wales.

References

Andersen, H. (1984) 'Thumbelina', in H. Andersen, *Fairy Tales: A Selection* (pp. 30–45), Oxford: Oxford University Press.

Brodzinsky, D. and Palacios, J. (2005) *Psychological Issues in Adoption: Research and Practice*, Portsmouth, NH: Praeger.

Brodzinsky, D. and Pinderhughes, E. (2002) 'Parenting and child development in adoptive families', in M. Bornstein (ed.) *Handbook of Parenting: Children and Parenting*, Hillsdale, NJ: Lawrence Erlbaum Associates.

Brodzinsky, D., Smith, D. and Brodzinsky, A. (1998) *Children's Adjustment to Adoption: Development and Clinical Issues*, London: Sage.

Dept. for Education and Skills (2006, November 16) http://www.dfes.gov.uk/rsgateway/ DB/SFR/s000691/SFR44–2006.pdf, retrieved May 8, 2007.

Dept. of Health (2001) *National Adoption Standards*, London: Dept. of Health.

Fonagy, P. (2001) *Attachment Theory and Psychoanalysis*, New York: Other Press.

Fonagy, P., Gergely, G., Jurist, E. and Target, M. (2002) *Affect Regulation, Mentalization and the Development of the Self*, New York, NY: Other Press.

Performance and Innovation Unit (2000) *Prime Minister's Review of Adoption*, London: Cabinet Office.

Rushton, A., Mayes, D., Dance, C. and Quinton, D. (2003) 'Parenting late placed children: the development of new relationships and the challenge of behavioural problems', *Clinical Child Psychology and Psychiatry*, 8 (3) 389–400.

Secretary of State for Health (2000) *Adoption: A New Approach*, London: Dept. of Health/ HMSO.

Selwyn, J., Sturgess, W., Quinton, D. and Baxter, C. (2006) *Costs and Outcomes of Non-infant Adoptions*, London: British Association for Adoption and Fostering.

Siegel, D. (1999) *The Developing Mind: How Relationships and the Brain Interact to Shape Who We Are*, New York, NY: Guildford Press.

2　Why is early development important?

Sally Wassell

From its earliest writings, psychoanalytic theory has endeavoured to understand how the mind develops within the context of relationships. Through clinical work, it became clear that many issues in adult life have their origins in early childhood experiences and relationships. Bion (1962), in particular, drew attention to the importance of the repeated interactions between an infant and their primary caregiver and placed emotionality at the centre of psychic life and development. Over the last forty years, there has been a burgeoning of research that has both supported and enriched this psychoanalytic perspective.

This chapter will focus on three main areas of research which have had a profound impact on our understanding of child development and are of particular relevance to thinking about adopted children and their parents. First, attachment theory will be considered in relation to our understanding of what promotes the healthy growth of a child, facilitating exploration and learning. Adaptive mechanisms in the context of abuse and neglect will be outlined, and linked with the impact of different attachment patterns on outcomes in adoption. Second, the significance of the childhood experiences of adoptive carers will be explored in the context of the ways in which caring for hurt children may trigger unresolved issues. Third, recent research on the effects of abuse and neglect on the developing brain will be summarised. The chapter returns to reflect upon what is known about the core features of a caregiving environment most likely to promote emotional healing in a hurt child, emphasising the importance of the adoptive parents' awareness of the unique predicament of their child.

Attachment and the impact of abuse and neglect?

Effective practice in adoption has long been informed by our developing understanding of the significance of children's early, close relationships for their healthy maturation in all the developmental domains. Bowlby (1979) first explored the importance for a child of a 'warm, intimate and continuous relationship' in the early years of life in promoting mental health in later childhood and adulthood. He noted that the quality of early experiences with caregivers, and experiences of separation and loss from these relationships, affects a child's fundamental sense of security, developing sense of self and the quality of later relationships.

In the area of adoption, a child's early attachment relationships need to be understood in order to inform the emotional caregiving within the new adoptive home. In this context it is helpful to think about the ways in which the child has adapted to less than adequate caregiving and specifically to understand the survival mechanisms or strategies they have developed which were necessary within their previous attachment relationships.

There are four key systems of behaviour which inform the careful assessment of the impact of previous learning on a child's attachment security. The first governs a child's need for closeness and the strategies developed to alert their caregiver to their need for reassurance, as well as accurate and prompt responses to experiences of distress or arousal. This is commonly described as the attachment system, which is illustrated by the child's attempts to gain proximity to their attachment figure – commonly known as attachment behaviours. These behaviours are most clearly seen when the child feels anxious or stressed.

Second, the caregiver needs to be attuned to the child's signals of need in order to respond in a sensitive way. The cycles initiated by the carer, first in responding to the child's signals (the arousal relaxation cycle) and second in reaching out to the child (the positive interaction cycle) have been identified by Fahlberg (1991: 26) as pivotal in the promotion of attachment security. The adult's behaviours, both in responding and initiating socio-emotional interaction, make up the caregiving system. A vital consideration, when observing the 'dance' of interaction between parent and child, is the adult's capacity to think about the meaning of the child's signals in order to respond in an attuned manner. As Schofield and Beek (2006: 12) comment:

> The child's experience of having needs met and then of relaxation and well-being is also a learning experience at a psychological level. It shapes beliefs and expectations. The caregiver and the child communicate what it is in their minds by their behaviour.

Third, when a child's basic need for reliability and responsiveness is met, they are free to devote their energies to exploring their environment. These behavioural initiatives are described as the exploratory system. The sensitive caregiver offers a base from which a child is encouraged to venture away from the relationship, in the knowledge that they can return if they experience anxiety. This 'secure base' is therefore fundamental to a child's capacity to develop competence in task completion, promoting resilience and mastery.

Bowlby (1969) also originated the idea of a fourth behavioural system, described as 'sociable or affinitive', emphasising the increasing importance of other relationships with adults and peers for an overall sense of security in the outside world. This is expanded in the work of Dunn (1993), who describes the importance of friendships and close interaction with peers and siblings for children as young as three years. Additionally, attachment theory places at the centre the child's developing capacity to experience, and to make sense of their feelings. Attuned caregivers are vital in promoting the child's ability to manage and regulate their emotions. Through reflecting back to the child what they understand of the child's experience of feelings, they become central to the child's developing ability to process their own emotions. These processes enhance our understanding of the reasons why children who have been abused or neglected appear unable to make sense of their own feelings, much less the feelings and responses of others.

The question of how to explore these key principles was expanded by Ainsworth *et al.* (1978), who developed the Strange Situation – a set situation in which an infant is engaged in play with their mother or caregiver and then left for brief periods with an unfamiliar person. How the young child reacts on separation from their mother and responds to her return provides detailed observational material which can be studied. Through repeated observations of these sequences, three patterns of attachment were identified: secure attachment, insecure ambivalent and insecure avoidant.

Children within the secure group have experienced attuned, sensitive and responsive caregiving which not only promotes exploration, but also builds the foundations of positive self-esteem. Securely attached children view their caregivers as reliable and also perceive themselves as lovable. Additionally, they both express and understand a wide range of emotions within themselves and in others, and are able to tolerate mixed feelings. This promotes healthy social development. They are confident in exploration and have a sense of mastery and self-efficacy, important foundations of resilience (Daniel and Wassell, 2002). Securely attached children are 'mind-minded'; in other words, they are able to think about how others are thinking which, in the context of secure caregiving – including both active prohibitions on cruel or unkind behaviour and strong affirmation of kindness and generosity – promotes the capacity for empathy. Crucially, they are able to 'pause for thought' before responding or acting, thereby reducing impulsivity.

Children with an avoidant pattern of attachment, however, have experienced parenting which is rejecting of their emotional needs, leading a child to demonstrate a false self-reliance and pseudo-independence as a strategy to cope with this particular caregiving style. The message from the carer is, 'if you need comfort, don't come to me, but I will respond to demonstrations of your ability to manage on your own'. These children often hide feelings of low self-esteem behind a mask of apparent confidence. They do not understand their own feelings nor those of others, and possess little capacity for empathy and have poor self-efficacy. Crucially, these children may be mistakenly assessed as resilient, because they have learned not to express distress or signal their emotional needs. This is an organised strategy, which enables the child to achieve the best from their emotionally dismissing caregiver. In adoptive homes, their hidden anger often emerges and may distance their new parents. As Schofield and Beek (2006: 93) remind us, 'By deactivating their attachment behaviour, they are not avoiding a relationship – they are achieving the best kind of relationship that is available, by avoiding direct expression of emotion and demand'. In contrast to the secure child, these children may be socially awkward and poor at understanding the perspective of others. They may be both bullying and controlling and are at risk of conduct problems.

By contrast, children who have an ambivalent attachment, rather than inhibiting their attachment behaviours, adopt the opposite strategy of hyper-activating their signals of need in the context of inconsistent, uncertain and unpredictable responsiveness from their caregivers. These children have great difficulty in regulating their own emotions and behaviour and consequently have problems identifying and responding empathically to the feelings and needs of others. They are both angry and needy and make constant demands on their caregiver as a strategy to elicit maximum response. They view themselves as unlovable but their attachment figures as potentially, although unpredictably, loving. These children are often experienced by adoptive parents as exhausting, because of their incessant needy demands, combined with angry resistance. This again is an organised strategy. Typically, these children are unable to manage or regulate emotions or behaviour. They may be more at risk of depression and demonstrate poor self-efficacy in problem-solving and low self-esteem combined with high levels of frustration.

Further research (Main and Hesse, 1990) identified an additional pattern of disorganised attachment behaviour. Children with disorganised attachments have experienced frightened or frightening caregivers who, rather than soothing their anxieties, have proved the source of fear and uncertainty. Either the attachment figure frightens the child with their behaviour, or they may abdicate their caregiving – experiencing themselves as helpless, as a result of unresolved trauma in their past or current lives. The child is therefore unable to develop an effective and organised strategy of responses to protect them from anxiety when in close proximity to their attachment figures. Disorganised patterns are more commonly seen in children who have experienced abuse and neglect. Main and Hesse (1990) describe the experience of these children as 'fear without solution'. They have an internal working model of themselves as unlovable, others as hostile, frightening or helpless and close relationships as unpredictable and unsafe. In order to survive such unpredictable caregiving, the child may develop strategies for controlling the relationship – typically through aggressive, compulsive caregiving or compulsory compliant behaviour. These are role-reversal strategies involving the child acting as the 'persecutor' or 'rescuer' of the attachment figure (Liotti, 1999). These strategies are constantly changing, as the child attempts to anticipate the carer's actions and to protect themselves. The child, therefore, has 'multiple and contradictory models of the self and others' (Schofield and Beek, 2006: 117).

It is important to stress that not all maltreated children develop disorganised patterns of attachment, as some children have parents who – whilst they fail to resolve losses and trauma – do not abuse or neglect their children. George and Solomon (1996: 664) emphasise the importance of their findings that disorganised children experience abdicated caregiving. They comment, 'What frightens the child is the mother's simultaneous abdication of care and impermeability to the child's cues or bids for care'. In terms of the impact on the child's behaviour, Perry *et al.* (1995) note hyper-vigilance, hyper-compliance, defiance or dissociated, numbed or aggressive responses – all of which have significant developmental consequences. These children present the most complex challenges to adoptive parents, who meet confused and confusing responses when attempting to offer nurturing. These children's ability to regulate emotions is greatly diminished and they may be punitive and controlling, both with adults and peers. They are often lacking in empathy and may be aggressive in their responses – misreading the cues and behaviour of others – leaving them at risk of developing conduct problems or antisocial behaviour.

Howe (2005) and Schofield and Beek (2006) stress the importance, first, of distinguishing between secure and insecure patterns of behaviour and second, of distinguishing between organised and disorganised attachment patterns. This crucial element of analysis is vital to our understanding of the individual child's adaptation to previous caregiving, informing clear strategies for re-nurturing within the adoptive family. Schofield and Beek (2006) emphasise the impact of neglect and abuse on the adopted child's difficulty in trusting their new carers:

> These children will transfer their negative expectations of adults into their new environments, along with the patterns of behaviour that have functioned as survival strategies in the past. They find it hard to let adults come close enough to establish trusting and supportive relationships.
>
> (Schofield and Beek, 2006: 153)

The disorganised child is most puzzling to adoptive parents, as they have developed a range of strategies to discourage their new carers' efforts to establish and sustain supportive intimacy. Howe (2005) distinguished most helpfully between the impacts of various forms of maltreatment – physical, emotional and sexual abuse – and the impact of different forms of neglect: specifically disorganised, depressed, passive and physical neglect but also severe deprivation and chronic neglect, including institutionalised care. His thorough and careful analysis helps practitioners to identify key characteristics of the caregiving environment which impact on the emotional predicament of the individual child in different ways. His analysis underlines the vital importance of good information about the quality of early caregiving circumstances of a child placed with adoptive parents, which may facilitate their ability to attune to the child's emotional and behavioural defences.

Significance of the adoptive carer's own attachment history

The work of Main and Goldwyn (1984) in developing the Adult Attachment Interview has contributed much to our understanding of the trans-generational link between attachment security in parents, their child's behaviour in the Strange Situation (Ainsworth *et al.*, 1978) and the child's later representation of attachment-related situations. Main comments, from her research into exploring these links:

These studies have shown significant correlation between the quality of the infant's attachment to the parent (secure, insecure avoidant, insecure ambivalent or disorganised and disoriented) and:

1. the adult's construction of his or her attachment history as well as
2. the child's later representation of self and others.

(Main, 1991: 127)

The Adult Attachment Interview is a semi-structured process which seeks to elicit an account of the adult's memories, emphasising attachment-related material. For example, the adult is asked to generate five adjectives to describe each childhood attachment figure and then prompted to provide specific examples of memories for each adjective. In the studies described, the strongest correlation with infant security was the overall coherence of their parents' narrative of their own attachment history – whether they had insecure or problematic childhoods, or loving relationships and securely attached children.

The significance of these accounts lies less in the content of the account than in the manner in which it is given, specifically the degree to which it is a 'coherent narrative' of remembered experiences of caregiving. What is important is not merely whether or not the adult recalls positive or negative experiences of nurturing, but rather, the degree to which the experiences have been processed, both at the time that they occurred and since. The degree to which these experiences have been rendered coherent is highly predictive of the degree to which the adult will be equipped to offer secure experiences of attachment in their caregiving of a child.

Some adults, who have experienced highly compromised caregiving, nevertheless demonstrate an ability to reflect on their childhood experiences in a coherent way. They may be rated as demonstrating 'earned security' (Howe *et al.*, 1999). For example, one carer with a neglectful history commented:

I used to think it was my fault that I wasn't looked after properly when I was little, but now I realise that my mother was abandoned by my father and was overwhelmed because she was very young and alone, without family or friends to help her. It wasn't her fault and it wasn't mine, but it didn't stop me yearning for love and care.

This carer's ability to reflect on her own history and to render it coherent, allowed her to remain sensitive and available to her very angry adopted child. Secure caregivers are able to persist in offering care, and remain emotionally attuned and engaged, even in the face of confusing and contradictory messages from the child.

The link between adoptive parents' own experience and adoption outcome was explored in a study by Steele *et al.*, 2001. The study compared the data from Adult Attachment Interviews and a structured format of questions called the Experience of Adoption Interview, given to twenty-five adoptive parents who were identified by the family placement workers of the Thomas Corum Adoption Service as having 'successfully' adopted children with a varied range of developmental disability.

The Adult Attachment Interview results found that, whilst 32 per cent were assigned to the autonomous-(secure) group, and 16 per cent to the preoccupied (ambivalent) group, 52 per cent were rated as dismissing (avoidant). These results compare with findings in the general populations of 70 per cent in the secure group, 10 per cent preoccupied and 20 per cent as dismissing. Despite the fact that many of the adopters were not identified as autonomous-(secure), they demonstrated resilience not only in the face of past or present personal hardships, but also in the day-to-day task of caring for a child with disabilities. The dismissing group communicated as a distinct feature their pride at having overcome adversities and in keeping a distance from preoccupying or painful emotions. As the authors comment, 'It would seem that this stance toward close relationships might inform an optimistic frame of mind that would be of tremendous benefit when dealing with the day-to-day care of a child with special needs' (Steele *et al.*, 2001: 33).

The findings from the Experience of Adoption Interviews revealed that 80 per cent of the carers had specifically chosen to care for a child with special needs. Many also had prior experience of work with such children. When comparing the two Interviews, the following findings emerged. There was a correlation between having experienced their parents as loving and their views of their child as being capable of independence. In addition, some parents assessed as 'dismissing' valued the relationship with the child – in spite of less than loving early childhood memories of their attachment relationships. The study is viewed as confirming the observations of Macaskill (1985), that those who chose to adopt a child with special needs often have a background involving significant adversity.

When children have experienced trauma, it may be anticipated that the impact will be felt by their adoptive parents in particular, and also by any other children within the new family. Despite the efforts of adoption agencies to prepare adoptive parents for the effects that caring for a hurt child may have on them, their powerful feelings can often take them by surprise. The distress and pain in the placed child may trigger unresolved pains and losses in the carers' early history, or reveal in them new areas of hurt which assume significance in the present. The stress generated by this process can lead to exhaustion, confusion and even secondary trauma (see Chapter 5). Adoption agencies need to be alert to this possibility in any adoptive family and to provide training and well-informed support systems for adopters, to help them to remain emotionally available and resilient.

Recent neuro-biological research on brain development

In the last decade, there has been a burgeoning of research into the importance of early experience of close, reciprocal relationships with caregivers for the healthy growth of the infant's brain. Although the component parts of the brain are largely formed by the time babies are born, cell growth, specialisation and connections will continue, especially during the first three years of life when brain growth is most rapid. The work of Perry *et al.* (1995) and Schore (1994) illustrates the vital importance of early interaction upon the physiology of the brain, emphasising the importance of the quality of relationships with caregivers in the early years.

Much has been learned in the last decade about the way that the human brain develops, and the role of experience in both the establishment of synaptic connections and the role of neuro-chemical responses. As Balbernie (2001: 237) notes, 'It is now accepted that a baby's emotional environment will influence the neuro-biology that is the basis of mind. From the infant's point of view the most vital part of the surrounding world is the emotional connection with his caregiver'.

The capacity of the brain to alter its own structure is referred to as 'neuroplasticity' and the brain is especially sensitive and responsive to experience in the first three years of life. In these early years, multiple connections are made between neurons in the context of the baby's caregiving environment. Interaction with this environment of relationships is necessary for healthy growth of the brain. As Trevarthen and Aitken (2001: 21) comment, 'The emotional communicative precocity of human newborns indicates that the emotional responses to caregiving must play a crucial role in the regulation of early brain development'. At this time, many synapses are formed whereby one neuron links with another.

> Connectivity is a crucial feature of brain development, because the neural pathways formed during the early years carry signals and allow us to process information throughout our lives. How, and how well we think and learn – both as children as adults – has a great deal to do with the extent and nature of these connections.
>
> (Schore, 1997: 22)

The degree to which the environment is rich with experiences of close, attuned interaction has a crucial bearing on the pathways which develop. The limbic system in the brain plays a key role in the processing of attachment experiences. The orbito-frontal cortex is occupied with processing inter-personal interaction, containing neural networks particularly sensitive to such intimate experiences as eye contact, communication and tone of voice. Schore (2001: 35) states that, 'Attachment transactions are imprinted into implicit-procedural memory as enduring internal working models, which encode coping strategies of affect regulation'.

Impact of abuse and neglect on the developing brain

Those young children with severely compromised attachment histories are less able to cope with stress and with regulating their emotional states. Moreover, in circumstances of stress or danger which characterise abusive experiences, the child's brain accommodates by becoming hyper-aroused and ultimately dissociated, cutting off from the intolerable stress. The more severe the maltreatment, the more likely it will be that the infant's brain will be 'wired' for these experiences of threat. 'In a very real sense, traumatised children exhibit profound sensitisation of the neural response patterns associated with their traumatic experiences. The result is that full-blown response patterns (e.g. hyper-arousal or dissociation) can be elicited by apparently minor stressors' (Perry *et al.*, 1995: 271). The earlier the abusive experiences, and the more persistent, the more likely it is that the brain's 'hard-wiring' will be fundamentally shaped for the 'fight or flight' response.

Balbernie (2001) also comments on the profound negative effect of prolonged maternal depression which inhibits or reduces the formation of crucial connections in the brain responsible for processing socio-emotional interaction. It is the severity and persistence of the depression, and linked emotional unavailability, rather than the mere diagnosis, which is harmful. Maternal substance abuse also affects brain development in utero, the neurological impacts differing as gestation proceeds.

The experience of the abused and traumatised child is one of fear, threat, unpredictability and pain. Experiences of abusive treatment result in hyper-arousal and may lead to persistent hypervigilance in the face of chronic fear. Since the areas of the brain involved in the acute stress response also affect regulation, anxiety and arousal, it is easy to appreciate the dilemma for the abused child in trusting in the nurturing responses and initiatives of their adoptive parents.

Just as experiences of close, attuned responsiveness generate (within the limbic system of the brain) connections which facilitate the young child's capacity to process socio-emotional experiences, equally the absence of such reassuring intimacy undermines this vital process of development. This experience of neglect is often referred to as 'the trauma of absence'. Whereas the abused child may be hypervigilant or aggressive, the neglected child may be profoundly inhibited in their exploration and learning. As Perry (1997: 131) comments: 'Both lack of critical nurturing experiences and excessive exposure to traumatic violence will alter the developing central nervous system, predisposing it to a more impulsive, reactive and violent individual'. Therefore, since the growth of these connections is experience dependent, the neglected child may be as profoundly affected as the child who experiences other forms of maltreatment. Many repeated experiences of attuned responsiveness may be necessary if the chronically neglected child is to develop a capacity to recognise process and understand their own feelings and behaviours and those of others.

These findings clarify our appreciation, not only of the importance of early intervention, but also of the new carers' persistence in offering the child many rich experiences of stimulation within the intimacy of their new adoptive families, so that their brains gradually alter. Schore (2001: 219) suggests, 'Affectively focused therapeutic experience may literally alter the orbito-frontal system'. That is, 'The opportunity to grow up in an adoptive family provides a nurturing and reparative family experience, which can help to redress the impact of earlier adversity (Hodges and Tizard, 1989; Howe, 1998; PIU, 2000; Tizard and Hodges, 1978; Triseliotis and Russell, 1984)' (Steele, 2006).

In summary, the development of crucial brain functions, dealing with the processing of emotion, is stimulant-dependent and occurs in the context of early relationships, hence the vital importance of formulating a picture of the child's experience of early caregiving in understanding their responses to their adoptive carers.

Impact of the child's early experiences on adoption outcome

There are several helpful studies which consider the impact of the child's early experiences on adoptive homes. First, David Howe (1998) considers the evidence from studies of adoption outcome, in particular the influence of the child's attachment style. He considers specifically the effects of secure, anxious, angry and avoidant patterns for the process and progress of the adoptive home.

In terms of the behaviour, characteristics, achievement and personality of secure children, the view emerges of positive development in the child including healthy self-esteem, self-efficacy and self-confidence, good social understanding and empathy and the capacity to trust peers and adults. As Howe (1998: 146) states, 'On the whole, because these children are not distracted and disturbed by undue levels of emotional anxiety, they are likely to realise their potential'. These children evaluated their experience of adoption in a positive and satisfactory manner, as did their adoptive parents.

Equally, those children who were mildly anxious and insecure – although often being described as having low self-confidence, being slightly immature, sometimes impulsive and remaining anxious at times of loss and separation – were nevertheless positive in their views of their experience of adoption. Their adoptive parents had a positive and satisfactory view of the placement, as Howe (1998: 159) comments: 'Parents of this group of children speak warmly of the adoption. There are never regrets; indeed, the children's slight vulnerability encourages parents to feel protective. These are sensitive and responsive children and great pleasure is taken in their upbringing'.

Children in the angry group, however, are experienced by adopters as much more challenging to parent. In general terms, their behaviour is described as often resistant and ambivalent in close relationships and they often produce conflict. They may be involved in oppositional behavioural problems and they find it difficult to give and receive comfort and affection. In the school years, they often show poor concentration and under-achieve academically. They can also be very disruptive in the classroom. A significant minority of children are aggressive towards parents, lie and steal and may also experience despair or depression. A further minority misuse drugs or alcohol and commit criminal offences outside the home. A noted characteristic of later adolescence and early adulthood for these children is the fact that they tend to leave home early, possibly returning in an aggressive and hostile manner. However, a significant number of these young people establish more secure attachment with their parents at this stage of development and gradually develop more trust and a willingness to be loved and accepted. It is no surprise, therefore, that the adopters' evaluations of the placement of this group of children were mixed. Whilst they reported a negative view if the relationships remained poor or broken in adulthood, adopters gave a qualified positive view if there had been later reconciliations or healing in the parent–child relationship.

In summary, it would appear from Howe's detailed exploration of the outcome studies of adoption that an accurate assessment of the quality of the child's early experience and attachment style developed in response to particular styles of early caregiving are crucial both in preparing adopters for the nature of the challenge ahead and, furthermore, identifying those placements which may need long-term close support.

In relation to recent psychoanalytical informed research, over the last ten years, the Anna Freud Centre, Great Ormond Street Hospital and the Thomas Coram Adoption Service have collaborated to undertake an impressive and growing range of research. This research included following the changes in internal representations of maltreated children between the ages of 4 and 8 years who have been placed for adoption. Hodges and Steele (2000) describe the development and adaptation of the narrative story stem technique they used – which involves seeing a child individually and giving them the beginnings of twelve 'story stems', which they are asked to complete by playing with doll and animal figures. In one of the story stems, a little pig suddenly becomes lost; in another, an elephant stomps angrily; in a further story stem a child brings a picture home from school; in yet another, a child accidentally spills juice all over the table, and so forth. Each story stem intimates a particular problem or dilemma for which there are no set answers; instead they provide a 'frame' in which the child can respond through play, verbally and non-verbally. While the stories are not an exact representation of reality, the play allows access to what a particular child might make of experiences in the context of parent–child, sibling or peer relationships. Over the series of stories, theories emerge that give indications of what Bowlby (1973) has referred to as an 'internal working model', which is based on the experience of being with an attachment figure and serves as a way of anticipating or predicting responses to them.

In their study – which involved videoing, recording and scoring the stories – they found that the stories of children who were seen for assessment and who were currently living in an abusive situation were often dominated by frightening encounters, unexpected, bizarre or incongruous responses, or sequences in which the identified parent dolls were aggressive or rejecting. When compared with children from non-abusive homes, who had a secure attachment, there were significantly fewer instances of realistic or pleasurable domestic play.

In their subsequent study, they compared a group of children who had been removed from abusive situations to permanent adoptive homes (Coram group) and a group of children in foster or residential care, with two comparison groups – one from a more disadvantaged background and one from a predominately middle class background. A full description of all their findings would not be possible in this short chapter. Instead, I will focus on their findings in relation to the Coram group, who were given the narrative story stems soon after placement and again at one- and two-year intervals after placement. Their findings were fascinating. In the first year after placement, negative themes such as extreme aggression and catastrophic fantasies increased – they thought in part because these themes could be engaged with and not avoided. However, their stories were generally more coherent and there were more representations of pleasurable domestic play and more positive representations of parents as helpful or protective. These positive responses seemed to reflect the more positive caregiving the children were receiving. They concluded that it was, 'not so much that earlier, negative internal working models fade away, but rather that alternative, competing ones get developed and may even become dominant' (p. 452). That is, rather than 'forgetting about the past and looking to the future', the children needed time to make sense of their previous experiences, while forming new relationships and getting to know about new ways of interacting with parents, siblings and peers.

Importance of resilience

> Resilience – the capacity to transcend adversity – may be seen as the essential quality which care planning and provision should seek to stimulate as a key outcome of the care offered.
>
> (Gilligan, 1997: 14)

When placing children for adoption it is helpful to consider those factors which may act as a buffer, enabling the child to withstand difficult life events such as separation from important adults. This strength in the face of adversity appears to be a combination of individual temperament, resources available to the child and skills developed in the context of adult support:

> It is the particular coincidence of individual personality factors, the nature of supportive relationships available to the child or young person and the relative vulnerability or resilience at the time as shaped by the influence of past history, which is most likely to inform the child's need for support.
>
> (Daniel and Wassell, 2002: 59)

Rutter (1985) identifies three key factors associated with resilience: first, a sense of self-esteem and confidence; second, a belief in their own self-efficacy and ability to deal with change and adaptation; and third, a repertoire of social problem-solving approaches. However, unless there is careful assessment of the *impact* and *meaning* of life events, relationships and circumstances on the individual child, the child's resilience may be over-estimated. As Luther (1991) cautions, some children may appear to be coping well with adversity, whereas in fact, they may be internalising their symptoms. This may be a particular issue for children with an avoidant style of attachment who have accommodated their early caregivers' emotional unresponsiveness by minimising their own demands for care, and signals of need, appearing falsely secure. Their presentation represents an effective and necessary survival strategy in the face of low adult responses to their emotional needs, rather than true resilience.

A further point to bear in mind is that it may be assumed that, merely because a child has a sense of confidence, this alone will not be predictive of adult resilience. As Newman (2004) notes, 'self esteem is more likely to grow and be sustained through developing valued skills in real life situations, than just through praise and positive affirmation'. Adoptive parents can do much to enhance their child's resilience by creating a sense of security for the child, through remaining sensitively available and maintaining links with important adults from the past, as well as within their own extended family. They can promote the child's ability to learn and to benefit from school, to establish positive relations with siblings or peers and to support their child's talents and interests. With regard to social competencies, studies have shown that helping the child to develop a 'language for feeling' is an essential factor which may contribute to self-control and provide a fundamental basis for the capacity to attune and respond to the feelings of others. The close, attuned support of adoptive parents in relation to these various domains can provide numerous opportunities for enhancing new attachment relationships and promoting resilience.

Conclusion

This chapter has explored the effects of abuse and neglect on the healthy development of the child, in the context of highlighting the importance of early development.

The role of attachment theory in adoption has been explored in relation to the experience of the adopted child prior to placement, the pattern of attachment derived as an adaptation to early experiences, and in relation to the relevance of the adoptive carer's own attachment history. The concept of resilience has been discussed. There are many implications derived from attachment theory for effective adoption practice, which includes the sensitive matching of children to carers who are more likely to be able to meet their needs for healing, reparative care in the long term.

It is vitally important that, when placing children with adoptive carers, there is careful 'mind-minded' reflection upon the feelings and thoughts which drive the child's behaviours. This will help, not only in selecting the appropriate placement for the child, but also in identifying appropriate therapeutic services and other supports to the healing unit of the adoptive family.

Equally important, however, is the development of a wide range of therapeutic and support services for the adoptive child, the adoptive carers and their relationship, if the healing opportunity which the experience of living in a new family can provide is to enhance the potential for the recovery, and later adult resilience, for abused and neglected children (see Chapter 5).

Howe (2005) emphasises what we have learned about the needs of older children and more traumatised infants in terms of the way we assess and think about the skills and persistence required from adoptive carers. He summarises:

> Although older children and more traumatised infants may require more time, more thought and more effort, we are learning that even in these cases, change and recovery, at least to a degree, is possible. Those who can stay with and touch these children, emotionally and psychologically, have the capacity to heal young minds. If relationships are where things developmentally can go wrong, then relationships are where they are most likely to be put right.
>
> (Howe, 2005: 278)

References

Ainsworth, M., Blehar, M., Waters, E. and Wall, S. (1978) *Patterns of Attachment: Psychological Study of the Strange Situation*, Hillsdale, NJ: Erlbaum

Balbernie, R. (2001) 'Circuit and circumstances: the neurobiological consequences of early relationship experiences and how they shape later behaviour', *Journal of Child Psychotherapy*, 27 (3): 237–55.

Bion, W.R. (1962) *Learning from Experience*, London: Maresfield Reprints.

Bowlby, J. (1973) *Attachment and Loss*, Volume II: *Separation, Anxiety and Anger*, London: Hogarth Press.

Daniel, B. and Wassell, S. (2002) *Assessing and Promoting Resilience in Vulnerable Children*, London: Jessica Kingsley.

Dunn, J. (1993) *Young Children's Close Relationships: Beyond Attachment*, London: Sage.

Fahlberg, V.I. (1991) *A Child's Journey Through Placement*, London: British Association for Adoption and Fostering.

George, C. and Solomon, J. (1996) 'Representational models of relationship: links between caregiving and attachment', *Infant Mental Health Journal*, 17 (3): 198–216.

Gilligan, R. (1997) 'Beyond permanence? The importance of resilience in child placement, practice and planning', *Adoption and Fostering*, 21: 12–20.

Hodges, J. and Steele, M. (with Hillman, S. Henderson, K. and Neil, M.) (2000) 'Effects of abuse on attachment representations: narrative assessments of abused children', *Journal of Child Psychotherapy*, 26 (3): 433–55.

Hodges, J. and Tizard, B. (1989) 'Social and family relationships in ex-institutional adolescents', *Journal of Child Psychology and Psychiatry*, 30: 77–97.

Howe, D. (1998) *Patterns of Adoption, Nature, Nurture and Psychosocial Development*, Oxford: Blackwell Science.

Howe, D. (2005) *Child Abuse and Neglect: Attachment, Development and Intervention*, Basingstoke: Macmillan.

Howe, D., Brandon, M. Hinings, D. and Schofield, G. (1999) *Attachment Theory, Child Maltreatment and Family Support*, London: Palgrave Macmillan.

Liotti, G. (1999) 'Disorganisation of attachment as a model for understanding dissociative psychopathology', in J. Solomon and C. George (eds) *Attachment Disorganisation*, New York: Guilford Press.

Luther, S.S. (1991) 'Vulnerability and resilience: a study of high risk adolescents', *Child Development*, 62: 600–12.

Macaskill, C. (1985) 'Pre-adoption support: is it essential?', *Adoption and Fostering*, 9 (1): 45–9.

Main, M. (1991) 'Metacognitive knowledge, metacognitive monitoring and singular (coherent) vs. multiple (incoherent) model of attachment: findings and directions for future research', in C.M. Parkes, J. Stevenson-Hinde, and P. Marris (eds) *Attachment Across the Life Cycle*, London: Routledge.

Main, M. and Goldwyn, R. (1984) 'Adult attachment scoring and classification system', unpublished manuscript, California: University of California.

Main, M. and Hesse, E. (1990) 'Parents' unresolved traumatic experiences as related to infant disorganised attachment status: is frightened and/or frightening the linking mechanism?', in M.T. Greenberg, D. Cicchetti and E.M. Cummings (eds) *Attachment in the Pre-School Years: Theory, Research and Intervention*, Chicago, IL: University of Chicago Press.

Newman, T. (2004) 'Children and resilience', unpublished training material.

Perry, B. (1997) 'Incubated in error: neurodevelopmental factors in the "cycle of violence"', in J. Osofsky (ed.) *Children in a Violent Society*, New York: Guildford Press.

Perry, B., Pollard, R., Blakeley, T., Baker, W. and Vigilante, D. (1995) 'Childhood trauma: the neurobiology of adaptation and use dependent development of the brain. How states become traits', *Infant Mental Health Journal*, 16 (4): 271–91.

PIU (Performance and Innovation Unit) (2000) *Prime Minister's Review of Adoption*, London: Cabinet Office.

Rutter, M. (1985) 'Resilience in the face of adversity: protective factors and resilience to psychiatric disorders', *British Journal of Psychiatry*, 147: 598–611.

Schofield, G. and Beek, N. (2006) *Attachment Handbook for Foster Care and Adoption*, London: British Association for Adoption and Fostering.

Schore, A. (1994) *Affect Regulation and the Origins of the Self: The Neurobiology of Emotional Development*, Hillsdale, NJ: Lawrence Erlbaum.

Schore, R. (1997) *Rethinking the Brain: New Insights into Early Development*, New York: Families and Work Institute.

Schore, R. (2001) 'Effects of a secure attachment relationship on right brain development, affect regulation and infant mental health', *Infant Mental Health Journal*, 22 (1–2): 7–66.

Steele, M. (2006) 'The "added value" of attachment theory and research for clinical work in adoption and foster care', in J. Kendrick, C. Lindsey and L. Tollemache (eds) *Creating New Families: Therapeutic Approaches to Fostering, Adoption and Kinship Care*, London: Karnac.

Steele, M., Kanuik, J., Hodges, J., Haworth, C. and Huss, S. (2001) 'The use of the Adult Attachment Interview: implications for assessment in adoption and foster care', in *Preparing for Permanence: Assessment, Preparation and Support*, London: British Association for Adoption and Fostering.

Tizard, B. and Hodges, J. (1978) 'The effect of early institutional rearing on the development of eight year old children', *Journal of Child Psychology and Psychiatry*, 19: 99–118.

Trevarthen, C. and Aitken, K.J. (2001) 'Infant intersubjectivity: research, theory and clinical applications', *Journal of Child Psychology and Psychiatry*, 42 (1): 2–48.

Triseliotis, J. and Russell, J. (1984) *Hard to Place: The Outcome of Adoption and Residential Care*, London: Heinemann.

3 Understanding an adopted child

A child psychotherapist's perspective

Lisa Miller

This chapter sets the scene for the chapters based on detailed clinical material which follow. Why should psychoanalytical psychotherapy with individual children, whether or not in conjunction with other forms of support, have a place as treatment of choice for many adopted children and young people who are in difficulty? What form does this work take, and what are its distinguishing characteristics? What are the problems in relationships and communication which face children who have been exposed to early deprivation or damage? And how is this particular form of treatment, with its understanding of unconscious processes, adapted to deal with disturbances which are being expressed not only in words but also at a pre-verbal and non-verbal level?

Deprived and damaged children – the importance of early experiences

Research reveals in ever more depth and complexity how our earliest experiences are of critical importance in forming our future personality (see Chapter 2). Nature and nurture, genetic make-up and environment, work together and combine from the moment of conception to determine what kind of a person we will grow up to be. This is true physically and mentally; good nourishment is needed to build a healthy body, and good experiences enter the psychological system and build a healthy, resilient character in the same way. Nobody can have only good experiences, so part of building a healthy system is support, kindness and understanding for a baby in its anxious, troubled times. A lack of goodness, warmth and affection fed into the child's system, a lack of help when things go wrong, or, even worse, the actual introduction of painful, hostile experiences, will all destabilise and distort the baby's development. It is hard to bear the idea that serious and long-term harm can be inflicted on a very young child, or even for some to believe that experiences in babyhood leave their mark at all.

A couple, the Smiths, in their late thirties, had been fortunate (they felt) in adopting a baby boy soon after birth. This little boy, Michael, had done well and they applied for a second adoption. Their second son, Luke, was eight months old when he arrived. The parents confidently expected Luke to take his place as a family member with no more disruption than might have been expected in any family with a new baby. But they were rudely surprised when Luke turned out to be a very difficult baby indeed. Quiet when he arrived from the foster-placement where he had spent five months, he soon developed into a baby who regularly rejected food, cried desperately and woke continually during the night.

The parents consulted a professional at a time when they felt their whole family life was in disarray. Michael, who was now four years old, was having sudden and unprecedented sleeping difficulties. He behaved aggressively to the baby and had started to talk in an anxious way about the fact that he himself was adopted, asking if his parents would send him away. The parents felt that Luke had brought discord into the cheerful and happy home they had enjoyed before. They were considering not proceeding with the adoption process and worried there was something inexplicably wrong with Luke. Exhausted, they were consumed by guilty doubt; their conflicts were also expressed in family rows and never-before-experienced marital quarrels.

How can this example be used to draw out some general thoughts about the adoption situation? First of all, let us think about Luke. The first three months of his life had been spent with his young birth mother. Fundamentally unsupported – almost certainly deeply depressed – she relied on drugs, alcohol and a series of partners to try to still her anxiety and calm her fears. The part of her which had Luke's best interests at heart seems to have been the part which agreed that she could no longer care for him. This slender adult side to her character knew what good-enough mothering could be like, and saw that Luke wasn't getting it. The mother–child relationship was constantly intruded upon by the behaviour of that other aspect of Luke's mother – the part of her that was no more than a disturbed child herself. This part had been in no state to think about Luke, to remember to feed him or to understand how frightening it would be for such a baby to be shouted at. Luke arrived at his foster carer's underweight and neglected, and his care had been as inadequate in the emotional sphere. He picked up well in foster care, but his next experience of separation and loss, when he left to go to his adoptive home, re-awoke a feeling of panic, fear and bewilderment. Primitive anxiety spilled out of him, so that he could neither eat nor sleep and his new parents were filled with horror.

'Filled with horror' is not merely a figure of speech. Luke really was – in a psychological sense – broadcasting an unprocessed fear of abandonment. His parents were functioning like receiving stations and they certainly got the message: the whole family system became flooded with anxiety. It filled Michael, who in turn became a demanding, clingy, sleepless child. It filled both parents – they started to blame and criticise each other, each feeling let down, and each secretly believing that it was the *other* one who had wanted this wretched baby in the first place. Each family member started to feel abandoned and lonely. Perhaps this can be traced back to Luke's earliest infantile experiences, when his normal baby crying (panicky, bewildered and angry at times) did not meet with a mature adult mind capable of managing it. His most primitive fears seemed to have been re-activated, and what's more, they were infectious.

The remedy – or rather, the partial remedy – was the re-establishment of his parents as a working couple and in a better state of mind. This was a state in which they were able to think about what was happening to them, what was happening to Luke and what was happening to Michael. It was a profound relief to them to be introduced to the idea that Luke was likely to be difficult. This was not because they were, as they feared, inadequate parents; nor was it because Luke was some kind of inexplicably difficult baby. At one level, there was nothing inexplicable about it at all: Luke had not had the start in life which would have given him resilience and would have enabled him to command the resources he needed to manage another major change in his life.

Gradually, they came to see that an eight-month-old baby with Luke's former experiences would naturally tend to be a difficult little person – and certainly a different proposition from Michael, who had come at the earliest age possible. Luke's arrival was not the equivalent of having a new baby, because Luke was not new. However, once they had realised this, they began to see that some of their experience could helpfully be related to the ordinary stress and strain of having a second child. When a second child arrives in any family, sibling rivalry enters the scene for the first time. Have the parents got room in their hearts for two? Very often the ousted child simply doesn't think so. And sometimes the parents doubt it too – will they be able to manage the contrary and diverging demands of two children? What do they feel about rivalry, envy and jealousy? Often the rivalry between the children sparks off something competitive and rivalrous between the two parents. The couple stop being an adult pair – devoted in the main to understanding and responding to the various needs and tasks within the family – and start feeling competitive themselves. Soon the whole family scene is one of a nursery, where there isn't enough grown-up attention to go round.

Under stress, the fault lines show and crack. In addition, the parents were upset to find that Michael had become preoccupied by thoughts about his own adoption. His parents knew that they had done everything they were supposed to do in the way of sensitive, cheerful openness about Michael's adopted status. However, they had, without realising it, been assuming that anxiety can be 'explained away'. Small as he was, Michael wondered in his own way about what it meant to be adopted. The explanations given about Luke, whose mother could not look after him, had made Michael feel uncertain. Is this what happens to boys who are too much for their mummies? Do they get sent to another one?

Then, of course, when Luke seemed to be getting too much to cope with, everyone felt worse. The parents felt less and less like two mature and competent adults. Significantly, both parents had past difficulties connected with the advent of younger siblings. Earlier problems in their lives had been brought to life again. Michael felt less and less like a nice boy. Full of jealousy about the newcomer, he also felt that his angry and rivalrous wishes must be having an appalling effect upon Luke – look how Luke was yelling! Michael, instead of feeling like the boy his parents adored, felt like a thoroughly nasty person. He wondered what would happen. As for Luke, he was catapulted back into his earliest uncertain infancy, a time of suffering insufficiently relieved.

We have to hypothesise, I think, that the projected force of Luke's infantile fears was considerable, and that the situation was different from that of the birth of a new baby. In this case it was important to be able to rely on the insights into emotional development that are available to us from the discipline of psychoanalytic psychotherapy. Child psychotherapists, with infant observation at the heart of their pre-clinical training, are aware of primitive anxieties and the way in which these feelings may be communicated to others. One obvious way to address the problems presented here was to work with the whole family, after the model of Under Fives Counselling Service at the Tavistock Clinic (Emanuel and Bradley, 2008). In this service, appointments are usually given within two weeks and up to five meetings are offered. The aim of the service is to provide consultation to parents with infants to discuss whatever problems *they* are concerned about or to assist them in seeking further help if there are serious problems.

In Luke's case, it would not be realistic to think that he could ever grow into quite the child he might have been if his earliest weeks and months had proceeded well. But from the point where his parents began to get to grips with what was going on, the family was able to progress more smoothly with the task of assimilating its new member. The parents began to be able to absorb Luke's projections of distress, and to regard him as an ordinary baby for whom things had gone wrong. They began to deal with Michael's unsettled and jealous state as though it was comprehensible, rather than going along with his conviction that the advent of Luke was the end of the world as he knew it. Consequently Luke began to trust his new parents more. He ceased to have paranoid fears about his food and turned into an ordinary finicky eater; he stopped feeling he had to stay awake for fear of what would happen and started to sleep properly. Michael felt huge relief as Luke became calmer. He began to take an interest and a pride in him, and the family moved forward and out of professional hands.

Damage that has become entrenched within the child: the child who has been ill-treated

It was hard for Michael and Luke's parents to understand what was going on, partly because it is hard to grasp what effect early experiences can have on a baby. We have no wish to believe it. Our minds shy away from thoughts of a harmless baby's pain. Equally, it is painful to think of the damaging experiences that must have occurred for a small child to be placed for adoption. Social workers and adoption workers do their best in most cases to prepare prospective parents for the potential difficult time as they receive a small child into their family. Yet it remains hard to remember that the years before adoption do not go away, and that the problems may not be temporary.

Keith was adopted at the age of five. He had been in the care of two or three foster families, who had found him hard to handle – a child who had tremendous destructive tantrums, who smeared faeces on the wall and who displayed a whole range of unsettling behaviour. This was hardly surprising, since he had come from a home where domestic violence was ingrained. Keith himself had been deliberately and badly injured by his stepfather. However, he also retained a sweet and engaging side to his character: it was clear that he had been loved as well as hated, and a good deal of lively intelligence remained intact. The Taylor family decided to take him on.

They had plenty of information about Keith and some good support. Unlike the Smiths, who adopted Michael and Luke, the Taylors knew that they were taking on a challenge. Keith was not going to be like their other children. But they were a well-organised, active family and it was plain from the start that Keith was going to be expected to behave as much like the others as he could possibly manage. Smearing poohs was out. Indeed, a combination of good humour, clear boundaries, determination and patience did a great deal for Keith, whose warm and attractive side flourished. His parents worked extremely hard to understand him.

But three or four years later, he was still showing entrenched signs of difficulty in making relationships. At school he was only able to concentrate if he had an adult giving him sole attention. Problems cropped up round him: his Learning Support Assistant found herself not only devoted to him, but also in opposition to the class teacher, who found Keith something of a bully – dishonest and hard to like – though naturally she felt bad about this and kept most of it to herself.

Keith had a destructive side to his character, which was identified with bullying, treachery and violence. His 'better self' – who was talkative, affectionate and ingenious – seemed quite at odds with this destructive side. Keith's parents had visions of the future where his violence would spring out dangerously. They felt he was manageable in the context of a strong family unit or a sympathetic, well-functioning primary school, but the destructive part of him was alive and well and biding its time.

In this situation, more than family work or parent counselling was required. Keith's mother and father were clear that while the good experiences he was having were feeding the side of him which genuinely wanted to please them and felt an authentic attachment to them, a dark and resentful, rebellious side was unaffected by this. From time to time Keith would say that he was just waiting till he was grown up, when he could see his 'real' mum. He displayed the idealisation of his birth mother, so common and so agonising in cases like this. But idealisation, with its converse, denigration (here, the worship of 'Mummy Sue', his birth mother) carries a problematic charge of scorn – in this case for his adoptive mother, constantly felt not to be up to the job. The grim corollary of not being able to wait to get back to mum was Keith's unconscious wish to get back to dad – a dad who in his imagination was powerful, alluring and dangerous.

Keith's internal world – the world of his memory and imagination, the world of his thoughts, dreams and feelings both conscious and unconscious – had been formed early and continued to dominate his everyday life. In the world of his imagination with phantasy, lovely things like 'Mummy Sue' were forever linked to danger and destruction. The child psychotherapist who saw Keith three times a week for some years had to grapple with this fact. As soon as Keith had had a good experience – a feeling of being liked or understood, a feeling of being pleased or satisfied – another feeling came blasting willy-nilly into his mind. This was a sense of fury, hatred and rejection. This had little to do with what the other person had actually done: it was an automatic response, generated in early infancy, consolidated in early childhood, which said that good experiences do not last. They are all too quickly succeeded, undermined or even obliterated by damaging bad experiences.

It is discouraging for adoptive parents like Keith's, who are well-motivated, well-equipped and energetic, to find their endeavours frustrated by the dominance of their child's internal world – a situation created long before they knew him. It arouses both anger and pain to be forced to remember that the child you have adopted is still ruled from within by experiences which took place in infancy and toddlerhood.

What do child psychotherapists do?

Thinking of Keith and many children like him, we have to consider what psychoanalytic child psychotherapy has to offer. To do this we must consider its distinguishing characteristics. Psychoanalytic psychotherapy looks into the unique individual. It does so in the context of the relationship between therapist and child, a relationship which brings into action all those unconscious processes, the difficulties in communicating and relating, which are preventing the child from getting on with life in the world. While the philosophy and training of, for example, the psychologist and the psychiatrist, move from the general to the particular, child psychotherapy works the other way round. Although a warm interest in the child is a necessity for any good child and adolescent mental health practitioner, other professionals will be likely to start by fitting this child into a general context: is this little boy's presentation typical of autistic spectrum behaviour; attention deficit disorder? Is he functioning at the level of a normal eight-year-old? Does he fit into a pattern often observed in looked-after children? These kinds of questions are vital, of course, and no child psychotherapist would wish to ignore them. However, after the child has been viewed in the general context of development and behaviour, the question of his or her uniqueness remains. No two children are alike. No set of experiences is replicated exactly. The task of the psychotherapist is to find out in depth and detail the nature of this particular child's internal world.

Before we continue to look at the techniques involved in this kind of work we need to think about the question of the child's inner world. There are an abundance of examples in the following chapters of what is meant by the internal world of the child, but perhaps it is worth defining more clearly at this stage the way in which this idea is conceived of and used. In 'Our adult world and its roots in infancy', Klein (1959) put forward the idea that all experience has its effect – nothing that happens to us really goes away, although it may not be reclaimable as a memory. Our adult personality encompasses the infant we were, as well as the toddler, the child and the adolescent. We hope that the most mature part will mainly be in charge: as grown-ups, we would like to think that the adult, thinking, balanced part of ourselves is looking after and managing the adolescent or the child in us.

No one, however, is unfamiliar with their own childish outbursts, and everyone has times when, in crisis and under strain, anxieties of a powerful and primitive nature are released and rush out to trouble us.

Children or adolescents who are in trouble cannot rely on their most mature side; in other words, their ego-functioning. This is why forms of therapy which rely heavily upon a child's being able to talk things over and think about themselves are of limited value for these children. The sensible, self-aware, functioning aspect is constantly being disturbed by eruptions of irrational, anxious behaviour from the baby emanating within. In the case of Luke's birth mother, the adult maternal side of her personality was too weak (through early deprivation) to manage the fearful and delinquent child in herself; and neither could she manage Luke's baby needs – the baby in her was in constant angry competition. In the case of Keith, his eight-year-old self wanted to be a co-operative, cheerful schoolboy, but his behaviour was constantly influenced by up-rushes of something very different. Without meaning to, without understanding why, he would find himself frantically unable to tolerate somebody else having the teacher's attention and would attack another child; at the age of five or six, he had expressed what a mess he felt himself to be in by wiping faeces over the walls.

This last example illustrates something of the second aspect of Klein's concept of the internal world. Keith's internal experiences – feelings of rivalry, aggression, of being 'in the shit' – were enacted in external reality. Things which really belonged to the inner world of thought, phantasy and emotion, rushed across the boundary and became actions. Klein, in an illuminating way, saw the inner world of the mind as a *place*, a place as important and as real as the external world of people and events. We carry around with us our own world of the imagination, which contains both conscious and unconscious thoughts and feelings. Much exists below the conscious level.

When we sleep, we dip down and have glimpses in dreams of what is going on below the surface. We see that our inner world is peopled, as a theatre is peopled, and that things are happening in our mind all the time. Just as our vital organs – heart, kidneys, liver – carry on all the time without our conscious volition, so do our minds. All the time, our minds are interacting with external events; what our minds do, how they react, depends upon our mental state at the time.

In this book we are considering children whose minds – or parts of their minds – are not in a good state, and we are thinking about how to change internal worlds, and hence states of mind. There are some things we cannot change – we cannot change what has happened to children in the past. We cannot change things or people who are in no sense under our control. When Kevin's therapist heard him talking with longing about his birth mother, she knew that nothing could transform this person into the sort of mother Kevin imagined and longed for. The contrast between imagination and reality was poignant. But what *can* be changed? There was truly some hope that Kevin's internal world might alter to accommodate a different idea of a mother: not a super-idealised one, unreachable, to be longed for (and perpetually, if distantly, attached to the idea of a brutal but exciting father), but one that was more realistic. The internal concept of a mother with down-to-earth good qualities – annoying perhaps, but dependable and sound – would help Kevin in his relationships a great deal. As long as he was yearning for something long lost, that never even existed – a person who would fulfil all his wants by magic – Kevin could not appreciate the ordinary good parents he had in real life.

How does a child psychotherapist hope to effect change?

The setting

The psychoanalytic psychotherapist wants to get to know the patient in as much depth as possible. Children sometimes talk, but they have many other ways of communicating: via action, play, drawing, or in more subtle non-verbal ways. The therapist's task is to focus upon the child in a receptive way and to receive communication – no matter how disordered, obscure or upsetting – and to try to make something of it. Containing and managing the emotion generated in the room is a prime task, as the therapist works to understand the meaning of what is happening – much as a parent might, despite anxiety, puzzle away at an infant's cries of distress.

To enter into a close relationship with a disturbed or troubled child, a therapist needs to work within well-defined and secure boundaries. First of all, it is essential that sessions should be regular and reliable. Whether they are weekly or more frequent (and for those most damaged children intensive treatment is often appropriate), the sessions need to follow a pattern. They need to take place in the same room at the same time of day each week. It is no use having a room that can be easily dirtied and spoilt, because this will only arouse severe anxiety when the inevitable happens and damage occurs. Nor is it sensible to have a room full of communal toys, which can seem like an over-stimulating Aladdin's cave to a child already on edge. A child will have his or her box of toys, which will not vary. Cancellations – even planned breaks – are of great significance for the child, for whom the therapy becomes an important event.

Therapy and therapists are, however, important in a different way from the way the child's parents are important. Parents, siblings, teachers, friends are real people in the outside world, people with whom the child has relationships of another kind. Therapists are not like friends and relatives, but they accrue significance, which is a different matter. Therapists work best as part of a team, and parallel work needs to be undertaken with the child's parents or family. Parenting a child who has been through traumatic experiences is a hard task. Bringing the child to therapy is sometimes demanding and perplexing. We have to remember that a child is a dependent being who lives in the context of family, school, and perhaps other agencies with whom close links have to be maintained. Within the framework of careful support for the parents, of conscientious and reliable sessions, the task of looking into the relationship which springs up between patient and therapist can start.

How the child communicates

I have already said that children, like adults, communicate in many different ways – speech, body language, action and even subtler methods of unconscious projection. Mainly however they do not have the well-balanced adult's capacity to talk about themselves. This is a capacity which only develops gradually during childhood and adolescence: even in good circumstances it is not always easy for people to observe their own thoughts and actions and to identify clearly what they are thinking and feeling and why. Children's thoughts and feelings are enacted and demonstrated in their play: indeed, learning to play is intricately linked with learning to think.

With this in mind, the child psychotherapist provides each child with the tools for the work of thinking: a personal box of toys that will be kept safe and separate in between sessions. These are usually basic: little dolls, cars, wild and domestic animals; perhaps a light spongy ball, a small soft toy; plasticine, sometimes a cup and bowl for water. There are drawing things and stationery according to the child's age – pencil, rubber, ruler, sharpener, colouring things, paper, string, glue, scissors, sellotape. Children are free to use these things as they feel like, as long as it is not dangerous. Wholesale destruction is never helpful, but a degree of latitude is essential because there will always be negative emotions like hostility and aggression to communicate. Children can make and destroy things, can play, draw and write; they can also play out games using the furniture in the room, which includes a blanket and pillow. The box of toys facilitates the work of communication. It comes to carry much significance and must be carefully looked after between sessions and not disturbed.

Of course, many highly disturbed children are too anxious to play, or at any rate to play in a coherent and meaningful way. Then the child psychotherapist's training in observation comes into use. A particular feature of that training has been close observation of a baby (Miller *et al.*, 1989) where the trainee visits a family every week for two years to observe a baby growing up in its family context. Trainees do not only learn how to regard every little bit of behaviour, every nuance of response as meaningful; they also learn the power of the projection of primitive anxieties (see Introduction to Part III), as they become able to observe and understand the emotions that are stirred up in themselves by close contact with infantile pleasures and pains.

The work in the session

I shall use the account of a session made by a child psychotherapist to illustrate the way in which she observed the detail of what was going on, looked for meaning in what happened, and employed the observation of her own reactions as a clue to what was occurring in the unconscious mind of this adopted boy. Terry, a primary school age child, had a background not entirely unlike the one outlined earlier for Keith. The following session from Terry's three times weekly psychotherapy starts with Terry arriving with his father and grinning with pleasure when he sees

Kate, his therapist. This is the last but one session before the holiday break. At first Terry seems excited that the holiday is coming: he 'can't wait', he says – and indeed he had dashed off at the end of the session before. However, as the play unfolds, he does not seem so happy.

> Terry takes a little toy lion from his box, sticks it with plasticine to a car, uses a paper clip to join it to the fire-engine and tows it around. He lies on the floor in the same attitude that the lion lies. When he is reminded that he did this last time, he gets into a muddle about the days he comes. After another assertion that he can't wait for tomorrow, he disengages the fire-engine and loses the clip that joined them. He behaves as though this is a funny game, but hurts his finger, saying he damaged his elbow earlier, and tips his chair nearly over.
>
> It looks as though Terry wanted to feel attached to something, like the therapist who might be a sort of emergency fire-engine. He needs his dangerous feelings extinguished – feelings of panic engendered by the threat of loss which the break evokes. But when he is reminded that the end is in sight, that time exists and time is passing, his thoughts become confused: he loses his grip on the fire-engine and conveys the very picture of somebody feeling wobbly, unbalanced and at risk of injury.
>
> Things get worse. As the therapist talks about his getting into a risky situation, Terry says the lion is pesky, annoying – not risky. The engine becomes a breakdown truck and Terry says the lion is going to be stripped. He tears away the plasticine mane that he had given it, talks about ripping it off, ties up the lion's paws with string and puts it to roast in a pretend oven. On hearing Kate talk about cruelty to the lion, Terry grins. The lion dies.

It seems as though the lion – who began by needing to be towed along – has now become not only a nuisance, but the focus of triumphant, sadistic glee. No longer the object of some degree of concern, the lion became 'pesky'. And if you get 'pesky', it seems that no punishment is too bad for you.

> There follows a curious passage where Terry sings at length in a tuneless and hypnotic voice, quite unlike his usual nice schoolboy soprano voice. He keeps on asking Kate if she likes it. She writes, 'There followed a very disturbing experience when I felt suddenly sleepy. I found it extremely difficult to be alert to what was happening. This persisted for some time. I felt I was in contact with Terry through a sort of haze. He seemed absorbed in his songs. I was acutely ashamed of the way I was struggling to keep awake and "in touch"'.

In the countertransference – that is to say, as an actual experience in the room with Terry – Kate struggles to hear and remember him. A deep confusion and disturbance permeates her. She is receiving a bombardment of primitive, infantile projections. It is not at all a comfortable experience. The only consolation must be that nobody else in Terry's life is in the position where they are likely to do this service for him.

> Terry jumps up. He gets a baby doll. He says he is looking after Baby because Baby has nightmares. Then he proceeds to enact giving the baby nightmares – scaring the doll by putting the blanket over his own head and making noises.'How much time is there left?' Terry asks. On hearing there are only fifteen minutes, Terry darts to the end of the room. He is singing 'Rock-a-bye-baby' in a hideously sarcastic, jeering manner. He makes a fenced enclosure and puts the doll in. As Kate is commenting that it's hard for Terry to believe anyone wants to look after the baby, he hurls the doll across the room and shatters the enclosure.

This is not quite the end of the session, but it is enough for the purpose of demonstrating the close attention that Kate gives both to her own and Terry's reactions. The session turns out to be a study in saying good-bye. It takes place within the setting of the transference relationship of therapy, where the 'good-bye' in question is good-bye to three regular weekly sessions until next term. However, the matter of separation and loss is a fundamental one – linked as it is to all questions of thinking for ourselves and standing on our own feet – and it is coloured in an extra way for children who have been adopted.

In this session we see how the idea of a good-bye stirs up thoughts in Terry that, without prompting, take him back to the idea of babyhood. From conscious pleasure at the coming holiday the session moves through the various unconscious ideas, enacted in play, which the parting evokes in him. First the lion is offered some measure of help; then he is dropped, and then he is tortured. Next there is the obscure passage where Kate feels as if her alert, professional self is being put to sleep and that something destructive to thought – certainly disturbing at depth – is happening in the contact between her and Terry. Finally all becomes clear: the person who is supposed to look after the baby gives the baby nightmares; then the baby is treated with mockery and scorn and finally flung out to destruction. Thus we see that an ending is construed at an infantile level in terms of a violent act, possibly fatal.

Terry was in no position to tell Kate what was bothering him. He had no idea. What is significant is that this sort of work takes time. Sessions like this result in no instant changes, although Terry feels calmer at the end. Terry's character was formed in the earliest years of his life, and he is deeply accustomed to living according to its dictates. We all have an unconscious push to recreate the world as we know it – to change that world is a long task.

Psychoanalytic psychotherapy acknowledges this. Change takes time. It is hard to contemplate the degree of damage and pain involved in some of these cases – and perhaps it can only be done in short bursts, as by a therapist in a session. Parents need to be available to do the job of parenting, infinitely more important than anything a professional can do. But they may need to be able to proceed with the job without too many disabling intrusions from the part of a child's personality which is traumatised and unavailable to the good influences of ordinary upbringing. The therapist is there to try to contact the disturbed infant who is giving nobody a moment's peace, and to link with her colleagues who are providing regular support to the child's parents.

Working with parents

Working with parents is an integral part of Child and Adolescent Mental Health Services (CAMHS), and adoptive parents may need additional levels of support (see Chapters 5, 6 and 11). The CAMHS team will include professionals from a number of disciplines, including psychiatry, clinical psychology, nursing, family therapy and social work. The combination will vary, but the need for a multi-disciplinary group of CAMHS workers is very clear in these cases; there may be psychiatric issues, and links with the educational services or social services may need to be made.

But equally important is the direct support offered to the parents in an ongoing way by some members of the team. Bringing a child for therapy arouses mixed feelings in parents. On the one hand, they are grateful to a service which sets out to take their anxieties seriously and offers the hope that matters will improve. On the other hand, no matter how sensitively they are dealt with, parents may have a lurking sense of failure and of resentment. These feelings cannot of course, simply be explained away. Living with an unstable child is very taxing, as we all realise.

Effective support for those burdened parents will not only consist of encouragement and advice – it will also include some measure of acknowledgement of the powerful cocktail of ambivalent feelings aroused within them. Parents take on the adoptive tasks from a mixture of motives, including the zeal of rescue, and finding that a child is hard to save is discouraging. For most adoptive parents it is difficult to accept the fact that our generous and reparative urges have a limit set upon them.

Thus it is important that the parents should feel part of a team – a team which includes the therapist seeing their child. They need to talk to someone about the general situation, but they also need to be able to discuss therapy itself. Why doesn't the therapist stay on after the session for a chat? Why is information about what happens in the therapy room not immediately available? What does confidentiality mean in the context of a child's life? Why do they only see the therapist for review and feedback once or twice a term? All these questions are linked to the necessity for a clear, watertight arrangement of the setting. Within a strong framework the therapist can start to work.

Many of the chapters that follow are an attempt to demonstrate the child psychotherapist in action.

References

Emanuel, L. and Bradley, E. (2008) *What Can the Matter Be? Therapeutic Interventions with Parents, Infants and Young Children: The Work of the Tavistock Clinic's Under Fives Service*, London: Tavistock Series.

Klein, M. (1959) 'Our adult world and its roots in infancy', in M. Klein (ed.) *Envy and Gratitude and Other Works*, London: Hogarth Press, 1980.

Miller, L., Rustin, M., Rustin, M. and Shuttleworth, J. (1989) *Closely Observed Infants*, London: Duckworth.

Part II

Unconscious dynamics in systems and networks

Introduction

Graham Shulman

> ... the fact that these transactions are shaped by an underlying dynamic is unlikely to be perceived ... Here we seem to be dealing with repetitious actions which transfer a pattern of relationships from one situation to another in which new participants become the vehicles for the reiterated expression of the underlying dynamic ... The cast changes but the plot remains the same.
>
> (Britton, 1981: 48–9)

> Like individuals, institutions develop defences against difficult emotions which are too threatening or too painful to acknowledge.
>
> (Halton, 1994: 12)

There is a rich and diverse tradition of applying psychoanalytic understanding to dynamics that occur in families, groups, institutions and social systems (Freud, 1921; Jaques, 1953; Bion, 1961; Box *et al.*, 1981; Britton, 1981; Menzies Lyth 1988, 1989; Obholzer and Zagier Roberts, 1994; Hinshelwood and Skogstad, 2000; Sprince, 2000; Huffington *et al.*, 2004; Armstrong, 2005; Cooper and Lousada, 2005; Emanuel, 2006). This approach involves the concept of unconscious group, institutional or social processes; people within different parts of a family, institution or a system (Lewin, 1947; Miller and Rice, 1967; Zagier Roberts, 1994) interact or act in consort, but without conscious awareness, in ways determined partly by unconscious anxieties, feelings, defences, beliefs and assumptions. Specific anxieties, feelings and so on may be more at play according to the nature and task of the group or system; thus, for instance, anxieties about madness are likely to be more active in the context of a mental health service.

These unconscious dynamics in groups and systems affect interactions and relationships – personal or professional – between individuals in a variety of ways; they also influence ways of seeing (or not seeing), ways of thinking, and decision making in families and professional networks. They may cause behaviour and perceptions to be unwittingly organised around endorsing or sustaining a collective assumption or fantasy about how things are or should be; similarly, they may serve to protect groups or families from the emotional pain and awareness of how things actually are.

The concepts of unconscious group or institutional processes, and of institutional defences, have been usefully applied to professional networks, which constitute a system, and which psychologically speaking in many ways function like institutions or organisations. One particularly helpful idea is that relationships and powerful unconscious dynamics in a child's family can be unconsciously 're-enacted' (Britton, 1981) or 'mirrored' (Reder *et al.*, 1993) in the professional network – an idea that has been applied and elaborated more systematically in, for instance, the field of child protection (ibid.) than in the field of adoption. As Britton (1981) describes, professionals may unconsciously identify with different members of the family and take up positions or act in ways that correspond to these unconscious identifications or dynamics.

Professional networks in work with children are made up of a number of professionals from different agencies and departments who have involvement with a particular child or family. In the case of children who are adopted, the professional network around the child invariably changes at different stages in the process, i.e. the period before the child is taken into care, the period while the child is in care, and the period around the time of adoption and after. The degree to which these professional networks overlap or are more discrete may vary significantly, depending on circumstances and geography. In addition, it is not uncommon for a child to experience serial changes of professionals with particular roles – most commonly social workers – within one or more of these periods, due to staff turnover, re-organisation, long-term sick leave, or other reasons. These often repeatedly changing and 're-constituted' professional networks around a child make unconscious re-enactment in the professional network more possible or likely to occur, in the same way that a less consistent and 'stable' structure around children in any context provides less protection against powerful psychological pressures and dynamics.

When a child has been adopted this unconscious process of 're-enactment' can also occur within adoptive families. Powerful and often destructive dynamics from a child's birth family can be unconsciously re-enacted in the adoptive family – a theme that from different perspectives is addressed in the three chapters in this section. This has extremely distressing and disturbing consequences in families with an adopted child or children who have experienced severe abuse, trauma or neglect in their birth families. In an adoptive family, unconscious re-enactment can also occur in relation to painful or traumatic experiences of an adopted child's birth parent even where these were not experienced directly by the child (e.g. parental bereavement, abuse, or separation). A further complex dimension of re-enactment in an adopted family is where an adopted child's patterns of behaviour or response unconsciously resonate with painful issues and vulnerabilities of the adoptive parents, as Rustin and Sprince discuss in their chapters.

In her chapter 'Multiple families in mind' *Margaret Rustin* explores 'how the complex internal worlds of participants in adoption dramas influence ongoing relationships within substitute families'. Rustin describes the disorganising and confusing effects that 'multiple family life' can have on the inner worlds of adopted children. She goes on to highlight the way in which '[the] shadow of earlier turbulence is liable to fall on the [adoptive] family'. Rustin illustrates with clinical material both from individual child psychotherapy and from work with an adoptive parent how the inner worlds of adoptive children and parents may impact on or interact with each other at an unconscious level. The chapter demonstrates the contribution of clinical interventions to an understanding of 'these complex interactions'.

Kate Cairns, in her chapter 'Enabling effective support: secondary traumatic stress and adoptive families', describes the phenomenon of 'secondary traumatic stress' in which caring for others who have been traumatised has a traumatising effect on the carers. Cairns draws on this model to explain the distressing and disturbing process by which 'human beings move from caregiving into disorders of thought, feeling and behaviour'. She argues that an understanding of this is essential in relation to providing professional support for families who have adopted a child who experienced trauma earlier in life. Cairns makes the point that for adoptive parents the task of parenting a child who has experienced trauma is 'a professional-level task' and not merely one of ordinary parenting. She highlights the contrast between the requirement for support structures to manage occupational stress for people who are employed to provide care, and the difficulty and complexity of providing corresponding support for adoptive parents. While this chapter is not specifically psychoanalytic in its perspective – the conceptual framework derives primarily from attachment theory – it nevertheless complements a psychoanalytic model in relation to the ways in which people's inner worlds impact on each other at an unconscious level, and how this can affect relationships, and in relation to the idea of 'splitting in the network' which Cairns touches on.

In the chapter 'The network around adoption: the forever family and the ghosts of the dispossessed', *Jenny Sprince* discusses some conscious and unconscious emotional dynamics in professional networks and adoptive families. She links these dynamics to the children's abusive or traumatic histories prior to adoption, and to difficulties for professionals and adoptive parents in facing the extremely painful emotional reality of adopted children's inner worlds and how severely emotionally damaged some of these children are. Sprince argues that where this painful reality is unbearable for people, professional systems and adoptive parents may unconsciously 'unite to obliterate the past' – that is, obliterate its emotional meaning and consequences. Drawing on both her consultation work with professionals in the field of adoption and her clinical experience with adopted children and parents, Sprince elaborates how destructive aspects of an adopted child's early attachment relationships may unconsciously be re-enacted in the relationship between adoptive child and parents. She suggests that an essential role of the network around adoption involving emotionally traumatised or disturbed children is to facilitate an understanding of 'the complexity of the child's needs and the impact of their disturbances (or pain) on those around them'.

Some readers may find these chapters particularly uncomfortable or painful to read. It is an inherently painful and disturbing idea – perhaps even shocking – that professional groups or families whose intentions are unquestionably good, and whose aim is to provide children who have experienced often severe deprivation, abuse or trauma with a better alternative experience and life quality, may sometimes unwittingly act in ways that re-enact or mirror the dynamics of the damaging and destructive experiences they are aiming to protect a child from. It is perhaps an equally painful and disturbing idea that professionals or adoptive families may quite unconsciously act in ways that are part of an unhelpful or destructive dynamic that they may be entirely unaware of (just as it is undoubtedly a painful discovery for well-intentioned agencies or institutions to find that the collective effects of different parts of the system may be prejudicial if not detrimental to people or groups of people they are intended to serve). However, psychoanalysis offers an understanding of *unconscious* determinants that may be at work in repeated dynamics within families and systems, and that which can be understood is more likely to be amenable to change.

References

Armstrong, D. (2005) *Organization in the Mind: Psychoanalysis, Group Relations, and Organizational Consultancy*, London: Karnac.

Bion, W.R. (1961) *Experiences in Groups*, London: Tavistock Publications.

Box, S., Copley, B., Magagna, J. and Moustaki, E. (eds) (1981) *Psychotherapy with Families: An Analytic Approach*, London: Routledge and Kegan Paul.

Britton, R. (1981) 'Re-enactment as an unwitting professional response to family dynamics', in S. Box, B. Copley, J. Magagna and E. Moustaki (eds) *Psychotherapy with Families: An Analytic Approach*, London: Routledge and Kegan Paul.

Cooper, A. and Lousada, J. (eds) (2005) *Borderline Welfare: Feeling and Fear of Feeling in Modern Welfare*, London: Karnac.

Emanuel, L. (2006 [2002]) 'The contribution of organizational dynamics to the triple deprivation of looked after children', in J. Kenrick, C. Lindsey and L. Tollemache (eds) *Creating New Families: Therapeutic Approaches to Fostering, Adoption and Kinship*, London: Karnac. Original version published as 'Deprivation × 3: the contribution of organizational dynamics to the triple deprivation of looked after children', *Journal of Child Psychotherapy*, 28 (2): 163–79.

Freud, S. (1921) *Group Psychology and the Analysis of the Ego, S.E.* 18.

Halton, W. (1994) 'Some unconscious aspects of organizational life: contributions from psychoanalysis', in A. Obholzer and V. Zagier Roberts (eds) *The Unconscious at Work: Individual and Organizational Stress in the Human Services*, London and New York: Routledge.

Hinshelwood, R.D. and Skogstad, W. (2000) *Observing Organizations: Anxiety, Defence and Culture in Health Care*, London and Philadelphia, PA: Routledge.

Huffington, C., Armstrong, D., Halton, W., Hoyle, L. and Pooley, J. (eds) (2004) *Working Below the Surface: The Emotional Life of Contemporary Organizations*, London: Karnac.

Jaques, E. (1953) 'On the dynamics of social structure: a contribution to the psychoanalytical study of social phenomena deriving from the views of Melanie Klein', in E. Trist and H. Murray (eds) *The Social Engagement of Social Science*, Volume 1: *The Socio-Psychological Perspective*, London: Free Associations Books, 1990.

Lewin (1947) 'Frontiers in group dynamics, Parts I and II', *Human Relations*, 1: 5–41; 2: 143–53.

Menzies Lyth, I. (1988) *Containing Anxiety in Institutions*, London: Free Association Books.

Menzies Lyth, I. (1989) *The Dynamics of the Social*, London: Free Association Books.

Miller, E.J. and Rice, A.K. (1967) *Systems of Organization: The Control of Task and Sentient Boundaries*, London: Tavistock Publications.

Obholzer, A. and Zagier Roberts, V. (eds) (1994) *The Unconscious at Work: Individual and Organizational Stress in the Human Services*, London and New York: Routledge.

Reder, P., Duncan, S. and Gray, M. (1993) *Beyond Blame: Child Abuse Tragedies Revisited*, London and New York: Routledge.

Sprince, J. (2000) 'Towards an integrated network', *Journal of Child Psychotherapy*, 26 (3): 413–31.

Zagier Roberts, V. (1994) 'The organization of work: contributions from open systems theory', in A. Obholzer and V. Zagier Roberts (eds) *The Unconscious at Work: Individual and Organizational Stress in the Human Services*, London and New York: Routledge.

4   Multiple families in mind

Margaret Rustin

The structure of the inner world

The structure of the internal world of adopted children and their families is influenced in many subtle ways by their atypical life experiences. This is also the case for foster children and parents when long-term placements are made. In this chapter I describe how the complex internal worlds of participants in adoption dramas influence ongoing relationships within substitute families. This is an evolving process, and has a span beyond one lifetime because of intergenerational transmission. There is now a well-established understanding that adoption cannot be meaningfully understood as a one-off event or moment and needs to be seen as a process, whose meaning is re-worked throughout the life cycle (Rosenberg, 1992). Individual psychotherapeutic work can offer detailed descriptive accounts of adoptive experience from the perspective of internal reality, thus taking account of unconscious elements, and this is the primary evidential base from which this chapter is written.

An important feature of a young child's picture of the world is that it is only gradually integrated and organised. In a framework of good enough external care, the infant mind structures the varied fragments of experience and two pictures of mother take shape, one of a good trustworthy mother with all those attributes that gratify the infant, and a contrasting picture of a bad, unreliable and disappointing mother. This process is a fundamental achievement in psychological development which permits us to organise our mental lives in a differentiated way. Good and bad, beautiful and ugly, right and wrong, love and hate, are primary polarities on which we depend to order experience (Klein, 1946).

As the baby develops, it becomes possible for a well-supported infant to perceive the connection between the good and bad mothers of the inner world. The baby can also begin to struggle with the task which occupies us all internally throughout our lives, that is the bringing together of our diverse and contradictory feelings towards the objects of our passionate feelings, and of partial pictures of ourselves. The growing capacity to sort out self and other is the bedrock of persons becoming individuals. It is interfered with when the care of the young child is not consistent enough to assist processes of discrimination and not attuned enough to the infant's needs to modify early infantile anxieties.

The care received in the early months or years of many of the children who are subsequently adopted is likely to have lacked these helpful features. We need to bear this in mind when we try to grasp their experience of themselves and the impact they have on their new families. The care they require may be of a quite different order from that which their chronological age would lead one to expect. Their internal worlds are very often confused, lacking in meaningful differentiations (Boston and Szur, 1983).

Some features of multiple-family life have a striking impact on the nature of the child's inner world. The markers of familiar places, so important to young children, may be confused or lacking. Sounds, smells, the view out of the window may have changed unpredictably, as did the humans in view. There has to be space in the mind for not only birth parents and adoptive parents, but in all likelihood also for significant prior foster carers who have provided periods of care. In addition, there may be an area of disorganised experience where individual carers did not feature strongly enough to acquire a recognisable or consistent shape in the child's mind. This can be a consequence of multiple indiscriminate care in an institution, of multi-adult disorganised care in a severely dysfunctional family, or of the experience of being cared for by a mentally ill parent who did not seem to the infant to be a recurring recognisable figure. These examples are not exhaustive, but may serve to help us imagine a child's response to particular sorts of care. The social worker is an additional significant figure, and sometimes has provided the greatest continuity over a considerable period.

Anxieties caused by 'contact'

Current practice places an expectation on adoptive families of coping with a range of forms of contact with the original family. But such contact can be disturbing to a child, because it very often entails exposure to emotionally intense conflicts and stirs up distressing memories which intrude into present realities.

Katy, aged 9, in a recent conversation with her adoptive mother explained that she did not want any contact with her birth mother. Specifically, she did not want her adoptive mother to write the agreed annual letter to her birth mother giving a brief account of her and her brother's progress. She was very relieved to reassure herself that photographs were not being sent and she certainly did not want to send a card or note herself. Why not? Because, she anxiously confided to her adoptive mother, she feared that her birth mother might be able to trace her via her finger prints. Katy has recurrent nightmares that she will be kidnapped by her mother even though she has been in her adoptive home for a number of years and there is no contact.

It is as if Katy's sense of safety in her new family is intruded on quite out-of-the-blue by this figure of a mother-kidnapper. From Katy's point of view, the nightmare could always start to happen in real life. Explanation and reassurance about her position does not help her, for in her internal world she remains at the mercy of an all-knowing, all-powerful and terrifying mother. This is the legacy of the neglect and abuse she suffered as a small child feeling helpless in the face of cruelty. Sometimes her behaviour in the adoptive family seems to have the meaning of an attempt to pass on this horrific experience of being explosively intruded into, as in her recent symptom of sudden long piercing shrieks, right into someone else's ear. Katy is so frightened of these attackers that she is not able to acknowledge the reality of her own difficult behaviour – from her point of view, she is engaged in necessary self-protection. Sometimes she provides a glimpse of the simplified idealised world she seems to be in need of. Her current delight is in learning to canoe – the snug fit for one within the firm structure of the canoe, the special clothes and life-jacket, could represent the absent longed-for link to a caring sustaining mother, who holds the baby up above her terrors instead of plunging her into them.

Katy's opportunity to achieve basic splitting into good and bad was probably undermined in her early development. This building block of the mind has to be in place before integration can occur. From greater integration can flow the capacity to take responsibility and to feel concern for others.

Small nuclear families are not particularly characteristic of humankind over the centuries. There is some sense in likening the network of foster homes to the more extended families of other periods and indeed of some minority ethnic cultures within modern-day Britain. In some local authorities, the fostering support services enable foster parents to get to know each other and to provide respite care between foster homes to facilitate holidays and cope with crises in much the way grandparents and uncles and aunts sometimes support a family in need of help with childcare. What is difficult for these children is to get a grasp on what a mother, father, brother or sister is, when they have such a patchwork of broken-up experiences to draw on.

This element of confusion can further complicate the degree of conflict, particularly conflicts of loyalty, which such children often face. The crucial process of making sense of things, although it will in part be a conscious process, and can be assisted from outside by work of a life-story type and in other ways, is to a significant extent, an unconscious process, taking place in the depths of the mind.

A contribution from clinical research

In exploring this matter of conflict, a research project of a child psychotherapist colleague, Debbie Hindle, has yielded significant data (Hindle, 2000). She used careful observational assessment of siblings in care, together with meetings with the network of adults involved, to examine the decision-making process with respect to siblings being placed together or separately, and to try to refine some useful criteria for such decisions. She has worked with two sisters, aged 3½ and 1½, who at that point were living in separate foster homes. This arrangement was a consequence of a judicial decision that rehabilitation of the older child with the natural mother should be attempted once more. When the child was again abandoned, she was returned to a different foster home, though contact visits with her younger sister were maintained.

When the children were seen together their play was animated. The older girl, Kelly, made many moves to include, refer to, and take care of her little sister Susie. When Kelly left the room briefly to go to the toilet, Susie flopped on the floor and remained huddled and lifeless until she returned. The girls used each other's names frequently. When Kelly was seen alone she was markedly more disturbed, and was suspicious of and hostile towards the therapist. The story stem technique developed by Hodges and Steele (1995) for research with children with disrupted life experience was used as an additional instrument. Kelly's stories contained no evidence that she expected children who got lost or hurt to receive any help from adults, and threatening intruders seemed to be all-powerful, totally overwhelming the inhabitants of the doll's house. There was no model of a relationship imbued with concern between adult and child. Yet Kelly had been observed to provide quite tender care-taking for her baby sister – between sisters, something protective did seem to operate. When Susie was seen alone, there was repeated reference by name to her absent sister.

The conflict that this material highlighted was as follows: both foster mothers maintained that the child in their care had no memory of having lived with the other, and that the children did not know they were sisters. Kelly was said to have no particular relationship to Susie, 'She's like that with everyone,' said Mrs A, and Susie was said by Mrs B to have forgotten the time Kelly lived with them. Yet both foster mothers were identified with their foster children and protective towards them. How can we account for this sort of blind spot?

Each foster mother may perhaps be fearful that a shared placement could endanger the interests of 'their' child. Mrs A was angry with Mrs B that Kelly had not returned to the Bs following the abortive attempted rehabilitation with mother. She perhaps carried Kelly's feelings of rejection by Mrs B and the failure to protect her from yet a further chapter of hurt. Mrs A had been enthusiastic at first to keep Kelly as a long-term foster child, in the light of her mother's refusal to free her for adoption (Susie had been given up for adoption at birth), but this optimism had waned sharply and she was now seeing herself as providing a short-term placement. She, too, was thus feeling unable to hold on to Kelly in the long term and perhaps her guilt about this was pushed in Mrs B's direction.

Mrs B who had cared for Susie since birth knew that Susie was in pretty good shape, and that although as elderly foster parents she and Mr B could not offer an adoptive home, there was every chance that she would be placed in a good home where they might perhaps remain in a quasi-grandparental role. Thus, without the additional complications attached to Kelly's presence, in particular her not-yet-resolved link to her birth mother and to two older half-brothers, Susie could be seen as part of a new 'ideal' family. Kelly's presence would bring back into play all the uncomfortable elements in Susie's background.

There is an obvious disjunction between the evidence that the children's link with each other is of importance to them and the denial of this by the foster parents. One way of thinking about this is to note that the foster mothers' interpretation of the facts tends to reduce both the pain and uncertainty that the story presents. If we are in touch with the children's sense of investment in each other, it is very painful to imagine what each has felt about their sudden separation and it seems clear that maintaining their relationship is a priority. If we argue for a joint adoptive placement, we have to recognise that this will probably involve a delay in Susie's permanent placement and an element of risk, since Kelly might again evoke in a family an initial wish to have her, followed by an equally strong feeling of rejection. It is obvious that she is a little girl who will place great strain on any family's emotional resources, and that therapeutic help should be sought for her in conjunction with placement plans being made. All this means that the prospective adoptive family is going to need to be exceptional and, in particular, able to accommodate two children who will easily offer themselves as stereotypical opposites – the nice and the nasty one, the responsive and the non-attached. The family would also need to be able to tolerate sharing the care of one of their newly adopted daughters with a therapist. This is rarely a palatable idea for adopters, who usually hope that the 'forever' family will do all that is needed to put right a child's problems.

Clinical intervention

Once humans get close to each other, their internal worlds are in a dynamic relation to each other. All the earlier experiences of each member of any significant intimate relationship (dyad, triad, family, group, etc.) contribute to the landscape of the new relationship. Events in the present can throw into prominence troubling aspects of the past, both providing a chance for a new way forward but also often engendering confusion and distress.

Clinical interventions take us to the heart of these complex interactions. My first clinical example concerns work with an adopted boy aged 9. In this case, the internal world of the adoptive mother became a powerful organiser of the child's developing personality. This intergenerational intertwining of unconscious imaginative lives can create particular quandaries within adopting families. In the second example the emphasis is on the process going in the opposite direction, the impact of child on parent. Both examples raise some of the cultural complexities so commonly associated with adoption.

First clinical example

Sam, aged 9, is the adopted son of a couple who have lived in England for some years. He was referred for help with severe sleeping difficulties based on an acute phobia of snakes. At the time he was unable to sleep alone and woke in panicky states several times a night. The parents were exhausted and at their wits' end. Other difficulties noted were his jealous relationship with his younger sister (also adopted) and his intensely combative spirit when confronted with parental authority. He seemed unable to accept that adults had any rights commensurate with their responsibilities. I offered to see Sam once a week for psychotherapy after two assessment sessions in which he gained some immediate relief, but which also gave me a sense of the entrenched defensive impasse which was being enacted at home. The GP had written of a brief focal intervention in relation to the sleeping problems, but I thought that something more extended would be needed.

In the first term, Sam was reasonably communicative about all sorts of matters except anything that might pertain to the difficulties at home, of which I heard nothing. The parents continued to express extreme exasperation. Sam seemed very enthusiastic about coming to see me, using his time to the full, but for the purpose of interesting or occupying me rather than receiving anything from me. He would listen politely to what I said, but then brush it aside and enquire if he could now continue with whatever game he was engaged in. I struggled with growing frustration.

When working within a psychoanalytic framework, the therapist anticipates that the breaks within the regular treatment rhythm will be of significance, because attention is being paid to infantile aspects of the therapeutic relationship and this usually means that separations have a major emotional impact. However, the extent to which Sam's way of relating to me shifted prior to the first holiday break was a considerable surprise to me as I shall describe. More often, we find that breaks acquire significance once they have been experienced. For children with earlier disruptions in their history, however, they may be felt as a repetition of earlier abandonments and make their impact felt before they have actually happened. This always seems extraordinary at the time, but in my experience the child is relieved when it is possible to speak about feelings suddenly erupting into the therapy from an unfamiliar area of the personality.

The last session of the term brought a dramatic shift. Sam was in the waiting room together with the rest of his family, tearful, turning away from me to hide in his coat, and completely unwilling to come to my room. I decided to invite his parents to join us to get things underway. They both spoke volubly, while he remained slumped in a sad heap, and mother left after a few minutes to return to the younger sister. Father then spoke warmly about how proud he was of his son, who was now able to go to bed on his own and was not waking them up at night. This had the quality of both affectionate support of Sam, but also an implicit statement that he did not need to come to the clinic any more and that therefore what was happening in the room was unimportant, and should be brought to a close as soon as possible.

After a while, I decided to ask father to return to the waiting room, saying that although we could both see how upset Sam was, I thought he could manage to spend some time with me on his own, and stating to Sam that if he felt this was not so he could return to his Dad at any time. Father left, a bit reluctantly, and I then felt free to speak to Sam directly about his feeling that I had become quite a different Mrs Rustin for him now that I was going to be away over Christmas and not seeing him for two weeks. He could not find the Mrs Rustin he had liked talking to here today. I said that I thought he believed that I was leaving him altogether, as his long-ago first mummy had done, and that he did not trust what I had said about starting sessions again in January. Sam was able to stay for the rest of the session while I talked on these lines, linking his mistrust with his worry that

I would not remember him, did not like him, wanted to get away from him, and so on. He quietened and relaxed, although still looking very miserable.

When we resumed in January, a long sequence of sessions ensued spent on building armaments of defences – planes, missiles, laser systems, ever bigger bombs. Numerous wars were enacted in which the enemy, linked usually with the enemies of his country of birth, attacked and was held at bay by the superior defence system so carefully constructed. Each renewed attack required an escalation of the security system. He told me that he wanted to join the army when he was old enough. His world picture was of his country standing alone, taking on the whole world and surviving by monumental efforts.

I began to describe to him that the 'no', which became his virtually automatic response to anything I said, was like a kind of force field, a wall of 'noes' to keep me out, like the plasticine palisade he built around his camps. Occasionally he would allow me through for a second; a couple of times this took the humorous form of his saying 'Yes – I mean no' in response to what I said. Yet it seemed impossible to interest him in exploring these contradictions. I experienced him as impenetrable and could not see any way to convey to him that I might be able to help his beleaguered self.

I had tried on numerous occasions to make some link to the pre-holiday session, to no avail, but one day I roused myself to try afresh to locate the terrified and despairing Sam I had glimpsed just that once. Perhaps I spoke in a more imaginative way than usual as I described how puzzling it was to understand where that boy had gone, for Sam had been telling me repeatedly that he had no more problems now, echoing his father's words.

Suddenly he looked up at me and said, 'That boy left. That wasn't me. He's in Hollywood.' Thus began the story of the boy in Hollywood. Sam explained that the boy rings him every day to talk to him. The following week I heard more. The boy does not have any more problems at night because his nanny, Jacky, has helped him. She stays with him until he falls asleep, but the boy is still worried about being on his own. He thinks if he snuggles down inside his blankets so that he can't see the snakes, he might be all right, but he's not very sure.

Soon I learnt that the boy was getting very frightened because Jacky was going to leave to return to Canada – her sister was going to have a baby, and Jacky was going to help her. The boy was very sad indeed. 'I'll see her once more,' said Sam, quickly correcting himself, 'I mean he'll see her once more.' The boy supposed he would have a new nanny but he liked Jacky.

Now I will describe in more detail part of the session that followed this:

Sam began by fetching his huge war-plane construction, made of ruler, pencils, sellotape, and plasticine, together with his remaining plasticine, which is what he used to make missiles. I remarked that today he had an idea of needing to check up on being well protected. I had in mind the closeness of the Easter holiday but did not refer to it at this point. He then produced a large bag full of 'pogs' from his pocket (there was a wide-spread fashion for collecting these at the time), the metal type similar to large old-fashioned half-crowns, embossed on each side. Using the plasticine, he made what he called 'fake pogs' by imprinting them on the plasticine and cutting out matching rounds. He became more adept and drew my attention to how well the pattern came out. I talked to him about his wondering how well I would be remembering him over Easter and how well he might be able to keep me in mind in the weeks we did not see each other. I linked this back to the upset before Christmas, when he felt afraid I would not keep him clearly in my mind and would lose him and not come back to go on with our work. 'That was the boy from Hollywood,' he corrected me, but in a tolerant tone of voice which allowed our conversation to proceed. He then told me more about the boy when I enquired how he was. He was very sad and afraid since his nanny left; his cousin had been looking after him, but she would be leaving next week to go back to her family. I said I wondered if Sam could help that boy. He looked at me, a bit surprised. I explained that he might be able to talk to him as he knew something about being very upset when someone left. When I went away at Christmas he had been upset, but he also knew that I had come back, and that this was what would happen again at Easter time – we would say goodbye, but we would meet again after the holiday to continue our work. There was a brief pause and then he looked up and said he would see Jacky again one day. When he is 18, he will go to Canada to visit her.

Sam then began a game to see which were better, the real or the false pogs. He decided the fake ones were better because they were heavier and softer, more flexible. He showed me how they stick well to the pog they are thrown at and to the surface of the table, instead of just bouncing off.

I spoke about this making me think about his liking things that stick well, that don't get detached. I linked this with his feeling more hopeful about us sticking together, not bouncing off in opposite directions and losing contact. Then I went on to talk about his ideas about a contrast between his first mummy who had not been able to hold on to him, and his adoptive mummy who might feel like a fake mummy in one sense, because he had not grown inside her, but seemed to him to be better for him because she stuck to him. He said quietly 'my belly Mummy'. I asked was that his way of referring to his first mummy? 'No,' he said, 'it's my Mum's way. She doesn't like me to call my original Mummy my Mum.' I said it would be good for us to use the words he liked for thinking about her – was that his name for her? He confirmed thoughtfully, 'Yes, my original Mum.' I talked about his having lost her a long time ago but perhaps still having a lot of thoughts about her. Losing people that were important had started right at the beginning of his life. 'I was only two weeks old,' Sam said. 'My memory doesn't stretch that far back.' I agreed and added that in his imagination his original mum probably was still important.

There was some further reference to the idea of a new nanny and Sam thought I said 'Nana' and corrected me. I asked if he had a nana too. He was puzzled and I explained some people called their grandmothers 'nana' and I had wondered if he did. He looked up and calmly summarised for me precisely described details of his mother's traumatic early history as the child of two holocaust survivors, and added a painful episode from his father's family history.

Towards the end of the session he began to crush together the fake pogs. 'How many of them are still alive?' he asked me, as if in a game. He showed me that it was still possible to disentangle from the lump of plasticine a complete fake pog with the image clearly visible.

I talked to him about memories of people who had died being still alive in people's minds, both his and his mother's. Perhaps this was also linked to his thoughts about his original mother – he might wonder sometimes if she was still alive. 'And her parents,' he added. 'People at school say I look like my Mum and Dad and my sister,' he said. I asked what he thought about that. 'I don't think I do,' he said. I spoke of his realising that other people sometimes found it difficult to allow him to be a boy who had had an original mother and father and therefore tried to pretend that his family now was the only one he belonged to. He did not feel like that, and he wanted me to help him to think about the pictures he also has in his mind of his original mother and father.

He asked me if I still had the building blocks he used to play with. I fetched them for him. For the last part of the session he built constructions with rather substantial foundations which were in fascinating contrast to the tall, wobbly towers of the earlier period of brick play, which had always collapsed spectacularly. This building turned out to be quite solid at the base, and a good portion survived when he built a spindly top section obviously destined to fall over.

I talked about his feeling differently about coming to the end of the session today. I suggested he felt we had had a good solid talk and that even though finishing was difficult (as usual he was very slow about clearing up, in an attempt to prolong the session) he felt there was something which would remain there in his mind and in mine for us to build on next time – it was not all just a heap of fragments. Like a comic echo of this, as he picked up his jacket, he scattered coins all over the floor and grinned at me as he gathered them together.

Discussion

I shall explore three different threads in this material. First, the story of the boy in Hollywood. I think it was crucial that I did not prematurely cut off this story-line. At a suitably great distance and for a brief time (London to Hollywood, the length of a phone call) Sam could make contact with the terrified boy within him. We could discuss the boy's fear that nanny and others left him because they were fed up with him and couldn't bear all his worries. We could picture the boy's wish to remember and be remembered and his great fear of being abandoned. Over a number of weeks, Hollywood got palpably nearer, and I think Sam needed to be allowed to manage the pace of this integration (Alvarez, 1992). It will probably continue to move back and forth. We have, however, found a place where terrible anxieties can be located and yet contacted.

The notion of the boy in Hollywood offers a way of working over anxieties which Sam needs to be able to externalise and hold at a distance. This manoeuvre is a creative solution to the problem of being easily overwhelmed by intense feelings. It would be unhelpful to interpret the projection and take away the space in which there is freedom for us to explore together.

This links to my second point. The horror of the mother's tragic history is spoken about by Sam coolly and rationally. Only a tiny hint of the emotional meaning of the holocaust is offered. When he told me later on in the session about his aunt, he referred to her ashes being in the wood where a memorial playground had been built. My mind registered the link between the crematoria of the death camps and his reference to his aunt's ashes in the forest. The interweaving of these images of catastrophe with the idea of children's play space provides us with a vivid sense of how little unimpeded space for play there may be in the family landscape of children whose parents are close to the holocaust. I think Sam's account conveyed to me how laden down he is with his mother's tragedies, how much detail he has been burdened with, how much she may have needed her children's mental space for her own painful memories.

The family history he has had to ingest is not one he is able to imbue with real significance. The headline quality of his announcement that he was going to tell me his mother's tragic story indicates the distance between what is hers and what is his. This is of course one of the subtle difficulties in intergenerational construction of narratives of family history, for the teller of the story has a particular inflection and point of view, and an adult view tends to crowd out the child's perspective.

The third point is that we are shown Sam's pained distance from other people's version of his life. He must have got across to me in his tone of voice that the phrase 'belly Mummy' was not quite right for him, as I think I questioned him in response to this half-perceived note of discomfort. More explicit was his complaint about the pressure he feels in the school and social world to go along with the fiction of a perfectly fitting family of four. This fiction involves disloyalty to his emotional link to his birth mother, and in so far as that link is weakened he is also more exposed to the impact of his adoptive mother's traumatic history. I found myself thinking about the possibility that some of Sam's angry rejecting behaviour towards his mother may be a desperate effort to hold her at a distance and protect himself to a degree from being sucked into her nightmares. It is interesting to see how much he has been helped by a nanny who is more able to respond to his need for an understanding of his fearfulness because she herself is not so easily stirred into states of panic.

We have here a dramatic representation of the traumata of the earlier generation which have not been digested in the mind or found symbolic representation. Probably the nightmare black snakes are in some way linked to Sam's picture of the horrors of death camps which his mother needs him to help her to deal with – perhaps associated with black leather Nazi gear or the black columns of smoke from the crematoria or with swastikas. I do not know yet how this particular symbol has been formed.

Let us consider the parents for a moment. Mother's capacity to contain and process her own appalling experiences has been further damaged by her inability to bear children. This may have made her feel that the Nazi curse had got right into her body, destroying her fertility. This additional loss, after so many early ones, sets the scene for the adoption to carry an enormous weight of hope and anxiety – if this parental couple can come together, the hope is that the nightmare of the holocaust can be set to one side and an area of new growth be established. But the dread of a repetition of disaster is extreme, making both parents ill-equipped for the ordinary ups and downs of raising children. Every reverse is experienced as the beginning of a destructive process which cannot be controlled. Hence Sam's tempers are described as quite overwhelming for both parents who each try to leave the other one to cope alone.

Second clinical example – an adoptive parent's struggles

Now what about the parental perspective? I have chosen an example which offers a glimpse of the processes of working through anxieties which have a double resonance, an echo for both parent and child. I think it shows how the fresh opportunities for dealing with fundamentals raised by our relationships with our children can lead to moments of resolution and change.

I am working with the single mother, Ms B, of an adopted 17-year-old boy who has had a very turbulent delinquent adolescence. Steve currently lives in an excellent hostel, and this physical separation has contributed to considerable rebuilding of their relationship. One day mother described to me the events surrounding Steve's birthday. They had gone on a shopping trip together to buy him new clothes. She had set a cash limit which had been made explicit to Steve, and which, as always, was generous in the context of her limited resources. To her delight, Steve had chosen items within a manageable price range so that he had a complete new outfit with which he was pleased. They had a snack together. As they were about to say goodbye at the bus stop in Oxford Street, Steve tried to extract from her the few remaining pounds up to her cash limit for the birthday gift. She refused, feeling flooded with anxieties about what he wanted the money for (usually drugs or debts to dealers), and with rage at the way in which her generous present was now being made to seem mean. Steve's threats and verbal and physical abuse of her escalated, to the numb astonishment of the many bystanders, and to the despair and horror of Ms B who felt herself reliving a hundred previous violent rows. Steve screamed among much else 'No mother would treat a son the way you treat me. You only think about yourself – you're not my mother, you bitch.' She managed to escape with the arrival of her bus, arriving home still shaking with fury and terror and having retaliated with this rejecting parting-shot – 'I don't want to see you for two weeks, Steve.'

Later, she calmed down, and thought to herself, 'I can't do that. It's his birthday. He's had enough of being abandoned by people. I'm his mother and I can't not be there on his birthday.' She then left a message for him at his hostel – would he like to arrange something for his birthday? If so, please would he let her know? (She was thinking maybe go to a movie.) Steve responded – could they have a meal together?

In this sequence of passionate emotions stirred so strongly by the particularly painful edge associated with birthdays for adopted children, things get out of hand, but each of the two struggles hard to avoid a repetition of the so-well-rehearsed breakdown of relationship, and thus to allow that the present can be more than the past repeated. Something new is always a possibility. Without this element of optimism, adoption could never have been invented as a solution to something that has not worked. But the complexity of the task never fails to fill me with wonder.

Conclusion

It is a life-long reality for adopted children and their parents that their lives will be affected in unpredictable ways by the earlier experiences of the child. This may be particularly difficult to comprehend when there is patchy knowledge of the child's early history – bad times may erupt in ways which are deeply puzzling, since there is an absence of ordinary family memories which help to make sense of things. This is one of the reasons why a proper provision for post-adoptive support for families is so important. The shadow of earlier turbulence is liable to fall on the family when developmental pressures are felt and when anxieties beset family members. Separation, divorce, illness, death are a special threat to children whose inner security has major fault-lines, but ordinary changes – going to secondary school, moving house, new siblings arriving, leaving home – can also arouse intense worry. Adolescent sexual development, with its accompanying questions for the adopted child about the nature of the sexual couple which gave him life, is a particularly threatening time. Such preoccupations are often expressed through sexual relationships dominated by unconscious re-enactment of fantasies about birth parents, and this can be a particularly troubling time for families. Their experience of the complexities of negotiating their children's adolescence can thus be interwoven with a stark encounter with the meaning given by the adolescent to his early history, which may feel alien in distressing ways.

The essence of the matter is that adoption creates extremely complex familial structures; the internal reality of this is the dimension I have mainly attempted to describe. Changing legal and social frameworks frequently ensure that the external dimension, the ongoing real experience of contact with the original family, is increasingly part of the picture. Understanding the interaction of these two dimensions of fantasy and experience is a continuing challenge for the families and all who work with them.

References

Alvarez, A. (1992) *Live Company: Psychoanalytic Psychotherapy with Autistic, Borderline, Deprived and Abused Children*, London: Tavistock, Routledge.

Boston, M. and Szur, R. (eds) (1983) *Psychotherapy with Severely Deprived Children*, London: Routledge.

Hindle, D. (2000) 'An intensive assessment of a small sample of siblings placed together in foster care', Doctorate dissertation, Tavistock Clinic/University of East London.

Hodges, J. and Steele, M. (1995) 'Internal representations of parent–child attachments in maltreated children', Paper presented to the Thomas Coram, Foundation Conference New Developments in Attachment Theory, September.

Klein, M. (1946) 'Notes on some schizoid mechanisms', *International Journal of Psychoanalysis*, 27: 99–110. (Republished in *Developments in Psychoanalysis*, by M. Klein, P. Heiman, S. Isaacs, and J. Riviera (eds), 1952, London: Hogarth.)

Rosenberg, E.B. (1992) *The Adoption Life Cycle: The Children and Their Families Through the Years*, New York: Free Press.

5   Enabling effective support

Secondary traumatic stress and adoptive families

Kate Cairns

Thirty-five years ago I was opposed to adoption. Like many oppositional stances, my aversion was largely based on feelings derived from unconsidered prejudice. My cultural origins permitted a considerable variety of family structures but considered adoption as a means for rich people who wanted a family to take over, and take ownership, of the children of the poor. This cultural prejudice was rationalised through my observation that adopted children seemed to be over-represented in the population of children I came across as a social worker in a child guidance clinic. And it was reinforced by the discovery that the dominant theme in such referrals was the unacceptable behaviour of the children, with responses in the adoptive parents of overwhelming sadness, anger and disappointment.

Thirty years ago my partner and I decided to establish a large family providing permanence for children for whom neither adoption nor fostering were, in those days, seen as an option. Over the years we offered a family for life to twelve children in addition to our own family of three. For fifteen years we had ten children living at home. Despite our shared aversion to adoption we believed that permanent family care was the most hopeful approach to enable sound development in children separated from their families. There were two particular differences between what we provided and adoption as it was then practised. We were able to maintain, or in some cases establish and maintain, contact between all our children and members of their birth families. And we were absolutely clear that professional support was essential for us to maintain the health of our family group.

Twenty-five years ago some of my best friends were adopters. Being a large and unusual family brought us into contact with others who had chosen different lifestyle approaches to the raising of children. I began to discover the range and diversity of the adoption community. I found that by that point in the history of adoption in the UK there were many different and usually benevolent motivations driving people to adopt children. It became clear that many people who adopted, far from being rich and privileged, were making lifestyle choices that meant considerable personal sacrifice in terms of both wealth and earning capacity. And the sacrifices were not just financial. It was evident that there were emotional and social costs for all of us in taking on the care of other people's children. We all had a great deal to learn.

The importance of a knowledge base

Children who have lived through adversity can bring many challenges into their new family. Making sense of the chaos that came into our home became a pressing concern for us, and remained at the heart of professional support throughout our time of caregiving. Understanding child development and attachment, recognising the impact of unmet needs, disruptions and distortions in early experience, gaining insight into the effects of adversity before birth, all these helped us to comprehend the nature of the task our children had taken on in coming to live in such a strange environment to them as our family presented. All these formed part of my discussions with the growing number of adopters with whom I was in touch.

More recently, the growing research and theory based on trauma and resilience has proved a rich source of benefit in fostering and adoption (see Chapter 2). In particular, developing an understanding of the impact of trauma on both children and their carers has proved transformative, removing blocks that have previously prevented children and families from receiving or benefiting from the support or the therapy needed to survive and to thrive.

Adopted children and trauma

Almost all children adopted in the UK have come either from the public care system or from overseas and will have lived through prior adversity. Even if a baby is adopted at birth, or early on, separation from the birth mother and/or foster carer may have a traumatic impact – albeit less visible than in the case of overtly traumatised or disturbed older children. It is now clear that such adversity has an impact on brain development, creating lasting changes in the patterns of thinking, feeling and behaving available to the child.

Impairments or distortions in brain function may begin before birth. Parental exposure to toxic substances such as ionising radiation, drugs or alcohol before conception, and maternal exposure to such toxins during pregnancy can have an impact on the growing brain of the baby. Children who have suffered such exposure before birth may have difficulty in learning, in processing sensory information, and in self-regulating: they find it difficult to manage their own behaviour or to make sense of the world around them and their relationships with others. They may then also be unable to gain developmental benefit from the nurture provided by their carers, so that we see some early adopted children who have been provided with sound parenting but who present as though they had unmet attachment needs.

If the baby is born without any such impairments or distortions of function, then attachment relationships from birth onwards help to create the developing brain, each interaction between baby and carer producing new connective tissue that shapes and sculpts the very structure of the brain. As the brain expects such interaction, neglect results in absent functions just as surely as abuse results in distortions and impairments in thought, feeling and behaviour.

One function in particular is worthy of comment: babies are not born able to regulate stress. They will experience stress as changes in the body and brain, indicating that the interchange between the individual and the environment needs altering. Hunger, thirst, being cold, overheating, fear – or any other discomfort – will produce stress hormones which the baby cannot regulate. Yet unregulated stress is risky for humans, causing loss of blood supply to key areas of brain function. By the end of the first year of life such unregulated stress in babies will be liable to create a change in brain function equivalent to the impact of disastrous terror in an older child or adult. Disastrous stress in mature humans reduces blood supply to the thinking brain, speeding up response time and providing the maximum potential for surviving the disaster. In babies who do not gain the ability to regulate stress through soothing relationships with their first carers, even relatively minor stresses can produce this disaster response.

This baby equivalent of emotional trauma may be called developmental trauma, and can produce injuries to the brain through altered blood supply. Such injuries may in turn create global impairments or distortions of function physically, psychologically, emotionally and socially. These are complex post-traumatic disorders. To add to the mix entering an adoptive family, many of the children moving from the care system into adoption have also experienced terrifying events which in themselves would constitute emotional trauma. They may have been abused or exploited physically, sexually and emotionally before intervention removed them from harm. At which point we may take the child away from the harm, but that does not remove the harm from the child.

Traumatised children need therapeutic parenting. The most positive parenting in the world will fail to meet their complex needs, unless the parents also have the knowledge and ability to adapt their role and provide therapeutic input. In birth families where children have lived through traumatic experiences, parents generally move into this role intuitively. They recognise that their child has been changed by the adverse experience, and they adapt their own behaviour to provide the milieu and the relationships that will enable the child to stabilise, to integrate the trauma into their life story and to adjust to their new reality.

When children enter adoption this seamless progression is critically interrupted. The adopters have no prior history with the child against which to develop their own responses. Their task goes beyond therapeutic parenting. It is therapeutic re-parenting, requiring them to engage as a parent with children who already have an internal model for attachment figures and an existing set of assumptions, expectations and beliefs about the world. In foster care it is increasingly accepted that this task of therapeutic re-parenting is a professional level task. Yet every year thousands of traumatised children are moved out of the care system into adoption, to be placed with people whose motivation is to be a parent and not to be a professional carer.

Secondary traumatic stress as a model for making sense of what happens in adoption

One consequence of these anomalies in the process of adoption is that many adoptive families find it difficult to make sense of life with their adopted child.

Nothing in their previous experience or thinking could have prepared them for the day-to-day impact of living with a traumatised child. Preparation sessions can do a great deal to help adopters learn what to expect from their children, but cannot prepare them for how they will feel or what it will be like.

Providing an explanatory model that takes account of all the dimensions of this experience is one way to enable adoptive families to contain and manage these powerful experiences. Understanding the impact of early trauma helps adopters to recognise the long path to recovery they are travelling with their children. And understanding secondary trauma helps them to grasp the impact of the early childhood trauma on everyone around the children, and especially on those who love them and live with them.

This way of thinking about the impact of traumatic stress on those who care for the victims of trauma was put forward by Figley (1995, 2002) in relation to the experiences of the families of Vietnam War veterans. The discovery that caring for others may injure us is not new. But setting out a process by which human beings move from caregiving into disorders of thought, feeling and behaviour enables those affected to recognise their own condition without fear, and also provides pathways back to health and stability.

What is secondary traumatic stress?

As social beings empathy is our greatest strength, allowing us to create complex social structures that can operate more or less harmoniously. But empathy is the attribute that makes us vulnerable to injury when we care for others who have been injured.

In psychoanalytic thinking, this identification and emotional resonance with others came to be seen as part of our earliest experience, described by Klein (1946) and Bion (1962) as both a way of ridding the self of painful or unwanted thoughts or feelings *and* as a primitive form of communication. From close observation of emotional interactions in therapeutic work, Bion's idea of containment developed. When this is available, in the context of a relationship between an infant and their mother, anxieties can be modified and modulated and the infant can introject a feeling of being understood and begin to build up a capacity to contain difficult and even contradictory thoughts and feelings. In the absence of the experience of a caring mind that can understand and modulate yet unthought experiences, anxieties can only be evacuated or evaded. It is these anxieties, unmodified, that adoptive parents either see in their children – manifested in a range of behaviours, including activity or bodily symptoms – or experience as being elicited in them. That is, empathy requires us to replicate in our own bodies a little image of the physiological state of another human. Traumatised people live physiologically in a state of terror. Empathic people will therefore replicate in their own bodies a little of the physiology of terror. The closer the bond between the two people, the more likely it is that this empathic response may destabilise the caregiver.

People are more vulnerable to this secondary stress response becoming overwhelming if they have experienced trauma in their own lives, and especially if they have unprocessed traumatic experience that may be triggered by the secondary stress response (Cairns, 1999, Van der Kolk *et al.*, 1996). But everyone is vulnerable to stress disorders, and even the most resilient people cannot be resilient all the time. The level of exposure to trauma in adopters is very high, as they share their life space with the traumatised child. Such high exposure raises the probability that at some time resilience will be reduced and the adopter will become vulnerable to secondary traumatic stress.

When that happens, people change. No longer able to regulate the secondary stress induced by exposure to trauma, they either become hyper-aroused, developing evident indicators of stress, or they may dissociate – shutting down emotionally and losing contact with their own sensory world. These are not choices made by the individual, but are automatic responses to overwhelming stress. These two possible automatic responses are then mirrored and cause splitting in the network around the child. Any couple or dyad may be split apart under the impact of secondary stress, and whole families and groups may be affected by such splitting.

In such circumstances emotional functioning changes. Hyper-aroused people become more emotionally unstable and volatile, dissociative people become more cold and withdrawn. Sleep patterns may alter, with hyper-arousal leading to difficulties in sleeping, and dissociation leading to sleeping longer or more heavily. Appetite and patterns of consumption may change in response to the altered physiology; people may crave food or drink that stimulate, or soothe, or produce a pleasure response, and use of mind-altering substances such as tobacco or alcohol may increase. It is common for people to become avoidant in relation to the traumatic material that goes with the child. Dissociative people become unable to enter the emotional space of the child, becoming more rigid and punitive in relation to this child than they are in other circumstances. Hyper-aroused people find themselves unable to escape from the child's emotional space, entering into that state of wordless terror in which the trauma cannot be confronted but instead takes over the core of everyday existence.

Adoption and secondary stress disorders

At times when resilience is reduced people may become overwhelmed by secondary traumatic stress, and they are then vulnerable to developing a stress disorder (Stamm, 1995). When this happens the induced stress has gone beyond their ability to regulate it, and has begun to injure the brain, producing noticeable changes in behaviour and day-to-day functioning.

People work harder, but achieve less and make more mistakes. They may avoid certain tasks, whilst quite unaware of that avoidance, or they may become perfectionist or obsessive in relation to other activities. They lose confidence in themselves, and become negative and demanding as they develop feelings of isolation, alienation and reduced worth. It becomes too painful to seek support, so that people withdraw from their own sources of support whilst at the same time feeling abandoned and uncared for. This subjective experience of abandonment and isolation leads either to feelings of helplessness and hopelessness or to angry demands to be provided for in some unspecific way.

When professionals working with traumatised children are subject to secondary traumatic stress there is at least the possibility that they work for an enlightened organisation that will have in place sound strategies to prevent and treat disorders. Such strategies are generally highly effective, and applying a secondary trauma model to such organisations can do a great deal to maintain the health and wellbeing of the workforce. Foster carers are the professional group most vulnerable to secondary traumatic stress, because the child shares their life space, but fostering agencies that take secondary trauma seriously are seeing that the wellbeing of care families can be monitored and nurtured.

Adopters are in a very different position. Their motivation is different – they want to be parents, not professional caregivers. Their access to support and input is different – once the adoption is completed there is no agency that has any right to monitor the family or to insist on the acceptance of support that may be offered. And adoption is much more intimate and personally engaging than any employment – parenting is a passionate activity that sits at the heart of human identity.

Prevention and treatment of secondary stress disorders

The three main strands of effective prevention of stress disorders among those who care for traumatised children are training, support and consultation. Training provides caregivers with the knowledge they need to become aware of their own stress responses and alert to signs of change in themselves and their colleagues. They may also seek – or be guided to seek – training that can increase their repertoire of available responses to stress, either in the form of straightforward training in stress management, or through learning other active routes to stress regulation such as patterned physical activity, meditation, activities that involve breath control such as singing, or self-help alternative therapies. If adopters come to understand the implications of secondary traumatic stress, they may well be able to gain access to training that will help to prevent such stress developing into disorder.

Support includes both informal and formal structures in the network that surrounds the traumatised child. The informal support network of family and friends has a vital part to play in maintaining the health of caregivers. The beneficial effects of such support are much greater if members of the network learn about the impact of trauma, and can keep an informed eye on the caregivers, watching for signs of developing disorder and helping the carer to accept the support they need to stay well. Formal support structures may include peer groups, mentors and telephone help lines. Again, adopters who understand the need for support are more able both to set up and to engage with such structures. But any support for adoption must recognise that as people become disordered they withdraw from support, so that effective support needs to be alert and proactive.

Consultation is a clinical necessity in working with traumatised children. It must be provided by professionals who thoroughly understand the dynamics of trauma, and who are able to offer both structure and emotional containment into the consultation process. It is essential that the expectations on both consultant and adoptive parents are clearly set out, and that consultation is regular and structured and has high priority. It is also important that there is in place some external review of the consultation, as consultants can be pulled in the direction of the trauma, and may develop a distorted view of the supervisee. Consultation is now built into foster care, and has been recognised as a vital contribution to stability and wellbeing. In adoption, however, there is no obvious capacity to provide or engage with consultation. By definition, consultation is linked to systems of accountability and power, and these do not exist in adoption after the legal process is complete. Perhaps the closest that can be hoped for is that adopters may become aware enough of these needs to set up their own clinical consultation as they travel with their child on the long and rocky road to recovery from trauma.

It is not possible always to prevent disorder. Living with traumatised children produces relentless exposure to trauma, and all sorts of events and experiences can reduce resilience and increase vulnerability. The key to maintaining health and wellbeing in caregivers is to ensure that they have access to sound treatment options when they do become disordered. There is then a high probability that they will recover and indeed gain added resilience from their journey through disorder.

Access to a range of therapeutic interventions and models can be helpful, including cognitive therapy to address any acquired distortions in thinking, behavioural therapy to help overcome any unwanted behaviour patterns developed in response to stress, couple counselling to heal any trauma-induced rifts between spouses or other dyads in the household, and family therapy to address disrupted function in the whole family group. The specialist Fostering, Adoption and Kinship Care team at the Tavistock Clinic, London offer a twelve-week parenting programme group based on a behaviour/cognitive model which they found fits well with other conceptual frameworks, including systemic, attachment and psychoanalytic. Rather than being contradictory, these frameworks were in fact complimentary as each provided a way of understanding and addressing different dynamics – in the family as a whole, within couples, and within the child. Granville and Antrobus (2006: 191) noted, 'while it was important and helpful to develop strategies to manage and change behavioural and interactional patterns, it was crucial also to think about the experiences and meaning of these for the children in parallel'. To this, I would add the need for adoptive parents to be able to reflect on their own experience as part of the healing processes in relation to trauma-induced rifts.

It is essential that any therapists working with adopters have a thorough grounding in the extraordinary dynamics of adoption. As an adult one of our children was asked to explain his experience to a group of social workers. He said that it had been clear to them as children that social workers were used to dealing with problem families, and that sometimes we were seen as a resource but at other times, when things were not going smoothly we suddenly became a problem. Nobody, he told the group, had ever asked him, but if they had he would have wanted to tell them that we were not a problem family before they placed the child in our care. This is a message professionals dealing with adoptive families would do well to remember.

Conclusion

Social policy in the UK places adoption at the centre of the public care of children, with thousands of children every year moving out of the care system and into private and unsupervised households. The threshold for entry to public care is high, and in general children who enter care will have lived through significant adversity. Many of them will be formally assessed as having suffered significant harm. These are traumatised children, and those who care for them will be vulnerable to secondary traumatic stress disorders.

Such disorders can usually be prevented and can always be treated, and it is relatively straightforward to build in structures for prevention and treatment where people are employed to provide care. Indeed, health and safety law requires employers to assess hazards and manage risks arising out of occupational stress. But it is much more problematic to provide strategies to prevent and treat secondary stress disorders in adoption.

Secondary traumatic stress can be extremely destructive. People affected by it change, losing key aspects of their function in how they feel, think and behave. Such changes can disrupt lives and destroy families. There is no accurate count of how many adoptions break down, since after the legal process adoptive families merge into the community and if the family disrupts that may never be seen as an issue of adoption. Certainly there is no way of counting pain, and many adoptive families do suffer pain.

Yet adoption can also provide great hope for the traumatised children in our community, and be a source of joy throughout life for adoptive families. Secondary traumatic stress in adoption is therefore an issue for the whole community. When we recognise and find a way to meet these needs, we will be able to ensure that the opportunity adoption offers for traumatised children to recover from harm is not achieved at too high a price.

References

Bion, W.R. (1962) *Learning from Experience*, London: Maresfield Reprints.

Cairns, K. (1999) *Surviving Paedophilia: Traumatic Stress after Organized and Network Child Sexual Abuse*, Stoke on Trent: Trentham Books.

Figley, C.R. (ed.) (1995) *Compassion Fatigue: Coping with Secondary Traumatic Stress Disorder in Those Who Treat The Traumatized*, New York: Brunner/Mazel.

Figley, C.R. (ed.) (2002) *Treating Compassion Fatigue*, London: Brunner-Routledge.

Granville, J. and Antrobus, L. (2006) 'From tired and emotional to praise and pleasure: parenting groups for adoptive, foster and kinship care', in J. Kendrick, C. Lindsey and L. Tollemache (eds) *Creating New Families: Therapeutic Approaches to Fostering, Adoption, and Kinship Care*, London: Karnac.

Klein, M. (1946) 'Notes on some schizoid mechanisms', in *Envy and Gratitude and Other Works*, London: Hogarth Press, 1980.

Stamm, B.H. (ed.) (1995) *Secondary Traumatic Stress: Self-care Issues for Clinicians, Researchers and Educators*, Lutherville, MD: Sidran Press.

Van der Kolk, B.A., McFarlane, A.C. and Weisaeth, L. (eds) (1996) *Traumatic Stress: The Effects of Overwhelming Experience on Mind, Body and Society*, New York: Guilford Press.

6 The network around adoption

The forever family and the ghosts of the dispossessed

Jenny Sprince

This chapter aims to describe the essential function that needs to be provided through an ongoing and attentive involvement of the professional network around an adoptive family.

The psychological importance of the first few months and years of life in the formation of personality and the establishing of emotional resilience is now better understood than ever before. The later in life that a child is adopted, the greater will have been the impact of their previous experiences on shaping personality and causing psychological problems that few ordinary couples are equipped to deal with.

Even babies adopted after only a few months within one stable, loving foster home will bring to their new family a personality already affected by the quality of their early attachment to these foster carers. They will inevitably be scarred by the loss of these first carers, and for this reason alone may need more expert parenting than ordinarily good parents may know how to provide. When older children who have been through early experiences of chaos, deprivation or abuse are placed in adoptive families, the complexity of their needs and the impact of their disturbances on those around them are much greater.

Experienced foster parents often struggle with the task of caring for traumatised children, even when supported by social workers and with the resources of a mental health team available to them. It can be extremely difficult to take on board the implications of what these children have suffered, help them to learn new ways of relating and enable them to form more trusting attachments.

The importance of permanency for such children is paramount: they need a new family that can continue to love and care for them rather than a series of temporary placements. However, providing appropriate ongoing love for deprived and traumatised children is a difficult task. Adoptive parents may not have the experience of bringing up their own children, let alone any expertise in working with victims of trauma or abuse. In their longing to become parents, they may easily succumb to the fantasy that late adoption can be a 'new beginning'. Their enthusiasm may sometimes lull the professional network into an equivalent optimism – a belief that an abused child can be assimilated into his or her new family without the provision of long-term ongoing social work and psychological support; or that such support need only be made available if or when things go wrong, rather than being provided as a matter of necessity from the start and over many subsequent years.

In this chapter I will attempt to explore some of the many pressures – conscious and unconscious – that contribute to this fantasy, as well as providing examples of what can go wrong when the difficulties that need addressing by the network are neglected. As a consultant child psychotherapist working in independent practice and for an organisation that provides therapeutic interventions for looked-after children in crisis, I am generally called in only when an adoption is under threat, so I know more about the failures than the successes. Likewise, in my role as consultant to Thornby Hall, a therapeutic community within Childhood First, I meet regularly with families and professionals who are only too aware of how much has gone wrong. This chapter therefore does little justice to the many examples of excellent work by professional networks that can be found throughout the country, and should be read with this in mind.

The context of adoption

A child who is freed for adoption will have long been at the centre of a large and complex network of professionals. Removing a child from the legal care of his or her birth parents, with or without their consent, is not lightly undertaken. Members of the network will have gone through a process that may include the initial response to worries about the family's functioning, attempts to support the family both long-term and at times of crisis, emergency and short-term residential or foster placements for the children, assessments of the parents' capacity to parent, and legal battles with parents who have disagreed with those assessments. Alongside that, there will have been the search for a new family, the assessment of prospective adoptive parents, the matching of such parents with particular children, and the preparation of both children and parents for the adoption. For the professionals concerned, the final placement for adoption constitutes the successful end of a long and difficult piece of work. Indeed, by the point of placement, many of the professionals will have already withdrawn from the case; these may include teachers, local health or mental health workers, foster carers and the Guardian ad Litem. If, as often happens, the adopters live at some distance from the child's original Local Authority, geography will limit any but occasional contact with the professionals that remain involved – the child's social worker, and the social worker responsible for family placement. Once the adoption has been finalised, they too may withdraw. Whether or not local professionals are called on to take their place varies from case to case.

Making the decision to take a child permanently away from his or her parents is a long and exhausting business, fraught with hugely painful emotions. More powerfully even than the trauma that surrounds the break-up of a marriage, the separation of children from their parents leaves everyone involved struggling with feelings of grief, failure, guilt and betrayal – even when there is mutual agreement that adoption is the best outcome.

How children feel about being taken away from their parents varies with the circumstances. They are usually confused and frightened, often angry. When they have contributed by letting adults know something of the family's distress or dysfunction, they will typically feel immensely guilty – quite apart from how much they may feel themselves to blame for the family's situation in the first place. Seldom or never do they feel straightforwardly relieved.

Often, losing their parents will coincide with a family crisis, which will have exacerbated whatever the family's difficulties were. Children may come into care because their parents' relationship splits up, or in the aftermath of a new baby's birth, or because of the deterioration of a parent's mental or physical health. Such circumstances leave the children with many unanswered and hugely troubling questions. It is important to stress that these children have seldom had life experiences that are conducive to a state of mind in which they could easily trust adults or openly convey their concerns.

The majority of children who come into care are placed in short-term foster placements; but this term can be misleading. In reality the work of such short-term foster carers may stretch out over months or years, as family finders search for an adoptive family, or while legal proceedings drag on. Some children will establish deep attachments to such foster families. They will long to stay where they are, and resent and fear the anticipated adoption. Other children may find themselves moved from one placement to another, compounding their experiences of confusion, loss and discontinuity. In the face of ongoing uncertainty about care plans, they may protect themselves with idealised expectations of a future adoptive family that no real family could hope to live up to. All of this can increase and complicate the difficulties of waiting (see Chapter 9).

Foster carers occupy a particular position within the network, somewhere between professional and volunteer status. They differ from most adoptive parents in some important respects: they generally accept that the children they are fostering will be troubled children, and that they may need the input of social workers and mental health professionals, and they do not expect these children to become a replacement for a baby born to their family. This can be an advantage. Foster carers can be more ready to take on the full implications of a child's past experience than adopters who long to make a child their own. As one sensitive carer used to say to me, 'You can take the child out of the family, but you can't take the family out of the child!'

Foster carers sit within the social work boundary, and can do vital work in helping children to make the transition from their birth families into care. Many short-term foster carers become expert in making their own relationship with troubled birth parents, and helping the children placed with them to make sense of the difficulties they experienced in their birth families. Unfortunately, constraints of time and geography do not always allow the same opportunities for foster carers to be involved in the transition from foster care to adoption. This can be a loss for all concerned (again see Chapter 9).

Dilemmas for the network

The impact of adoption work on the social services and foster care networks cannot be overestimated (Sprince, 2000). Often social workers are painfully aware that the birth parents' deficiencies are the result of their own childhood experiences of abuse. It can feel to social workers as if they are inflicting further abuse when they remove a child from a vulnerable parent. 'He's the only person who ever loved me,' one such mother said. The social worker who reported this to me was filled with the pain and outrage of the mother who was losing her little boy, and as much pre-occupied with her distress as with the danger to the child. Children too bring their own feelings of extreme distress and bewilderment: 'It was the worst day of my life,' said one such girl to her social worker, two years after being removed from violent and abusive parents.

There is often little or no opportunity for social workers to think together about feelings that are generated in them by traumatic work experiences. This can sometimes interfere with their capacity to recognise the full extent of the damage that trauma has inflicted upon these children and to make adequate plans to support them and the families that care for them (Hindle, 2000; Emanuel, 2006).

It is not surprising that adoption has become the first choice as a solution to the problem of how to provide for such traumatised children. There are often childless couples desperate to parent and children in desperate need of parenting: it is understandable that matching one with the other seems to make sense. It is important, too, not to overlook the pressing need amongst social workers to feel that they can do something worthwhile, finite and satisfying in a short time span, when so many cases seem endlessly long term, complex and problematic.

The search for a 'happy ending'

Adoption seems to offer that rare thing so much desired by the professionals who work with looked-after children: a 'happy ending'. It seems to offer a way of alleviating distress – recompensing the children for their previous lack of a happy family life, giving them the kind of family that they should have had, right from the start, or that everyone had hoped that the birth family might have been helped to achieve: a 'forever family' to provide them with the experience of unconditional love and attentiveness that will equip them to grow into happy, responsible and emotionally resilient adults. However, such a family is not so easy to find.

It is an unhappy fact that many children who have been physically, psycho-logically or sexually abused in early life are not easy to love, though parents longing for a child may find it easy enough to fall in love with them at first sight. Social workers who find themselves in the position of making matches, struggling to find good parents for damaged children, are understandably wary of drawing attention to those aspects of the child that may frighten off potential adopters, and frame advertisements so as to attract as much interest as possible and minimise much that is problematic.

'Sunny and friendly, loves to please', may indicate a child so cut off from feelings that they are unable to show anything but a numb compliance; or, just as worryingly, one who will make indiscriminate or sexualised overtures to all comers. 'Loves running and playing games', may mean hyperactive and unable to concentrate or relate to other people. Often, social workers try their best to hint at the difficulties they know are there: 'Loving, but can be naughty', may mean behavioural problems of a tall order; 'Will need lots of individual attention', may point to a child whose crippling jealousy could disable a marriage, or who would not be able to withstand even the occasional presence of other children.

This issue can be compounded by the hope that a child's behaviour will settle down once they are given the security of a safe and permanent home, with clear rules and standards. Alternatively, the apparently good behaviour of children when they are first placed in care can be misread as an indication of only minor emotional problems. Youell (2002: 121) describes the way in which characteristics such as being 'independent', 'self-reliant' or 'undemanding' can be seen as indications of resilience, when they may in fact be evidence of a deeply entrenched distrust of all relationships, a state of mind which can interfere with a capacity for intimacy and be highly detrimental to future development.

One seven-year-old girl, Pauline, was moved from one foster family to another during the nine months she waited for an adoptive family to be identified. In the first foster family she chose to dress neatly in frilly, girly clothes; in the next family, she wore sporty jumpsuits. Her social worker realised that she was modelling herself on each foster mother in turn – the first one very feminine and well groomed, the second, athletic and keen on jogging. However, the degree of emotional disturbance underlying this behaviour was not recognised until her adoptive parents, distraught at their inability to make any real relationship with her, brought her to therapy. Throughout her therapy sessions, she drew endless pictures of ghosts, monsters and witches, explaining how they could change shape and look like ordinary people on the outside, tricking other people into believing that they were harmless, while planning horrible deeds of revenge.

Pauline's adoptive parents were virulent in their anger against social services, feeling that they had been tricked into taking a child who was described to them as 'resilient' and 'without severe problems', when over time it became clear that she was very seriously disturbed. But the fact is that social workers are caught between contradictory imperatives. They need to find adoptive families for children as quickly as possible but are well aware that in the competition for adoptive families children can be disadvantaged if they are seen as having severe emotional problems. When I suggested to one social worker that a couple should be warned about the inevitability of emotional disturbance in a little boy of six, whose mother had killed his baby sister, she protested strongly: 'We don't want to stigmatise him, after all he's been through already', she said. 'He has a right to be seen by prospective adopters as an ordinary little boy!'

If the pressure to place a child can sometimes lead to an over-optimistic appraisal of the extent of that child's disturbance, a similar dilemma can interfere with the selection of adoptive parents. While it is relatively easy to assess an adult capacity to care physically for a child, and to provide ordinary, loving reliability, the capacity to understand and withstand the psychological effects of trauma may be much harder to judge (see Chapter 5).

Preparing adoptive parents

Adults looking to adopt a child do not typically come from a position of expertise about the impact of early neglect, trauma or abuse. They have not volunteered because they are looking to rescue a traumatised child. They simply want to have a family. Often, they have struggled with issues of infertility and have gone through many years of painful longing for a baby. Although some adults seeking to adopt will have come from a background of fostering, or have had birth children of their own, the majority of adopters have never had the experience of raising children. Their expectations may be at a considerable distance from the reality of the task, and it can be hard to know in advance how they will respond to the challenge.

Social workers think deeply about the assessment and preparation of adoptive families. Although the details may vary from one authority or agency to another, it is always a rigorous process. However, many prospective adopters can experience the assessment procedure as yet another hurdle on the route to parenthood, rather than as an opportunity to prepare for a complex and difficult task, and to decide for themselves whether or not they really wish to undertake it. In their eagerness to be selected, parents may miss out on crucial opportunities for preparation. Many couples do not get as much help as they may need to explore their reasons for wanting to adopt a child, or to think about the differences between adopting an older child and the experience of having a baby of one's own.

But however rigorous the process, the preparation of prospective adopters comes before the experience itself, not in conjunction with it, and this is an intrinsic difficulty. Almost the first thing that many adoptive parents have acknowledged to me, when I have met them at a later stage, is how unable they were to take in what was said to them in their excitement about a forthcoming adoption: it all meant very little to them without the reality of their ongoing life with their adopted child. However much information adoptive parents may have been given, its implications can be hard for them to understand or to hold in mind. Most parents, after all, whatever they have heard from friends and family, are shocked by the impact of having their own first baby. 'You just have no idea till it happens to you', as one ordinarily happy mother of an ordinarily happy child said to me. This is still more the case with adoptive parents.

Benny, aged 6 years

In one consultation, I was asked to see a couple whom the placing social worker felt were 'looking at everything through rose-tinted spectacles'. They were delightful, but unreachable in their excitement and enthusiasm. It felt as though they expected six-year-old Benny to arrive in their home as free from his past experiences as if he were a new-born baby. When I talked about this they laughed and said they were 'only too happy to be missing out on the horrible stage – the dirty nappies!' They told me they knew about Benny's background – the violence between his parents, how his father had beaten him. 'We're putting it to the back of our minds,' they said, 'We're going to try to forget all about it. We don't want him ever to have to think about it again.'

I said that I didn't think they could prevent the fact that Benny would have dreadful memories and that these might affect him all his life. They looked sober for a moment, and then started to describe all the treats they had planned for him, how much they wanted to give him to 'make it up to him and help him to forget'. They talked about their family and friends, the cousins who would be the same age as Benny. When I tried to suggest that although he might have lived the same number of years, he would not be the same age emotionally, they told me how they planned to help him 'catch up' with extra educational tuition.

Nothing I said could dent their impenetrable optimism. The social worker agonised over her decision: should she take a chance on this family, or leave Benny in temporary foster care for yet another year while an alternative adoptive placement was found? In the event, she took the gamble, strongly recommending that the family should come for regular consultations over the first three months of placement. They agreed enthusiastically. But they did not take up the offer: they lived at some distance, the journey was too long, and they did not feel the need. The adoption failed after eighteen months.

It would clearly be of immense value if the network of professionals who have known the child in his or her birth family and previous placements could continue to be available to such adoptive parents, to interpret the information, and link it to the adoptive family's current experiences of the child. However, the practicalities of adoption and of social work can make this hard to achieve, even were the resources always available. Adoptive parents are often geographically distant from the local authority where the child was born. The information held by social workers may be limited, the social workers responsible for the case may have changed several times since the child first came into care, and there may be no workers left who hold a continuity of personal knowledge of the child.

The new beginning

A child's sense of his or her identity is built on the experience of the parents of their infancy; nothing that comes later can replace this foundation. However much a child who has lost these parents may seem to forget them, he or she will always be haunted and preoccupied by them, and by the quality of the relationships they had with them, whether or not they are consciously remembered.

It is tempting to believe that very young children will not be damaged by discontinuity and trauma: that they are resilient, adapt easily and will forget about their earliest experiences. Children may, indeed, appear to forget – but the memories and experiences will be built in: hardwired, as it were, into their whole way of experiencing the world and their expectation of what the world is like (see Chapter 2). Going along with such children's apparent obliviousness may leave them feeling that they are not really known and understood, even if they cannot themselves explain what part of them is being ignored.

This was vividly demonstrated to me through clinical work with a young man who had been adopted at the age of two. He had come from a refugee background, and his adoptive parents had been of the same original ethnicity as his birth parents.

Mark

Mark came into therapy at the age of twenty. He had in many ways been very successfully adopted, and described his adoptive parents as loving, generous and considerate. However, he had left home at the age of eighteen and now had very little contact with them. He had been studying languages at university, but felt alienated and lonely, could not concentrate on his work, and had dropped out. We came to understand his choice of subject as related to his long-term search for what he described as his 'mother-tongue'. He knew that he had been sent to this country as a refugee by parents who were desperate to give him a safe home when they could not. But he felt that he had never been at home with the English language. He thought he had felt alienated all his life. In the course of therapy we came to think that his difficulty in making relationships was connected to his fury with his birthmother for relinquishing him, and to his inability to forgive his adoptive mother for adopting him: for her expectation that he should speak her language and feel himself to be her child, without realising his deep attachment to his birth family. We came to the conclusion that he was rejecting his adoptive parents as he felt they had rejected the part of him that was his birth-parents' child. However, he loved his adoptive parents too. When I wondered why he couldn't talk to his adoptive mother about what we had been discussing he said, in a tone of surprise, 'But how could you expect me to do that? It would hurt her too much.' He honestly believed that such a conversation would hurt her more than his continued lack of contact with her – and this was at a time when he had not spoken to her for two years, despite her many letters to him. We came to think that his belief that his adoptive mother would be deeply hurt by his pre-occupation with his birth mother was at the root of his difficulty in studying. He felt that her love for him was conditional on his denial of the first two years of his life, and their meaning for him. We understood that his need to punish her for two years was related to his age at the time of the adoption.

This young man had come from a non-abusive background, and had kind and loving adoptive parents. When he was able to talk to them about his interest in tracing his birth family, they were able to respond and acknowledge the mistakes they had made in wanting him to be too much 'their own' child. The young man himself began to think about how his feelings about them were confused and mixed up with feelings about his birth parents. 'They did the same thing, really,' he said, 'They all wanted to protect me from something they thought would hurt me, but they only made things worse.' He felt that he would have preferred his birth parents to keep him with them, whatever the risks, but he understood that they had thought they were acting in his best interests. And in the same way he would have preferred his adoptive parents to keep talking to him about his first two years, and what it meant to be adopted, rather than behaving as though he was their own child, even though he knew that in doing this they had wanted to protect him from feeling unloved or different. He had, similarly, tried to protect them from something he thought would hurt them, by staying out of touch with them, and in doing so had caused them greater pain. His ability to use psychotherapy to gain insight into his predicament, his birth parents' predicament, and the predicament of his adoptive parents, bears witness to the good parenting he had had throughout, however greatly the abrupt and traumatic discontinuity between his experience with his birth parents and his life in his adoptive family had scarred him.

Forgetting and remembering

Mark was lucky. For children adopted from abusive backgrounds, the difficulties are much greater. Like Mark, they suffer from a sense of discontinuity, from a sense of anger and loyalty to parents they may or may not consciously remember, but unlike him they may not have had the kind of parenting in their earliest years that lays down the foundations for a belief in the basic good intentions of adults, and of their willingness and ability to help small children make sense of their confusing experiences of the world. Adoptive parents, expecting to love and be loved unreservedly, can find the emotional rejection meted out by their adoptive children very difficult to take unless they can fully embrace the importance of the ghosts of dispossessed parents, and understand how these ghosts may interfere between them and the children they have adopted.

This does not mean that adoptive children are necessarily keen to talk openly – or at all – about their early experiences. Any child who has suffered the impact of trauma, neglect and abuse will want to escape the feelings that these experiences, and the memories associated with them, have generated: terror, pain, rage, despair. But this will necessitate burying other feelings too: their love, loyalty and identification with their birth parents, their guilt about what went wrong. When placed with adoptive parents, they may be frightened to remember or talk about the experiences of their childhood – experiences that led to feelings they have no safe way of expressing: their love for their original parents or the contradictory emotions associated with their abuse or neglect. They may become extremely upset by contact with anyone who knew them in their past lives, and sympathetic professionals may very understandably think that it is in their best interests to 'draw a line' under these experiences, and help adoptive parents to do likewise. But the ghosts of dispossessed parents are not so easily exorcised.

Both the professional network and the adoptive parents may find themselves feeling under strong pressure to behave as though some or all of the elements of a child's past could be wiped out, as though everyone could start afresh with a blank page. The phrase so often used to children being prepared for adoption – the 'forever family' – can easily seem to carry the misleading implication that foreverness stretches both ways: into the past as well as into the future.

Adoptive children may collude all the more eagerly with this fantasy if they feel it will please their new adoptive parents, and this can add to the difficulties for the professionals. Children who have lived in chaotic families have often had to watch adults very carefully for their own survival: a father or mother, for instance, who could be loving when sober but might become suddenly violent if they had been drinking. They may have had to protect their families by putting on an act at school, so as not to alert the social workers. They may have had to accommodate to sexual abuse by one member of the family and keep it a secret from others. So they are often very aware of the importance of 'fitting in', of trying to be what adoptive parents want them to be. In their longing to feel safe and to feel loved, they can make their adopted parents feel gratifyingly needed and adored, especially during the first few 'honeymoon' months of their placement, which can bolster their belief that there will be no necessity for professional support.

However, the children's pre-occupation with their original relationship soon shows itself, often in very subtle ways, over which they have no control, and which evoke responses in the adults around them that are hard to understand; adoptive parents can feel at a loss to explain what they find so disturbing. But this may not encourage them to look more closely into the background of their adoptive child, or to link what they are feeling with their child's early experiences. Indeed, their adoptive children may make it very hard for them to do so. Instead, they may find themselves making links with their own past in ways that can feel extremely distressing.

At Thornby Hall, a therapeutic community that works with troubled adolescents, many of whom are adopted, we have evolved a way of working that tries to understand the children by exploring the impact of these 'ghosts' on the adults around them – the same approach that I use with adoptive parents and foster carers in other settings (Sprince, 2002).

I include a very brief example below.

The children I will discuss in the brief descriptions that follow each had loving adoptive families, but the impact of their disturbance was such that their parents found themselves unconsciously replicating aspects of their children's early experiences of abuse and neglect, in ways they did not understand and could not control.

Sammy

Sammy, aged five, threw dreadful tantrums with his adoptive mother, Caroline. However, they were always followed by tearful promises that he would be good and declarations of his love for her. She felt sure that things would come right once he had settled in.

It wasn't the tantrums that caused the near-breakdown of the adoption after eighteen months: his adoptive mother couldn't really explain what was so unbearable. 'He just makes me feel such a horrible person', she said. I asked what her partner felt about Sammy. 'Oh, he's very supportive', she replied, 'But he doesn't know what to do about it any more than I do.'

Caroline and her partner Greg told me what they knew of Sammy's background. His birth mum had enjoyed teasing and provoking him till she got him into a rage, and had then punished him severely – beating him and burning him with her cigarette.

The three of us discussed why they had wanted to adopt Sammy in the first place. They had not been able to conceive their own children. Greg 'wasn't very fussed' about whether or not they had a baby, but Caroline had desperately wanted a little boy she could protect and love. Her younger brother had died of cancer when she was a little girl, and she had so much longed to bring up a boy successfully, make him feel good about himself, prevent harm from coming to him. But this little boy made her feel like a cruel sadist – she couldn't bear who she became when she was with him. Greg couldn't bear watching it all: 'I never really wanted Sammy in the first place, but now he's here I'm quite fond of him. I can't cope with all the rows, though, and whatever I do, I end up in the wrong.' Greg had been a bullied younger brother, himself. I thought that he found it easy to identify with Sammy, and Caroline agreed: she felt that he took Sammy's side against her.

As Caroline, Greg and I worked on disentangling what both they and Sammy brought to the relationship, we came to see that the experience of being with Sammy compounded something unresolved in Caroline's own past – and in Greg's. Caroline realised that she had so longed to make things right for a little boy because of her own guilt at having jealously teased her own younger brother, who subsequently became ill and died. But this little boy wasn't her own younger brother. Unfortunately, Sammy had had a birth mother who behaved like an extreme caricature of a jealous and cruel older sister: that was the Mum he had in his head, the Mum he recreated with Caroline. That was what made Caroline feel so horrible that she simply couldn't bear it. What was worse was that Greg, in identification with Sammy, saw her that way too. The son Caroline wanted was one who would have been free to see her as the loving Mum she longed to be, the Mum she could easily have been with a child who had had no former abusive experiences.

Greg realised that he had always allowed Caroline to take the lead in emotional matters. But now she needed him to intervene to protect her from the intensity of what happened between her and Sammy, without taking sides with either of them. Over four years, as they worked on how they could parent Sammy together, I was relieved to see that their attitudes to one another changed as much as their feelings for Sammy: they became far closer as a couple, and were able to understand one another much better, as well as understanding Sammy. The process was long and painful, and we often had doubts about whether or not the adoption would break down, but the depth of relationship they achieved as a family reassured me that Sammy was well placed – as, indeed, proved to be the case.

Belinda

Unlike Sammy, Belinda was not the kind of child who showed her disturbance overtly, through tantrums or other behaviour, and this meant that for many years her difficulties remained unrecognised or unacknowledged. Belinda was adopted at the age of three. Her adoptive parents knew that she came from a background of violence, neglect and drug abuse. They were a well-educated middle-class couple, and both were high achievers in academic fields. Belinda never coped well at school: 'We never tried to push her: we always knew that we couldn't assume that she would be academically bright', her mother told me, 'But I think she has always felt she was a disappointment to us, however hard we've tried to show her that wasn't true.' Belinda became sexually promiscuous as a teenager, and made a serious attempt at suicide at the age of seventeen. This was when I first met her.

I saw Belinda on three occasions and felt strongly that her difficulties in school were related to her emotional pre-occupations, not to any intrinsic lack of intelligence. However, Belinda refused to attend any further sessions, and she and her adoptive parents assured me that the suicide attempt and her sexual promiscuity were all 'in the past' and that Belinda would know better than to do such things again. At first I was bewildered by such an apparently self-deluding judgement from seemingly intelligent parents, but then found myself wondering what it was about Belinda that made it so hard for anyone to insist on facing reality with her. A few months later the parents contacted me again, to tell me that Belinda had left home to live with a young man who was a pimp and a drug addict. Her adoptive parents felt pretty sure that she was 'on the game' and taking drugs, too, and over several sessions they explored with me their own longstanding difficulties in facing up to who Belinda was. Both parents had been the children of unhappy marriages, and we came to recognise how much as children they had retreated into books in order to hide from the turbulent emotions within their families. We related this to Belinda's own need from a very early age to protect herself from the realities of neglect and abuse. Belinda's mother had had a series of violent short-term boyfriends and had used drugs to protect herself from the reality of her own emotional pain. Belinda had a way of coping that mimicked the use of drugs: she just went into a private fantasy world where she could tell herself there was nothing wrong, in the face of the most convincing evidence to the contrary. Challenging this defence felt like cruelty to Belinda. We discussed how she used to dress up in a fairy dress as a little girl, put lipstick and eye shadow on her face, and then sit and stare at herself in the mirror for hours on end, while listening to her stereo. Her parents had told themselves that this was just 'girlie' behaviour, and, later, had thought that she might be seriously interested in becoming a beautician. 'But it was as if she was hypnotising herself. We never asked her what she saw in that mirror – ghosts, perhaps?' They came to feel that they had, over many years, colluded with Belinda's wish to cut herself off from reality, at the expense of her long-term emotional wellbeing as well as her education. Belinda's adopted mum talked movingly about her own mother, who had insisted on seeing her little girl's obsessive studying as wholly positive. 'I didn't realise it before, but she was really ignoring what I felt, just like we did with Belinda, and just like Belinda's birth mother did with her. I don't suppose that any of us meant to do that. It just somehow happened.'

Dylan

Dylan was placed at Thornby Hall a year after his adoption failed. He had been adopted at the age of three and a half. His adoptive parents knew very little about his background except that it was neglectful and that he had been left for hours on end in filthy nappies for the first eighteen months of his life. After that he had been in a short-term foster placement for two years. His adoptive parents had decided they couldn't keep him when he was fourteen. He had gone into a placement with foster carers that had swiftly broken down, then into a children's home. The staff there didn't know any details. They said that he wasn't a difficult child, but he was quiet, seemingly detached, unable to make relationships. His parents had refused to have anything more to do with him. No one could quite understand why they were so determined in their refusal. 'They seem a really nice couple when you meet them', said Dylan's social worker, bemused. 'How can they be so cruel and neglectful? They just don't seem to see what they're doing!'

Once he was living in the community, the staff group soon began to understand what had got into Dylan's adoptive parents; what at first had seemed timidity in Dylan quickly started to feel like sadism – he rejected any affectionate approach with cold, derisive contempt. It seemed clear that Dylan had dealt with early abuse by withdrawing into himself in a way that made other people feel as he had felt as a baby – left in the dark, smelly and not worthy of any attention. Without meaning to, people ended up paying him back in his own coin.

Fortunately, our own experience of Dylan made it possible for us to empathise with his adoptive parents without blaming either him or them. As Dylan began to make progress, and recognise the impact of his state of mind on the other children and adults in the community, he became able to see how unremittingly rejecting his adoptive parents must have found him. Eventually, he wrote to them through his social worker, expressing his understanding of his behaviour but making it clear that he did not want to return to them. This led to a meeting, and a partial reconciliation. Dylan's parents began to talk regularly to his key-worker about aspects of their own backgrounds: his adoptive mother had been abandoned by her own mother as a five-year-old child, and both parents had been sent to boarding schools at a very young age. Gradually, they all came to feel that some tentative relationship could be salvaged. His parents continued to maintain contact with Dylan and eventually when he obtained independent accommodation and a place at college, they all agreed that it should be nearby. Their relationship continues to grow in mutual understanding and respect.

Discussion

These clinical examples are greatly condensed, and raise many questions which are beyond the scope of this chapter. However, they all illustrate the extent to which the unacknowledged trauma of late adoption can have a profound and destructive impact on the relationship of children with their adoptive parents. In the cases I have described, the adoptive parents did not feel that the professional network had impressed upon them the depth and complexity of their adopted child's disturbance, how it was linked to his or her early history, or the necessity of professional help in making sense of it. Instead they felt they had been allowed to believe that they would have sufficient skills through their ordinary life experiences to be left to get on with the job on their own, like any other parents. But despite their best efforts they found themselves caught up inadvertently in re-enacting some destructive aspects of the relationship between their child and their child's birthparents, in ways that were intensely distressing to them and potentially harmful to their children.

Which aspect of this early relationship they found themselves re-enacting, and the way in which they re-enacted it, was intimately dependent upon their own childhood experiences. Through their empathic intimacy with their adopted children, something painful and unresolved in their own lives was subliminally evoked, in an intense and unexpected form. If they had had children of their own, or adopted newborn babies, they might well have been put in touch with some of the same issues, but not in the same way. A baby would not have brought to the situation the same compulsion to distort a comparatively mild problem into a replica of extreme trauma. In all probability, a baby would have allowed their parents a reparative experience: the opportunity to give their child something better than they had had themselves, and to watch them benefit from it. Belinda's parents were keen to offer a happy marriage, unlike the marriages their own parents had raised them in. Dylan's parents were determined to give him all the cuddles and affection they felt they themselves had missed. But tragically, Belinda and Dylan were not able to make use of what was good in their adoptive families. On the contrary, they were driven to find and to latch on to those parts of their new parents that could be made to re-evoke and replicate the worst aspects of the parents they had lost – neglect and cruelty. That their parents tried so hard to persevere, despite the difficulties, bears witness to their love, commitment and generosity. They persevered, without asking for help, for many years, and in some ways that made the situation worse.

For adoptive parents trying hard to prove themselves, and often with no preliminary experience of parenting their own birth children, it can be hard to allow themselves to recognise how impossible the situation has become. It can take many months or years for parents to admit to themselves that the family needs help, and by the time they do so their feelings may have hardened into a fixed hatred or despair (Kenrick, 2006: 75). Unfortunately this can often be entirely consonant with their child's expectations of a parent.

Conclusion

For the professionals who work with dysfunctional families, and particularly for social workers, the tragedy of the damage done to children who are left in abusive situations is hard to bear. It can be hard to accept that whatever happens next needs to include a full recognition of the reality of that damage.

If it is hard for the professionals to accept, it is even harder for adoptive parents, who long to feel that they can give their adopted child what they would have wanted to give to a baby of their own – a safe and happy experience without discontinuity or trauma.

Adoptive children, in their confusion and distress, are torn between their innate loyalty to their original parents and their wish to believe that they can make a fresh start, be 'born again' to their new families. Unfortunately, in trying desperately to fit in, they can key into aspects of their adoptive parents that match their own experience only too well – as was the case with Sammy. Belinda and Dylan, too, pulled their adoptive parents into a 'fit' that matched their own unconscious expectations. It was only through understanding the nature of the parental figures in the minds of the children and their parents, and the match between them, that this mutually destructive way of relating could be disentangled.

Bringing up children puts every parent in touch with his or her own childhood; that can be complicated enough, with two adults struggling to come to terms with what is evoked from their own past, and trying to understand each other through the process. But as compensation, parents hope to pass on what was good in their own early experiences, and to repair anything that went wrong in their relationships with their own parents through giving something better to their children. Bringing up traumatised children can feel as if it gives them the opposite experience: all their worst experiences are revived, all their worst fears are realised.

Adoptive parents are not responsible for what the children bring to the family. But if they do not fully understand their children's past, they may find themselves allowing it to be recreated.

The more that professionals and adoptive parents unite to obliterate the past, the less they can help late-adopted children to come to terms with the reality of the damage that has been done to them. Unless the professionals can support adoptive parents to fully understand and adopt their child's history as well as their child, the child's unconscious memories of their dispossessed parents will return like vengeful ghosts to haunt and attack the adoptive relationship.

References

Emanuel, L. (2006) 'The contribution of organizational dynamics to the triple deprivation of looked-after children', in J. Kenrick, C. Lindsey and L. Tollemache (eds) *Creating New Families: Therapeutic Approaches to Fostering, Adoption, and Kinship Care*, London: Karnac.

Hindle, D. (2000) 'An intensive assessment of a small sample of siblings placed together in foster care', Doctorate Thesis, Tavistock Clinic/University of East London.

Kenrick, J. (2006) 'Work with children in transition', in J. Kenrick, C. Lindsey and L. Tollemache (eds) *Creating New Families: Therapeutic Approaches to Fostering, Adoption, and Kinship Care*, London: Karnac.

Sprince, J. (2000) 'Towards an integrated network', *Journal of Child Psychotherapy*, 26 (3): 413–44.

Sprince, J. (2002) 'Developing containment: psychoanalytic consultancy to a therapeutic community for traumatised children', *Journal of Child Psychotherapy*, 28 (2): 147–61.

Youell, B. (2002) 'The relevance of infant and young-child observation in multidisciplinary assessments for the family courts', in A. Briggs (ed.) *Surviving Space: Papers on Infant Observation*, London: Karnac.

Part III

Primitive states of mind and their impact on relationships

Introduction

Graham Shulman

> Infantile feelings and phantasies leave, as it were, their imprints on the mind, imprints which do not fade away but get stored up, remain active, and exert a continuous powerful influence on the emotional and intellectual life of the individual.
>
> (Klein, 1936 [1981: 290])

Primitive states of mind are pre-verbal emotional states which have their origins in early infancy. These of course contrast markedly with mature adult emotional states, forms of mental functioning and ways of relating. The emotional states of mind that have their origins in infancy are commonly felt – and expressed – in the body as much as in the mind. Moreover, at this very earliest stage of post-natal mental life a baby has not yet developed the 'mental equipment' and capacities to organise and make sense of experience. It is because this 'mental equipment' or thinking capacity has not yet developed to deal with states of mind and body in earliest infancy that the baby is dependent on the mother or primary attachment figure for the processing and containing of these.

Winnicott (1958 [1945]: 150*n*), writing of 'primitive emotional development', refers to 'our most primitive selves whence the most intense feelings and fearfully acute sensations derive'. Klein thought of these pre-verbal emotional states as linked to the newborn or young baby's situation of total dependency on the mother or primary carer for their psychological and physical survival. Psychoanalytic writers have formulated these primitive states of mind partly in terms of the emotional, subjective pre-verbal experiences corresponding to states of integration, unintegration, disintegration, containment, uncontainment, and the like; the emotional subjective experiences of these early infantile pre-verbal states are conveyed by phrases such as feeling 'held', 'held together', 'at one with', or feeling 'unheld', 'falling to pieces', 'torn apart' or 'overwhelmed'.

An everyday example from early infancy is the newborn baby whose babygrow is removed, who seems quite literally to 'fall to pieces' and to scream in panic and terror. Another example is the young baby who cries desperately every time they are put down – here the baby appears to be dominated by a fear that physical separateness or separation spells disaster.

A further dimension of primitive states of mind in infancy is the ordinary baby's passionately possessive and even territorial attitude towards its mother which develops over time; at a primitive level this is underscored by the fact that for the young baby the mother is felt to be the primary source of love and goodness, on which the baby's psychic survival and growth depend as much its physical survival and growth depend on nourishment.

Primitive states of mind obviously mediate the relative balance of a baby's loving or hating feelings towards, and internal picture of, the mother (or primary attachment figure). Klein discovered through her clinical work with children and adults that these primitive, pre-verbal states of mind continue to exert a powerful influence on the emotional life of the individual, and as a result on relationships. However, in optimal development these are balanced by a more mature part of the personality, and do not unduly impact on everyday life and relationships (though at times of stress they may predominate over more mature ways of functioning and relating).

In the ordinary development of a baby within ordinary family life, 'primitive states of mind' are not a phenomenon that requires special understanding or knowledge by parents. Rather, they are part of the emotional ebb and flow of their daily life and relationship with their baby, and are something that parents respond to and process at an intuitive, empathic and more unconscious level, in the course of normal caretaking and interactions with their baby. (A useful analogy here is that of storms or bad weather that are part of the normal variation in climactic conditions, which we are aware of but which do not unduly trouble us or threaten our everyday lives and well-being, in contrast to extreme and persistent weather conditions that cause major disruption to our everyday lives and routines, cause significant damage, can threaten our lives or well-being, and may be frightening.)

Where a baby's or young child's primitive states of mind become extreme, persistent and/or pervasive they may begin to interfere with everyday life and, importantly, they can have a serious and even lasting negative impact on attachment relationships and on the developmental process. For instance, a baby who cries piercingly and continually and who seems unable to settle or to be comforted despite the best efforts of the parents, is likely to have an extremely unsettling, if not disturbing, impact on the mother's and father's states of mind; if this situation is passing, it will soon be forgotten, but if it is recurrent – and if things remain bad enough for long enough – this can have a damaging effect on the relationship between mother and baby, between mother and father, and on family relationships in general. Such a situation may result in a range of typical feelings and responses in the parents including distress, frustration, helplessness, tension, resentment, anger, guilt and even hatred. Where primitive states of mind persist in older children they may not be recognised or understood, or they may be disapproved of, or they might be censured and deemed unacceptable.

Children who have suffered neglect, abuse, trauma or disrupted attachment relationships in infancy or early childhood are likely to have less developed mental 'apparatus' (Bion, 1962 [1967]) and capacities to deal with and process primitive, pre-verbal emotional states. At the same time, their experience of these states is likely to have been far more extreme, intense, persistent and pervasive than in ordinary development and family life. The effects of these may be obvious and visible, but can often be complex, more subtle, intermittent or even delayed, only manifesting themselves at a later stage of development or life cycle which presents particular emotional challenges for the child.

The task for adopted children of forming new primary attachment relationships inevitably revives and re-evokes intense and extreme primitive emotional states linked with the trauma of early emotional experience and original attachment relationships; these revived primitive states of mind are likely to be felt by the child as disturbing, threatening or even dangerous to the self, and may give rise to pre-verbal anxieties, feelings of fragmentation or fear of disintegration. The nature of primitive emotional experience that is revived at the time of adoption may range from the profound rupture of separation from the mother at birth or in early infancy, to severe emotional neglect and deprivation, the trauma of abuse, or the disorganising effects of pervasively confusing, chaotic and inconsistent patterns of interaction and contact.

Primitive states of mind seemed to underlie aspects of the adopted child's functioning and ways of relating to others as described by *Caroline Case* in her chapter 'The mermaid: moving towards reality after trauma'. Although SIX years old at the time she was referred for therapeutic help, the girl's primary mode of communication with, and way of relating to, others remained non-verbal and physical, despite the fact that she was able to speak, and this did not seem to be sufficiently accounted for by her learning difficulties. During the course of individual psychotherapy it became possible to understand the child's selective mutism and bodily 'moulding' or physical invasiveness as ways of attempting to preserve a primitive state of being psychologically merged or fused with others, in order to avoid experiencing separateness and primitive anxieties linked with separation. The understanding gradually gained from intensive long-term individual psychotherapy in turn enabled the parents to better understand the nature, severity and complexity of their adoptive child's emotional functioning and difficulties; this gave a framework for making sense of what they knew at an experiential level but could not reasonably be expected to make sense of without professional help. It also helpfully contributed to the decision-making process about appropriate schooling for the child.

Primitive states of mind also seemed to be at the heart of the adopted child's behavioural and profound emotional difficulties discussed by *Judith Edwards* in her chapter 'On being dropped and picked up: the plight of some late-adopted children'. Much of this SIX-year-old boy's behaviour seemed to be driven by primitive catastrophic anxieties of psychic fragmentation and disintegration related to not feeling 'held together'. The boy's preoccupation with falling, his denial of physical danger and his physically risk-taking behaviour came to be understood by Edwards as primitive bodily expressions of a 'fear of being dropped' psychologically, linked with feeling emotionally 'unheld' and uncontained; his behaviours could then be thought about – both with the boy in his therapy and with his adoptive parents in meetings with them – as attempts at overcoming or mastering these primitive anxieties. Similarly, his disturbing preoccupation with cruelty and violence, his murderous feelings towards babies and his mindless destructiveness were understood as products of primitive, extreme fears of vulnerability and helplessness from infancy.

In both cases the adoptive child's behaviour and underlying primitive anxieties were having a profound affect not just on their development and learning but on the quality of their relationships with their adoptive parents. Within the safe and secure setting of therapy, it was possible for the child's primitive feelings and anxieties to be expressed, enacted and worked through; in this way the child is sufficiently freed from the worry of the impact of their states of mind on their parents, while the therapist is not prey to the natural and often severe anxieties and stresses felt by adoptive parents in response to their child's extremely worrying and disturbing behaviour. Finally, it is noteworthy that in both these cases the child was referred and seen only after a significant period of time in their adoptive family – the first after two years and the second after one year.

References

Bion, W. R. (1962) 'A theory of thinking', in *Second Thoughts*, London: Karnac, 1967.

Klein, M. (1981 [1936]) 'Weaning', in *Love, Guilt and Reparation*, London: Hogarth Press.

Winnicott, D.W. (1958 [1945]) 'Primitive emotional development', in *Through Paediatrics to Psychoanalysis: Collected Papers*, London: Heinemann.

7   The mermaid

Moving towards reality after trauma

Caroline Case

In this chapter, I want to consider the impact of early trauma and neglect on one child's developing mind, which affected her learning, speech and interaction with others, and inhibited her relationship with her adopted family. In the clinical work to be described, I hope to show how psychotherapy provides a specific way of 'seeing the child' in a context of trauma and damage. I suggest that the difficulties of being aware of or acknowledging such trauma and damage can significantly interfere with the attachment process between adopted child and adoptive parents.

The child, whom I shall call Alison, was initially dominated by an illusion – tyrannically held onto – that she was an 'inside baby'. That is, still unborn, inside her mother in phantasy. Therapy led to the breaking down of this illusion and, in time, a move towards the acceptance of being an 'outside baby'. That is, both physically and psychologically born in the outside world. The French psychoanalyst Rey (1975), in describing such children, used an interesting image of a marsupial baby to define a child that is physically born into mother's 'pouch', but not yet psychologically born. This psychological situation can be carried over into new attachments and may impact on the adopted child's task of forging new relationships with adoptive parents.

A crucial turning point in the therapy and in the child's life came when her parents accepted that she would be better served educationally at a special school. This shift came about partly as a result of the therapeutic work with the child and also through discussions with the adoptive parents and school, which led to a change in their understanding of the nature and severity of her difficulties.

The clinical material that follows raises questions about how young children under age five may forget or retrieve traumatic experiences (particularly experiences during the pre-verbal stage of development) and how traces of those experiences may remain in the mind and in the memory. Neuroscience research provides an explanation of the ways in which early experience – and in particular experience in the pre-verbal stage of development, or before conscious memory – is laid down in the neural pathways and circuits of the brain. First, I shall outline some of the significant findings of neuroscience to highlight their relevance to understanding the impact of trauma in infancy and to the therapeutic work.

Trauma, memory and neuroscience research

There has been a blossoming of research into the workings of the brain by neurobiologists over the last ten to fifteen years, which has greatly altered our understanding of how early trauma in childhood affects the personality (Balbernie, 2001; Pally, 2000). First of all, neglect has been seen to cause actual damage to the developing brain by the failure of the needed stimulus at the right time, so that neural pathways atrophy (Glaser, 2000; Nelson and Bosquet, 2000; Schore, 2001a, 2001b). Further, actual trauma which initiates primitive flight/fight or freezing responses fosters these patterns of reaction over the more elaborate reflective processes, where thought takes precedence over action (Perry *et al.*, 1995). Primitive states of mind or defences can predominate, in response to traumatic early experiences, and shape the interactive relationship with carers.

It is possible for neural pathways to connect where previously there have been none; and it is also possible for reflective thinking processes to develop in therapy – but it is a slow and uphill task (Schore, 1994; Fonagy and Target, 1997).

Turnbull and Solms (2003) discuss how our inherited memory mechanisms are modified and individualised during development. Our memories will be organised by different parts of the brain in a standard way but the capacity of the brain to do this task will be affected by our personal experiences, shaping the way that the brain is wired. Neurobiologists suggest a number of different memory systems which may interact or act separately (see Chapter 3 of Pally (2000), and Turnbull and Solms (2003), for readable accounts of the brain structures involved).

Memory starts with sensory input, resulting in an iconic memory lasting a few seconds, as information is processed. This passes into working or short-term memory, which enables us to hold several relevant pieces of information together and use them. Some of these may have been retrieved from long-term memory, which is the permanent storage of information. Long-term memory can be divided into explicit/declarative and implicit/non-declarative. Explicit memory is the conscious recollection of previous experience which may be actual facts (semantic), or memories of specific events (episodic). An experience which recalls something familiar may move an implicit memory to an explicit one.

There is also a continual interactive process, as we project our previous expectations of the world on to it and filter our perceptions of it. As memories are encoded in more than one way, it is commonplace for experiences to influence our behaviour and beliefs, without us consciously remembering the experience in question (Turnbull and Solms, 2003). We have a source memory that aids us in the source of the information we seek. Pally (2000: 52) discusses how the immaturity of children's pre-frontal cortices may make them susceptible to 'source memory errors' – that is, as to whether information 'originates from within themselves (imagery, fantasy) or from external events'.

Not having developed an adult memory system, newborns and young children rely more on perceptions in the 'now'. The encoding of memory is affected by the conscious attention towards the information at the time. If a child is emotionally aroused, they will remember the event with greater vividness or intensity, as stress hormones affect the way that the memory is encoded in the brain. However, extremely stressful situations can impair episodic memory due to hippocampal dysfunction. In babies and young children the hippocampus is not fully functional in the first two years of life and infantile memories are stored as bodily memories and implicit knowledge of how the world works. We are helped in retrieving a memory if there is a degree of similarity between the present situation and the past. In this way a word, gesture, scent, or even a piece of music may trigger a retrieval of an experience. This experience is remembered again, but modified by the current situation.

Implicit, or non-declarative, memory is the name given to memories that are non-consciously processed. This may include our memory for shape and form, and emotional memory as well as known skills, habits and routines. Bodily changes to our autonomic nervous system – such as heart rate, feeling sick or sweating – form part of our emotional memory. Due to their immaturity, infants and young children may not be able to recall an actual traumatic event – that is, an explicit memory – while having the somatic memory of the traumatic event – i.e. the implicit memory (see Gaensbauer, 2002). Adults may be more likely to present with a story of a traumatic incident without the accompanying emotions.

Therapeutic work may be able to link these two separated memory traces, which are parts of one trauma. It is thought that the verbalisation of traumatic material, together with the therapist making sense of what the child is experiencing in the present, will help the processing of the trauma. This process gives it a narrative and helps it to become part of explicit memory, rather than a disturbing physical symptom unconnected to an event, or a story of an incident without the accompanying feelings (Schore, 1994; Fonagy and Target, 1997). Turnbull and Solms (2003) discuss how the 'recovery' of a memory by an adult patient or older child may actually be the recovery of a link between the 'feeling self' and procedural and semantic memory, which in turn is linked to a current feeling state in the present.

However, they suggest that children under two years of age are unlikely to consciously recall specific events because, as mentioned above, the hippocampal memory system has not developed in any viable sense. Affect-based learning systems are available, which they suggest are like a feeling of intuition or a hunch, based on the implicit memory system. They hypothesise that, because episodic memory is not available, the world is unreliable and unpredictable. The child is therefore dependent on a reliable care-giver or facilitating environment, to help them organise their experience.

Background

The history, in brief, is that Alison had been taken into foster care at 10 weeks old after her mother – who had severe mental health problems – had been unable to care for her. When Alison was three her foster family wanted to adopt her but were assessed by social services and were not considered suitable as permanent carers. She was then swiftly adopted, without necessary preparation, because it was thought that she would not understand.

Alison was adopted into a caring middle class family, who had two older children of their own. She had moderate learning difficulties and was selectively mute – that is, she talked to a few adults and some known children. She was successful in using her adoptive mother and other adults to express or do things for her. For instance, she exerted pressure on her class aide to help her, to such an extent that it obscured her limited abilities and lack of progress in school. Alison's projection of helplessness and her wish to possess her class aide's abilities proved a powerful defence and a block to her own learning.

Alison was referred, aged six, when her adoptive parents became increasingly worried about her lack of progress over the previous two and a half years. Her parents' request for help reflects the fact that her way of relating caused concern, but was also very puzzling. Although appearing to be affectionate, she related through a puppy-like contact of sensual physicality, not words (Case, 2005a). Alison's symptom of selective mutism (where a child is able to talk but will not do so in selected settings or with selected people) did not allow her ready contact through speech, so that her main way of engaging, when she liked someone, seemed to be to throw herself at them physically. She physically moulded to the adult that she was with and in an invasive way thrust into other people's personal space, as if she were not aware of their separate existence. By the time Alison was referred for therapy, her horseplay had become a cause for anxiety, although it had not originally been seen in that way.

Although Alison had a reasonable grasp of language, over time I found that she lived in a phantasy world which was being kept intact through not speaking to adults outside the family and only speaking to children in a whisper. I came to understand that one aspect of her phantasy – which she struggled to maintain – was that she was part of another person, and not a separate individual, thus becoming physically and mentally entangled with whoever she was with.

Horseplay

The first months of working with Alison were characterised by this floppy, breathy, rag-doll-falling-into-me play. In fact, it was not at all playful and made me feel uncomfortable, so much so that I missed that enjoyable feeling of being with another person in play. It gave me cause for concern about her vulnerability to others who could take advantage of the lack of ordinary boundaries, having no sense of a 'me' and a 'you'. It was bossy, controlling and intrusive and began the moment she saw me – leaping from her escort straight to me, and touching me in a possessive, tickling, patting way in the corridor – but became more insistent once we were in the room. It was perhaps possible to see some remnants of toddler behaviour, in wanting to scramble over an adult and poke at their tongue or eyes – or in Alison's case trying to prise my forehead off to get inside. An example follows:

As I went to collect Alison she rushed to me, grabbing my hands and leading me to the door, where she dropped them and ran on, only to leap out at me, tickling and then grabbing my hands and swinging back so that she skidded along the floor behind me. I felt like a playground toy, an object being used, and was aware of her intense excitement and giggles and breathy laughing. She jumped up onto a chair in the playroom and flopped straight into me as I approached so that I had to catch her or she would have crashed onto the floor. When I sat down she began falling from the window sill behind me over my shoulder and into my lap, breath coming out in short gasps, so actually there was a quality of tension. My attempts to get her onto a chair of her own failed and she was lying across her chair and onto mine, rolling about a lot, showing her bottom and later trying to get her head up my skirt, muttering, 'You're a heavy baby!'

The normal boundary around touch was missing and in its place was a confusion of self and other, an 'entanglement' (Tustin, 1992). There was no sense of our getting to know each other and the work that is involved in this. There was also no sense of a gap between her leaving her escort and then meeting me, or of a gap between the sessions, when my absence might be noticed and I might be missed. In the apparent excitement, there was no room for any upsetting feelings like hurt, worry, losing someone or being lost. There was a lot of surface-to-surface contact (Bick, 1986), sticking like glue, or trying to force her way inside me by intrusive attacks or launches, prising my forehead up, or trying to dive under my skirt.

When Alison was little there had been a delight in her gambolling behaviour, and the serious nature of it had been missed. The quality of Alison's physical play was sensuous and excited, characteristic of an infant's desires for the mother's body (when children are in these primitive emotional states of mind the body-to-body play has a different emotional resonance from the sexualised play of abused children). Alison's play suggested a wish to possess the mother's body so as to obliterate separateness, loss, and abandonment. Thus, the behaviour can be seen to be a survival mechanism which has a protective function in an adverse early care situation: it shields the child from the reality of their separateness and the terror of realisation that they are outside of mother and thus dependent on her, and that mother is not sufficiently mentally or physically available.

In trying to understand what kind of person Alison thought she was with, it seemed that the play implied a mummy that you have to catch by surprise. Under the breathy giggles there was a lot of tension, quite a desperate feel to the interaction; it was as if it were a matter of life and death. There was no place for a mummy to offer the baby a breast, metaphorically speaking; instead the mummy had to be seduced (by tickles and pats) or assaulted (by launching attacks). It evoked a situation of an abandoned baby and a mummy with no capacity to look after a baby, but the baby's accompanying feelings to this situation were 'missing'. Instead of a sense of absence or loss, there was an omnipotent feeling of control and bossiness and of being 'the heavy baby'.

As a baby, Alison may have had a feeling or phantasy of being 'too heavy' in a physical or psychological way for her birth mother. A further extract from the following session will give a clearer sense of her wish to be an 'inside baby', and therefore not separate or in touch with her separate existence:

> The session began in a similar way with my asking her if we could walk together in the corridor, which she managed for part of the way. In the playroom, she repeated her attempts to throw herself at me, to take over the chairs, to grab at my body, as if to take over parts and bits of me. I had unsuccessfully been trying to get her off my lap onto her own chair and she lay heavily on her back across my lap. I asked her where she was. She replied, 'In your tummy.' She began to make struggling, tiny, baby movements. She got up and tried to reach the ceiling after I had talked of her wishing to be an 'inside baby'. She stood on the table to touch the ceiling, saying, 'I'm the mummy.' Looking down at me through her fringe, she whispered, 'I want to be the mummy.' There was for a moment a different feel to her, as if there was a separate person looking at me. She giggled and then said, '*You're* giggly!' She crawled across the floor and pretended to eat my shoe/foot. I said that she wanted to eat me up, to take me inside. She said, 'I'll eat you and then I'll be you and you can be me.' I replied, 'If you eat me, it is as if you have me inside and will become me.'

In this short extract it seems as if there are only two positions: either to be an 'inside baby', where you will not have to experience being both separate and dependent and the possibilities of loss that that involves; or to be the 'mummy', in which case I become her, as with '*You're* giggly'. This results in a confusion of identities. An exchange of identities takes place either through incorporation – 'eating up' – or by an exchange of parts of each other in phantasy. Parts of oneself that are too painful to bear can be passed to the other person ('*You're* giggly') just as parts of the other person that are desirable can be taken into oneself ('I'm the mummy'). In other words, the child's characteristics can be attributed to others, or the child can take on some of the characteristics of others.

In contrast, there was a moment when Alison looked through her fringe at me when she was in ordinary contact and could say, 'I want to be the mummy' – not 'I am the mummy' – and at this moment I felt as if I was with a different person. In a sense, the therapist is trying to make contact with this more reality-based part of the child, to aid her in taking on the pain of ordinary life.

The mermaid, who cannot walk or speak on land

One of the interesting things about Alison was the affection that she could inspire; people liked her, and wanted her to talk to them. They were disappointed when she remained mute, talking to very few. At the start of therapy the only man she talked to was her adoptive father. She talked more to women, and to selected children at school. The outside world and communication with it was very frightening, but she was also very bossy and controlling, using her mother and others as part of her expressive apparatus. In one of the school reviews her educational aide in the classroom was honest about actually doing the work for her – rather than encouraging her own efforts – to enable her to keep up with the other, more able children. Alison's appealing helplessness evoked the maintenance of this defence against a realistic awareness of her limitations.

Alison attended a normal primary school, but as she got older the gap between her and her classmates widened. In therapy, our interactions around drawing in the second year give a flavour of both the helplessness which she communicated, and the huge struggle involved in helping her to do things for herself. This was absolutely necessary if she was ever to develop. Her own limited abilities needed to be faced before she could start to learn. It is important to note, however, that there was a hopeful aspect to Alison's communication of 'helplessness', in that she still held on to the possibility of a helpful adult. Rhode (1997) suggests that a 'life-seeking part of the child's personality' remains strong in children like Alison, who can inspire involved adults with feelings of love and a desire to help them.

Six months into therapy Alison became fascinated by the story of *The Little Mermaid*. The Disney film was popular, and she had the accompanying dolls, figures and videos. Mermaids are half human and half fish and this immediately suggests the psychological dilemma of whether one is to live in the world of the senses – a liquid, foetal world – or whether one can survive on land, in a conscious world. The mermaid has characteristics of both worlds. In the half-human, half-animal form, we sense that emotion remains unspoken, not humanised (Case, 2005a). To articulate can be painful, but allows one to enter a world of shared communication. It is significant that, in the story, Ariel (the Little Mermaid) trades her voice for a pair of legs, so that she can enter the human world. It was as if Alison was trying to preserve a pre-verbal state of self through her defences.

Following a half-term break, Alison brought a photocopied picture of Ariel to her session. She drew the curtains and leapt onto my lap with a lot of the type of giggling and leaning back that had happened at the start of therapy. I talked about the break and about 'being in the dark', and about the mermaid; Alison ran off to the toilet, as frequently happened after I talked to her, as if to concretely get rid of the words. When she came back she showed me that she had begun to colour in the mermaid, just a tiny amount, but the rest was an empty shape. I found the crayons and she then wanted me to colour it in, saying, 'You do it'. I compromised in the end, so that I would colour in with her as long as she did some too. While I was doing this I was able to talk to her about her struggles to do things for herself. She then wanted me to cut it out and to put a string on it, so that she could take it with her.

It was as if she had an outline of a self, and the beginning of a sense of boundary, but no content. The previous year she had made enclosures on paper, and had also made a tiny little figure so that I thought she did have a rudimentary sense of self. Fordham has suggested that the drawing of a boundary is the first evidence of a developing sense of self in children (Astor, 1985).

I thought after this session that I had done much more for her than I would normally. I continued to struggle with this in the weeks that followed. When Alison would want me to draw I worked very hard to encourage her, but after the session felt that I had given in, as she was so persuasive. I found myself in the crux of a dilemma. If I played within her phantasy world she would speak to me, because I played alongside her and did not challenge her position. However, if I tried to provide an outside perspective, she used every defensive means possible not to listen or take in what I said. Similarly with drawing, she was delighted if I drew – as if she were completely helpless – but was enraged if I tried to facilitate her own drawing.

The next month she wanted a mermaid cut out and as she took her, she said, 'She's still wet', shaking her, as if she had come out of the water in being cut out of the paper. In this action, it is as if the background paper represents the mother environment or foetal sea; and the cutting out represents the coming onto land, or being born psychologically (Case, 2005a, 2005b).

In the original story the Little Mermaid decides to die when her love is unrequited. It is in effect a suicide, a turning of one's face to the wall suggestive of the huge struggle to stay attached to life. I think in the case of Alison the potential for this was reflected in the underlying life and death dimension of experience that became evident in her therapy.

The stolen baby: forward movement is abandonment and loss

It was difficult to know how Alison understood her move to an adoptive home when she was three and a half. One of her adoptive brothers recalled her arrival as a traumatic day, because of her screaming protest. One theme that ran intermittently throughout the five years of therapy was of a baby being stolen and moved forward and backward between two people or groups. This phantasy of being a stolen baby, or adoptive parents unconsciously feeling that they have stolen a baby from its mother, is not uncommon (see Hodges (1990) for variations on this theme). In the first year of therapy Alison imagined being a baby pony that was taken from its mother by a giant in the middle of the night and padlocked in a garage. The mother then stole it back and this was played out repetitively, backwards and forwards, week after week. One day when I asked how the baby felt when the giant and the mother both wanted her, she whispered, 'Dead inside'. However, she never returned, in this game, to this moment of being in touch with what had felt a piercing sadness.

Such traumatic early changes in her life left her very vulnerable at times of different but necessary change. In the second and third year of her therapy she played at being 'a lovable puppy' before breaks. This had its own haunting quality, because the communication suggested that I could not possibly abandon a little defenceless puppy, whereas children could be abandoned – a perspective on human life sometimes shared by looked-after children in their play (Case, 2005a).

In the middle of the fourth year of therapy, Alison's adoptive parents and the network around her were in general agreement that a move to a special school for children with moderate learning difficulties would aid her progress at school. This was a painful time for her parents, who held a belief in equal opportunities for all and had fought long and hard for provision for her within the local mainstream school. The gap between Alison and her peers was widening and the move to the new school had several advantages. She would be with other children with learning difficulties and in reading, for instance, would be able to shine in the new situation. The curriculum would be geared to her individual needs and she would be able to continue at the same (very good) school, into secondary age.

Alison reacted characteristically to news of the impending move – regressing in the sessions to being a crying baby, and then to being a puppy. She searched for somewhere in the room to hide, making baby or puppy noises. Late in one session she responded to my wondering what had happened to the 10-year-old Alison, and told me that she might be moving school. She did not want to move and she wanted to stay at home all day. Change was equated with abandonment and being thrust out of security, into the unknown. Here, two phantasies ('being stolen' and 'forward movement as abandonment') converge, and the effect was to make any progress problematic for her.

She went back to much earlier play, but in the weeks that followed became interested in the character of Simba, a lion cub in Disney's *The Lion King* who struggles to grow up in the face of parental loss. In the first session after her start at the new school Alison drew a picture – with a sun and ground in the right place, for the first time – while pretending to be at school. She also looked through her box and folder of drawings, and this had the quality of a review of where we had come from and where we were going. Two months later some interesting material surfaced around drawing, stimulated by the change of school.

A sense of time and a past tense

Alison had settled very well into her new school, and her work was improving – possibly spurred on by being in the more able group. Mother reported that she was joining in more activities with her brothers at home. She was more able to live in external reality, but still found it difficult, and was very resistant to accepting unwelcome facts.

After a two-week holiday break from her therapy, Alison returned to her floppy behaviour, as if her backbone kept collapsing. She made a bridge with her body, from her own chair over to my chair. I talked about the feelings aroused by the break and she was able to start to play with the toy lions. She was playing part of *The Lion King* story but the props she was using got tipped over. It seemed to represent a part of her that felt tipped out by the holiday break. At first she was cross with me for talking at all and hid herself in the curtain. She made ghost noises and came out with the blanket over her as a ghost, but then she decided to paint.

At first I was excluded from this activity because of her crossness about the break but then, after a while, I was allowed to sit with her at the table. She started with areas of colour with very little form, and a sun lower down the picture so that it felt like a topsy-turvy world – disorganised, despite her quite intense work on it, so that I thought it reflected her difficulty in 'putting things into order inside'. She asked me about two techniques, 'crayon and wash' and then 'crayon rubbings' – where an object is underneath the paper and a crayon reveals a pattern. She attempted both of these with a desultory feel, because it was not clear what she was aiming for. She then added a blue sky. All through this quite lengthy sequence it was very difficult to understand her. She was half talking to herself but I was meant to know what she was saying and she got very angry when I could not in fact hear her – refusing to repeat what she had said and saying, in response to my asking her to repeat, 'Nothing'.

She then folded a new piece of paper in half and drew 'a scary house'. It was a tall thin house with tall thin windows and a big, tall, thin door. She wrote 'wichs [i.e. witches] house, ha, ha, ha', and put her own door number on it. There was a slight sense of a figure. I talked about how scary it seemed. The thin windows and doors made it look difficult to get in or out. I asked if her house had ever seemed scary in the past. She said, 'No' but then drew underneath, on the other half of the paper, a scarier house. This house had taller, thinner windows and door, and again was labelled 'wichs'. At the end of the session she hid these drawings and took them away.

It was possible that the separation in the break had evoked thoughts of past separations and that Alison had more mental equipment to begin to be able to attempt comprehension of the past. In the present, one aspect of this drawing was that the therapist was a 'witchy Mrs Case', due to her absence on holiday. The play at being a ghost, together with the pictures, made me wonder if a memory of the adoption move had been pieced together in some form. The ghost play suggested literally that ghosts from the past were present in her mind. The two techniques that Alison was trying to use in her first picture are both ones where the shape of something is revealed, either by the crayon wash or by the crayon rubbing of a shape under the paper. In the trying out of these techniques there was a first play with depth – a move towards three-dimensionality – which continued in the following session.

When I had first started work with Alison she had only ever used the present tense. There had been no idea of past or future. Now she was coming to therapy and telling me sometimes about things that had happened at home, or at school, or about an outing she would be going on – past and future had developed. Alison seemed to be developing a mind in which there was a sense of depth and things below the surface, and of memories that could be held and re-evoked. In a session at this time:

> Alison arrived for therapy in a rush, running ahead of me, and hiding in the room. She very soon let me know where she was, wanting me to find her. She came out from behind a folder and said that last week's painting was not

finished. She got paints out and began to add colours to it. She began to lift the corner of the painting several times, looking under and putting it back. Then she said that she was pretending to copy a picture under the painting. She did this but then said that it was difficult as it wasn't there. She said that she would draw this picture first. I said that there seemed to be another picture present that was hidden by this top picture and she nodded. She put the painting on the ground, got white paper and began to draw in felt tip. She drew a sun with a face, sky, and a red circle, an orange/brown shape. The painting then had to go back on top, and she began to paint, lifting it up to look underneath. She added a sun at the top of the picture, some red paint, and what appeared to be rain or tears. I was very moved by what appeared to be an attempt to organise something that seemed to be in pieces.

She said, looking under, that the one on top and the one underneath were not at all alike. I agreed they were different. She then hid behind her folder to do some crayoning on the pictures, asking for my help in fixing the paper so it did not slide about. I talked about the missing drawings and the importance of having her work all together, so that we could try to understand all the things that made up Alison. She was able to say that they were scary and that this clearly evoked a wish to hide them. I talked about the different pictures, and how scary things can make us feel in pieces, and how she seemed to be trying to put something back together. She was rummaging around in her box but said clearly, 'I am listening'.

At the next session she bought the two scary drawings back and put them in the folder.

In the last two sessions described above, Alison was struggling to represent the sense of having acquired a past with memories in sensory form that could be evoked with appropriate stimulus from the external world. It was as if she had previously lived like an infant and pre-school child, in a present tense mixed with dreams and wishes. The 'wichs house' pictures gave her traumatic affective memory a visual form, together with the experience of re-living the trauma in the present, with the therapist trying to make sense of it. I think this allowed some of the pain to be borne. It acquired a shape and form, a somatic memory released through the physical act of drawing, and was now part of a shared narrative.

Separateness, memory and the mind

When children are in a confused state of being, mentally entangled with others, life experiences will be missed and the child's development is affected (Bion, 1957; Tustin, 1992). For example, to have a memory it is necessary to have separated sufficiently and to be able to bear the pain of absence, in order to have something to remember. If you are stuck like glue to another, there is no past and future, only the now, in the present (Meltzer, 1975). In the past, Alison had been determined to be an inside baby or a mummy – but definitely not a child of the age she actually was.

In contrast, in the last of the clinical extracts, Alison seemed to be trying to understand how one thing in the past (underneath) might affect the present (on top). She seemed to be interested in the novelty of that and was able to progress from the crayon and wash, to the crayon rubbing – both giving evidence of something underneath that can be revealed – to the idea of a picture underneath the picture she was working on. This development of a sense of past and present was linked to the emergence of affective memories in the therapy; it went hand in hand with the development of a sense of self, based on being an 'outside' 10-year-old girl with an inside mind in which one can have 'thought-images'.

When Alison first began to try to copy an imaginary picture, it may have been a way of expressing a memory from a time when she could not verbalise. Painting and drawing are particularly useful to express pre-verbal experience and for Alison re-evoked something from her past that was about a world fragmenting into pieces. At the same time, through her use of materials, a new form was taking shape in a reparative way. The therapy setting, the relationship, and the paper and materials all acted as elements of a frame that allowed this new organisation to take a shape.

The impact of trauma on development and attachment relationships

Confusional and entangled children, like Alison, have frequently had a traumatic experience of being unable to make contact with their main carer – usually mother. This may be as a result of the mother or carer's mental illness, or severe depression; or it may be the sensitivity of this particular child to a trauma or disruption (Dubinsky, 1997). Explorations into traumatic states of mind have shown that such experiences – which have been so emotionally overwhelming that they could not be assimilated, leading to feelings of helplessness – may cause the trauma to stay in the person's mind like a concrete object: played out repeatedly, yet bringing no relief (Garland, 1998). In Alison's case, there had clearly been trauma as a tiny infant – in the experience of living with a psychotic mother unable to care for her – as well as later traumatic separations in the move to her foster family and then to her adoptive family.

The therapist struggles to bring the child into a shared world with others. Through my own struggles, it could be appreciated how difficult it was for parents to parent Alison in a way that facilitated growth and development, and for staff in school to work with her learning difficulties. Her family and the whole network around Alison had to struggle with a tougher approach that could surmount the challenge of her learning difficulties and could deal with the realisation that perhaps her current school placement was not the correct one.

In these circumstances, both therapist and adoptive parents face the daunting responsibility of keeping hope alive in the child and being open to any fragile move towards a real relationship in the external world, as an alternative to a phantasy life that can be very attractive for the child. This may be an unrewarding task initially, as attachments are weak, and there may be little sense of the kind of engagement that makes parenting fulfilling. Supportive parental work, alongside individual therapy, is essential in bearing the pain of the strength of the child's impulse to turn away from life.

Awareness of this is essential for effective and appropriate parenting of such a child. In her play with puppets in therapy sessions, Alison enacted a mother who 'plays dead' in relation to the baby, not communicating with or feeding the baby. She also played a father character, who would dump the babies and bury them as soon as they were born. Her play did not reflect the loving parenting she received in different ways from foster and adoptive parents, but rather how her inner life inhibited and coloured her perception of being parented.

Conclusion

Alison and I continued to work together for a further two years, until a change in circumstances bought the work to an end. Alison had made progress but was still in need of support. She returned to therapy in adolescence, but with a new therapist. When children have had such a poor start their emotional needs are great. Trauma combining with such early deprivation in life is crippling on the development of mental capacities. There can be a powerful dynamic in child, adopted family and the network, for the child to 'be normal' and not different: to be accepted in ordinary school and with ordinary friends; to put the traumatic past *in* the past.

Unfortunately, it cannot just disappear with a loving family and needs to be addressed with professional support, as well as from the community around the adopted family. Being able to remember the past, in some form, may enable adopted children to integrate disturbing and previously split-off emotional experience, as well as aiding the development of identity (autobiographical memory). In this context, by 'remember' I do not necessarily mean exact (explicit) memories, but what Klein (1957: 234) referred to as 'memories in feeling' – that is, implicit memories. Early situations and states are revived, played over and worked through in therapy in a way that fosters development and frees up the relationship between the child and adoptive parents. It is during this process that the child may develop a different attitude towards what were crippling frustrations.

Note

Illustrations of artwork discussed in this chapter can be found in the original version of the article in Vol. 31 No. 3 of the *Journal of Child Psychotherapy*.

References

Astor, J. (1985) *Michael Fordham: Innovations in Analytical Psychology*, London and New York: Routledge.

Balbernie, R. (2001) 'Circuits and circumstances: the neurobiological consequences of early relationship experiences and how they shape later behaviour', *Journal of Child Psychotherapy*, 27 (3): 237–55.

Bick, E. (1986) 'Further considerations of the function of the skin in early object relations', *British Journal of Psychotherapy*, 2 (4): 292–9.

Bion, W.R. (1957) 'Differentiation of the psychotic from the non-psychotic personality', *International Journal of Psychoanalysis*, 38: 266–75.

Case, C. (2005a) *Imagining Animals: Art, Psychotherapy and Primitive States of Mind*, London: Routledge.

Case, C. (2005b) 'Thinking about cutting up, cutting out and sticking down', *International Journal of Art Therapy, Inscape*, 10 (2): 53–62.

Dubinsky, A. (1997) 'Theoretical overview', in M. Rustin, M. Rhode, A. Dubinsky and H. Dubinsky (eds) *Psychotic States in Children*, London: Duckworth.

Fonagy, P. and Target, M. (1997) 'Attachment and reflective function: their role in self-organisation', *Development and Psychopathology*, 9: 679–700.

Gaensbauer, T.H. (2002) 'Representations of trauma in infancy: clinical and theoretical implications for the understanding of early memory', *Infant Mental Health Journal*, 23 (3): 259–77.

Garland, C. (ed.) (1998) *Understanding Trauma: A Psychoanalytic Approach*, London: Duckworth.

Glaser, D. (2000) 'Child abuse and neglect and the brain: a review', *Journal of Child Psychology and Psychiatry*, 41 (1): 97–116.

Hodges, J. (1990) 'The relationship to self and objects in early maternal deprivation and adoption', *Journal of Child Psychotherapy*, 16 (1): 53–73.

Klein, M. (1957) 'Envy and gratitude', in *The Writings of Melanie Klein*, Volume III, London: Hogarth Press and Institute of Psychoanalysis.

Meltzer, D. (1975) 'Dimensionality in mental functioning', in D. Meltzer, J. Bremner, S. Hoxter, D. Weddell and I. Wittenberg (eds) *Explorations in Autism*, Strath Tay: Clunie.

Nelson, C.A. and Bosquet, M. (2000) 'Neurobiology of fetal and infant development: implications for infant mental health', in C.H. Zeanah (ed.) *Handbook of Infant Mental Health*, 2nd edition, New York: Guilford Press.

Pally, R. (2000) *The Mind–Brain Relationship*, London and New York: Karnac.

Perry, B.D., Pollard, A., Blakeley, T., Baker, W. and Vigilante, D. (1995) 'Childhood trauma, the neurobiology of adaptation, and "use-dependant" development of the brain: how "states" become "traits"', *Infant Mental Health Journal*, 16 (4): 271–91.

Rey, H. (1975) 'Liberte et processus de pensee psychotique', *La Vie Medicale au Canada Francais*, 4: 1046–60, referenced in Steiner, J. (1993) *Psychic Retreats*, London: Routledge and Institute of Psychoanalysis.

Rhode, M. (1997) 'Discussion', in M. Rustin, M. Rhode, A. Dubinsky and H. Dubinsky (eds) *Psychotic States in Children*, London: Duckworth.

Schore, A.N. (1994) *Affect Regulation and the Origin of the Self: The Neurobiology of Emotional Development*, Hillsdale, NJ: Lawrence Erlbaum.

Schore, A.N. (2001a) 'Effects of a secure attachment relationship on right brain development, affect regulation and infant mental health', *Infant Mental Health Journal*, 22 (1–2): 7–66.

Schore, A.N. (2001b) 'The effects of early relational trauma on right brain development, affect regulation, and infant mental health', *Infant Mental Health Journal*, 22 (1–2): 201–69.

Moving towards reality after trauma 135

Turnbull, O. and Solms, M. (2003) 'Memory, amnesia and intuition: a neuropsychoanalytic perspective', in V. Green (ed.) *Emotional Development in Psychoanalysis, Attachment Theory and Neuroscience*, Hove and New York: Brunner/Routledge.
Tustin, F. (1992) *Autistic States in Children*, revised edition, London and New York: Tavistock/Routledge.

8   On being dropped and picked up

The plight of some late-adopted children

Judith Edwards

Happy are those who lose imagination;
They have enough to carry with ammunition.
Their spirit drags no pack,
Their old wounds, save with cold, can not more ache.
Having seen all things red,
Their eyes are rid
Of the hurt of the colour of blood forever.
And terror's first constriction over,
Their hearts remain small-drawn.
Their sense in some scorching cautery of battle
Now long since ironed,
Can laugh among the dying, unconcerned.

Wilfred Owen, Insensibility

An adopted boy who had been badly abused in his original home had two contrasting memories which emerged in a therapy session: a flowered stair carpet and a frightening shape at the bottom which he thought had something to do with hanging coats. (He had in fact been found, nearly naked, shut in a cupboard under the stairs.) Whatever the reality on which these images had been based however, I could simply take it up in his therapy in terms of fragments – good and bad, safe and unsafe – which he was used to carrying around, trying to piece them together. We all have these Proustian images which seem to exist in an area between waking and dreaming, but for the late-adopted child with perhaps little idea of parents inside his mind to help him think about his story, they can become persecuting and persistent. The non-adopted child in an ordinarily good enough home with biological parents has to struggle to unite the opposing ideas of loving and hating the same people. The process involves illusion and disillusion on the long road towards an adequate appreciation of reality. For the adopted child, this task may be severely compromised by the facts of early history and the fantasies constructed around them. These may remain dormant and then erupt with great force when the child is finally placed for adoption, and begins to have a sense of a secure base from which to express a rightful grievance. Are the birth parents bad? Is the child a bad child? Have the adoptive parents stolen the child from an idealised happier situation? It is sobering to note how the most abusive early situations can turn in the child's mind to something loved and lost in the face of the inevitable difficulties of fitting into a new family. As another child said to me, 'I just don't believe they did those things to me.' This was a child who had received substantial 'damages' through the courts for the treatment which he had received at the hands of his birth parents. The often very violent repudiation of knowledge may then re-enter the mind in a similarly violent way, causing further splits because of the difficulty of integrating facts and fantasies. This process is of course vital, in order that the child may achieve a realistic and inevitably mixed picture, both of the birth family and the adoptive family. Conflicts may either persist as an inhibiting factor towards settling down, or they may re-emerge at times of stress, as in the case I describe here, where the stress of a new baby caused a resurgence of ancient griefs and grievances.

In the case of children who are adopted, how can we ensure that they are able to achieve some integration of feeling, in order to be able to make satisfactory enough emotional and thus ordinary developmental progress? Often they have split off feelings, like Wilfred Owen's war-traumatised soldiers: the original trauma has rendered the pain often too great to be born, and their hearts do indeed remain 'small-drawn', with a resultant impoverishment of their emotional lives.

Oedipus and adoption

Perhaps the most well-known case in myth of an adoption which had disastrous consequences is that of Oedipus, cast out by his parents because of a prophecy that he would kill his father and marry his mother, abandoned on a hillside and subsequently taken up by another couple but not told of his origins. Then, in an attempt to escape the prophetic shadow, he leaves his adoptive parents whom he believes to be his birth parents. Casting himself adrift from them, he returns 'by chance' to Thebes, his actual city of birth. Even before entering the city gates, he begins to enact the very situation most feared by himself and his parents, by killing the father he does not recognise. The Oedipus Complex was one of Freud's core concepts, and has been of ongoing interest to psychoanalytic thinkers as a paradigm for some of our most central dilemmas. In a thought-provoking paper, Lupinacci (1998) reflects on the two couples involved in this tragic transaction: the parents of Thebes and the parents of Corinth. The Theban couple, in psychic terms, cannot bear the risk involved in bringing up this child, who may through his passion attempt to destroy their relationship (and this drama of the child who wants sole possession of mother to the exclusion of father is played out, particularly with a first child, with painful intensity in ordinary families). To save themselves, they expose Oedipus to certain death. The parents of Corinth accept Oedipus without question, and it is the love which Oedipus has for them which forces him to leave them, in order to spare them. However, as Lupinacci points out, there then exists a split between the idealised couple of Corinth, who do not have to bear the violent and turbulent feelings of the infant, and the negative abandoning couple of Thebes, who split off and expel aggression and murderousness, which then returns with greater force. As Lupinacci observes, being an adopted child is a common childhood fantasy for non-adopted children when there is rage and anger against the biological parents: somewhere, the child reasons, there are my real parents who would not treat me in this way.

Telling the story: memory and thinking

We begin at the beginning. But for a late-adopted child, as I have said, beginnings may have been painful, disrupted and chaotic. With late adopted children, we all become used to hearing the stories of early lives fraught with instability, comings and goings, toings and froings, before events finally become such that the child is 'freed' for adoption. The slow unravelling of emotional ties (or their swift rupture) accompanies the inevitably (and necessarily so) slow external procedures. Inside the mind of the child, there may be huge uncharted areas of confusion and doubt. The 'Life Story Book' which is our adult way of helping the child to make sense of these confusions may go some way to being a move forward, but may also inevitably leave untouched these uncharted areas of experience, and also impede further development. Social workers may spend many dedicated hours working on these books, which document, with photographs and words, the late-adopted child's fragmented experience. While this is a worthwhile enterprise, for some children there may then be a feeling that it becomes yet another burden. One adopted child I treated arrived with his weighty life story book under his arm. He was very surprised when I tentatively suggested he might let it go, so he could move on to what might come next now he was adopted. 'Oh, do you really think so?' he asked, with evident relief.

It is only during the last fifteen years that psychological research has shown that infants and young children are able to recall specific events in their lives. Freud noted that adults he saw had no recall of early life events and marvelled at 'this remarkable amnesia of childhood … the forgetting which veils our earliest youth from us and makes us strangers to it' (Freud, 1966 [1916/17]). He thought that early memories were repressed, and that children retained images and fragments of events, but not coherent representations of past experiences. The subsequent observational and clinical experience of child psychotherapists and analysts over the years has put the profession very much in touch with the powerful but unconscious nature of early memories. It is the attempt to make some of these conscious in the therapy that can bring relief, as I hope to show later in this chapter. Developmental research has now documented this early capacity to recall events. By demonstrating simple non-verbal sequences to children and infants over progressively longer periods it has been shown that as early as thirteen months, the capacity to construct and maintain memories of specific events can result in recall over extended periods of time (Bauer and Hertsgaard, 1993). What was discovered to be crucial was the nature of the events, the number of exposures, and the availability of memory-jogging cues. The researchers talk of 'enabling relations' and by this they mean events which have coherence. We might, I think, extend this concept to include the enabling relationships which are available or not, to render events meaningful for the child.

For the child that begins life in an environment characterised by its instability, lack of continuity and often its potential for significant harm, where no enabling relationship is available to process events, it is not surprising that there remains an unprocessed swirl of unlinked fragments. This is in stark contrast to the experience for the normal infant and young child within a biological family, whose fears and phantasies are contained, transformed and returned in more manageable form through the reverie of its parents (Bion, 1962). This vital early experience forms the foundation from which thinking and linking can emerge, and learning and growth can ensue.

Gary

The case I want to think about, that of a six-year-old boy called Gary, was the inspiration for the title of this paper. It was Gary's inexorable development in therapy from gently lowering himself onto the floor onto his head, to headlong and reckless throwing himself or deliberately somersaulting onto his head, which caused me to think most urgently about his core experience of being emotionally dropped, not once but many times, during the course of a short life, and about the desperate internal state of a child who felt he had nothing more to lose.

It was the head teacher at Gary's school who suggested to his adoptive mother that she should approach our Family Consultation Service, because of behavioural problems both at school and at home. The Head described him as a bright boy but restless and volatile, easily provoked and prone to attack other children, especially in the playground. When I met with the family – which comprised Gary's adoptive mother, her own son James (10) and her husband Edward – mother described Gary's ceaseless activity, and inability to be in a group. He was also apt to eat everything in the fridge at one sitting. He wet the bed and there had been episodes of stealing. His adoptive mother was exhausted, but was also able to be helped through our discussions to be in touch with developments which seemed to occur after outbursts: tearing James's books and then learning to read; eating James's Easter egg and then learning to dress himself. In a sense his destructive envy of James, the birth child, had the effect of driving him forward, but it was this desperate driven quality which caused his carers later to be concerned for his sanity. Peter Wilson (1996) in talking about Winnicott's concept of 'the anti-social tendency' notes what he calls 'the mark of justification' in stealing – 'It's mine!' The child is seeking to right a wrong. Wilson (1996: 395) quotes Winnicott, 'An antisocial child is a deprived child. In the psychopath and the delinquent and the deprived child there is logic in the implied attitude "the environment owes me something" … he is searching in some way to get the world to acknowledge its debt.'

Gary's birth mother had been a heroin addict and he had been born addicted and thus withdrawing from heroin himself as a result. In addition to the profound changes accompanying the normal 'caesura of birth', his first infantile experience

4

was of enduring the pains and bewilderment of 'cold turkey' as heroin addicts describe their experience of withdrawal. Gary had been premature and had spent some time in an incubator before being taken home to a house where other addicts lived. In retrospect, sad as this may seem, one may postulate that for Gary time in the incubator had at least offered some containment. At 'home' he had been passed round members of the family and had been looked after for a while by his maternal grandmother, who then took an overdose when Gary was in the house, because she felt at the end of her tether with the comings and goings of her daughter, who also had an older daughter by a different father. It was then that Social Services became involved, and Gary was finally taken into care at the age of two. He was placed in a large foster family where he stopped growing altogether and did not develop speech. The few words he did utter came out in a painful stammer.

In her paper 'On childhood stuttering and the theory of clinging' Klaniczay (2000) postulates that 'difficulties to do with the need for an "object" (*a primary figure*) are central'. For Gary at this point in his short life there had indeed been no primary figure for reliable identification, and the placement in a large foster family must have induced further internal chaos in a child already bewildered and catastrophically confused. His adoptive mother was distantly related by marriage to his birth mother, and Social Services had initially been doubtful about the wisdom of her proposal to adopt him. Gary's prospective adoptive mother however managed to convince them. He moved into their household when he was almost five, and indeed it has been in her care that Gary has begun to grow, to be extremely articulate (the stammer disappeared) and to feel properly held for the first time in his life. (In one of our sessions his mother described how she had been called to the house after the grandmother's overdose: Gary was hysterical and terrified, someone was trying to give him a bath, and as she then said, 'he was falling apart, but I calmed him down and held him'.)

Family work

In the Family Consultation Service where I then worked with a child psychotherapist colleague, we offered five sessions to each referring family in order to explore how much may be achieved by working with the family as a whole. The sessions might be spread over a period of several months. There might well be enough change within this structure for the family to progress without further intervention, but we also offered individual help according to resources available at the time. (For a fuller account of this approach, see Edwards and Maltby, 1998.)

Right from the first family session Gary (and his adoptive brother too) made it clear he liked having a space to think. His first act was to stick a drawing of himself on the wall. As the session progressed, he had the dolls fighting in the house, and there were crocodiles with teeth and fierce octopuses. The boys' mother said they fought a lot, and James said, 'Gary laughs when I hurt him'. Gary's confusion and anger about his situation were evident in his communication that his real mother had ten children: he could go back to her, and then if he was naughty again he would be sent back to his adoptive mother. His adoptive mother had previously felt rather despairing at this rejection. In the session, as we thought about Gary's guilt and his wish that someone should be punished, his adoptive mother was able to make some sense of the communication and to empathise with Gary's desperation.

As the meetings progressed Gary settled down considerably, both at home and at school. His mother was impressed that he could tolerate her talking to me in the sessions, as usually he tried to interpose himself in a demanding and controlling way. At school he was still compulsively spilling out his story, and was finding changeovers to playtime and lunchtime problematic. We could link this to his anxieties about being dropped, and what happened in gaps, and his mother felt more able to ask for support for Gary during these times, so he did not become, as she described it, a blitz or a whirlwind. Gary's play in the house revealed an internal world full of fighting, and a policeman had a fight with a bad baby, which we could link with his feelings that he must have been bad to be sent away by his birth mother. These sessions were helpful too for James, who could express some of his anger around being invaded by Gary and his difficulties. The family frequently arrived up to half an hour early for sessions, which I took to be a measure of the huge need for the thinking space. Gary's adoptive mother often looked exhausted, and there were difficulties with her husband, but he also attended some of the meetings. It was clear that our five family meetings would only begin to address Gary's predicament, and agreement was secured for weekly individual sessions which were funded by Social Services.

The later theme of being picked up and dropped was already present in the family sessions, both in our thinking and in Gary's play. He would line up the soldiers and then knock them down in a manically triumphant – rather than playful – way, as he and James played skittles: it was clear that he had identified with a powerful and controlling figure who would enact what he most feared, before it was visited on himself. His vulnerable self was heavily armoured in a suit of apparent invincibility, and I was to recall many times in the individual work what James had said about a Gary who laughed when he was hurt. As Wilfred Owen said, 'They … can laugh among the dying, unconcerned.'

However Gary was already making progress; he was calmer both at home and at school, less voracious and demanding. He was still wetting the bed, though less frequently: in one session he drew a 'monster' (who looked rather like himself) who he said was 'weeing everywhere'. He stoutly maintained he liked wet beds. He had started to draw what he called 'ghosts' on flimsy pieces of tissue, flitting them around my head, and I took this up in terms of thoughts and feelings which came and went, which he wanted to make sense of. It also made me think of Fraiberg *et al.*'s work (1975) with deprived families, where what she called 'ghosts in the nursery', the parents' unworked-through difficulties, come back to haunt the next generation and sabotage the parents' capacity to parent. It seemed to me that these 'ghosts' of Gary's might well represent residues of his mother's difficulties, whispering and fluttering in the unconscious atmosphere surrounding him both pre- and post-birth. Certainly there had been intergenerational difficulties in

Gary's family of origin which had affected his early life, and these 'ghosts', which seemed to me to be something to do with a transgenerational haunting, continued to appear in the individual sessions.

Individual therapy

Therapy began after the summer break. While Gary continued to stage interminable fights – 'mortal combat' where people were finished off – he denied anger, either with me or anyone else. But everyone in the play always ended up dead. My own feelings were often of boredom. When I said it was hard for him to think he could do anything else apart from killing, he stopped, surprised, and said, 'But don't you like it?' In his mind he was fused with the notion of a mother who could also revel in an orgy of killing. This state of mind was described by Maiello (2000), who differentiates motives of anger and aggression, which implies it is directed towards someone from a more cut-off state of mindless destruction. He played and replayed scenarios where he was a 'big bad turtle' who was greedy and selfish, eating all the ice cream, ordering pizzas loaded with numerous toppings. Issues about feeling abandoned emerged: Gary would lie on one of the soft chairs and lower himself slowly headfirst onto the floor. One of the small dolls would fly around the room and became called 'spider boy', then he would slide down a wall or a chair out into space, or into shark-infested waters, or be drowned in lava. I talked about a Gary who found gaps and breaks difficult, who then turned into a flying boy in order not to be a falling boy, and then killed off all the adults that might help, including myself, because he got into such a spin.

An unexpected event

Resources were such at that time, when there were only two of us managing quite a considerable caseload, that it was possible only for me to offer Gary's adoptive mother monthly sessions herself. These could help support her work with Gary, and we could think how to maintain the evident improvements in the world outside the therapy room, now that he had obtained a safe weekly space to begin simply to unload, but hopefully eventually to digest, some of his previously undigested experience. At one of these meetings his mother arrived saying that suddenly things seemed to have taken a turn for the worse. Was this part of the 'things get worse before they get better' pattern? The week before Gary had had an outburst of uncontrollable swearing at school, which had then been continued at home. He seemed much more unsettled again, and we thought around why this might be. At first we seemed to draw a blank. Then I asked mother how she herself was at the moment. She revealed that she had just had it confirmed that she was pregnant. While she was at first resistant about linking this with the swearing outbursts, she then said even the dog had noticed her lack of energy and was following her about! She was able then to think with me about Gary's feeling of guilt that people who look after him get tired (or even take overdoses as did maternal grandmother), and that he might be too much for them. We could then agree it would be important to be thinking about how to help Gary with this new turn of events.

A new character emerged in Gary's sessions: he was called 'Dyno-wrecker' and he was engaged in prolonged and bitter fighting. Occasional sad moments swiftly turned into contempt and self-loathing, and he would put himself in the bin. He was also concerned about me in an anxious way: 'You sound cross today'. I felt that he was monitoring my state of mind – as he was that of his adoptive mother's – for signs that he had overstepped the mark and was about to be pushed out again. I think that this new-found feeling Gary had experienced of a place to be safe had stirred up all his old anxieties about being ejected from his mother's mind and the reasons for this.

As his adoptive mother's pregnancy advanced so did my concerns about Gary. After the half term break he zoomed back into the room and deliberately dived off a chair straight onto his head. He told me that his Mummy had a baby in her tummy, and that she would call it Nina. Then with no time for me to comment he zoomed off in a spaceship, leaving me with the tissue 'ghosts', telling me seriously, 'they last a long time, you know'. I think in this way he was indicating the devastating remnants of his early trauma of being abandoned in an uncontained space, which returned to visit him as mother visibly grew larger with the baby inside her. During the next few months I was left on many occasions with the ghosts, while Gary went off in a space ship, hastily thrown together with a heap of chairs. Nina was chased by police, drowned, smacked and tortured. Meanwhile I was Sellotaped to my chair, forced to witness Nina's persecution. Different ways of killing babies were devised, and in many ways this seemed a helpful way of thinking about his murderous feelings so that they would not become enacted. In some sessions Gary's anger was cold and vengeful: in a way it had gone beyond anger to a state of vengeance cut off completely from links with better feelings. When I described his angry feelings as he talked of killing he said, 'It's not about feeling, I'll do it.' Maiello's (2000) paper was helpful in thinking about a link which had not so much been actively broken, but never experienced, so that the nameless dread of falling forever was not contained and became split off into mindless destruction, which in Gary's case was soon to become self-destruction. As Maiello (2000: 13) suggests: 'Falling or dropping is not necessarily the consequence of hostile primary feelings, but may also result from the introjection (or forging) of a weak link.' Gary's early experiences may well indeed have resulted in a link in his mind to a mother being almost non-existent.

As Maiello also points out, her thinking about deficit has been proceeding along similar lines to that of Alvarez (1998) in terms of links which have never been adequately forged. Gary started to threaten to swallow objects in the room, like pen tops, and I talked to him about how I should be very worried about what he might do. I think he was communicating to me most urgently the sense he had of imminent destruction, and as had become habitual, he would kill himself rather than be killed. He would leap dangerously from table to chair to table again, letting me know about a precarious and wildly veering emotional state where a second-by-second monitoring of the situation could even then barely prevent disaster. After many sessions I was left feeling exhausted as I attempted to hold onto Gary, both physically and emotionally, in order to contain his fragmented states of mind.

The most concerning feature of this deterioration was his increasingly frequent tendency to throw himself headfirst onto the floor, even one day as I was holding his hand to take him back to the waiting room at the end of a session. While at first he just laughed, Gary then rubbed his head and said he wondered if he would bleed to death and all his brains would come out. Finally he was beginning to be in touch with his desperate internal plight. His adoptive mother was understandably extremely concerned about the deterioration, as he physically hurled himself from high places and was nearly impossible for her to contain at all at times in her heavily pregnant state, and she requested with my support a psychiatric assessment. While I felt that Gary's state of mind was directly linked to a resurgence of feelings of traumatic abandonment because of the pregnancy, mother herself feared he might be having a psychotic episode. (Again here the ghosts of the past: Gary's mother had herself been mentally extremely unstable, and his adoptive mother linked his fragmented states with her fears of a repetition of this.) When a dissociated state changes and the patient is more in touch with his internal plight, work is vital but there may be the risk of suicide or suicidal attempts. In the event the assessment by the psychiatrist after some discussion with me of 'ADHD (attention deficit hyperactivity disorder) but not needing medication' was a relief to mother, as it disconfirmed her worst fears, and she in turn was more able to contain Gary's panic as he taxed her tired state with his often manic and uncontrollable behaviour. He settled down again, and while I offered a second weekly session during the crisis, she felt she was able to manage. The sessions were still exhausting, but did not feel so much on the edge of disaster. Gary could still move in and out of fragmented states, but seemed to be able to be more contained by my active technique. There was no question of my remaining on my chair holding Gary with interpretations alone: it was imperative that I follow him physically and link my interpretations to active physical contact at times of danger. In this context I thought of the earliest interactions between mother and baby, where the physical interactions involving feeding, holding and cleaning are so intimately bound up with what the baby takes in of the mother, the idea of a good mother being slowly built up in his mind (Bick, 1968).

On his adoptive mother's due date her husband brought Gary to his session, and this time he accidentally fell onto his head as he was holding onto a pillow. I was able to talk to him about shocks and how they made him feel he had been dropped on the head, but that it was important that we could think about them rather than him needing to hurt himself and become addicted to falling.

He weathered the birth of his sister at home, but the sessions were again a whirlwind of activity, and he told me darkly, 'my badness hasn't gone away'. Alvarez (1995: 172) talks of the need with potentially psychopathic patients for the badness to remain 'out there ... otherwise humiliation, shame, despair and revenge can lead to explosive and dangerous eruptions'. Gary was in many senses addicted to disillusion and pain, which in his case had resulted in characterological hardening and damage to himself.

Later on in the therapy Gary built 'spaceships' from the chairs in the room. I had to steer from the back while he crouched at the front in a foetal position, only to throw himself out violently and collapse in a heap on the floor. This I saw as a significant development of an attachment relationship, and also a re-enactment of his premature birth to a heroin-addicted mother. Maiello (2000) described work done with an autistic child who had been threatened in the womb by miscarriage. She talked of the foetus's sensitivity to tactile experiences and what might be engendered as the walls of the womb contract prematurely to expel the child too early into the world. One might speculate that for Gary, at a proto-mental level, there was even at such an early stage an impulse to hurl himself rather than passively wait to be expelled. Subsequently however there was a different birth enactment, where he emerged more quietly, 'with blood on my head' from under my chair. Gary is now beginning the slow work of integration of pain and guilt. In one session he called me 'Mummy' after one such birth enactment. I acknowledged this 'mummy feeling': the beginning of an idea of being held and not dropped. This seems to me not to be an illusion, but rather the first realisation of his previously unrealised preconception of 'something good'.

Trauma and the mind

I think it is clear that for Gary, his early experiences had affected his habitual responses. In his case he had attempted to master the experience of being threatened by threatening himself with danger and imminent destruction. As recent research has demonstrated, there is an intimate and early connection between external events, feelings, and brain formation (Schore, 1998). Schore (2001) went on to link brain research into early states with the concepts of psychoanalysis, in a way which helpfully linked the two disciplines. Such difficult early experience, encoded into the brain itself, may compromise the encounter with later experience, and complicates the picture when we think of the possible plight of traumatised children coming for the first time into a secure situation.

In his paper 'Precipitation anxiety', Houzel (1995) postulates what he calls a 'gradient of psychic energy' as the new baby relates to the world outside the womb, experienced initially as a precipice. This needs to be carefully regulated by the caretaker, in the ordinary everyday caretaking process, so that something gradual rather than precipitous is negotiated. It happens through physical care, and through mental communication; the understanding and managing of early mental states. As I have already suggested, Gary's premature emergence into the world withdrawing from heroin may indeed have felt like the most destructive and traumatic catapulting into life.

Gary's earliest experience of being prematurely born heroin-addicted to an addicted mother, of being in an incubator, and then in a chaotic home situation, unheld, had not given him the opportunity to experience regulation of the gradient. He may frequently have felt as if he were hurtling headlong into the precipice, and this profoundly felt anxiety was stirred up most painfully by his adoptive mother's pregnancy. By her own ability to be in touch with this through our work, and by my efforts in the therapy to provide regulation and a space for thinking about chaos without sliding into it, Gary has indeed been able slowly and painfully to achieve a new level of stability, although this could still at times be undermined by his terror of gaps and changes.

Conclusion

What I hope to have shown is how the devastation which external circumstances may have wrought on the internal worlds of traumatised late-adopted children can then impact on their environment, when they finally come to experience some safety. They can be most painfully vulnerable to change and development, which may then cause similar feelings to reverberate in their adoptive families and in the professional networks surrounding them. Ordinary life events may then re-traumatise a vulnerable child. It is vital to be able to work with these upheavals, not only to protect the children themselves and their placements, but in order to prevent later resurgence of seemingly intractable difficulties, particularly during adolescence. It is our awareness as professionals of the ongoing issues involved for adoptive parents, at different moments in the developmental cycle of their adoptive children, which can facilitate the giving of time and space to consider the traumatic outcome of being dropped, both externally and internally.

References

Alvarez, A. (1995) 'Motiveless malignity: problems in the psychotherapy of psychopathic patients', *Journal of Child Psychotherapy*, 21 (2): 167–82.

Alvarez, A. (1998) 'Failures to link: attacks or defects?', *Journal of Child Psychotherapy*, 24 (2): 213–31.

Bauer, P.J. and Hertsgaard, L.A. (1993) 'Increasing steps in recall of events: factors facilitating immediate and long-term memory in 13.5 and 16.5 month old children', *Child Development*, 64 (4): 1204–23.

Bick, E. (1968) 'The experience of skin in early objects relations', *International Journal of Psychoanalysis*, 49: 484–6.

Bion, W.R. (1962) *Learning from Experience*, London: Heinemann.

Edwards, J. and Maltby, J. (1998) 'Holding the child in mind: work with parents and families in a consultation service', *Journal of Child Psychotherapy*, 24 (1): 109–33.

Fraiberg, S., Adelson, E. and Shapiro, V. (1975) 'Ghosts in the nursery: a psychoanalytic approach to the problems of impaired infant–mother relationships', *Journal of the American Academy of Child Psychiatry*, 14 (3): 387–422.

Freud, S. (1966 [1916/17]) *Introductory Lectures in Psychoanalysis* (Strachey, J., trans. and ed.), New York: Norton.

Houzel, D. (1995) 'Precipitation anxiety', *Journal of Child Psychotherapy*, 21 (1): 65–78.

Klaniczay, S. (2000) 'On childhood stuttering and the theory of clinging', *Journal of Child Psychotherapy*, 26 (1): 97–115.

Lupinacci, M.A. (1998) 'Reflections on the early stages of the Oedipus Complex', *Journal of Child Psychotherapy*, 24 (3): 409–21.

Maiello, S. (2000) 'Broken links: attack or breakdown? Notes on the origins of violence', *Journal of Child Psychotherapy*, 26 (2): 5–24.

Owen, W. (1963) *Collected Poems*, London: Chatto.

Schore, A. (1997) *Affect Regulation and the Origin of the Self*, Hillsdale, NJ: Lawrence Erlbaum.

Schore, A. (2001) 'Neurobiology, developmental psychology and psychoanalysis: convergent findings on the subject of projective identification', in J. Edwards (ed.) *Being Alive*, London and New York: Routledge.

Wilson, P. (1996) 'Winnicott's clinical concepts: the anti-social tendency', *Journal of Child Psychotherapy*, 22 (3): 373–401.

Winnicott, D.W. (1971) *Playing and Reality*, London: Tavistock Publications.

Part IV

Belonging and becoming

Transitions

Introduction

Debbie Hindle

> New attachments are not meant to replace old ones. They are meant to stand side-by-side with existing relationships. Bowlby (1980) points out that the success of a new relationship is not dependent upon the memory of an earlier one fading; rather the new one is likely to prosper when the two relationships are kept clear and distinct.
>
> (Fahlberg, 1991: 160)

All growth and development involves the repeated negotiation of transitions. The first caesura of birth, through weaning and all subsequent separations in ordinary development, encompass the dual aspects of a sense of loss and the possibility of growth and the acquisition of new experiences.

Learning to negotiate transitions and the inevitable uncertainties and anxieties that are part of these is an ongoing process. Sorensen (2000) described the delicate and detailed interactions, both physical and emotional, between mothers and babies that she came to call transition facilitating behaviours. Gradually, through repeated interactions in which the mother attends to, imaginatively identifies with and emotionally 'anticipates, tolerates and mitigates the impact of shifting states and experiences through *unconscious* resonance' (p. 53), the infant begins to internalise these capacities. She links this process to the promotion of secure attachment and the development of capacities within the baby to begin to manage changing experiences and states of mind. The significance of this early experience cannot be over-estimated. To this I would add the importance of Winnicott's ideas about transitional objects and transitional space which is elaborated in Monica Lanyado's chapter (Chapter 9).

The repeated lack of understanding and/or the misattribution of the meaning of experiences from the child's point of view may lead to a sense of confusion, discontinuity, disorganisation or fragmentation. Children who have experienced significant disruptions in their early lives may have difficulty in gathering together their experiences in a way that can be made sense of, symbolised, played out or remembered so that the beginning of a narrative and a sense of coherence can emerge. What is often lost is a sense of continuity, affecting a child's capacity to orient themselves in time, to apprehend the past and to anticipate the future. One profound consequence of this may be the inability to distinguish – emotionally

– between past and present. This is likely to be compounded by the corresponding loss or absence of a parent's mind that both shares and remembers the child's history.

All children who are adopted must manage the transition from their birth parent or parents to their adoptive family, but many late-adopted children may have experienced other significant transitions: perhaps repeated receptions into care, in an attempt to support and maintain a child with their parent(s); or moves within the care system, from a short-term to a long-term foster home or to a bridging placement in preparation for adoption. At times, transitions can be planned and prepared for, at other times they may be precipitous, bewildering or traumatic. All these circumstances, both external and internal, impact on the way in which the transition to a new family is experienced.

In relation to transitions in adulthood, Clulow (1982, 1996) describes the impact of the birth of a first child and the complex emotional tasks involved in becoming parents, tracing partnering and parenting and back again as a journey with a circular route. Although this transitional process is unique to each parental couple, he highlights the significance and developmental nature of this experience. For each individual also there is an internal shift from a sense of identity as a daughter, sister, wife or partner to being a mother and a similar shift to being a father, and as a couple, they must make a further adjustment to include a third. If these are the developmental tasks for every new family, the process of adoption adds another dimension to what is already a challenging life experience. In writing about work with adoptive families, Tollemache (2006) describes reconciling what is often experienced as a gap between expectations and reality and the difficult work involved in living 'within the parameters of the possible' (ibid.: 144).

Dealing with transitions is, in part, relevant to all the chapters. However, the next four chapters consider how such transitions may evoke deeper levels of anxiety and consciousness and the way in which experiences of separation and loss and establishing new relationships may be facilitated.

Monica Lanyado considers therapeutic work with a four-year-old child at the point of transition from his foster home to his adoptive home and discusses the way in which 'transitional anxiety' and transitional phenomena may be encountered and understood. She explores the paradoxical task of having to manage what she calls the 'both-ness' (rather than the 'either-or-ness') of staying in touch with painful losses while being open to the potential of making and experiencing new loving relationships. Lanyado elaborates on Winnicott's ideas about the creative and developmental potential of transitional experiences, linking this to a child's capacity to play and to symbolically communicate internal conflict. She states that therapy, alongside restorative experiences in foster care and active cooperation within the professional network, can provide the kind of environment in which transitional phenomena can gradually emerge. Although this process can be difficult and often elusive, enabling a child to play and to find their way towards ordinary developmental processes is an important step at such a crucial turning point in a young child's life.

The following three chapters describe parallel work with an adopted child and his adoptive parents and the authors' reflections on their shared experience.

Francesca Calvocoressi explores the importance of a child's capacity to play imaginatively and symbolically in the therapy of a 5-year-old adopted boy. The lack of emotional containment in his early life was repeatedly encountered in sequences of play which gave expression to his terror of abandonment, fear of his own aggression and his difficulties in remembering, thinking and being able to emotionally digest all that had happened to him. As in Lanyado's chapter, Calvocoressi illustrates the way in which the therapeutic process can provide a catalyst for development and sets in motion the potential for recovery through the development of reflective functioning.

Molly Ludlam reflects on her work with the adoptive parents of the child described in the previous chapter. Although they dreamed of adopting a child who was 'just right' for them, the reality of getting to know 'their' boy involved a struggle to make sense of his desperate, confused and confusing attempts to claim them. Facing their disappointment, preparatory to mourning the loss of their ideals was an important step towards becoming the procreative couple they longed to be. Ludlam emphasises the importance of apprehending and tolerating what felt at times to be overwhelming anxieties. By holding the couple in mind, the parents were helped to have a better sense of belonging to each other and to their little boy and of being a family.

In the final chapter of this section *Francesca Calvocoressi* and *Molly Ludlam* describe their collaborative work and reflect on the way in which it provided a containing space where the respective relationships between the couple and between the parents and their child could develop. In the course of their work, several important themes emerged related to the linked developmental tasks of belonging (the process of forming attachments) and becoming (the process of establishing a sense of self and identity), and the unique journey for both adopted children and their adoptive parents in becoming a family.

Adoption involves a major transition for the child or children and parents alike. These four chapters open the door to thinking about some of the complex emotional issues that might arise. Although much hope is invested in any new placement, it does not mark a 'happy ending' (see Chapter 6), but the beginning of a new set of relationships which have implications for a sense of self and identity.

References

Bowlby, J. (1980) *Attachment and Loss*, Volume III: *Sadness and Depression*, London: Basic Books.

Clulow, C. (1982) *To Have and to Hold: Marriage, the First Baby and Preparing Couples for Parenthood*, Aberdeen: Aberdeen University Press.

Clulow, C. (ed.) (1996) *Partners Becoming Parents: Talks from the Tavistock Marital Studies Institute*, London: Sheldon Press.

Fahlberg, V. (1991) *A Child's Journey Through Placement*, London: British Association for Adoption and Fostering.

Sorensen, P. (2000) 'Observations of transition facilitating behaviour–development and theoretical implications,' *International Journal of Infant Observation*, 3 (2): 46–54.

Tollemache, L. (2006) 'Minding the gap: reconciling the gaps between expectation and reality in work with adoptive families', in J. Kendrick, C. Lindsey and L. Tollemache (eds) *Creating New Families: Therapeutic Approaches to Fostering, Adoption, and Kinship Care*, London: Karnac Books.

9   Playing out, not acting out

The development of the capacity to play in the therapy of children who are 'in transition' from fostering to adoption

Monica Lanyado

Anxieties about change and managing transitions are bound to be intense during the weeks in which a young – and inevitably emotionally damaged – child has to find a way of parting with the comparative security of a foster home and joining the (hopefully) lifetime adoptive family that will continue this caring. The responsibilities of all the adults involved, to try to make what feels like a bodily transplant of a young and vulnerable child from one family to another, 'take' rather than be rejected, are enormous. The child's anxieties are naturally greater, given all the failings of adults in their past.

What can be done, therapeutically, to help this change to fulfil its potential? This is the question that I wish to address by thinking about the nature of 'transitional anxiety' and how a growing ability to play can lead to the creation of transitional objects and experiences which can 'hold' this anxiety, so that it does not get acted out in destructive ways (Winnicott, 1951).

The ideas about transitions in life that I wish to discuss in this context inevitably move freely between internal and external reality, often attempting to stay in the paradoxical 'no man's land' which lies at their interface. This is a rather large grey area in which, during the actual process of change, two apparently conflicting internal and external realities have to co-exist as best as is possible. This is about the 'both-ness' of this extraordinary situation of a child being adopted, not the 'either-or-ness'. It is about trying to stay in touch with the painfulness of the loss of the foster and birth family – which inevitably re-evokes earlier losses – whilst trying to be as open as possible to the positive potential of making and experiencing new loving relationships in the adoptive family.

Generally speaking, it is has been thought unwise to offer psychoanalytic psychotherapy to a child whose external living situation is considered to be too changeable to withstand and adequately contain all the ups and downs of the child's therapy. However, this has at times led to children who are in stable foster homes and considered suitable for adoption being denied treatment which might help them to make the extraordinary emotional changes that are expected of them – in being able to form new loving relationships with their adoptive families.

Referrers, usually foster parents or social workers, have found this frustrating and difficult to understand.

Psychotherapists have responded by voicing their concerns about the potential for additional loss and discontinuity that will be experienced by the child becoming engaged in therapy, and then having to end therapy, if they are placed with a family who – for a variety of reasons – may be unable to continue to bring the child for therapy. One way of offering psychotherapeutic help in these circumstances has been for the psychotherapist to consult with the professionals, foster and adoptive parents over the process of transition. This has been helpful in many ways. However, this chapter argues that – providing that the therapist and all other professionals, as well as the foster and adoptive parents, work closely together throughout this process – it can be very helpful to offer therapy to a child who is 'in transition' from fostering to adoption. By working together in this linked-up way, the adults who are important for the child can create enough of a sense of a continuity of emotional containment for the child, for the therapy to feel grounded in the stable environment that is needed for it to 'work'. The surprising rewards of therapy offered under these conditions are illustrated in this chapter.

In order for this kind of treatment model to work, the therapist and the other adults who are concerned about the child need to make a commitment *before therapy starts*, to consult regularly and thoughtfully with each other, and to keep each other properly informed about the child's emotional state of health. It may be important to have a clear written agreement to this way of working from the most senior member of the social work team – so that, if there are changes in the child's social worker, key decisions about the child's future are not made without consulting with the therapist. Efforts to communicate as effectively as possible about the child – knowing that there will inevitably be many 'blips' in this communication – have to be maintained throughout the process. If there are significant doubts that this is achievable, then it might indeed be better not to embark on therapy but rather to offer consultation to the professionals already working with the child.

By stating these conditions for effective treatment to take place, it becomes clear that therapy with these children will require the therapist's readiness to be much more involved in the external world of the child than might ordinarily be the case. This is one of those clinical situations where the therapist, possibly as well as a colleague in the inter-disciplinary team, may need to attend review meetings, and meet with foster parents and adoptive parents on a regular basis. In addition, wherever possible, the therapy for the child needs to be supported by parallel therapeutic work with foster and adoptive parents, by a colleague.

In my clinical experience, it is important for the child's therapist to have direct contact with these important adults in the child's external life as well as working with the child's internal world. In this way the therapist can act as a kind of 'interpreter' of what is going on in the child's internal world to the important adults in their life. This is *in addition* to the therapeutic work and the case management that colleagues are offering to the adult network around the child. This is necessary because of the extraordinary external situation that these children and families find themselves in, which calls for a similarly 'extra' ordinary response from the child's psychotherapist. Indeed, these very deprived children seem to claim 'extra' in a multitude of ways from their therapists, as many accounts of therapy with 'looked after' children illustrate (Edwards, 2001; Gibbs, 2006; Hindle, 2000; Hunter, 2001; Ironside, 2002; Lanyado, 2006).

The active presence of the therapist within the professional network is very helpful in monitoring the risk of acting out in the network (Lanyado, 2004). Their intimate knowledge of the child's inner world enables them to spot the potential for destructive repetition within the network and thus reduce its possible impact. The difficulties of preserving a child's privacy whilst being in contact with so many people in their external world are, I feel, outweighed by the advantages of the improved level of containment of anxiety that results from the contact between all adults working with the child.

My interest in working with children who are 'in transition' arose out of a thoughtful referral from a social worker, who was concerned about a boy, Sammy, whom she was preparing for adoption. She was worried that he was going to find it distressing and possibly re-traumatising, to face the loss of his loved foster mother and family. The social worker was also very concerned that the loss would make the foster mother and family unable to face fostering any more children, even though they had clearly given so much to Sammy. I learnt a tremendous amount from my work with Sammy, which encouraged me to offer therapy to other children in similar circumstances.

Sammy was only four years old when he started to see me, and had spent half of his life with his foster family. He had been deprived and neglected as a young child, but had clear memories of his young birth mother, whom he had clearly loved, and who – despite her inadequacies as a mother – had very much wanted to keep him. Like many other young children in these circumstances, his behaviour in his foster home was often impulsive and aggressive. He could be very destructive of toys and furnishings, and when angry would deliberately wet and soil in the home. He had great difficulty concentrating on anything, and was unable to play in any age-appropriate way for more than a few minutes before he became distracted and moved onto something else. He was a 'handful', but he was also capable of being loving and remorseful, particularly when he had annoyed or upset his foster mother. When he first came for therapy, he was in a state of emotional turmoil, knowing that he was going to be adopted. His head was full of confusion and anger about three sets of parents – his birth parents, his foster parents and his fantasised adoptive parents – all of whom at various times he both idealised and felt rejected by. All of this was going on in the heart and mind of an emotionally derailed four-year-old child.

The disruption of ordinary emotional development

Children like Sammy are usually accompanied through their troubles by fat files of information about their short and highly traumatised lives. There are many reports, describing the abuse, neglect and trauma which led to them being 'looked after' by the social services. Within these reports there is the child's history of attachments, separations and losses – sadly repetitive accounts of parent–child relationships that have failed; adult relationships that have failed; mothers and fathers, and step-fathers or partners, foster families and adoptive families who come and go from the child's life; siblings, grandparents and extended family with whom there is now little or no further contact. The complex impact of all this on the incredibly sensitive emotional life of the baby and young child is enormous.

Winnicott's (1965) model of ordinary emotional development is very helpful in trying to understand what has crucially *not* happened for these children at the start of their lives. Winnicott emphasises the importance of the facilitating environment (emotional and physical) in providing the fertile soil that the embryonic 'self' of the infant needs if it is to achieve its unique potential. One only has to think about how hard it can be for ordinary devoted parents to be 'good enough' parents in their own eyes – providing protection, understanding and continuity as well as unconditional love – to realise what a nightmare world the children who end up coming into care have been born into.

Drawing further on Winnicottian thinking about emotional development, these children have not been held in the centre of a caring adult's mind in a totally pre-occupied way because the adults in their lives had so many issues of their own, which made it mostly impossible for them to do this, however much they may have wanted to. Their children have not experienced the quiet holding of their anxieties, or the fact that their parents are able to withstand their periods of primitive fury or terror and help them to survive these times. They have not felt safely protected from danger by their parents. Their utter helplessness and vulnerability in life often remains unthinkable, and only thinly masked by their infuriating defences of omnipotence and control in their relationships with those who subsequently try to help them. Their early, most basic, physical needs – which contribute vitally to their early emotional well-being, in terms of food, basic hygiene, or comforting when crying in pain or fear – have often not been adequately met. Most of the fundamental building blocks that are needed to 'create' a human being have been in some way compromised. It is in the details of how these experiences have been processed or not, by the growing child, that we find the full developmental repercussions of the innocent looking word 'neglect'.

Winnicott (1951) linked the development of the ability to play with what he called transitional phenomena and objects. He described these as, for some children, emerging in response to the need to bridge the space between one emotional state of mind and another. Classically, this is seen in ordinary development – in the baby or young child's need to have a particular toy or blanket, or particular rituals to help him or her to move from waking to sleeping. Much to many parents' embarrassment, this transitional object acquires a life of its own – together with a particular smell and feel that must not be interfered with. At the height of its emotional significance to the child, parents will go to enormous lengths to make sure that it is available when the child faces any anxiety-provoking situation, or needs it to go to sleep.

Children who have had very poor starts in life – such as those under discussion – often have not reached the developmental stage where they have been able to create such an important transitional object in their lives. And sadly, often if they have had these special toys and possessions, they have been lost in the moves from one placement to another. Their re-emergence, or emergence for the first time, is therefore an emotional event of tremendous consequence because of their ability to help the child to hold anxieties that would otherwise feel unbearable.

Not surprisingly, many of these children are unable to play in a free, communicative sort of way. They might play briefly with one toy, but then become distracted or dissatisfied with this and move on to another. There is likely to be little evolving fantasy or narrative in the play, and more probably a rather static or defensive quality to the play, which remains focused on the toy itself, rather than the fantasy world that the toy might potentially evoke for the child. Toys are thus 'things' rather than a means whereby the child is able to communicate non-verbally about internal pre-occupations. Many of these children may be described as having difficulties with attention, concentration, impulsivity and hyperactivity. Importantly, for the theme of this chapter, it is more than likely that the playing is barely able to hold aggressive fantasies within the play itself, before the child actually becomes aggressive or physical in some way. Thus the child 'acts out', rather than being able to 'play out' his or her deeper anxieties, pains and angers. And these children do have a great deal to be angry about. This primitive rage is evident in their violent responses to many apparently ordinary situations. Through these responses they are frequently expressing their *outrage* at what has happened in their short and traumatised lives.

The ability to play in a satisfying way is such a hallmark of a healthy childhood that it is easily taken for granted – until one is faced with a child who cannot play, and one realises what a sophisticated achievement this truly is. Here I am emphasising the *process* of playing itself and how this develops in early childhood, over and above the content of the play. This ability to play usually grows in the course of any child's therapy which is a going concern. However, my focus on paying attention to this ability in its own right has been intensified by my work with children like Sammy, whose developmental progression in the ability to play moved on significantly when their transitional anxieties were 'held' in therapy during the move from fostering to adoption (Lanyado, 2004). Becoming able to play out their internal conflicts and pains, rather then act them out, is an emotional and a cognitive achievement for children, which once reached paves the way for creative problem-solving as they grow up, and into their adult lives.

I now see one of the primary tasks of the therapy of children like this, as being to redress this emotional environmental failure, through providing a therapeutic environment in which the child can be offered the opportunity to take some vital emotional steps – with the relationship that develops with the therapist acting as a catalyst. When the therapeutic package described above is working well, what the therapist is providing (in a very pure and concentrated culture during the therapy session), the external world environment also provides through good fostering and adoption and good social work practice – which is supported in its understanding of the child in the ways already discussed above.

The emergence of transitional experiences and phenomena and play, during the crisis of 'transition'

Sammy reached this developmental milestone at a time when the anxiety within him, and in the system of adults around him, was at its height. The adoptive family had been accepted by the adoption panel, and planning was under way about how to introduce them to Sammy. Although he had not yet been told about this, he was finding the waiting for his 'new' family to arrive quite unbearable. It was striking that when Sammy was literally needing to tolerate the paradoxical experience of having to let go of one set of loving relationships before he could be open to potentially loving new and lifelong relationships, he became preoccupied with 'in-between' spaces – both physical and emotional – in his therapy. To my initial astonishment, transitional phenomena started to emerge in his therapy and helped him to contain this transitional anxiety.

I would now like to describe the way in which Sammy became able to make these developmental steps. From the start of therapy, a treatment plan was set up in which each session started with Sammy and his foster mother seeing me together, so that I could help them with their turbulent and rather passionate relationship. At some point, depending on what felt right in the session, I would then see Sammy alone. This very fluid arrangement (which was unusual for me) was well suited to the purpose of trying to help them to face their impending separation with as little defensiveness as possible.

For many months, when he was on his own with me, Sammy was a typically distractible child who found it hard to play. He was extremely physical – jumping around the furniture; running out of the room; throwing toys around when frustrated in the bits of play he managed. However, very gradually there were little oases of calm in this mayhem, when he was able to express his feelings. He liked to play 'Peter Pan', in which he was Peter and I was the wicked Captain Hook, with whom he had energetic sword fights. Somewhere mixed up in this play, I was able to understand and then talk to him about his identification with Peter Pan and the 'Lost Boys' who didn't have a mother and who didn't want to grow up. I was able to relate this to his fears about his future and his defensive fantasy that he didn't need a mother as she would only let him down.

There were times when Sammy started to enjoy playing with the sand in a quiet and absorbed way, during which I would also be very quiet as his absorption in the play felt very positive and healing for him. However these periods of calm where some kind of therapeutic reverie could emerge, really were very occasional oases (Ogden, 1999; Lanyado, 2004). When they happened, they were also times when Sammy could briefly have the experience of playing because he was 'alone in the presence of another' – where he was able to feel free to play because of my quiet presence (Lanyado, 2004). However, the norm was much more a situation in which I needed to be on constant alert because of his emotional and physical impulsiveness – uncertain of what he might do next.

This was the context of the build-up towards his introduction to his adoptive family. By this point in his therapy, he frequently complained that his 'new' family were taking a very long time to come and claim him from his foster home. He was angry as well as relieved about this. He knew that they were on their way, but the wait felt interminable to him and further proof of how unwanted he was. He started to express his sense of being at an in-between place in his life by insisting on spending a fair amount of time on the stairs between his foster-mother in the waiting area and the therapy room itself. This helped us to talk about how he felt in limbo and torn in two directions in his life, not knowing where to 'put' himself emotionally and physically.

During this period, at the end of a particularly painful session, Sammy was suddenly desperate to take a green ball from his box of toys home with him. As we had often battled about his – usually quite arbitrary – wish to take therapy toys home, this was very much against my better judgment. However on this occasion there was such an imperative in his wish to take the ball that I let him do this, as long as he brought it back to the next session – which he agreed to do. I then said to him that although he knew I did not normally allow therapy toys to go home, on this occasion I would, because I could see it was so important to him, and we would see together what came of this. In other words, I was giving his acquisition of the ball my blessing, rather than letting it feel to him like a theft or a triumph over me.

I agreed to Sammy taking the green ball home because I was intrigued by the way in which this ball – which he had barely noticed before – had suddenly and genuinely become special to him. He seemed to be claiming rights over it, in the same way that a baby will naturally discover and claim his or her own special blanket, or soft toy, that becomes the classical transitional object as described by Winnicott (1951). This felt potentially healthy to me and was quite unexpected in the midst of his generally disturbed behaviour at this time. I wanted to see what happened to this fragile beginning of what might have been his first transitional object.

Throughout the weeks that followed, during which time he was introduced to his adoptive family and left his foster family, the ball came and went from the sessions with Sammy. It was played with and carefully looked after (as well as at times aggressively knocked about), both in the therapy session and at his foster-home. His foster mother intuitively understood that the ball was important to him. Even when he forgot to bring it to the session, he always referred to it. It was very clearly neither his nor mine, but it was also both his and mine. This paradoxical state of affairs was very much in keeping with his feeling that he belonged to both his foster and his adoptive family, as well as at times that he belonged to neither of them. Winnicott describes how transitional phenomena serve the function of holding this type of anxiety. It was therefore fascinating to recognise that Sammy had created a new transitional object just when it was most appropriate and most needed – at the height of his anxiety about the transition between his foster parents and his adoptive parents. I think that Sammy's use of the green ball may have been important in helping him to cope with the anxiety of the paradoxes of moving from foster to adoptive home, in what became a manageable transition, as opposed to a traumatic discontinuity and loss in his life.

During this period, he also astonished me by his ability to express his growing tolerance of transitional anxiety in highly communicative and moving play. All the adults in Sammy's life knew when he was going to be told that his 'new' family had been found, and there was an inevitable build up of tension in all of us leading up to this time, each of us wondering how Sammy would cope with the move to his new home. I often found myself deeply preoccupied during his sessions (if I had the chance for this to happen) and in between his sessions, with trying to make sense in my mind of all that was about to happen to him. This intense preoccupation felt similar to primary maternal preoccupation during late pregnancy and was a state of mind in which I was very aware of having Sammy 'in my pocket', as a way of trying to hold and contain his transitional anxiety (Lanyado, 2004: 106).

In his session two days before I knew he would be told about his new family, he became quietly absorbed in 'making cakes' from wet sand. At first this felt defensive to me and I found myself musing aloud to him about how hard it might be for him, knowing that his new family would arrive soon, but not knowing quite when this would be. I wasn't even sure that he had heard me as he just carried on with his concentrated play. He came and sat next to me, again surprisingly quietly. I waited a few minutes and then asked him what was happening in his play, as he still seemed immersed in it. He told me, in a rather patient, teacherly way, that we had to wait a bit now. I wasn't sure what he meant, and then in one of those amazing flashes of connection that Stern *et al.* (1998) call a 'moment-of-meeting' between patient and therapist, I realised that he meant that we had to wait for the cakes to bake. We had to be patient and wait till they were ready.

This was a deeply moving moment on many levels. I was astonished at the appropriateness of the metaphor he had found in his play for expressing his understanding and trust that he just had to wait for his new life to unfold. He seemed to accept this and trust that the adults in his life knew what they were doing. This was a great achievement. His image of the oven with the cakes baking inside them, also implied that he felt contained in a creative way by these adults and felt that something good might come of all their efforts 'to bake' him a new family. Through his growing ability to play, he had found a means of expressing what was deepest in his heart, and then expressing it to me through his play. I don't think it was just me who felt I could smell those cakes baking. The tangible sense of something longed for, but which had to still be waited for, was alive in the room. I was then able to say – probably unnecessarily, as he already understood this – that he knew that it was important to wait till the time was right to take the 'new mummy and daddy cake' out of the oven. If it was too soon, it would not be ready – and if it was too late, it would be 'burnt'. Sammy's ability to communicate in this way, just when it might have been expected that he would be finding it most difficult to contain his anxieties was a tremendous *developmental achievement*.

This seemed to be a part of a combination of inter-related developmental steps, in which he was becoming able to use transitional phenomena to help him contain his transitional anxiety, and he was becoming able to internalise the containing presence of the important grown-ups in his life. It was an example of how a life crisis can have within it the opportunities for dramatic growth and change, as well as the potential for disaster.

The three weeks that followed his introduction to his adoptive parents were like an emotional roller coaster. Sammy brought out his full repertoire of awful confrontational and aggressive behaviour towards his adoptive parents, as well as being very volatile with his foster parents. The green ball was with him a great deal of the time, and it came and went from the therapy sessions as before. Slowly, Sammy was able to see that his adoptive parents really wanted him and that they tried very hard to understand his distress. He gradually became more able to accept them and the inevitability of saying goodbye to his foster parents. As the day approached that he would leave them, he often asked them whether they would cry when he went. They told him truthfully that they probably would – and in fact did. It was very significant for Sammy to know that he mattered enough to them for them also to be very upset at their parting. This was very different from the separations and losses of the past in which he'd felt that the grown-ups were glad to get rid of him.

In this case, Sammy was able to continue with once-weekly treatment for a further six months, with his adoptive parents bringing him some distance to see me. I had met his adoptive parents before he had, and we had talked about his life story and about the emotional difficulties that he had, and how therapy was trying to help him. However I don't think that I had re-negotiated his need for therapy as much as I would do now, and so his attendance for therapy became rather erratic and we eventually agreed on just a few sessions to bring his therapy to an end, although in many ways I felt that it might have been better for him to continue.

The need to be sensitive to adoptive parents' wish to 'claim' their child, and provide for all his or her emotional needs, must be respected by therapists. Adoptive parents have often been through so many personally intrusive hoops – before being accepted as adopters – that they understandably cannot wait to be left alone to get on with their lives. There can be a fear that if they admit to the inevitable difficulties that they face with their newly adopted child, they will be judged as being inadequate parents. It is important for the therapist to try to overcome this difficulty through the relationship they form with the adoptive parents during the transition and after the child goes to live with them. This can enable adoptive parents to see the therapist as an ally and not a threat during the difficult early stages of adoption.

The creation of transitional phenomena in therapy – the green ball

I would now like to turn to a more theoretical discussion of playing and transitional phenomena. The idea of transitions, and the manner in which they are not 'either/

or', but are paradoxically 'both', is extremely pertinent when thinking about children in Sammy's position. Sammy's use of the green ball as a transitional object helped him to cope with the paradoxes of his life during the transition to his adoptive home. By managing to hold so many paradoxical feelings within him, rather than becoming torn apart by the internal conflicts they represented, he managed to stay remarkably together during a period in his life where he might have literally felt that his mind was 'blown'. Transitional phenomena (objects and experiences) help to contain and transform transitional anxiety within what might be experienced as a terrifying void or chaotic gap, into experiencing that same psychic or external space as being potentially bearable and creative (Fransman, 2002). Harnessing the creative potential that is present within a transition can be seen as a significant aim of the psychotherapy of looked-after children.

Therapy, alongside restorative experiences in foster placements, can provide the kind of environment in which new transitional phenomena can emerge. One of the qualities of this facilitating environment is providing the quiet and often repeated experience of what Winnicott (1958) evocatively describes as being 'alone in the presence of someone'. This experience is very relevant to the child's developing capacity to play, which in turn relates to the ordinary developmental creation of transitional phenomena. Through this concept of being 'alone in the presence of someone', Winnicott describes the states of mind that are likely to be present in the 'secure base' image of a child being able to playfully explore the environment in a state of absorption, as long as an attachment figure is present (Ainsworth, 1982; Bowlby, 1988).

In essence, I see what I conceptualise as transitional space as emerging slowly from the many small and cumulative experiences that the patient has of being alone in the presence of the therapist. It is an experience that can be thought of as a space in between them, which does not belong to one or the other person. This in-between nature of the space is uniquely created and generated between patient and therapist as the therapy progresses, and is what makes it transitional. It has to do with 'two-ness' creating 'one-ness'. It is similar to the idea that you cannot clap with one hand. Building on Winnicottian thinking, the in-between-ness of the clap itself is what makes these experiences 'transitional'. Initially in therapy, these experiences may be momentary. But if the therapist notices them, and is able to let them breathe a bit and 'be' a bit in the session, they gradually appear more often. Over time the therapist is able to observe more fully formed ideas, and then ideas which are played with – again, briefly at first – begin to emerge within the session. This is the way in which young children developmentally start to play. The ability grows quietly, initially dependent on the presence of the 'other' to keep it going and growing.

So it is possible to postulate that a child who cannot play, nevertheless may have the potential to play, if the relational conditions allow for this. The therapist may be able to provide this kind of relational environment, through his or her concentrated attunement to the patient during the session, together with his or her capacity to notice the tiny beginnings of ideas and play, and then nurture and pay further attention to them. The concentrated attunement on the part of the therapist is what creates the ground for the patient to gradually become aware of being alone in the presence of the therapist, and indeed the therapist to recognise that this is starting to happen.

Lest this description should sound too much like Nirvana, I would like to emphasise that what emerges in the shape of children's play during these times, is often painfully and frighteningly appropriate to their internal dilemmas. The transitional space is a place in which these painful issues can be addressed because the *vehicle* through which they can be expressed – be it play in a child, or free association, dreams and creative thought or expressions in the teenager or adult – have become more available for use. Sammy's 'baking of cakes' is a good example of the painful expression of emotional truths that can become possible in these circumstances.

The transitional space that the child becomes able to enter has certain characteristics that can help the therapist to recognise that the therapeutic journey has reached this place. But it is rather easier to say what this transitional space is *not*, than to say what it *is*. Transitional space is the opposite of a space in which the individual feels trapped, and unable to breathe, think and play. The sense of being stuck in endlessly repeating negative emotional experiences is a frequent complaint of those seeking psychotherapeutic help. By contrast, a sense of freedom and spontaneity characterises experiences that take place within the transitional space. It is in the transitional space that new ideas and possibilities emerge and can be played with in a safe way. It can be like emerging into an open space after being lost in the woods. But it can be very difficult to reach this place.

It is the acceptance of the essence of this space – that it is neither inner nor outer, past or future, the patient's or the therapist's, but paradoxically both – that contributes significantly to the feeling that this is a space in which anything could happen. It is a space full of potential and surprises where paradox – defined in the Concise Oxford Dictionary as 'a seemingly absurd or contradictory statement, even if actually well-founded' – can be tolerated. The freedom of playing with ideas relies heavily on the suspension of the ordinary rules of reality, and the suspension of 'either/or' thinking. This is not about the conflict of two opposing forces or feelings, but about the acceptance of their co-existence. This leads to the contemplation of what may seem absurd – such as two opposing feelings being true simultaneously.

It is important to acknowledge that for many very deprived and traumatised children, the creation of a transitional space can prove enormously elusive. The specific difficulties within each treatment of enabling this space to become alive, is one of the processes that therapists have to work with as creatively as possible. A long period of time in therapy may be spent in trying to enable a child to dare to let him or herself to be free enough, just to 'taste' the transitional space for long enough, to become attracted and intrigued by it.

Part of the therapist's task is to keep the possibility of entering this space as alive as possible within the therapy, despite the endless setbacks that inevitably take place in this process. It is often a question of 'trying and trying again'. Winnicott (1971: 44) writes intriguingly that one of the major tasks of the therapist is 'bringing the patient from a state of not being able to play into a state of being able to play'. This chapter has attempted to describe how this process can evolve in the therapy of children for whom adoption is planned, who are desperately in need of this experience because of the severe environmental failure they experienced at the start of their lives. I have argued that one of the most important functions of therapy is to enable children such as these to play, and through this, find their way towards the ordinary developmental processes which will continue in their lives. This is the process of recovery that therapy and well-supported adoptions are able to offer to children who have had such damaging and traumatic starts to their lives.

Note

This chapter is an extension of the thinking in Chapters 5 and 6 in *The Presence of the Therapist: Treating Childhood Trauma* (Lanyado, 2004) and includes some sections from these chapters.

References

Ainsworth, M. (1982) 'Attachment: retrospect and prospect', in C.M. Parkes and J. Stevenson-Hinde (eds) *The Place of Attachment in Human Behaviour*, London: Tavistock.

Bowlby, J. (1988) *A Secure Base: Clinical Applications of Attachment Theory*, London: Routledge.

Edwards, J. (2001) 'On being dropped and picked up: adopted children and their internal objects', *Journal of Child Psychotherapy*, 26 (3): 349–69.

Fransman, T. (2002) Personal Communication.

Gibbs, I. (2006) 'A question of balance: working with the looked after child and his network', in M. Lanyado and A. Horne (eds) *A Question of Technique*, Hove: Routledge.

Hindle, D. (2000) 'The merman: recovering from early abuse and loss', *Journal of Child Psychotherapy*, 26 (3): 369–91.

Hunter, M. (2001) *Psychotherapy with Young People in Care: Lost and Found*, London: Brunner-Routledge.

Ironside, L. (2002) 'Living in a storm: an examination of the impact of deprivation and abuse on the psychotherapeutic process and the implications for clinical practice', unpublished PhD thesis, University of East London and Tavistock Clinic Library.

Lanyado, M. (2004) *The Presence of the Therapist: Treating Childhood Trauma*, Hove: Brunner-Routledge

Lanyado, M. (2006) 'The playful presence of the therapist: "antidoting" defences in the therapy of a late adopted patient', in M. Lanyado and A. Horne (eds) (2006) *A Question of Technique*, Hove: Routledge.

Ogden, T.H. (1999) *Reverie and Interpretation: Sensing Something Human*, London: Karnac.

Stern, D., Sander, L., Nahum, J.P., Harrison, A.M., Ruth-Lyons, K., Morgan, A., Bruschweiler-Stern, N. and Tronick, E.Z. (1998) 'Non-interpretative mechanisms in psychotherapy: the "something more" than interpretation', *International Journal of Psychoanalysis*, 79: 903–21.

Winnicott, D.W. (1951) 'Transitional objects and transitional phenomena', in D.W. Winnicott, *Playing and Reality* (1974), Harmondsworth: Pelican.

Winnicott, D.W. (1958) 'The capacity to be alone', in D.W. Winnicott (1965) *The Maturational Processes and the Facilitating Environment*, London: Hogarth Press and Institute of Psychoanalysis.

Winnicott, D.W. (1965) *The Maturational Processes and the Facilitating Environment*, London: Hogarth Press.

Winnicott, D.W. (1971) *Playing and Reality*, London: Tavistock Publications, and Harmondsworth: Pelican Books (1974).

10 Just pretend

The importance of symbolic play and its interpretation in intensive psychotherapy with a four-year-old adopted boy

Francesca Calvocoressi

The barriers which prevent some children from settling into an adoptive home are intangible, but make themselves felt through behaviour which puzzles and disturbs. A situation may arise whereby a child not only suffers the loss of his parents of origin, but subsequently appears unable to access the love offered by his new adoptive parents and so suffers a 'double deprivation' (Williams, 1997).

This chapter draws on clinical vignettes to describe my work with a young boy, Jamie, who was adopted, aged three. In the following chapter (Chapter 11) Molly Ludlam describes her work with his parents and in Chapter 12 we reflect together on our collaborative work and the way in which this created a containing space in which their sense of being a family could develop. Here I hope to illustrate how it is possible for even very young adopted children to allow their imaginations to find expression in therapy, and how symbolic play can help them to find their way to a new reality through a therapeutic process of transformation. Therapy provided a window into Jamie's inner world, and a safe space in which he could explore feelings, anxieties and disturbing aspects of himself which seriously interfered with his relationship with his adoptive parents.

Referral

Jamie was four years old when he was referred to the Children and Young People's Service, a year after his adoption. His adoptive parents, a childless couple, described their indefinable sense of a lack of connection between Jamie and themselves – a feeling which was not always present, but which was sufficiently troubling for them to seek help.

Jamie had been taken into foster care at the age of three, because of serious physical and emotional abuse and neglect. Initially he seemed to settle well in his adoptive family, but the transition to school threw up all kinds of difficulties. His solution to feeling vulnerable was to 'tough it out', getting into fights with other children, tearing and dirtying his clothes and wrecking his toys. He could not explain his distress, but could only externalise it through his behaviour – indeed, at that time he was probably unaware of being distressed and lacked the capacity to know his feelings. At the point of referral, Jamie was in danger of once again being received into care, as his adoptive parents felt unable either to tolerate or to manage his behaviour. Feeling at a loss as to how to understand Jamie, they could not identify with him and were afraid that he was too damaged to become their son.

The assessment team formed a hypothesis that Jamie was terrified he did not belong. His removal from his birth mother had been as abrupt as his departure from his foster parents. In addition, Jamie's early experience of rejection and cruelty – which had left him with a severely damaged sense of self – appeared to be colouring his view of his current home. It was therefore agreed to offer Jamie intensive psychotherapy three times a week for a minimum of one year, in order to help him to mourn the loss of his birth mother and his foster parents, and to modify the effects of the emotional damage and negative self-image resulting from his experience of abuse and neglect in infancy. It was hoped that this would help him to be more able to forge a new relationship with his adoptive parents. Concurrently, it was agreed that his adoptive parents would meet fortnightly with an adult psychotherapist (see Chapter 11).

Therapy

Jamie's struggle to try and make sense of past relationships and to move towards a new parental couple who could respond to his need for containment – and with whom he felt he belonged – was to dominate his therapy sessions. What Jamie was unable consciously to process, let alone verbalise, was gradually revealed through the material of the sessions and in his relationship with his therapist and his adoptive parents.

Lost child

Jamie was a tall, sturdy child for his age, with a round face and bright eyes. It was some time, however, before I felt that he really noticed me, or allowed any contact between us to develop. Characteristically, he would arrive, dash headlong into the room, play busily with the toys provided for him, and then rush away again at the end of the session without saying 'good-bye'. Out of this maelstrom, certain patterns and themes began to emerge over time in his play, allowing a glimpse into Jamie's inner world. From the beginning he was attracted by the toy animals and was anxious to sort them into family groups, often singling out a sub-group of a parental couple and two babies. In his game, these babies would – for a variety of reasons – repeatedly become separated from their parents. As a consequence they would be thrown into dangerous or even deadly situations – for instance, deep and fast-flowing rivers, or crocodile-infested swamps. Alternatively, they would become wildly over-excited and unable to control themselves in their frenzied activities. The smallest of these animals – a dog, a tiny monkey and a baby kangaroo which fitted into a mother kangaroo's pouch – were in reality easily lost in the room. As they came to symbolise the most vulnerable, unattached part of Jamie, I found myself repeatedly becoming anxious about their fate, as if their loss would confirm Jamie's vulnerability. It seemed that a scenario of loss and abandonment was to be played out, but with very little emotional involvement on Jamie's part, while I was left carrying the anxiety – not only about the fate of the tiny toys, but also about Jamie's state of mind. While this imaginative play appeared to echo much of his actual history, it soon became clear that attempting to clarify connections in words was wholly ineffectual. Interpretations were met with a blank look of incomprehension or denial. It seemed that Jamie needed to enact certain situations repeatedly in order to have his communication received and acknowledged, but without being able to link this to his own history.

A child's understanding of the reasons for his adoption are complex. The knowledge of having been given up by biological parents inevitably feeds into a self-representation of being unwanted. Fantasies of having been kidnapped (Hodges, 1990) can serve as an antidote to these profoundly disturbing realities. Conversely, there may be unconscious guilt and sadness in transferring feelings of love from one parental figure to another. In the following extract from an early session it is possible to track some of the confusion in Jamie's mind, particularly in connection with feelings of being lost, fantasies of being kidnapped by a counterfeit mother, and guilt:

> Jamie decides that the baby kangaroo and dog will go hunting alone. Their parents are asleep. He moves the dog from the table onto the carpet. The baby kangaroo in the meantime has disappeared. Jamie hunts about for her anxiously and is very relieved when he spots her, grey against the grey carpet. 'She's so small', he says. I find that I too am relieved that he has found her. In spite of this adventure, the kangaroo sets off hunting and encounters the Mummy kangaroo, which is not, however, *her* Mummy. The kangaroo puts the baby in her pouch but this is all wrong: wrong baby, wrong pouch, wrong Mummy. The daddy lion wakes up and comes to snatch the baby out of the pouch and return her to her real Mummy (the lioness). Jamie repeats this action again. The mother kangaroo is left on her own, some distance away from the other animals. I ask Jamie how she is feeling. 'Sad', he replies, using a small sad voice and looking at me.

For many months, during which the baby animals struggled to survive against all the odds, I made few interpretations. It appeared that if I suggested that the parents were being rather careless or neglectful, Jamie tended to excuse them by explaining that 'they couldn't help it' or that 'they were tired'. In the vignette which follows, I think it is possible to see Jamie's struggle to make sense of parents who are unavailable and also to cling onto a version of his own parents as having wanted him, but not being able to care for him:

> A Mummy zebra and Daddy horse are both asleep … It is morning time and the horses call their parents to wake them up. This has no effect and so they increase their noise, calling, 'wake up!!' Jamie begins to raise his voice

and finally shouts. The parents continue to sleep. I comment on how hard it seems to be to get this Mummy and Daddy to wake up and pay attention to their babies. Jamie agrees and fetches the elephant, saying loudly, 'trample, trample, trample', while making the elephant stamp on the sleeping parents. They still don't wake up. The rhino is brought into play to create a disturbance. Finally, the zebra (mother) gets up slowly and asks in a very tired voice what the matter is, then falls down asleep again. The baby horses go over to her and start to feed from her ... I comment on the fact that the parents are still asleep, that they can't seem to take care of their children, but Jamie replies in a serious voice that they can't help it because they've been up very, very late.

As time went on and he developed a more open and trusting relationship with me, Jamie became less interested in the plight of abandoned baby animals and bolder in his play. Fights – either between the animals or between himself and invisible opponents – were now regularly enacted. It was difficult to distinguish between the different types of fighting – on the one hand fighting for fun, or on the other, fighting as a defensive act where serious aggression was being presented. One sort of fight would quickly tip into the other and back again, but when I tried to clarify what was happening, Jamie denied it, confirming my sense that his confusion was deeply embedded in his internal world.

At the same time there were reports that Jamie was exhibiting a great deal more aggression at home and at school and this was naturally causing a lot of anxiety for his parents. It became obvious that while Jamie was making huge strides socially, with the help of his adoptive parents, the question of how to manage his natural aggression remained problematic.

In the case of children such as Jamie, the necessary healthy aggression which promotes the development of personality (Furman, 1993) is all too often over-shadowed by a primitive aggression which threatens to overwhelm the child and which can feel equally threatening to adoptive parents. Where early years are characterised by inconsistent parenting and domestic violence – or worse still, abuse – children are traumatised and confused because they have received contradictory signals. They have also suffered a deprivation in being denied the opportunity to develop an internal regulator (Schore, 1994) to help them to understand their own and other people's emotions and behaviour. A mother normally helps her baby to make sense of the world around them by her words and actions. Developmental psychologists emphasise the role of the mother as auxiliary ego in the second half of the infant's first year. Without understanding from the caregiver, a child cannot develop their own understanding of the difference between normal aggression and a terrifying destructiveness.

It follows that it is crucial for a child in therapy to be able to express their aggression, but equally important that the therapist should survive these onslaughts to mind or even body, and remain emotionally available while not colluding with the child's aggression.

Who cares?

Six months after beginning psychotherapy, Jamie introduced a new theme in his play. He created the character of a mother who did not care about her child and, in parallel, a boy who was equally unaffected by her lack of care. There was a pervasive absence of feeling. The striking element in this material was the physical presence, but emotional absence, of a maternal figure and the way in which he, as her son, appeared to collude with the notion that children were better off when adults relinquished all responsibility. Since no one cared about Jamie – neither a mother nor a father, nor anyone else in the world – he could, as he explained, do as he pleased without being told off. He played at being bad at school, bringing back notes from the teacher for his mother to see, and was gleeful when she tore them up and praised his bad behaviour. The dilemma for me was Jamie's insistence that I should play the role of this irresponsible parent. He was not satisfied if I stood back and commented, but demanded a convincing representation of this neglectful maternal figure. The following vignette from a session gives a flavour of this extraordinary play:

> Jamie says he wants to be the boy with the not-caring Mum. He goes over and, glancing at me, tips his box of toys onto the floor and pretends to kick them. He then picks up the cushion and hits it around, kicking it and then throwing it. He takes his shoes off and throws them any-old-how across the carpet. I comment on this and then am instructed to say, 'Oh, well, I don't care about your toys. You've thrown your new shoes, anyway I don't care.'
>
> Jamie begins to pretend to destroy the room. He tells me he's breaking the lights, the windows, the furniture, the walls, the doors, the heating. All gets bashed up and broken but I, the Mum, am to sit and say, 'who cares?' He hurts his leg in the game and I am not to care about this either. He insists that no-one in the world cares. He is quite agitated and caught up in this game and I find myself reminding him repeatedly of the difference between his game and the reality of being with me. I say things like, 'What a horrible house that would be, what a pity the Mum in your game doesn't care, how awful to be a little boy who had no one who cared.'

In this session and many similar ones, Jamie appeared to be conveying unconscious memories of his early emotional experience as they came to the surface. Klein (1957) evocatively described this as 'memories in feeling'. Children who are cruelly treated cannot react. It is too dangerous. Yet in his play, Jamie communicated a great sense of urgency about my participating in his games. My experience was that of walking a tightrope – on the one hand, I worried about 'becoming' the abusing or neglectful parent in his mind, while on the other hand the game seemed to be helping Jamie to recall and make sense of early experiences and to process a terrifying situation where everything was topsy-turvy.

Jamie himself exhibited very little affect in his sessions, while I was often left with a sense of terrible sadness. In these games, it seemed as if I became the mother who had lost her baby and that I was to carry the experience of that catastrophe. But although Jamie appeared oblivious to the emotional content of the scenarios he created, I was continually aware of how much it mattered to him that we re-enact these games. The urgency of his tone and the way in which he threw himself with all seriousness into his role, finding new refinements each time, spoke volumes. Nevertheless, making direct connections in words with his history continued to feel precarious.

While his adoptive parents were all too aware of his difficulties, Jamie was not at a stage where he could articulate feelings, which in fact he was hardly conscious of owning. It seemed that at some level it still felt unsafe to verbalise strong feelings to his adoptive parents for fear of rejection. What was impressive was how much he was using his sessions to sort out, to try to understand, and to be understood.

The bully and the victim

At home, Jamie's behaviour became more manageable: he was less destructive or inclined to get into sulky or distant states. Unfortunately, he became quite bullying at school and rough with local children – which was particularly painful for his parents, as they then felt rejected by neighbours. It became clear that being in control by controlling other children was an antidote to an emerging sense of vulnerability. The following vignette, in which Jamie brought the bully boy into a session, illustrates this dilemma and highlights once again the problem of the lack of a reliable adult in his mind:

> I am the class teacher trying to keep order. Jamie is the terrified little boy coming to nursery school for the first time. He cowers in a corner, whimpering and hiding his face. My job is to coax him to come into the group. He gradually becomes a little braver, but still doesn't dare come too close. Jamie tells me that some of the children are laughing at him. I am to bring the class to order. The whole class is laughing and staring. I am apparently unable to keep control. One of the 'silly' boys gets up and begins to taunt the timid boy. I comment on how I as an adult seem unable to protect this sad and helpless little boy.
>
> Then there is a switch and Jamie becomes the mocking and aggressive child. He pretends to kick the frightened boy. I say, 'Where are the grown ups?' Jamie answers, 'All the grown ups are dead, they died in the war.' I say, 'How terrible, and now there seems to be no-one to protect the small and shy children. The bullies can do what they want.'

Much of therapy is concerned with observing and appreciating 'defence mechanisms' which are used to protect the self from anxiety. Because many looked-after children are exposed to intense levels of unsupportable fear, their defences tend to be strong, rigid attitudes that repel many advances.

The greater the danger, the stronger the fear, the weaker the child, the more do psychological means of protection have to create an illusion of bearable safety. Impotent fear is turned to illusory power, omnipotence.

Hunter (2001: 120)

Jamie could gain this illusory feeling of power by using his strength to overpower children at school – as he was big and strong for his age, it was easy for him. But he had been told by school and his parents that he could not carry on with this sort of behaviour, that it was unacceptable. I think that in the above session, Jamie demonstrated how terribly small and insignificant he could feel, while at the same time he seemed to be clearly acknowledging that his solution to the problem – becoming the bully – was not satisfactory. Unconsciously denying and attempting to obliterate the small vulnerable part of himself with an overbearing and cruel self, left Jamie with a lack of helpful internal parents on whom he could depend. In fact, as his play demonstrated, Jamie was clearly communicating his wish for a restraining presence from the adults who would understand that the bully was the victim in disguise.

Internal mess and its containment

Early on in our work together, Jamie had created many sessions in which the toy animals were lost, abandoned or exposed to terrifying experiences which conjured up nightmarish medieval images of hell, not unlike Bion's ([1962] 1967) description of 'nameless dread'. Bion used this term to describe the extreme state of fear that an infant can experience in the absence of a mother who is able to provide a containing function for powerful primitive anxieties. About a year into his therapy, Jamie was beginning to conceptualise things from a more secure position. There were journeys and separations, but also reunions. He became freer to express his aggression – for instance informing me that he was fighting me and describing what he was doing in chilling detail. It was now safe to be very angry in the transference with a mother who had abandoned him. He was also less difficult with his adoptive mother at home. It became possible for him to have a more realistic view of her, free of internal projections belonging to the past.

Then came a session where an imaginative scenario gave way to conscious memories of a particularly significant episode of his past. Jamie was lying on the floor on his back with his head near my feet and as he spoke, he stretched out his arms towards me – as if he wanted to be held – almost touching my hands, and looking back into my face. He said that he remembered, and went on to give a coherent account of an episode of his early life and his eyes filled with tears. After a short pause, he broke off and told me that he didn't want to talk about it anymore.

As Jamie neared the end of his therapy, a new version of his game was created. I was to be the mum who *did* care:

He goes over to one of the small chairs and tips it over, then knocks over the waste-paper basket. The contents spill onto the floor. I say, 'Oh dear, you've knocked over the chair. Could you put it back please?', which he does. I add that I will put the rubbish back in the bin. Jamie stands on the furniture and indicates that I am to tell him to get down. He decides he's playing football outside with his friends. He's getting extremely muddy because it's been raining and he's the goalie. He comes back for tea. I am to comment on his state, which I do, without telling him off. I ask what clothes he's been playing in. Old clothes, apparently. He asks for Coca-Cola to drink. I say that I don't think this would be his usual teatime drink and he agrees, saying in an accepting tone, 'OK then, I'll have water.' He informs me that he's going out to play football again and is going to get even muddier. He mimes falling face down in the mud and getting completely covered, face and all. I am to be tolerant and ask him for his muddy clothes, which I will sort out and wash while he gets cleaned up in a bath.

Jamie, in getting into a pretend mess, was revisiting a most important but potentially dangerous theme. How safely could he get into a mess, or express the messy and messed up part of himself? Would there, in the transference relationship, be reprisals – or could something more ordinary happen? That is, could Jamie begin to envisage a more tolerant and helpful parental figure? At every stage of this piece of the game, Jamie directed my response, indicating that I could wash his clothes, that I was not angry and that he could have a bath at the end of the day. This brought to mind one of the first conversations with his adoptive parents, in which they had highlighted this very problem – Jamie's apparent need repeatedly to mess up his clean clothes – and their difficulty in dealing with this on an emotional level.

Concluding remarks

Jamie's struggle to try and make sense of past relationships and to move towards a new parental couple who could respond to his need for containment, and with whom he felt he belonged, was to dominate his therapy sessions. What Jamie was unable consciously to process, let alone verbalise, was gradually revealed through the material of the sessions and in his relationship with me.

Jamie was lucky in having been placed with a couple who became aware quite quickly that there was something wrong – that there was an obstacle preventing him from connecting with them – therefore they looked for help. He was able to make very good use of this opportunity and give expression through his play to what he faced in his internal world: terror of abandonment, fear of his own aggression and lack of control. At the end of therapy Jamie was reported to be more settled at school and there was a sense that he and his parents were beginning to feel like a family.

I hope to have illustrated the way in which it is possible for even very young children to allow their imaginations to find expression in therapy, and how this symbolic play can help them to find their way to a new reality. This new reality partly involves developing for the first time – or re-discovering – different aspects of themselves, and different internal representations of parental figures, which critically shape new relationships.

I would like to conclude with some insights about imagination from Britton's *Belief and Imagination* (1998: 121): 'when we imagine things taking place we do so in a space, therefore we also have to imagine the space they take place in'.

On the basis of his clinical work, Britton conceptualises this space as 'the other room'. He goes on to write:

> When we place our phantasies about events in this psychic 'other room' we know we are imagining something … If we are prepared to accept that the proper place for these phantasies is the 'other room' we can use our imagination.
>
> Britton (1998: 121)

References

Bion, W. R. (1962) 'A theory of thinking', in *Second Thoughts*, London: Karnac, 1967.

Britton, R. (1998) *Belief and Imagination: Explorations in Psychoanalysis*, London: Routledge.

Furman, E. (1993) *Toddlers and their Mothers*, Madison, CT: International Universities Press.

Hodges, J. (1990) 'The relationship to self and objects in early maternal deprivation, and adoption', *Journal of Child Psychotherapy*, 16 (1): 53–73.

Hunter, M. (2001) *Psychotherapy with Young Children in Care: Lost and Found*, Hove: Brunner-Routledge.

Klein, M. (1955) 'The psychoanalytic play technique: its history and significance', in *Envy and Gratitude*, London: Virago, 1988.

Schore, A.N. (1994) *Affect Regulation and the Origin of the Self*, Hillsdale, NJ: Lawrence Erlbaum Associates.

Williams, G. (1997) 'Double deprivation', in *Internal Landscapes and Foreign Bodies: Eating Disorders and Other Pathologies*, London: Duckworth.

11 The longing to become a family

Support for the parental couple

Molly Ludlam

This chapter presents parallel therapeutic work with a parental couple, whose adopted child was referred for psychotherapy (see Chapter 10). It also considers the challenges that adoptive parents, and those who seek to support them, might encounter in their progress towards becoming a family. The issues arising from the particular experience of engaging in parallel work with this family are further discussed in Chapter 12.

Idealisation of the family

Many adoptive families find there is a gulf between the idealised family which has developed in the minds of the parents and of their adoptive child, and the actual family which they discover in real life. The wish to form intimate relationships appears to be a fundamental characteristic of being human. Suttie (1935) and Fairbairn (1941) have helped psychotherapists to conceptualise the longing to seek and remain in relationship as innate. Fairbairn described a journey of personal growth, from the infant's state of complete dependence to the adult's final hoped-for destination of mature dependence, noting that dependence on relationships with others is essential throughout such a developmental journey. From the starting point of dependence on parents, he perceived the growing person as gradually widening that dependence, ultimately to rest it in culture and society.

Fairbairn's concept describes the ideal path, attainable when the environment during development allows for dependence. We know that, sadly, it does not always do so. At their best, the institutions of marriage and family facilitate an inherently vulnerable process. While they are often idealised, these human institutions inevitably also express human failings. Thus part of the crisis to be addressed by a therapeutic or helping relationship is to consider the loss and mourning of such idealisations.

Dependence and interdependence in nurturing relationships

Where there is a parental couple, the nature and strength of the bond between them as a couple is enormously significant in determining the nature and strength of the dependence available to their infant and growing child. The couple relationship becomes the equivalent of that 'secure base' which Bowlby (1988) defined as the essential resource from which children can take their points of departure and growth from parents.

When parents are under stress, as naturally happens at times of transition, such as with the arrival of a child, they experience challenges to their ability to provide their child with what Winnicott (1960) termed 'holding'. The holding environment allows children to experience dependence and the 'containment' (Bion, 1962) of their anxiety and distress. Psychotherapists therefore seek to mirror this, by offering a holding environment and containment through a temporary state of dependence on their security and trust. In this way a therapist working with the parental couple can help to strengthen the parental couple's resources, and thus also offer support to the whole family system. If the parental couple relationship can contain the couple's own anxieties, it is much more able to offer a containing resource to the child (Rustin, 1998; Cowan and Pape Cowan, 2001).

Supporting the creative couple

All of this lends weight to the belief in and the practice, where possible, of offering parallel work with parents when a child is offered individual psychotherapeutic treatment (see Chapter 3). Nevertheless, what is considered best practice may prove to be an obstacle, as it has cost and resource implications for both families and services. This can lead to resources being focused exclusively on the child as the presenting problem; this is at the expense of both the child and the parental couple, since in such circumstances the couple's own problems and concerns receive relatively little attention. In turn, this may serve to exacerbate the tendency, observed commonly in parental couples, to triangulate their own conflicts and difficulties, dealing with them vicariously by seeing them as belonging only to their child.

Couple psychotherapists have helped to define what it is that characterises the dependable environment which couples need from a therapist in order to feel safe enough to work through a relationship crisis. This process may usefully be considered in relation to the 'crisis' of the arrival of an adopted child, especially when it is the couple's first child. Morgan (2001) describes the therapist as needing the capacity to hold a 'couple state of mind' through which containment and a holding environment can be achieved. Morgan built on the concepts of marriage as a 'psychological container' (Colman, 1993) and of the 'creative couple' (Morgan and Ruszczynski, 1998), and concluded that the couple in the mind of the therapist is experienced as truly containing when it is conceptualised by the therapist as a 'creative couple state of mind', one which can envisage mutual nurture and growth. This capacity might be considered to be especially important when working with adoptive couples who have been unable to conceive their own children and whose sense of being creative, both physically and emotionally, has been profoundly challenged by that experience. The psychotherapist must be aware of the couple's need to grieve, whilst also acknowledging and nurturing the longing to be creative.

These issues are illustrated in the following account of work with Fiona and Bob, the adoptive parents of Jamie (see Chapter 10) who was referred for therapy when his placement with them was at risk of breaking down.

Case illustration: work with Jamie's parents

From the outset, the agreement to offer Jamie three times weekly child psychotherapy for the period of one year was part of a treatment package in which I would also meet fortnightly with Bob and Fiona, his parents. A great deal of care went into making these arrangements, as we were aware that Jamie's behaviour and his whole future were causing enormous concern. So much seemed to be invested in the success of his psychotherapy that we were concerned that if it (and we) failed to help him, he might be returned to foster care. If that happened, would his parents' hopes of creating a family then be lost forever?

Jamie's therapy thus became a focus for very powerful anxieties and fears about failure and loss. On reflection, fear of such compounded losses was probably central to the family's crisis. Thus, although my primary task was to support Jamie's parents during his psychotherapy and to help them to create a tolerant space for him in their family, I was also aware that this would depend on whether they could be helped to think about other pre-occupations. These were their understandably overwhelming fear of the permanent loss of their son, their grief at the non-arrival of birth children, together with their hope that they might yet create a family.

The team in which Jamie's psychotherapist and I worked was part of a wide network of services for this family, involving many relationships and boundaries to be negotiated. The network around the family, which provided the wider holding environment for our therapeutic service, unwittingly reflected many of the family's needs and characteristics. Fiona's mother having died two years before the adoption, the network, albeit unconsciously, offered her many other mothers on whom she could be dependent and who could witness her transition to motherhood. Reverberations of the family's anxieties were also felt in the network, and washed back in waves to our team. My ongoing working relationship with Jamie's psychotherapist proved invaluable for thinking about this, and, in time, in helping to contain this dynamic therapeutically (see Chapter 12).

At our first meeting, I learned that Bob and Fiona had originally applied to adopt more than one child and that they still hoped, in time, Jamie would have more siblings. I soon appreciated that they were wary of any enquiry on my part which might suggest their rejection as suitable parents. Bob made it clear at the start – as if pre-empting any focus on them – that they were just there to sort out Jamie. There would be no need for anything like the 'third degree' pre-adoption enquiry. Fiona added, 'What Bob means is that we have gone through all those hurdles. We know why we want children and that we are OK. We just want Jamie to settle, so we can love him like our very own.' I imagined that our meeting might be evoking painful echoes of the uncertainty and critical enquiry experienced during the pre-adoption assessment. I would need therefore to try, delicately, to separate this work with them from that previous experience.

From my experience of meeting with adoptive parents, I am aware that the pre-selection assessment may leave prospective parents feeling exposed and needing to protect themselves. This raises a dilemma, since careful pre-adoption scrutiny is vital and may even serve to test a couple's resilience and the strength of their motivation. But it may also deter parents from seeking the help and support they need early on in the crucial immediate period following the adoption, for fear that being seen to struggle then would be considered as an indication of failure. Sometimes adopted children bring with them damage or disadvantage which goes unrecognised or unacknowledged. Sadly, early unattended difficulties can become entrenched and so much more difficult to address when they are compounded by subsequent disappointment and resentment about a lack of foreknowledge or support.

I therefore acknowledged Fiona and Bob's deep concern about Jamie: that I thought they were right to bring him to my colleague for her help, and that, at this time of crisis, we appreciated that they too needed support. Jamie would probably find his sessions sometimes disturbing and thus our own meetings would be somewhere they could think about what was going on for him and how that affected them both.

They appeared relieved at this, but keen to be business-like. Fiona quickly produced some notes they had brought and plunged into an agenda, filling the space with a 'shopping list' of questions. Even though I appreciated their need for something structured, I had to struggle not to feel inadequate. I could see that the list provided them with some security, whereas free-floating thinking might overwhelm them, or my own questions might expose them. I felt unable to ask them to put it aside. This and subsequent meetings often seemed to be driven by worries, more like school parents' meetings than a place to reflect on hurt and disappointments.

With meetings so pre-occupied by anxieties, I felt inhibited about asking what might be considered intrusive, or critically loaded, questions, for fear of upsetting their seemingly tenuous place with me. Nevertheless, I felt curious about their childlessness and about how much they had felt supported by each other in the loss of having no children of their own. To explore such issues would have felt like venturing on rather thin ice. Their paramount need was for time to pour out all their frustrations and concerns and the time allotted was easily filled. In this way, Bob and Fiona kept a hold on the agenda. While Jamie was their prime pre-occupation, they also worried about future siblings they still hoped to adopt and who seemed to represent lost children. These pre-occupations maintained them primarily in their parental roles, almost eclipsing thoughts about their couple relationship.

The work of the first few months was primarily that of hearing their complaint, of recognising their disappointment and of trying to give them another emotional language with which to make sense of Jamie's desperate, confused and confusing messages. This was a slow process because their appointments with me could only be made, at best, every fortnight, and for a phase, once a month. Understandably, sometimes it was only possible for one of them to attend. Although they faithfully brought Jamie for his individual sessions, they were sparing in what they could allow for themselves; it felt like a minimum toehold in the door. Giving Jamie's needs such priority had the effect of putting his parents in a defensive relationship with us and of marginalising them. It seemed as if most of their needs, their own hunger, had to be met through him. In this way Jamie risked becoming like a cuckoo in their nest, with themselves as anxious parent birds – so pre-occupied with meeting his insatiable appetite, that they could not afford to be aware of their own needs.

Unconsciously, Jamie needed to test the strength of their resolve to remain his parents and, understandably, they were often outraged by him. At times Fiona and Bob appeared surprised by and unprepared for such testing of their love. Bob's upbringing had taught him never to be physically aggressive and when Jamie got into trouble at school for fighting, he could not identify with him. Both parents felt troubled by the anger and rejection Jamie's aggression aroused in them. Sent to his room, Jamie would wreck his bed and his toys, so confirming his parents' conviction that his placement wasn't working and that he would have to go.

At these times, I found myself caught up in the anxiety everyone involved seemed to share, that Jamie would be sent away. I had to remind myself that my role was to try to contain these feelings, so as to enable Bob and Fiona to understand and tolerate this little boy's turbulence. There was a delicate line to tread in translating the possible messages of his behaviour, whilst at the same time supporting his parents as adults. It seemed to be helpful to them to interpret the dynamic of the situation by explaining that Jamie communicated with them by getting them to feel as he did, that is, frightened, rejected and angry. Now that he felt relatively safe with them, he was in effect asking them to help him express all the feelings which originated in his relationship with his birth family, as discussed in the previous chapter. Having established this way of thinking, it was possible to explore all the infantile feelings which Jamie aroused in Fiona and Bob, which they then needed one another to understand and contain. We could also think about how Jamie looked for ways of coming between them, as if to separate them whilst unconsciously testing the strength of their relationship, to see whether, unlike his birth parents, they would stay together for him.

When, after several months of his psychotherapy, the threat of the breakdown of Jamie's adoption receded, it was apparent that Fiona and Bob's assertion of their parental roles in our meetings had, in part, expressed their fear that losing Jamie would mean the devastating loss to them of parenthood itself. I could appreciate then how I might be seen as a superior, powerful parent. It made me wonder how much their concept of themselves as a couple was dependent on being procreative, like their parents, and I then felt able to ask about their inability to have children of their own. I also acknowledged that it had not always been easy to meet with me. Bob shook his head, 'I think we just longed to be a "normal" couple, no questions asked. Two reasonably happy adults with two reasonably happy kids.' I concluded that their ideal internal couple was complete with two children, certainly not with only two adults.

Fiona said, 'I wonder if we need a problem. You know, like other people need a drink – or a dog! Somehow we can't let it go, as if we need a problem to worry about.'

I said, 'And Jamie has become the problem you can't let go?' Fiona replied, 'Yes, perhaps. After we talked here about what our parents expected of us, I've been thinking how it's wrong to expect Jamie to be the child we dreamed of having. There's no such thing as a perfect little boy, or a perfect person. I was watching him playing the other day and he was having a lovely time covered in paint, and I thought I wouldn't change him for anything. It's enough to see him being himself. We have decided that just now is not the time to be going ahead with adopting more children. We don't think Jamie's ready yet for that.' Bob nodded. He said he knew how much Fiona had wanted the family she had dreamed of, and that he wished he could have helped make that dream come true. It seemed to me they were both able to grieve a little more and to let unrealistic hopes go.

Afterthoughts about this engagement

As I have explored above, the process of this therapeutic work with adoptive parents involved me in witnessing a very gradual process of their relinquishment of feelings which were at one and the same time unbearable, and yet so hard to let go. My hypothesis is that the void left by the birth child who could not be theirs was unconsciously filled by Fiona and Bob with a dream of a child who was 'just right' for them. That such a child might not exist aroused intolerable disappointment and this in itself became problematic for them. To let that disappointment go would involve mourning for so much that could never happen, for without mourning there can be no letting go. Seeing that their disappointment and their sense of an ever-present problem had become interchangeable for these parents, helped me to understand that holding on to a problem was akin to holding on to disappointment. Because the parents' disappointment was unbearable however, their worry and the problem were projected onto the child. When his parents identified Jamie with their disappointment, he easily took this on and readily expressed it, because being a disappointment was a familiar role he had brought with him to his new family. But this meant that his parents' own grief for the perfect child who could never be theirs was not openly expressed.

We might also hypothesise that Fiona and Bob, like many adoptive parents, had unconsciously hoped to contain their loss of a child by assuaging another child's losses, an issue which is discussed in the next chapter. They had seemingly, however, been unprepared for what felt like an undeserved attack that such a damaged and deprived little boy could make on their love and idealisation. On top of this they had undergone the normal crises which a recently reconstituted family might expect, experiencing all the trauma of the arrival of a new baby, but without the emotional and psychological preparation usually afforded by pregnancy. There was not even a period of physical infancy. Jamie had arrived feeling that he must immediately prove his acceptability and so not display any vulnerability, straight into the laps of parents who were concerned that they should prove their adequacy. In their turn, they had to discover how to see themselves as a couple, without being the ideal family they had envisaged they should be.

Might this couple also have been relating unconsciously to internal parents who seemed critical and withholding as parents towards their own inner child and who thus denied them the right to put their needs first? If so, such inner parents might have been felt unconsciously by Bob and Fiona to be embodied in the hospital services, the social services, our service and their own bodies. Perceptions of this kind however remained hypotheses and could only have been explored once their child's psychotherapy had safely ended. In the event, Jamie's psychotherapy ended after one year, prompted by the conclusion of the contract and the funding arrangements. Although it seemed, in psychotherapeutic terms, an early ending, Jamie was already much more settled both at home and at school. Important work had been accomplished by his parents in helping them all to have a surer sense of belonging together.

In summary, my initial role was to help support Jamie's parents, to strengthen the holding environment by keeping it in mind. This meant tolerating the parental transference, the anxiety about not being adequate. As work with this parental couple developed however, it became evident that in order to help them become a family, it would also be necessary creatively to hold in mind this couple's grief and their fear of further losses. With the integration of all these feelings, the belief in the potential of their relationship to become the creative couple they longed to be was allowed its rightful place.

Note

This chapter is a substantially revised version of the chapter 'Psychotherapy for the parents as a couple', in J. Savege Scharff and D.E. Scharff (eds) *New Paradigms for Treating Relationships*, New York: Jason Aronson.

References

Bion, W. (1962) *Learning from Experience*, London: Heinemann.

Bowlby, J. (1988) *A Secure Base*, London: Routledge.

Colman, W. (1993) 'Marriage as a psychological container', in S. Ruszczynski (ed.) *Psychotherapy with Couples*, London: Karnac.

Cowan, P. and Pape Cowan, C. (2001) 'Transmission of attachment patterns', in C. Clulow (ed.) *Adult Attachment and Couple Psychotherapy*, London: Brunner Routledge.

Fairbairn, W.R.D. (1941) 'A revised psychopathology of the psychoses and psychoneuroses', in *Psychoanalytic Studies of the Personality*, London: Routledge and Kegan Paul (1952).

Morgan, M. (2001) 'First contacts: the therapist's "couple state of mind" as a factor in the containment of couples seen for consultations', in. F. Grier (ed.) *Brief Encounters with Couples: Some Analytical Perspectives*, London: Karnac.

Morgan, M. and Ruszczynski, S. (1998) 'The creative couple', unpublished paper presented at Tavistock Marital Studies Institute 50th Anniversary Conference.

Rustin, M. (1998) 'Dialogues with parents', *Journal of Child Psychotherapy*, 24 (2): 233–42.

Suttie, I.D. (1935) *The Origins of Love and Hate*, London: Kegan Paul, Trench Trubner.

Winnicott, D.W. (1960) 'The theory of parent–infant relationship', in *The Maturational Processes and the Facilitating Environment*, London: Hogarth (1965).

12 Shared reflections on parallel collaborative work with adoptive families

Francesca Calvocoressi and Molly Ludlam

This chapter brings together two perspectives based on our respective separate narratives of our collaborative work (see Chapters 10 and 11). We aim to convey through our reflections some of the challenges to be processed together when working in parallel. Our discussion here represents a distillation of the dialogue which we had both during and after our involvement with Jamie's family, and which we believe served as an important container for their and our work.

Our experience of working together has prompted us to draw a number of conclusions; some of them are drawn from our general experience of working with adoptive families, others derive from this particular collaborative experience, for which we are indebted to Jamie and his parents. We discuss what makes parallel collaborative psychotherapy effective, instancing how working together enables anxiety to be contained and the capacities to bear loss and to mourn to be nurtured. We also stress the importance of being aware of defences against disappointment and of the significance of memory, history and narratives of self. Finally we conclude with thoughts about endings in this kind of work.

We begin, however, by reflecting on two particular developmental tasks for both parents and children as the context in which therapeutic work must take place.

Belonging and becoming as developmental tasks

The psychological processes of belonging and becoming encompass two profoundly important and linked developmental tasks. In belonging, we form attachments to others with whom we identify. They become our own kith and kin. Once a kinship attachment has been formed, we can embark on becoming, the process of establishing a sense of self and identity. These two processes take place within the containing environment of the family. Some families however, offer an uncertain and unstable environment, in which the experience of belonging and becoming is fraught with risk and disappointment.

The bonding between mother and baby, parent and child is sometimes compared with falling in love. Falling in love is a heady process of recognition of likeness, of 'identifying with'. In the process of adoption such recognition may accrue more slowly. The aim of the careful assessment in the pre-adoption phase is to maximise matching and promote the recognition of positive shared characteristics. When a sense of belonging together is found, parents and child can become a family, and each member can grow to discover their potential.

In *every* family, this sense of belonging has to be found, it can never be imposed. When we are called on to assist a family where the adoption may irretrievably break down, we have to step aside from our own desires for a happy ending, to allow and to contain the fear of falling out of love, and to permit the respective family members to retrieve what they feel they can own. It can be a heart-wrenching experience for the practitioner who is working alone, and when working collaboratively we may find ourselves taking up the opposing split positions, mirroring the love/hate or the love/loss-of-love splits in the family. As our experience bears out, at such times it is crucial for practitioners to be able to digest together the unpalatable feelings which they have been asked to take in and 'swallow'.

What makes parallel collaborative psychotherapy effective?

Our experience endorses the widely accepted principle that when individual psychotherapy is offered to a child, it should be conducted, whenever possible, in the context of ongoing support for his or her adoptive parents (see Chapter 3). Such parallel work provides an essential forum for thinking with the parents about the child's development and changing needs. We would moreover argue that the efficacy of a parallel service of this kind lies in the concurrent establishment of close collaboration between the respective psychotherapists; hence our stress on parallel *collaborative* therapy. This collaboration requires not merely that the two psychotherapies run concurrently, with occasional meetings between them, but also that they should work to maintain their professional relationship so that they can monitor how the stresses experienced within and between them may be mirroring what is happening in the family. (We instance this below with particular reference to containing anxiety.) We see this professional relationship acting as a lynchpin in the whole system, parallel with the position of the parental–couple relationship in the family system.

What implications do we see for both family members and professionals of recommending parallel work? Parents may understandably have feelings about their adoptive child forming a relationship with a therapist at a time when their own relationship with their child is in the process of being established (see Chapter 14). Nevertheless, parallel work may offset potential difficulties, while providing an opportunity to consider complex changes involved in becoming parents, as well as understanding difficulties the child has that can interfere with forming new attachments.

Working together to contain anxiety

There are two particular, related tasks which collaborating psychotherapists must undertake. These are to contain anxiety and to nurture capacities in the family to bear loss and to mourn.

Our joint work and shared reflection helped us in particular to make sense of the way in which anxieties were being processed separately, by the child and by his parents. Our common psychotherapeutic language and training greatly facilitated joint thinking and the processing of our experience – our 'countertransference'. It proved essential to know that the other was 'there', and potentially available should a need arise. This allowed us to consider what might be being communicated in the atmosphere of almost overwhelming anxiety – the sense of precariousness about survival and the focus on the work with Jamie, as if *his* psychotherapy alone had to bear the greatest strain. This seemed to mirror an apparently fragile hope that all would be well if only Jamie were 'cured'.

Jamie's struggle to try and make sense of past relationships and to move towards a new parental couple, who could respond to his need for containment, and with whom he felt he belonged, was to dominate his therapy sessions. What Jamie was unable consciously to process, let alone verbalise, was gradually revealed through the material of the sessions and in his relationship with his therapist.

We can now see that his parents, Bob and Fiona, were, in parallel, undertaking their own journey. Initially this entailed learning to contain Jamie's terror of rejection, as well as their own anxieties about proving adequate as parents, and particularly as parents of a boy who had been deeply affected by his early experiences. As argued in Chapter 11, the attainment of a positive mutative outcome was dependent on recognition of their shared grief, as well as acknowledgement of their hope and their potential to become a creative couple. We have learned from this that, not only is parallel work with parents important in supporting child psychotherapy, but also where possible the psychotherapy offered to parents should take account of the significance of their couple relationship, as it plays such a crucial role in the family system.

Defences against disappointment

Our general experience has helped us to understand that problems may arise particularly for parents who have been unable to have their own child: such parents have to manage simultaneously re-emerging disappointment about their lack of fertility alongside realisation of their resentment about the damage that has been done to their adopted child. Disappointment can so easily spill over from a sense of personal loss to disappointment that their child is carrying significant damaging losses of his or her own. At this point, the strength of the parental couple's relationship is an important bulwark in helping them to contain their own disappointment. If they cannot do so, they may resort unconsciously to requiring their child to bear it.

Nurturing capacities to bear loss and to mourn

We assume that, by definition, all adoptive children and the majority of prospective adopting parents will approach the task of making a new family with separate histories of losses, the nature of which may never be fully understood by each other, no matter how much each wishes to do so. When unmet expectations cannot be easily reconciled, or there are difficulties in tolerating the pain and anxiety arising from the child's earlier traumatic experiences, an assessment of the whole family system, so as to locate appropriate foci for the therapeutic work, is as important for adoptive families as for all therapeutic endeavours with parents and children.

The correlation between the adoptive parents' capacity to mourn their own loss and their ability to provide a supportive enough environment in which the child's mourning can find expression is crucial. As Winnicott (1958) has pointed out, the complex process of mourning is dependent on the maturity of the individual. Therefore an infant or small child who does not yet have the capacity to mourn, nor even possibly the conscious knowledge of what was lost, will need the ongoing long-term support of an environment in which sadness and anger can find expression, before a working through of the mourning process is possible.

From our experience, we hypothesise that there are indeed profound underlying dynamics which continually make it difficult, for families and psychotherapists alike, to hold such compound losses simultaneously in mind. In our discussions with each other, we discovered difficulties in making space to consider the interaction of the family's newly compounded loss. We say this because we experienced a compulsion invariably to consider Jamie's needs first, as the more vulnerable, before Bob and Fiona's needs were also thought about. That is, we were aware of a powerful tendency to separate the child's needs from, rather than to link them with, those of his parents. With hindsight, we see that this might also have come about because of our steadfast attempts to hold the boundaries between our work; for, despite communicating regularly together, we maintained a confidentiality between us about the factual content of our respective psychotherapeutic sessions.

In the light of the above, it may not be surprising that we also often spoke about the pervasive presence of anxiety which continually prompted reaction and threatened to overwhelm everyone's capacity to think. When we appreciated that the stupefying feeling was a response to fear and was a countertransference communication, we were then able to wonder together about how the family's interaction might be affecting our thinking. This proved significant because it helped to inform how we responded in our separate subsequent meetings with Jamie and his parents. For example, as Bob and Fiona's anxiety was better contained and the meaning of their anxiety was thought about, Jamie in turn became progressively freer to express his disturbance in his psychotherapy sessions. In understanding this process, Bion's (1962) notion of container–contained is helpful. Thus parental anxiety aroused by Jamie's angry and upset behaviour, which his parents found difficult to accept, could, over time, be thought about, 'de-toxified' and de-personalised, and fed back in discussion with his parents – and then, in turn, to him – as something that was manageable and understandable. A further example of this lies in the provision of thinking space for us in our psychotherapeutic service. The work with Jamie was conducted within a Child and Family Service, and we therefore had access to consultation from an experienced supervisor who was skilled in creating space for thinking. That space for thinking can be seen to have been mirrored in Jamie's own moment of reflection as he lay on the floor (see Chapter 10).

It appears that the creation of a multi-layered holding environment, as conceptualised by Winnicott (1960), was also important in enhancing capacities in the family for learning and growth. The picture evoked by this concept resembles a series of concentric onion rings, each with a semi-permeable membrane allowing for movement between the layers. At the outer ring, there is the container of supervision; then, progressively moving inwards, there are reviews with the parents, joint thinking between therapists, Jamie's individual sessions, and so on, to interaction between the parental partners, and finally, at the centre, the relationship between the parents and their child.

As professional partners in this work we were fortunate on having a good ongoing working relationship. Nevertheless it is interesting to note how often we spoke in reaction to a family crisis, in addition to our regular three-way supervisory meetings. This leads us to observe how important it is, in principle, that busy practitioners set up regular opportunities to confer, rather than to rely on meeting only when crises arise. We can now appreciate that the pattern of our discussions also allowed us to construct an additional narrative to those which we were hearing from Jamie, Fiona and Bob, so that together we engaged in a dialogue, of the kind which we hoped might emerge between the parental couple and between the parents and their child.

Memory, history and narratives of self

Our shared experience of working with this family has highlighted the place of memory in constructing narratives. Initially, the family members were only able to focus on what was happening in the present, as might be expected in a time of crisis. With encouragement, they were subsequently able to reflect on earlier stages of their lives. In so doing, they might be said to have been looking after their own inner child, and in the process, creating and re-creating narratives about that child.

As a child who had been passed from one family to another, Jamie did not know how he should appear in order to be acceptable. In the process of his adoption, Bob and Fiona had been given a negative account of his birth family and were frightened that if Jamie was not like them, his adoptive parents, he might then grow to be a replica of his birth father. It is not uncommon, particularly where behaviour problems threaten to destabilise the home, that there may be worries about imagined adverse inherited character traits or genetic factors. It was our task to enable them all to tell and retell their individual memories and histories, allowing new narratives to emerge and giving space for Jamie's own separate identity to be recognised. In this we aimed to contain fears and anxieties of different kinds, both conscious and unconscious. Experience has taught us not to underestimate the difficulty and delicacy of the task. Experiences in infancy may not be accessible to conscious memory and the painfulness of early childhood experience often blocks memory in children so powerfully that the memory loss can persist into adult life. Whilst such blocks may serve as vital short-term defences, they can of course impede parents and psychotherapists alike in the task of helping children to mourn their past.

Adoptive parents may struggle fully to understand the meaning of their child's experiences: it is however crucial that they appreciate something of the nature of their child's infancy and life before joining them in a way that enables them to hold it in mind, without letting their concern or distress about it distort their perception of their child. This is an extraordinarily difficult psychological task. Sometimes referring to life with the birth family in front of the child can be experienced as punitive, especially when abuse or neglect is repeatedly referred to as an explanation for present misdemeanours, or as an expression of parents' disappointment for their less than perfect child. In this way, early abuse may be unwittingly repeated. By providing a separate thinking space for the parental couple, the meaning of such painful re-enactments can be understood and 'de-toxified'.

Endings

When it comes to assessing whether psychotherapy has been 'good enough', and judging when it is time to stop, it is necessary to distinguish between the abatement of the child's troubling behaviour, which might appear to happen quite quickly, and the longer-term process of internalisation and ego strengthening which allows the growing child to know and express more of his authentic self.

When Jamie's psychotherapy came to an end after the agreed year at his parents' request, we felt somewhat concerned that this ending might be prompted by a premature sense of relief at the apparent lessening of his disturbance. Jamie had initially presented as a boy who could not bear to think – an 'all action' boy. At the end of a year, his parents were indeed better able to tolerate and understand the meaning of his behaviour, although he remained over-active, still needing to externalise feelings. Perhaps Bob and Fiona also needed to relinquish their dependency on their therapist/parental figure and to prove themselves, through reclaiming Jamie, as parents in their own right. Given the significance for all the members of the family of endings and losses, of the intolerable drawing out of transition phases and the ambivalence about dependence, we feel that we should not be surprised that there was a sense of something hurried and not completed with this ending.

Nevertheless, we assessed that the joint work provided a secure base which Jamie and his parents could draw on for support and nurture during a period of transition and growth and one that they could let go when the internal integration was felt to be good enough to sustain the next phase of their journey.

References

Bion, W. (1962) *Learning from Experience*, London: Heinemann.

Winnicott, D.W. (1958) *Collected Papers: Through Paediatrics to Psychoanalysis*, London: Karnac (1992).

Winnicott, D.W. (1960) 'The theory of parent–infant relationship', in *The Maturational Processes and the Facilitating Environment*, London: Hogarth (1965).

Part V

Being part of a family

Oedipal issues

Introduction

Debbie Hindle

> The entry into the Oedipus complex involves the introduction of a distinctly
> new form of otherness into the mother–infant dyad that requires a radical
> psychological-interpersonal reorganisation.
>
> (Ogden, 1989)

Being part of a family is a developmental task which under ordinary circumstances both children and parents have to negotiate. From the infant's earliest relationship with their primary carer, usually their mother, and the wish for an exclusive relationship with each parent, there is a growing awareness and acceptance of the parents' relationship with each other and the separateness and independence of others. The complexity of this process for young children has been conceptualised by psychoanalytic literature over time and in different ways, but there is general agreement that the successful negotiation of the Oedipal complex contributes to a sense of self and the growth of the capacity for love and concern. As Britton (1989: 86–7) states, 'the "triangular space" bounded by the three persons of the Oedipal situation and all their potential relationships ... provides us with a capacity for seeing ourselves in interaction with others and for entertaining another point of view whilst retaining our own, for reflecting on ourselves whilst being ourselves'.

For children who have suffered early deprivation or abuse, the security engendered by the intimacy of the infant's relationship with a primary carer may not have been established. Thus, tolerating ordinary frustrations or establishing emotional closeness with others may be problematic. Not only may children in these circumstances have missed important developmental opportunities, but also trauma may have interfered with their capacity to master anxieties and to think symbolically, leaving them with an ongoing sense of deprivation and loss. Where this has been a primary feature of very early experience, and where the dyadic relationship with the mother has been problematic, relationships involving a third (triangular relationships) can be experienced at a primitive level as a dangerous intrusion and a threat to an already precarious situation.

Added to this are the special psychological tasks for children who are adopted, so aptly described by Brinich (1990). In the ordinary course of development, children have to manage feelings of love and hate in relation to each parent and towards the parental couple, but how can these feelings be managed in relation to two sets of parents? Further, can aspects of development, such as this, that have been missed, be re-visited at a later stage or in more benign circumstances?

In relation to later development, Freud (1909) described young children's idealisation and identification with their parents and their gradual disillusionment in the face of ordinary frustrations, disappointment and resentments that are part of growing up. A common fantasy to offset this, he proposed, was characterised by the idea that a child's 'real parents' were different, more exciting or of a higher standing and that they themselves were a step-child or adopted. This fantasy, which Freud came to call *family romances*, often encompassed feelings of revenge towards the parents and rivalry in relation to siblings. But he concluded that the fantasy also represented a longing for an earlier period when parents were exulted in their children's eyes. Both Oedipal development and these later fantasies about oneself and one's parents may have particular meaning for children who are adopted.

Brinich (1990) goes on to describe the way in which each area of ambivalence or vulnerability may also be experienced consciously or unconsciously by adoptive parents. Similar to the family romances of children, adoptive parents may harbour feelings towards and fantasies about a longed-for birth child or an idealised adoptive child that may be at odds with their experience of their real child. Parent's own unresolved Oedipal issues may also interfere with managing these powerful feelings as they emerge in a newly formed family. Being part of an adoptive family raises many issues and important dynamics for both children and their parents.

Developmental and Oedipal issues are addressed in *Debbie Hindle's* chapter where she describes her work with a five-year-old girl who had been placed for adoption at a few weeks of age. In this family, their hoped-for future was disrupted by the tragic death of the adoptive father through cancer when Annie was three years old. At this point, early developments seemed to have come to a standstill, leaving her in a 'developmental vacuum', unable to grieve the loss of her father and inhibiting her ability to play, form relationships and to learn. Gradually, in the context of intensive therapy and in relation to important changes in her home, the problem of 'how to love two daddies' arose. This opened the door to thinking again about her adoptive father, forming a new relationship with her mother's new husband and revisiting Oedipal issues. By eight years of age, she was beginning also to think about her adoption in a more meaningful way and to be able to hold 'multiple families in mind' (Rustin, 1999).

Powerful dynamics can also take hold in the 'triangular' relationship between a child in therapy, the therapist and adoptive parents, as described by *Pamela Bartram*. In her chapter, Bartram gives several examples of clinical work in which the structure of therapy, established to protect the confidentiality of the child and to support the parents, can leave parents feeling excluded and rivalrous. In these cases, she hypothesises that feelings of unresolved loss were enacted through the premature ending of the therapy. Bartram points to the need for thought to be given to this 'missing link' – a sufficiently strong and resilient alliance with the adoptive parents – and highlights the importance of attending to this dynamic in work with adopted children and their parents (see Chapter 11).

References

Brinich, P. (1990) 'Adoption, ambivalence and mourning: clinical and theoretical inter-relationships,' *Adoption and Fostering*, 14 (1): 6–17.
Britton, R. (1989) 'The missing link: parental sexuality in the Oedipus complex', in R. Britton, M. Feldman, and E. O'Shaughnessy (eds) *The Oedipus Complex Today: Clinical Implications*, London: Karnac Books.
Freud, S. (1909) 'Family romances,' *Standard Edition*, IX, London: Hogarth Press.
Ogden, T. (1989) *The Primitive Edge of Experience*, London: Karnac.
Rustin, M. (1999) 'Multiple families in mind', *Clinical Child Psychology and Psychiatry*, 4 (1): 51–62.

13 Loss, recovery and adoption

A child's perspective

Debbie Hindle

For children placed for adoption within the first few weeks or months of life, there is a hope shared by the adoptive parents and professionals involved that all will be well. As the preoccupations of caring for and establishing a relationship with the new arrival takes precedence, it is hard to imagine that tragedy may disrupt an anticipated future. Yet adopted children are subject to the same uncertainties and changing circumstances that may befall any family.

This chapter follows the developments of a five-year-old girl who was placed for adoption shortly after her birth, but whose adoptive father died when she was three years old. During the course of her psychotherapy from the age of five years, her capacity to grieve the loss of her father enabled her to develop a closer relationship with her adoptive mother and to grapple with earlier stages of development at a later stage. The complexity of this young girl's struggle to be part of a family and to begin to think about the fact that she was adopted is described.

Annie

Annie was five years old when she was referred to the Child and Adolescent Mental Health Services by the family GP and simultaneously by a paediatric registrar because of encopresis and speech delay. Although full descriptions were given of Annie's toileting problems, no mention was made in either referral of the fact that Annie was adopted or that her adoptive father had died. It was only after the community nurse specialist had visited the family at home that we understood how long standing the problems had been.

When I visited Annie at school for an initial assessment, she was anxious and inhibited. She took the toys I had brought with me out of the box, only to put them back again, a sequence repeated over many sessions. The class teacher described Annie as being withdrawn and regressed. She was not able to concentrate in class, did not mix with the other children and spent most of her time sucking her fingers. She wet herself and also soiled. Although encopresis and speech delay were the presenting problems, it became obvious that these were symptoms of a more profound delay affecting every area of her life. In light of such severe problems in such a young child, intensive psychotherapy was recommended. I began seeing Annie three times a week, while the community nurse specialist visited her adoptive mother at home on a weekly basis. Social Services arranged and paid for volunteer transport to enable Annie to attend sessions.

Annie was seven and a half weeks old when she was placed with Mr and Mrs M, her adoptive parents. She was collected by them from hospital. She had not been premature nor had she had any complications. Her adoption had been planned prior to her birth through a private adoption agency, with the consent of her birth mother. We had no information as to why Annie had been placed for adoption, nor why she had remained in hospital following her birth. From her adoptive mother's descriptions, Annie was a bright baby who had reached all her early developmental milestones.

When Annie was nearly two years old, her adoptive father developed cancer. He was in and out of hospital and was nursed at home during his illness until he died when Annie was just three. Mrs M, who had cared for her husband throughout his illness, described this as a very stressful time for them all. In relation to Annie, Mrs M was both angry towards her for the problems she was presenting and overwhelmed by feelings of guilt that she might have 'caused' them. Mrs M described how Annie had to attend nursery and was often sent to relatives to stay, so that she could look after her husband. Added to this were feelings of ambivalence about continuing to care for Annie now that she was on her own. The plans to adopt a child had been shared with her husband. Now she harboured regrets about having adopted Annie. 'If I had known what would happen …' The relationship between Annie and her adoptive mother had deteriorated to the point that we feared Mrs M might 'give up' and that Annie might have to be received into care.

Initially our aim was to create a therapeutic space in which to think about all that had happened. For Mrs M, time was needed to grieve the loss of her husband and the loss of their shared hopes and dreams. For Annie, the situation was compounded by the fact that her adoptive father's illness and subsequent death effectively marked the loss of her adoptive mother as well, as much of Annie's care shifted from adoptive mother to nursery or relatives. In addition, Mrs M's preoccupation with her husband's illness and her own grief following his death left Annie emotionally isolated. Where the demands of a young child had previously delighted her adoptive mother, they were now a source of irritation.

'Lost'

Initially Annie was unable to play, much as she had been during the assessment. Instead, she took the toys in and out of the box or wandered aimlessly about the room. She presented as a much younger child than she was, so much so that I came to think of her as 'stuck' developmentally at the point at which her father had died. Speech and imaginative play seemed to have come to a standstill. Important steps in her development, such as toilet training, had never been achieved. It was many months before a livelier Annie began to emerge as she became more involved in the therapy. Repetitive games gave way to games of hide and seek, and livelier games of skipping using string from her box. Yet her increased wish to involve me in her play coincided with an insistence that I should also do as she said: 'Come here!'; 'Hold this!'; 'Watch!' Annie commanded.

From feeling helpless about how to reclaim what I had felt to be a 'lost child' I became bewildered by her apparent self-assurance and control of the sessions. We played endless games of 'Freeze', in which I had to stand statue-like until either I moved and 'lost', or Annie said, 'go!' Annie conveyed a need to keep things fixed and also under her control. Her presentation as a 'little Miss Bossy Boots' exasperated her adoptive mother, as more cooperative efforts between them gave way to battles over who was in charge. In one session, Annie expressed her wish to grow up quickly: 'I don't want to be little, I want to be BIG!' 'Why?' I asked. 'Because I have to …' she said. Only gradually could I fully understand how Annie had turned to self-reliance and pseudo-maturity as a defence against anxiety and loss. Yet Annie remained unable to control her soiling, which now occurred regularly in her sessions. A problem that had been located at home, in relation to her mother, became focused in therapy.

Many months passed before Annie could begin to accept my help – for example, with climbing down from the filing cabinet. Her wish to maintain a high-up position (literally on top of the filing cabinet) was not easy to relinquish. Similarly, only gradually could Annie begin to accept my help in identifying when she needed to go to the toilet, instead of denying she had soiled. As omnipotent defences gave way, and Annie was able to be in touch with her dependency needs and a more vulnerable part of herself, she began to experience anxieties. In sessions she played out complicated material about ghosts, while at home she had nightmares and was clingier towards her adoptive mother.

'Found'

During the second year of therapy, Annie struggled to sort out what she could do for herself and what she needed help with. Often in sessions she would demand help in an imperious way for things she could easily do, but found it hard to ask for help with things she was genuinely struggling with. At times she could behave as if she were the busy mummy who had so much to do that she hardly had time to notice me. At other times, she demanded to be carried to and from the room or pretended to be a baby who needed everything done for her. Annie demonstrated how tangled she could feel inside by literally tangling herself in a long piece of string and asking me to untangle her. Using physical processes, such as soiling to rid herself of bad or unwanted feelings and the confusion around how to process such feelings inside her, gradually gave way to increasing confidence in her ability to communicate. Annie would shout, 'Take that, Mrs Hindle!' as she scattered the toys across the room and actively made a mess. Alternatively, Annie would empty a pile of toys and pens into my lap, saying, 'Sort them out!' The idea that someone was available to 'take that' or to sort out something seemed an important step in our work together.

Scattered amongst this ongoing work was something I could only describe as a 'heavy feeling' inside me. Later Annie was able to demonstrate through her play what I felt represented this feeling. Annie piled pillows, her blanket and overturned chairs on top of herself, as if she were partially buried. In another repeated sequence, she pretended to be in a deep hole – a pit. She was falling, alone in the darkness. In both sequences I had to rescue her. The idea that someone needed to rescue her, graphically played out in sessions, mirrored the urgency I had felt early in her therapy when Annie had been so lost and withdrawn. In retrospect, I am struck by how close my actual attempts to engage Annie were to what Alvarez (1992) refers to as 'reclaiming'. Only in writing this could I see how Annie's commands: 'Come here! Look at this!', although not my actual words, may have echoed Annie's perception of my attempts to reclaim her. I also thought of Annie's loss of her adoptive father and the problem for such a young child to describe feelings of depression. Annie remembered her adoptive father, but at three years old, how could she have fully understood his death or communicated her own sense of loss? When I tried to talk to Annie about this, she said, rather imperiously, 'I know all that.' Like the fact that she knew she had been adopted as a baby, she knew what she had been told. What was more complicated for Annie was to begin to make sense of her feelings about what had happened.

Preparing for the wedding

Throughout this period, Annie was developing a closer relationship with her adoptive mother. However, nearly four years after the death of her husband Mrs M had met someone and was preparing to re-marry. Much time and thought had gone into introducing Mrs M's new partner to Annie. Annie was both interested in her new daddy and pleased by his interest in her. As Mrs M's thoughts turned to the impending wedding, Annie demonstrated anxieties about the changes in her family. On some occasions she actively played out a wish to have her adoptive mother or me all to herself, with 'no daddies' or 'no Mr Hindle!' On other occasions she openly expressed her pleasure at having a new daddy who, as she said, 'does everything for me!' In several sessions, Annie took down the half net curtain from the window, placed it over her head and went into the hall. When she knocked on the door I was to open it to see 'Annie the Bridesmaid', only to be surprised when she removed the veil to reveal 'Annie the Bride!' It was perhaps not surprising that her longings to be her new daddy's little girl were muddled with a wish to be the bride and to take mummy's place.

The struggle to be part of a family seemed paramount. In one session, while looking at a children's picture book called *Family*, we identified each member in turn. When I commented that her new daddy would be joining the family soon, so that there would be 'mummy, her new daddy and …', before I had the chance to say her name, Annie said with some alarm, 'Don't forget me!', forcefully adding her name to the list. Annie's fears of being left out or excluded were compounded by her jealous, sometimes hostile phantasies. What often began as the toy animals playing together, ended with vicious attacks between them, the room in a mess and Annie having soiled herself. It was hard to feel part of a family when she felt besieged by angry, jealous or left-out feelings. In one sequence, after playing with two horses that were running and bumping together, she searched for the elephant family. The baby elephant attacked the two horses and killed the father elephant. Almost immediately, the mother and father elephant joined together, saying in a menacing tone, 'Shall we?' Using the mother and father elephant, Annie dropped the baby elephant in the bin 'for being naughty'. After an angry interchange, the baby was retrieved from the bin, and the family reunited, with conciliatory words of 'I'm sorry' and 'Glad to see you'.

Annie's ambivalence towards her new daddy made me wonder whether earlier wishes for an exclusive relationship with her mother had unconsciously implicated her in her father's death (the baby elephant killing the father elephant). In this story, the parents joined to attack and punish the baby, yet in the end all was forgiven. I talked to Annie about wanting her family to be happy and together and her wish that angry or jealous feelings would not spoil or destroy her loving feelings, or those of her parents. It felt as if Annie was involved in an important struggle in moving from a two-person to a three-person relationship. During this time, Annie tried to learn to juggle in her sessions, using her ball, a cup and a toy. Although neither Annie nor I mastered juggling these three items at once, we found we could keep one in the air by tossing the items back and forth between us. I felt this represented the difficulty involved in juggling a three-person relationship, a problem that required both help and some practice.

The impending marriage also raised questions in Annie about the possibility of there being another baby in the family. Phantasies about her mother and new daddy having a baby – Annie being put 'in the bin' – alternated with the plight of the baby piglet, who was repeatedly rescued 'just in time' before going down the plughole. Perhaps this represented Annie's ambivalence about what she might want to do with a new baby. At other times she pretended to be a mummy, having a baby of her own (Teddy) whom she gave surprisingly realistic birth to. Not only did this play seem to express a wish to be in mummy's shoes, but also conveyed a sense of hope that she could identify with a mother who could have children of her own. Although Annie knew that her adoptive mother could not have children and that she was adopted, her adoptive mother was her 'psychological mother' – to use the term described by Goldstein *et al.* (1980). In this sense, her identification with the possibility of her mother having children seemed an important developmental step. There was clearly much to think about in becoming part of a new family!

These struggles coincided with my growing ability to identify when Annie needed to use the toilet. When she was in a co-operative mood, something akin to toilet training – long overdue – was beginning to occur within the sessions. On one such occasion, Annie called for me with some alarm. As I opened the door to the toilet cubicle, I could see Annie's glasses just about to go down the drain. I reached into the toilet and grabbed them. I could see in a glance what had happened. After using the toilet, Annie had flushed it and leaned forward to look at what she had done as it disappeared. Like the piglet she had so often rescued 'just in time' before it went down the plughole, now I too had managed to rescue her glasses 'just in time'. This incident elicited in me a sudden panic and an immediate response which made me wonder whether a contributory factor in Annie's soiling had been fear about loss as well as holding on to her faeces as a way of keeping things under her control. Her growing ability to turn around and look, rather than rushing out of the toilet without flushing it, seemed like a step in the right direction; the rescue, a turning point.

How can I love two daddies?

It is in this context of growing awareness and developmental struggles that the problem of how to love two daddies arose. In one session I ventured that Annie seemed to be telling me that she thought she loved her 'new daddy'. Annie stood arms akimbo and with some irritation in her voice said, 'How can I love two daddies? I have one daddy in heaven and one down here, I can't love them both!' At home, Mrs M described Annie as actively trying to work out the differences between her adoptive father and her 'new daddy'. Annie repeatedly looked at old and new photo albums, moving from one to the other, pointing out who was who. On one occasion, Mrs M inadvertently observed Annie dancing in front of a picture of her adoptive father. This scene reminded Mrs M of the way in which Annie, as a two-year-old, had danced and entertained her ill father. This memory reawakened an awareness in Mrs M, as well as sadness, about how close Annie had been to her adoptive father.

Later in Annie's therapy, the volunteer driver, Mr N, who had brought her to her sessions three times a week, died suddenly. This gentle, older man had throughout this time been consistent and reliable and Annie, her mother and I had grown fond of him. He had in a sense made Annie's therapy possible. We all responded with letters of condolence and appreciation. Although this loss felt like a cruel repetition for a child who had lost her adoptive father, it was an experience that was shared and could be openly discussed in her therapy and at home. As Annie said, 'We will miss him'.

It was another six months before Annie drew a picture of a girl (herself) all in yellow. She then added two blue tears that joined to form a 'pool of tears' at her feet. The idea that Annie could symbolically communicate complex and contradictory feelings, such as her bright sunny side, as well as a deep sadness within her was an important development. Annie had lost her adoptive father, but during the course of her therapy and in getting to know a 'new daddy', she had also recovered her attachment to and love of her adoptive father.

Annie's story

As relations within the family began to settle, Annie played out a scene which at first was fragmented and hard to follow. It took several months before these scattered 'excerpts' developed into something resembling a story. In this story, a woman died in a fire. Following this, I was to knock on the door and enter the room to find a baby (Annie) laid out on the small table. Annie instructed me to cry.

'Why?' I asked. 'Because the baby is dead.' I pretended to cry, but Annie insisted that my tears had to fall *into* her eyes (the eyes of the dead baby). As my 'tears' touched her eyes, the baby (Annie) 'came alive' and stretched out her arms to be picked up and carried around the room to a waiting car. I was to 'drive' us both home and carry the baby around the room again to place her on my desk, her 'new home'.

Throughout the development of this story, I could see that Annie wanted me to play a part, but I could not at first grasp what was going on. Rather, I dutifully followed her directions until this clearer picture emerged. Only in writing this could I see how my puzzlement may well have mirrored Annie's difficulty in understanding her adoption. As such a young infant she could not have consciously remembered what had happened. However, she knew what she had been told, that she had been adopted as a baby and taken from hospital to her new home. Was this her way of beginning to think about what had happened and why?

Discussion

The death of Annie's adoptive father constituted a loss that was remembered by Annie and shared with her adoptive mother. This loss had a profound effect on Annie, her development and their ongoing relationship. Bowlby (1980) wrote extensively about the trauma of loss, the various responses of children given their age and stage of development, and the difficulty in identifying bereavement in childhood. In my early contact with Annie, she was withdrawn, her defensive structure more of a carapace, as I struggled to 'reclaim' her from her isolated position.

What was striking was her absence of feeling, her inability to concentrate, her regression and later her self-reliance and insistence on being in control. Nagera (1970) describes how 'withdrawal of cathexis from the lost object [can] leave the child in a developmental vacuum, unless a suitable substitute is found'. (Here Nagera is referring to the emotional relationship of a child to his or her primary carer that is so important in helping them negotiate different stages of development which necessarily takes place within the context of relationships.) Sekaer and Katz (1986) state that a bereaved child must deal not only with the immediate loss, but also with the impact of the loss at subsequent stages of development. The fact that her father's illness also precipitated increased periods of separation from her mother, who was both involved in her husband's care, preoccupied and later herself bereaved, compounded Annie's isolation.

Annie's adoptive father's death, not mentioned in the initial referrals, implied that her presenting problems, encopresis and speech delay, were not perceived as being related to what had happened. That is, the request for help did not take into consideration the complexity of the situation for the child. Although not showing any outward signs of sadness and grief, taken together, her symptoms and presentation were an indication that her experience of loss had affected her accomplishment of important developmental phases and had indeed left her in a 'developmental vacuum'. Only later in treatment was I able to detect a 'heavy feeling' as Annie demonstrated through her play being 'weighed down' (by the pillows, blankets and chairs), or in a deep hole – a pit, perhaps concretely a 'vacuum'.

Annie needed her omnipotent defence and underlying anxieties addressed before she could establish a relationship with me and re-establish a closer relationship with her adoptive mother. However, I would argue that only in the context of a relationship could feelings of loss or depression be explored. We can only hypothesise that Annie's response to her adoptive father's death and consequent lack of involvement of her adoptive mother, might also have been influenced by her early period in hospital. The three-year-old Annie was too young to understand the concept of death. She could only have experienced her adoptive father's absence, perhaps as abandonment – a replication of her earliest experience of abandonment by birth parents?

Annie's position as an adopted child in this family also made her more vulnerable to the possibility that her adoptive mother might 'give up' on her. Her adoptive mother's anger, guilt and ambivalence, aroused in part by Annie's problems, made her doubt her ability to care for Annie. The loss of her husband marked the loss of shared hopes, creating mixed feelings about shouldering the burden of parenting a child on her own. Mrs M too needed time to recover. The ongoing work with Mrs M – undertaken by the community nurse specialist – cannot be underestimated. Added to this was the adoptive mother's change of circumstances, her meeting someone who cared for her.

The struggle to be part of a family

Annie's dilemma – so aptly put when she asked, 'How can I love two daddies?' – seemed to fit with an idea that love is quantifiable, or can only be allotted to one person at a time. Annie's problem also related to her jealousy of her mother's new relationship and the difficulty she was having in adjusting to the idea that her mother could love her *and* a new partner. Annie's love of her adoptive father, her growing ability to understand and to grieve his loss, as well as her loyalty towards him, conspired to make this a 'complicated situation' (her words). Yet reaching a stage where she could experience Oedipal jealousies and express her dilemmas was in many ways a developmental achievement.

Getting to know her 'new daddy' also reminded Annie of her adoptive father. What had previously been an absence gradually became a memory, as she contrasted and compared pictures of her adoptive father and her 'new daddy'.

The problem of how young children encompass multiple attachments, in the face of what may be experienced by them as divided loyalties, is a poignant and often recurring theme for children who are fostered or adopted. Love of and loyalty towards a parent, or idealisation of a dead or absent parent, can leave children unable to form new attachments. Fahlberg (1991: 160) aptly describes the way in which new relationships are not dependent on displacing previous ones, but the importance of these different relationships standing 'side-by-side' in a way that is both clear and distinct.

This case illustrates many issues relevant to working with children who are adopted. The importance of the grieving process, highlighted in a case where there had been a natural death, has similarities for children who may have experienced multiple losses as they moved through the care system. In considering such cases, Fahlberg (1991: 133) states that: 'unresolved grief interferes with forming new attachments, thereby inhibiting continued positive growth and change'. She continues by emphasising that: 'in focusing on facilitating the grief process we help counteract factors that work against developing new attachments'.

Thinking about adoption

For Annie, it was hard to think about the fact that she had been adopted when there were so many other issues to deal with. It was perhaps significant that in therapy the issue of her adoption did not emerge until things had 'settled down'.

Annie knew that her adoptive father had died, and she knew that she had been adopted as a baby – as she often said, 'I know all that'. But what was increasingly apparent to me was the difference between what had been a real experience with her adoptive father, whom she deeply missed, and her understanding of her birth parents, whom she had never known. Bion (1962) makes a distinction between 'knowing about' and 'learning from experience'. How could Annie allow what she knew to have meaning and emotionally digest an experience she had never had? The idea of Annie having had a 'third' daddy – who was in fact her 'first', birth father – was not yet available for thought. However, in Annie's later play, the possibility of her raising questions about an unknown birth mother began to emerge.

'Annie's story', replayed over many sessions, resembles a myth. Like the pool of tears in her earlier drawing, here tears seem to have life-giving properties. I thought of Annie's early experience, in hospital, perhaps alone for long periods, with no one person to care for her. It might have felt as if she had been left to die, and that the presence of her adoptive mother had brought her back to life. Perhaps at some level 'Annie's story' encompasses the woman's grief about her own relinquished or unborn children. I also thought of the way Annie and her adoptive mother had been both separated and, over time, united in their loss of adoptive father.

Freud (1917) refers to the 'work of mourning', the 'mental pain' involved, and the subsequent strengthening of the ego. Certainly Annie and her adoptive mother's relationship strengthened as they gradually came to terms with her adoptive father's death.

However, in 'Annie's story' – prior to the sequence about the child – a woman died in a fire. Is this Annie's phantasy about what may have happened to her birth mother? Had her adoptive father's death become entangled with an idea that her birth mother may have died? For all individuals the primal scene, conception and birth, is essentially a mystery. For the adopted child, this mystery can be experienced more as a void. Important facts about birth parents, their relationship and the circumstances around their conception and birth may or may not be known. The question seems to be whether what is not known can be tolerated and perhaps imaginatively thought about.

In writing about adopted children in psychoanalytic treatment, Hodges (1984) describes the problem for children who have 'no contact with biological parents outside earliest infancy, no organised experience, no memory to draw on to construct a representation of a parent'. Yet, for most of the children seen, there seemed to be an 'internal, psychological need or wish to know … a wish for a mental representation, without, as it were enough bricks to build it'. Hodges says information about birth parents creates a gap. Feelings and phantasies influenced by the child's phase of psychosexual development may coalesce into a mental representation, but one 'not modified by everyday reality experiences'.

Preoccupation with phantasy can be detrimental to development. But in Annie's case, the move from not being able to play imaginatively to allowing a 'myth' to emerge seemed an important step in her development. Klein (1980) acknowledges the importance of playing and phantasy 'to the instinct for knowledge and to a child's achieving real stability of mind'. Segal (1994) emphasises the interplay between phantasy and reality and the way in which it 'moulds our view of the world … affects our personality and influences our perceptions …'. Bion (1959) points to the importance of curiosity to the capacity to learn and the detrimental effect when this impulse is inhibited, or when anxiety or aggression combine in a hostile way to interfere with curiosity, which may result in a severe arrest in development. For Annie, I would hope that her early attempts to understand not only what happened, but also *why*, might be the basis for allowing thoughts to develop which later in life she might want to compare with reality.

In therapy with Annie, I often felt one step behind her. Sometimes it seemed as if I needed to bear witness to what unfolded in her play. At other times, it seemed crucial to begin to recognise and put into words what was experienced more as feeling states, the 'heavy feeling', her need to go to the toilet, feelings of sadness or loneliness. It was, I felt, the interplay between her imaginings and mine that allowed for something resembling the story of her life to emerge.

Attachment and Oedipal issues

This case highlighted the difficulties for a child when their primary need for attachment had been fractured – for Annie, first through abandonment by her birth mother, and subsequently by the death of her adoptive father. It was, however, the emotional unavailability of her adoptive mother due to her own grief, which catapulted Annie into a 'black hole', a void re-evoking the experience in her first few days and months of life in hospital. She needed active help to draw her out of her withdrawn state and to enable her to engage and to 'find' her mother and me.

The loss of her adoptive father also threw Annie back into a pre-Oedipal stage of development. Only later, when her mother re-married did Annie have a chance to re-negotiate the Oedipal phase of her development, now in the context of her new family configuration. She could begin to think again about her adoptive father and to apprehend her parents' relationship with each other and her relationship to a parental couple.

Conclusion

In my work with Annie and her family, I felt it was important to attend to the immediate trauma: adoptive father's death, the consequences of this on Annie's development, and the centrality of the changing family relationships. Adoption was an additional component in the life of this family. But, as Hodges (1984) states: 'in the child's inner world as well, adoption may function as an organiser, a focus for various anxieties'.

In writing this, I was interested in the fact that I have gone on thinking about Annie and her family long after the end of her therapy. I wondered if this paralleled the way in which issues particularly around adoption may need to be revisited at later stages of development or in light of new experiences or information. Annie's early attempts at juggling may well be a precursor to her need to 'juggle' these ongoing issues, perhaps herself gaining different perspectives on them at different times in her life.

A year following the end of therapy, as agreed, the community nurse specialist and I visited Annie at home to follow up our work together. At the end of this visit, to my astonishment, Annie, now ten years old, said, 'I don't have to miss you, I can think about you.' The idea that something could end, and not be missed, but remembered and thought about seemed an important and remarkable distinction.

References

Alvarez, A. (1992) *Live Company: Psychoanalytic Psychotherapy with Autistic, Borderline, Deprived and Abused Children*, London: Tavistock, Routledge.

Bion, W. (1959) 'Attacks on linking', *International Journal of Psychoanalysis*, 40: 308–15.

Bion, W. (1962) *Learning from Experience*, London: Maresfield Reprints.

Bowlby, J. (1980) *Attachment and Loss*, Volume Ill: *Loss, Sadness and Depression*, London: Hogarth Press.

Fahlberg, V. (1991) *A Child's Journey Through Placement*, London: British Association for Adoption and Fostering.

Freud, S. (1917) 'Mourning and melancholia', *Standard Edition*, Vol. XIV, London: Hogarth Press.

Goldstein, J., Freud, A. and Solnit, A.J. (1980) *Beyond the Best Interests of the Child*, London: Burnett Books.

Hodges, J. (1984) 'Two crucial questions: adopted children in psychoanalytical treatment', *Journal of Child Psychotherapy*, 10: 47–56.

Klein, M. (1980) *The Psychoanalysis of Children*, London: Hogarth Press.

Nagera, H. (1970) 'Children's reactions to the death of important objects: a developmental approach', *Psychoanalytic Study Child*, 25: 360–400.

Segal, H. (1994) 'Phantasy and reality', *International Journal of Psychoanalysis*, 75: 359–401.

Sekaer, C. and Katz, S. (1986) 'On the concept of mourning in childhood: reactions of a two-and-one-half-year-old girl to the death of her father', *Psychoanalytic Study Child*, 41: 287–314.

14 Oedipal difficulties in the triangular relationship between the parents, the child and the child psychotherapist

Pamela Bartram

In this chapter, I reflect on work with adopted children in therapy – where it has been useful and has promoted development and change and where difficulties have arisen that have resulted in premature termination of therapy. I suggest that these difficulties have to do with the triangular relationship between the child, the parents and the therapist and consider the importance of thinking about the forces both within and between these three 'parties' which may be negotiated with greater or lesser degree of success.

The chapter is based on my experience of families who come for help when life with an adopted child is proving difficult. I have found that arrangements for setting up and sustaining individual psychotherapy for adopted children are frequently more problematic than with non-adopted children. Of course, not all adopted children need psychotherapy. Many adoptive families do not need professional help to support and promote their child's development. This chapter, however, draws on experience of children whose development has needed specialist intervention.

Oedipal development

In the course of normal development, a child moves towards an understanding of and accommodation to the knowledge that mother and father have a potent relationship which, at times, appropriately excludes them. Feelings of exclusion thus have their origins in, and are intimately linked with, the Oedipal situation. Psychoanalytic thinking stresses the importance for mental health of navigating this psychological terrain. Oedipus – whose name is associated with the task – was blind to its landscape and his journey through it, long and fraught with tragedy. The developing awareness of the reality of a child's relation to the parental couple goes hand in hand with a process of mourning (Britton, 1989). The idealised good parents of an earlier developmental stage, fantasised to be always and exclusively available to the child, are gradually understood to be a more ordinary mixture of good and bad, capable both of satisfying and disappointing. At the same time, the Oedipal situation offers 'the possibility of being a participant in a relationship and observed by a third person as well as being an observer of a relationship between two people' (Britton, 1989: 86). Whilst this awareness brings an experience of expanding psychological space within which the child can grow, it also brings pain, humiliation, envy, rivalry and a sense of helplessness. It is when these feelings can be managed that the union and potency of the parents is discovered to be reassuring and the reality of relationships between the generations acknowledged and accepted.

Material gathered from adopted children in psychotherapy shows that the negotiation of this psychological process, difficult for all children, can prove particularly demanding for some adopted children (Canham, 2003; Edwards, 2000). This very likely has to do with the lack of stability in their early relationships, complicated in some cases by trauma and abuse. That is to say, the conditions within which these children might acquire an emotional understanding of these facts of life have not pertained.

Children from these circumstances may benefit from psychotherapy which allows both the emotional and cognitive working-through of their confused (and in some cases perverse) misunderstandings. This psychological work can result in a fundamental change in the child's experience of themselves and their place in the world, with corresponding changes in their emotional life and their behaviour.

Nevertheless, I have found that setting up and maintaining psychotherapy for adopted children can be problematic. This, I believe, has to do with some of the Oedipal difficulties I have described, expressing themselves in another triangular relationship – the triangular relationship between the child patient, the therapist and the adoptive parents.

Child psychotherapy assessment and treatment

To put this in context, perhaps it is useful to begin by thinking more generally about what is entailed in setting up individual psychotherapy for any child. In my experience this process always has to be handled sensitively. By the time parents come for help they may feel a sense of failure at not having been able to sort out their child's problems without professional intervention. When, as a result of careful assessment, a child is offered individual psychotherapy, parents, while grateful and recognising the need for therapy, may feel an added sense of failure.

Some parents will turn down this treatment intervention, although they may seek the therapist's guidance and help for themselves as parents. There may be a number of reasons for this. Some may find it hard to accept the nature of the work of child psychotherapy which is based on establishing and working within a one-to-one relationship with the child. Therapy takes place in a boundaried space with regular attendance and a degree of confidentiality suited to the child's developmental stage. We advise parents that children may develop intense feelings, both positive and negative, about their therapy, or indeed, about their therapist. We ask parents to be prepared for resistance and to continue to bring the child even if he seems not to want to come. The ending of therapy is planned well in advance allowing plenty of time, in some cases as long as a year, to work through issues which arise in its anticipation. In all these ways, we convey that we expect to have an intense relationship with their child and that we are committed to weathering difficulties encountered within it.

As the heart of the work is to understand how the child experiences himself and the world around him, the relationship between therapist and child in some ways reproduces, when the process is going well, aspects of their real and internal or phantasy relationship with their parent or parents.

Adoptive parents usually have their own worker whom they see regularly to discuss difficulties from their point of view. This therapist may, at times, act as a useful link between the parents and the child's therapist, passing information in both directions. However, as well as acting as a link between the parents and the child's therapist, this therapist also stands between the parents and their child's therapist, part of a structure which defines the boundaries of the psychotherapeutic relationship. In addition to their own allocated worker, parents will meet the child's therapist once a term or so, to hear directly about how their child is progressing in therapy and to update the therapist on developments at home.

This is what I think of as the ordinary framework for therapy within which helpful developments can take place both in the child and in his parents' ways of thinking and managing, for the mutual benefit of all. The partnership between therapist and parents, whether or not the child is adopted, is of central importance to the well-being of the therapy. However, as I mentioned at the beginning, in the case of adopted children I have found these arrangements to be frequently more problematic to set up and sustain and the optimum framework for the psychotherapy, less clear. I would suggest that there is a specific difficulty for these families, of managing the three-way relationship between therapist, child and adoptive parents. Some aspects of the difficulty may mirror difficulties with threesomes (and all the emotional challenges they bring) with which the adopted child himself struggles, while others may have independent origins in the adoptive parents themselves.

In some cases, adoptive parents abruptly terminated the child's psychotherapy for reasons which seemed to do with their unconscious responses to their child's treatment, rather than conscious reasoning.

It should be noted that siblings and members of the extended family also, of course, make an important contribution to family relationships. However in this chapter, I confine myself to a consideration of the key three-way relationship between parents, child, and – when the child is in treatment – the therapist. The following clinical material relating to Ian, Sarah and Molly will provide a focus for thinking further about these issues.

When things go wrong

Ian

Ian, aged nine, had been removed from his birth mother at the age of two and a half because of neglect and abuse – the details of which were not known to his adoptive parents. He lived in several foster placements prior to his adoption.

After an initial honeymoon period, Ian become verbally and physically abusive towards his adoptive mother and was referred to the clinic after he began to smear and eat his own faeces. At the point of referral, Ian had been living with his adoptive parents for two years and they felt they could no longer manage without professional help.

The work began with several family and parent-only meetings with myself and another worker. We heard how Ian had broken all his toys, wrecked his room, and 'spoiled' family life, especially any outings which were supposed to be family treats. After a few meetings, some improvements took place in Ian's behaviour at home. He quite quickly stopped smearing faeces and punching his adoptive mother. However, his attitude towards her, as reported by the parents, remained very negative. He continued to speak to his mother with contempt and disgust, as if from on high. Ian subverted her attempts to be a 'good enough' mother – she was never allowed the satisfaction of feeling she had understood him, or even momentarily had met any of his needs. It was interesting to note that in the family meetings, Ian never displayed this behaviour, but always made loving pictures for his mother, or played games which showed aspects of his vulnerability rather than his aggression. However, given his mother's increasing desperation for things to change at home, we offered an individual psychotherapy assessment for Ian, feeling that as much change as possible had been achieved within the parental or family framework. It seemed that there were powerful and potentially destructive thoughts and feelings inside Ian which were not amenable to family work.

I was aware of feeling considerable sympathy towards Ian, who looked like a little waif – making it hard to reconcile the way he presented in family meetings with the picture of home-life portrayed. I thought of how difficult it may have been for a childless couple to suddenly find themselves not only with a seven-year-old boy, but also with a boy who had been neglected and abused. Their wishes and expectations of happy family outings might perhaps have to be reviewed in the light of Ian's history and his unexpectedly swift arrival in their home.

Ian was responsive to being seen individually and we agreed that he should begin psychotherapy. However, once therapy was underway, I was able to see how very difficult he could be. He was contemptuous and disdainful of any idea that he might need someone to help him. In the first review with the parents, they were relieved that I too had a first-hand understanding of what it was to be with this little boy who resisted so strongly the possibility of a warm and dependent relationship. I talked to them about my understanding of why this might be so difficult for him, and linked it with what we had begun to piece together about his past history. It seemed that Ian's father, in particular, found this way of thinking helpful. At first his mother also seemed comforted to think that anyone in her position would be in line for the experiences to which Ian subjected her.

As psychotherapy continued, this sense of alliance between the adoptive mother and myself became more strained. Within his sessions, after several months dominated by negative transference, spoiling and destruction, Ian had begun to bring a more vulnerable part of himself. Whereas previously he had represented himself in his play with an invincible little boy doll, he now introduced a doll who was more ordinarily vulnerable. This boy doll, unlike the earlier version, could not fly, rather he hurt himself if he fell, or was injured if attacked by wild animals. Ian was able to draw a beautiful picture of his mother which he managed not to spoil and he began to make cardboard buildings which were not destroyed at the end of each session, but carefully preserved week after week.

As I reported these developments to his parents, I found that although father was now saying that he felt that he could manage Ian, and that generally things were better between the two of them, mother had a different reaction. She felt that while it was all very well for me to be having an easier time with Ian, she still found life with him very difficult, and at times, intolerable. Although it seemed there were signs of improvement in Ian's psychotherapy sessions, and at home with his father, his mother's distress and disappointment increased.

I began to be aware of a sense of a 'missing link' in the work with Ian and his family, a link that should connect the progress Ian was making in his therapy, with his adoptive mother's experience of him. Without that, the improvements in Ian and in some of his relationships seemed unable to express themselves in his relationship with his adoptive mother.

Ian spent his last session before the Christmas holiday making a board game out of cardboard. The aim of the game was to move via various obstacles from the start to the finish point on the board. As the session came to an end, he talked for the first time about leaving his foster mother to live with his adoptive parents. It was as if we had arrived at a point where we could begin to understand the nature of the problems we had for so long been struggling with. We looked at his holiday chart and confirmed the date of his return after the break. However on the day before he was due to return, his parents withdrew him from therapy and he was never brought back to say goodbye.

As well as considerable emotional pain, I was left with questions about this situation viewed as a whole. Ian was responsive to psychotherapy and seemed able in that context to develop an internal sense of a mother who could be helpful and resilient, rather than merely stupid, lazy and inadequate (his version of mothers until then). However he did not seem able to see his adoptive mother in this way, although his relationship with his adoptive father had improved. He seemed to need to keep his therapist and his adoptive mother separate in his mind and perhaps too his adoptive mother and adoptive father.

I was also left wondering about my own unconscious contribution to the situation. I had not been aware until he was withdrawn from therapy of the extent to which I had thought of Ian as 'mine'. I wondered whether the unconscious rivalry between his adoptive mother and myself, of which I had been aware only from her side, had also been a factor in her needing to remove him so abruptly from treatment (at the very point at which his relationship with his foster mother came into the frame in his therapy). Britton (1989) talks about the 'special relationship' with the analyst which can be part of the Oedipal illusion of the patient. Perhaps, in the transference, when a positive relationship with the therapist emerges, it is unconsciously felt to be at the expense of the relationship with the adoptive parent.

This may mirror the adoptive mother's own sense, perhaps quite unconscious, of having the child at the expense of the birth mother. Children's fairy tales are full of references to 'stealing' children, indicating the universality and primitiveness of these thoughts and fears. These issues highlight the difficulty of holding onto a sense of collaboration between two parties in the interests of a third. Instead, the triangular relationship is experienced as malign rather than benign. Two parties are felt to get together not in the interest of, but in order to exclude the third. In such circumstances the alliance between the therapist and the parents is of paramount importance and may require special attention if the therapy is to continue. Although I made every reasonable attempt to foster that alliance, it was not strong enough to allow the therapy to continue. It also seemed that the grief of the adoptive parents – which had emerged in the parallel work of my colleague with the parents – about their own childlessness may have been too overwhelming for them to manage to know about consciously. For whatever reasons, the parent/therapist couple in this case was not resilient enough to sustain the therapist–child relationship.

Sarah

In the case of five-year-old Sarah, her adoptive mother became distressed and agitated when Sarah started to say that she did not want to come to her therapy sessions. Sarah had been very destructive and difficult in the early months of psychotherapy. However, after a week when she had dared to bring with her a book about *The Creation Story* and to think with me for the first time about the origins of life, she told her mother she did not want to come to her sessions anymore. As soon as this happened her mother agreed with her that she could stop therapy. I was shocked by the idea of a sudden ending at this point, but managed to work with them together for a few sessions. This seemed to allay the mother's conscious fear that the therapy was causing Sarah unbearable pain. She had the chance to hear how I spoke to Sarah and how she responded. Nevertheless, mother felt that she could not expect Sarah to continue therapy if she said she did not want to. Eventually her mother agreed to let Sarah stop coming on her birthday, which was some months away.

It seemed significant that Sarah's therapy would be ending on her birthday – as if something to do with her original separation from her birth mother was to be re-enacted now, with myself. I wondered whether in adoptive mother's phantasy, I came to represent the birth mother with whom the child had her original, deepest bond. At the moment when Sarah began to find it difficult to attend, perhaps because of the fear and longing evoked by her newly developing interest in her own origins, I was perceived by her mother as a danger from which Sarah had to be rescued. I am not sure whether it was my perceived 'badness' or 'goodness' which was experienced as most dangerous, but adoptive mother's feelings, fears and phantasies seemed indistinguishable from Sarah's. There was little capacity to think about them – either in relation to the past or the present. Instead a painful enactment took place.

Molly

In the case of Molly, who was seen by a colleague, something powerful seemed to be re-enacted between her mother and her therapist. Exactly nine months to the week after Molly began psychotherapy, her mother said that she thought that the therapy was 'not working' and that she would like to bring it to a speedy end. As in Ian's case, although developments in Molly had taken place – in terms of the emergence of a more positive relationship and a new-found capacity for thoughtfulness with her therapist – Molly's mother reported that there were no changes in the difficulties she had with Molly at home.

When this was discussed further she said that, if anything, Molly was becoming 'more distant' and the therapist was struck by her sense of loneliness as she said this – as if she was afraid that she was losing Molly to her therapist. It seemed that whereas in therapy the opening up of a more thoughtful space offered the possibility of closeness, in her relationship with her mother it seemed only to represent the distance between them. The adoptive mother did not take up the offer of more frequent review meetings and did not want to meet with another colleague to think about the difficulties in her relationship with Molly. For her part, Molly had always found the prospect of review meetings very upsetting. It was painful to see that her worst fear now seemed to be confirmed – her mother and her therapist could not in fact team up to think about her in a helpful way and provide her with an ongoing therapeutic space. Instead, there seemed to be a rivalrous dynamic between them which centred upon the question as to who could nurture Molly's development and who could not. At the end of the final session, the therapist was left with a powerful experience of identification with an inadequate birth mother who had to relinquish her child to a new mother who seemed to have all the advantages of the Western economic lifestyle on her side.

Discussion

It will be seen that these cases which I have described ended too soon – from both the therapist's and the child's point of view, though not the parents'. It would be foolish therefore not to question whether such endings could have been predicted or avoided by a more thorough or a more expert initial assessment, but I do not believe that this is the case. It seems to me that some premature endings can be understood as having come about because of the transference of the parents to the child psychotherapist, which did not begin to 'take hold' until the work was underway and the effects of the work with the child were beginning to be seen or sensed by the parents. By this I mean that in the parents' minds, the therapist came to represent a powerful parental figure with the power to create and to destroy. It may be important that in all the cases described above, none of the adoptive parents had their own biological children. Where adoptive parents come to adoption because of an inability to give birth to children, perhaps they had not been able to assure themselves of their own creativity in that particular and very primitive area of human experience. In addition, more often than not, they had also missed out on important developmental stages in the family life of parent and child, such as teething, weaning, taking first steps and the beginning of speech. It is difficult to quantify such losses when these developmental and psychologically important experiences have not been shared. In normal circumstances, parent/ child relationships are not only expressed through the mutual negotiation of these developmental experiences, but also shaped by the way that parent and child go through them together. Parents of an adopted child may lack the security which comes from weathering and rejoicing in the sharing of important milestones. Furthermore, when adopted children are disturbed, difficult to care for and seemingly unresponsive to the parents' efforts to help them, the parents' experience of themselves as deficient may be underscored and deepened. By contrast the therapist may be seen in phantasy as a creative agent who can nurture children or bring them to psychic life.

I referred earlier to the possibility of the adoptive parents' unconscious sense of having stolen the child away from the biological parents. In parallel with this, they may also unconsciously identify with the parents from whom they feel the child has been taken away, weakening their own confidence as parents. It may be that these thoughts and feelings became enacted when therapy was ended without planning or preparation. It is because these feelings are so hard to know about and bear that they may be expressed through an enactment between adoptive parents and therapist.

In terms of creating a framework within which psychic change in the child and the adoptive parents can take place, it is difficult to generalise about what works best. Often it is chance or availability of resources which determines what is offered. The 'ordinary' framework of child psychotherapy, within which the parents are seen by another worker in parallel with the child's individual psychotherapy, may contribute to problems and in some cases create the conditions for a premature ending of the child's therapy. In the case of Ian and Sarah, I was aware that their parents experienced their own worker less as a helpful link to the child's therapist, and more as an obstructive barrier standing between them and her.

A different outcome

It may be useful at this point to think about two cases which helped me to understand something about what might allow therapeutic work to survive the pressures upon it.

Zara

Zara, aged eight, had been adopted as a young baby from a poor country, given up by a mother who could not afford to keep her. She was referred because of her phobias, anxieties and problems with learning. The work had a somewhat unpromising start. A colleague and I undertook an assessment which included family meetings, meetings with parents and three individual sessions for

Zara. She was clearly ready for individual psychotherapy, but I was unsure as to whether her parents wanted this for her. Her adoptive mother, in particular, seemed subtly resistant to the idea, while her father was more openly supportive of it. I was concerned at being perceived by mother to side with father against her in pursuing therapy. However, I couldn't find a way to explore these impressions and experienced my attempts to talk about them as being deflected or somehow just not engaged with. At the same time I was aware, from my sessions with Zara, of her wish, indeed her intense hunger for a space for playing and thinking. I felt torn, unsure whether the foundations of my colleague's and my relationship with the parents were strong enough to support the work, yet aware of Zara's desire and need for it. In the end I was encouraged to offer treatment, remembering that when we first met the parents they talked about not wanting to increase unnecessarily the long list of assessments Zara had already undergone. They wanted not a brief information-gathering exercise, but a solid and reliable intervention. As I weighed up these considerations, it seemed particularly important that I had confidence in my colleague's capacity to hold the parents in a helpful and creative way. I felt our partnership was a good one. Given, therefore, that there were no overt objections, I began to see Zara for once-weekly psychotherapy.

For the first year of work, Zara's parents met my colleague from time to time and met me once a term for reviews. In Zara's sessions the emotional temperature was high and Oedipal passions such as rivalry and possessiveness ran deep. By contrast, review meetings were low-key, somewhat oblique and puzzling. After several months of work, my colleague left the clinic on maternity leave and I worried about the effect this would have on Zara's therapy. However, it seemed to have no destabilising effect on Zara's punctual and regular attendance and Zara's parents seemed shyly pleased about their worker's pregnancy, asking for news of her from time to time.

Half way through the second year of our work together, Zara's mother came for a review meeting. She seemed unexpectedly full of feeling as she arrived and before I sat down, showed me a certificate Zara had received from school commending her generous and loving attitude to other children. It seemed that Zara had a sense of abundance within her, allowing her to be generous to others. Mother and I were both very moved by this and I felt that she had brought this information partly as an expression of gratitude for the help they too had received. Mother went on to talk about how she had always worked hard to keep her child in touch with her original culture, and how important she felt it was that Zara understood what had been good about her birth country and her birth mother. She reminded me of the judgement of Solomon in the Old Testament and said that in the story, the real mother was the one who would not allow the child to be sacrificed, but let the child go rather than have her suffer or die. Zara's mother was talking about this in the context of her relationship (in her mind) with Zara's birth mother, but I felt that it also had meaning in terms of her relationship with me. I felt that she was letting me know that it had indeed been hard to let Zara come for psychotherapy, but that she had struggled with her fear of loss and her feelings of rivalry, to let Zara have this help. She had stayed quite emotionally distant from me, but as changes took place in Zara which she linked with the therapy, she had now come closer to express her gratitude.

Zara had four years of psychotherapy which was brought to an end by mutual agreement of the therapist, the parents and Zara herself. The family arranged to continue to bring her to termly reviews and there was contact between Zara's school and the clinic which supported her educational progress. When Zara said she no longer needed to review with her therapist, it was left open that the family could make contact again if and when it might be useful to do so.

It is very difficult to say why this piece of work took the direction it did, whilst others took another direction. There are simply too many variables, too much that is unique in each case, to draw any simple conclusions. Zara had not been an abused child, but had been given up by a birth mother who wanted her to escape a life of poverty. Perhaps this made it more possible for her adoptive parents to hold in mind a good link with the birth mother, to which the child could then more easily have access. For whatever reason, Zara's parents' gratitude for Zara, and for the changes in her, more than balanced any sense of rivalry with the birth parent or the therapist. I sensed that it had been important in this case – as in some others – that the adoptive parents were able to stay at an emotional distance from the child's therapy, at least for some periods.

Sally

Sally was another child whose parents supported her therapy to its conclusion. Sally was removed from her mother's care when she was three years old and adopted along with her older sister some two years later, after a number of institutional and foster placements. She had been subject to neglect and abuse by her mother, and probably also to sexual abuse by men friends of her mother. After a few months in her adoptive family, Sally's behaviour began to deteriorate. The levels of her disturbance and violence were so great that the stability of family life was threatened. When Sally was nine her adoptive parents sought professional help, and following assessment she started four times weekly psychotherapy.

Her parents were a thoughtful and capable couple who both worked in professions connected to children's care and mental health. They had a good understanding of what the therapy would involve and made solid arrangements for her to be brought to the clinic. They agreed to attend termly reviews with the therapist as well as fortnightly meetings with a co-worker to think about how to live with and manage, as well as possible, Sally's emotional and behavioural problems at home.

To their worker's surprise, her parents often came late or cancelled their own appointments, although Sally attended her sessions with great regularity. This concerned Sally's therapist who wondered if it was a sign of their lack of commitment to what had been agreed. The co-worker found it difficult to explore this issue with Sally's parents. Nevertheless, productive termly reviews with Sally's therapist and the co-worker took place as scheduled and the work seemed to go well.

In effect, little or no work with the parents took place other than in the review meetings. The parents seemed to want or need to relate only to the child's therapist, and not too often at that, but not to their worker who was in effect made redundant. The triangle of therapist, parents and child seemed to work well for Sally and her therapy ended, like Zara's, when there was mutual agreement that well-established changes had taken place inside Sally as well as in her behaviour within her family.

Discussion

By contrast with Ian, Molly and Sarah, Zara and Sally's therapies ran their course to good effect. In both cases, however, the parents, by their own choice, kept only a minimal contact with the worker allocated to them. Although previously uneasy about this, I now wonder whether it might have been their way of allowing their child to have a separate space in therapy into which they did not feel unduly drawn. Perhaps it was also a way of managing their more difficult and potentially destructive feelings – that is to say, by keeping at a distance, but continuing to work hard at home to parent their child.

How can therapeutic work with adoptive parents and their children be informed by the ideas and experiences explored in this chapter? First, the likelihood of powerful and unintegrated Oedipal forces at play must be borne in mind from the outset. The therapist's awareness of these should inform her exchanges with the family during the assessment, and where possible, should be openly explored with them. Second, an extended period of family work may be helpful. Any pressure for the child to be seen individually may provide the opportunity to explore parents' sense of helplessness as well as their hopes and expectations of the outcome of therapy. Third, the usefulness of the usual framework for child psychotherapy, in which parents are seen by another therapist may benefit from adaptation. It may be good for the child's therapist to make herself more frequently available to the adoptive parents than usual in order to facilitate a benign triangular relationship between parents, child and therapist. Klauber (1991) describes her work with an adopted adolescent which involved her also meeting with the whole family in parallel. This came about by chance rather than by design, and there were considerable difficulties in working on her own, without a colleague to see the parents. However, this framework unexpectedly facilitated helpful links to be made between family issues and the presenting problems of the adolescent. Finally, in common with all clinical work, the therapist's own supervision – as well as her ability carefully to monitor her responses to the child and his parents – will of course be of paramount importance in the navigation of this difficult terrain.

Conclusion

Whatever the framework, doubtless the important thing to keep in mind are the forces at work in triangular relationships. These forces include primitive feelings of exclusion and inadequacy as well as those of rivalry and jealousy, often at an unconscious or only partly conscious level. There may be a strong tendency to revert to a 'black and white' view of the world which spares us the sadness and discomfort of knowing that good and bad co-exist. These forces will certainly be at play within the individual child. Those intimately involved with the child are bound to come under their influence. When these forces are not contained, they may interfere with a good working alliance between the adoptive parents and the child's therapist to the child's detriment.

The negotiation of Oedipal problems is inherently linked with the work of mourning (Britton, 1989). Oedipus himself was a child abandoned and then adopted. For the child, the task of mourning the birth parents and the life (however deprived) that he might have had with them is enormous. Often foster parents have also been loved and lost. All this, the child brings into the adoptive family which may reel from its impact. For the adoptive parents too, the task of mourning if they did not have their own children, and of mourning the adopted child who would have brought them only comfort, not more pain, is enormous. Failure to acknowledge or sufficiently work through the task of mourning – for adoptive parents or child – may seriously interfere with the working alliance between adoptive parents and their adopted child's therapist. The supportive framework for the work of the child's psychotherapy, whatever its shape, must be sufficiently resilient to contain the painful shock of loss as well as the weight of jealousy and rivalry.

References

Britton, R. (1989) 'The missing link: parental sexuality in the Oedipus complex', in R. Britton, M. Feldman, and E. O'Shaughnessy (eds) *The Oedipus Complex Today: Clinical Implications*, London: Karnac Books.
Canham, H. (2003) 'The relevance of the Oedipus myth to fostered and adopted children', *Journal of Child Psychotherapy*, 29 (1): 5–19.
Edwards, J. (2000) 'On being dropped and picked up: adopted children and their internal objects', *Journal of Child Psychotherapy*, 26 (3): 349–67.
Klauber, T. (1991) 'Ill-treatment in the counter-transference: some thoughts on concurrent work with an adopted girl and with her family by the same psychotherapist', *Journal of Child Psychotherapy*, 17 (2): 45–60.

Part VI

Adoption and adolescence

The question of identity

Introduction

Debbie Hindle

> ... the task of becoming oneself, now and always, involves relinquishing the denigrated and idealised version of the self, of other people and of relationships, in favour of the real. It involves re-negotiating dreams, choices and hopes, whether self-generated or imposed from without. It involves tolerating opportunities lost and roads not taken.
>
> (Waddell 1998: 159)

In writing about the 'family life cycle', Carter and McGoldrick (1989: 17) note that adolescence 'ushers in a new era because it marks a new definition of the children within the family and of the parents' roles in relation to their children'. For adolescents, the physical changes of puberty require a fundamental change in their sense of self. The emotional preoccupations of being part of a family, give way to a fuller engagement with the wider world – in relation to friends and peers and also to education, and in time, employment. Yet the process of separation and individuation can be painful. Parents too can feel bereft at the 'loss' of their child and at a loss as to how to understand and respond to the 'stranger' in their midst. But adolescence also provides an opportunity to revisit and rework earlier stages of development, to explore different aspects of the self and to embrace the challenge of new experiences.

In an ordinary way, the turmoil of adolescence is difficult enough to negotiate, but for young people who have experienced earlier deprivation or abuse, adolescence may prove particularly problematic. For some adolescents who were adopted, there may be a growing urge to understand and reflect on earlier experiences – to gain a perspective on their lives in light of what has happened. But others are powerfully overtaken by a wish to avoid thinking by all the means now available to them – drink, drugs, sexual activity – often re-enacting aspects of their own experience through their actions or the responses they elicit in others: anger, rejection, or further abuse.

Brodzinsky *et al.* (1998: 31) state that 'The most fundamental task for the adopted teenager is establishing a stable and secure sense of self.' They go on to outline the unique psychological issues for adolescents who have been adopted, particularly in relation to integrating their psychical self and establishing sexual maturation. Questions about their own origins, their adoptive parents' procreative capacities and what their own sexual development might mean to their adoptive parents may come to the fore. For many adopted young people, conscious fantasies give way to a deeper understanding of the reality of their lives and the implications and meaning of adoption. To these issues, Sorosky *et al.* (1975) add the importance of 'genealogical continuity' and the confusion and uncertainty that can accompany having limited knowledge of one's birth family and ancestors.

How these issues are explored and whether they can be thought about depends increasingly on what the young person has made of their experiences and whether they have been able to integrate different aspects of themselves. The move to understanding the reasons for their being adopted – in a more realistic way – may involve painful truths and raise difficult feelings. For some adopted adolescents, problems associated with their early experiences may have lain dormant and may arise in quite unexpected ways in response to the onset of adolescence. Whilst the two chapters that follow draw on clinical work with adolescents who were experiencing quite serious problems, they also poignantly illustrate the way in which earlier experiences of being unheld or prematurely self-reliant can interfere with development at this stage.

In the chapter 'Deprivation and development: the predicament of an adopted adolescent in the search for identity', *Tessa Dalley* and *Valli Kohon* describe the psychotherapy of an extremely troubled adolescent who had been adopted at the age of five after severe deprivation and neglect in infancy and early childhood. Dalley and Kohon explore the issues and difficulties that puberty may present for children who have been adopted. They consider the adopted child's experience of bodily changes in puberty, in the context of the fundamental importance of a mental representation of the body to the development of a secure sense of identity. The authors highlight the fact that the body constitutes a biological and psychological link to the birth parents. The significance of this is explored in relation to issues of identification and individuation linked to the developmental task of establishing a secure identity in adolescence. The chapter illustrates the depth and severity of emotional disturbance that can remain undetected or unrecognised in some adopted children until they are faced with the challenges and tasks of adolescence.

In 'Adoption and adolescence: idealisation and overvalued ideas' *Sheila Spensley* discusses the psychotherapy – which she supervised – of a 14-year-old who had been adopted at the age of 10. Spensley elaborates the problems of negotiating the move toward separation from family in adolescence, for those adopted children for whom 'the childhood attachments that require to be loosened … have never been authentically formed'. She delineates the emotional and psychological plight of adolescents who were adopted, whose experiences in infancy and early childhood have resulted in a 'poverty of psychic life'. Spensley suggests that for these children, the move toward separation from family in adolescence gives rise to 'catastrophic anxiety' linked to the trauma of 'premature psychological birth' in their early years, and to the fear of not being wanted or loved. This can lead to an extreme and hostile rejection of the adoptive parents when the adopted child reaches adolescence – as a way of defending against catastrophic anxiety

– accompanied by an idealisation of birth parents or family, and over-valuation of the adolescent's view of himself as having no ties to, or need of, his adoptive parents. Spensley argues that if adoptive parents can be helped to understand what lies behind this behaviour, it may enable them to avoid a downward spiral of embittered mutual recrimination and rejection, and to respond with more realistic expectations.

Both these chapters describe aspects of adolescent experience that adoptive parents and professionals need to be alert to in the face of what might appear inexplicable behaviour. Holding in mind the added psychological tasks of adopted adolescents is crucial to being able to 'hold on' and to provide ongoing containment and thought, so needed for a young person to begin to establish a coherent sense of self.

References

Brodzinsky, D.M., Smith, D. and Brodzinsy, A. (1998) *Children's Adjustment to Adoption: Developmental and Clinical Issues*, London: Sage Publications.

Carter, B. and McGoldrick, M. (1989) 'Overview: the changing family life cycle. A framework for family therapy', in B. Carter and M. McGoldrick (eds) *The Changing Family Life Cycle,* London: Allyn and Bacon.

Sorosky, A.D., Baran, A. and Pannor, R. (1975) 'Identity conflicts in adoptees', *American Journal of Orthopsychiatry*, 45: 18–27.

Waddell, M. (1998) *Inside Lives: Psychoanalysis and the Growth of the Personality*, London: Duckworth.

15 Deprivation and development

The predicament of an adopted adolescent in the search for identity

Tessa Dalley and Valli Kohon

This chapter sets out to explore how the onset of adolescence and the inevitable changing bodily experiences resonated with the cumulative trauma of early neglect and subsequent adoption of an adolescent who began individual psychotherapy at the age of 12. The fundamental role of mother in the formation of a mental representation of the body – known as the 'body schema' – is a complex predicament for the adopted adolescent and particularly in Tony's case, as both his biological and adoptive mother were also adopted. The sense of loss and search for the birth mother in the development of identity become more urgent with the anxieties of leaving home and the possibility of finding her in reality.

The adolescent's relationship to her/his body

Adolescents manifest many of their conflicts and anxieties in the body schema. The rapid bodily changes of puberty create an experience of alienation that is acutely felt by adolescents. They ask themselves, 'Whose is this hardly recognisable body?' On reaching puberty, adolescents may experience their sexual maturity as a trauma that threatens the idealised pre-pubertal image of the body, which is felt to be free of conflicts. Moreover, powerful sexual impulses in adolescence may be felt to endanger the fantasised ideal union between mother and child.

Puberty requires a radical adaptation in the adolescent's relationship to her/ himself. The adolescent has to take possession of a body which, by changing in drastic ways, confronts her or him with profound issues of identity.

As Freud (1923: 26) said, 'the original ego is a body ego, rooted in the sensations and perceptions that a baby has of its physical experience'. Torras de Bea (1991: 176) writes: 'At the beginning the body schema is the representation of an undifferentiated body; as development proceeds it is transformed into a representation of an articulated body that not only has external borders and surfaces but also a certain context and "organs" with differentiated parts that have specific functions. We must also add that the body schema is in fact a symbol.' In other words, the body schema is a symbolic representation of the body.

The role of the mother in the formation of a mental representation of the body is fundamental, not only because of her handling and attitude towards the body of her baby and later child, but also because of the relationship to her own body. The child's appearance, the similarity to the father and other family members and what this evokes in the mother, also plays an important role in the child's body schema. For normal development to take place, a double mourning has to evolve from birth onwards: the mother's mourning for the dependent baby that is lost with every step her child takes towards independence, and that of the child who progressively loses the idealised mother, totally devoted to him.

In infancy and latency the child's body does not change drastically, and the idealisation of the pre-pubertal body can be retained. Laufer (1991) writes that for the adolescent to achieve the image of an integrated mature sexual body after puberty, he has to be able to include the idealised pre-pubertal image of his body in order to feel secure and loved. Puberty ushers in a transformation of the adolescent's body from its infantile and pre-pubertal form to an adult, sexually mature one. This necessitates a fundamental change in the body schema. The adolescent's attitudes toward and treatment of his body reflect his internal relations, especially between different parts of his personality. Instincts and impulses reactivated from infancy may lead to disturbance that had not been evident during childhood and latency, but can emerge in adolescent sexual life.

Adolescents who are adopted

The predicament for the adolescent who has been adopted is complex. In adolescence the ego has to reorganise itself to accommodate internal changes and maturing genital functioning in order to take 'ownership of the body' (Laufer, 1968). Blos (1967: 163) describes adolescence as 'the second individuation process, the first one having been completed toward the end of the third year of life': what in infancy had been a process of individuation (Mahler, 1963) out of the mother–infant dyad, in adolescence 'becomes … the shedding of family dependences, the loosening of infantile … ties in order to become a member of society at large or, simply, of the adult world'.

The role of mother in encouraging adaptation remains crucial. 'In conceptualising the genesis of the eventual "sense of identity", I tend to regard demarcation of the body image from the image of … the mother as the core of the process' (Mahler, 1963: 309). The experience of mother's nurture and emotional containment gives the infant the sense of developing a body schema. The adolescent may experience his body and body sensations as foreign and dangerous to his whole functioning. If this process has been distorted through disruption or failure in the early mother–child relationship, the adopted adolescent may be unable to experience the mature body as belonging to himself and may regard his changing body as either his enemy, or something separate from – and alien to – the rest of himself.

For a child adopted from birth or early infancy, his body may be the only concrete link to biological parents, knowing that this was all his parents knew of him as an infant. With bodily changes in adolescence, the sense of loss from the ties to the biological parents is often compensated for by the resurgence of a need to find them. There is a constant reminder of them, due to the lack of physical resemblance to the adoptive parents as the adolescent reaches sexual maturity and, as a young adult, grows to look more like his biological parents. The search for mother or father by the adopted adolescent can partly reflect the need to find someone who has similar facial features and with whom there is a family resemblance.

Adoptive and biological parents – two representations

Alongside distortions in the body ego, other representations are complex for the adopted adolescent. The adopted child must include two separate sets of parents within his representational world (Brodzinsky *et al.*, 1998), which creates difficulties at each stage of development. Hodges (1984: 49) writes, 'Where the child has no contact with the biological parents outside very earliest infancy, there is no organised experience, no memory to draw on to construct a representation of the parent.' The gap is filled by the mental representation of the parent, to which the child attaches feelings and fantasies of his own, unmodified by the reality of everyday experience.

In adolescence, adoption presents problems in the establishment of a sense of identity in relation to the task of separation and individuation. Without knowledge about and experience of biological parents, it may be difficult for the adolescent to build a firm sense of identity by locating his own personal history within his adoptive family. Curiosity about his origins and early life may be experienced as conflictual and dangerous.

When the separation–individuation issues come to the fore in the search for a coherent independent identity, this can lead to challenging behaviour – in particular, attacks on the body by self-harm, drug misuse and so on. With non-adopted adolescents bodily self-harm can sometimes be understood as an unconscious attack on the parents; with adopted adolescents it can sometimes represent an unconscious attack on the *biological* parents. Bodily self-harm can also be understood as a test of whether the adopted adolescent is loved and wanted, or of the adoptive parents' commitment.

Tony

In the discussion that follows, we explore these issues about the onset of puberty and the relationship to the body in an adolescent who had been adopted. When thinking about Tony there are particular aspects of his behaviour that we would like to consider in some depth. He had a tendency to dismantle and take apart all sorts of objects until they were in tiny fragments. He also searched for various forms of containment, including the use of nappies. Both of these communicated the relationship that Tony had with his internal world, his early experiences and his identity as well as revealing elements of his body schema. Lacking a stable primary relationship with his birth mother, his fantasy about his adoption gave rise to a sense of self that was damaged, unloved and rejected, a perception which was not modified by his adoptive mother, in spite of her best efforts to be emotionally available to him. By turning away from a difficult relationship with his adoptive parents to fantasies about an idealised biological mother, these feelings about himself were not open to change by everyday experience, but persisted instead in disassociated states of mind. As a result, he was continually threatened by imminent disintegration.

Tony was referred to a Child and Adolescent Mental Health Clinic when he was 12. On transfer to secondary school, he was constantly distracted, had poor concentration, and showed attention-seeking and immature behaviour which included baiting older boys. His self-esteem was very low and he seemed confused most of the time: he was overwhelmed by anxieties which affected relationships with his peers and development towards independence, such as an inability to catch a bus or train on his own. His mother reported excessive secrecy, hoarding penknives, ropes and sharp objects in his bedroom. When she found him with a rope tied around his neck, she realised the extent to which he was becoming depressed with suicidal thoughts. One persistent problem was that Tony continued to wear nappies at night, and left them occasionally soiled with urine in this bedroom. If Tony did not have nappies, he resorted to using any item of linen such as a pillowcase to wrap around his genitals.

As an infant, Tony suffered severe deprivation. His young mother – who was adopted when she was one year old – had learning difficulties and was probably schizophrenic. His father left home when Tony was two years old. Tony and his sister, two years older, were always dirty, undernourished and remained behind in their developmental milestones due to under-stimulation. Tony was four years old when he was placed in care and both children were adopted when he was five. His adoptive parents, a caring professional couple, had two teenage daughters, but following the death of their son, they decided to seek to adopt. Both parents found it very painful to think about their son who had died, and their sense of loss and feelings of guilt undoubtedly influenced their decision to adopt two traumatised children. Tony's adoptive mother had herself been adopted, but was reluctant to talk about her experience and consequently found it hard to think about the emotional experience of the children.

At the time, Tony's behaviour was 'like a whirlwind'. He was out of control and totally unaware of danger. He was both encopretic and eneuretic, and had significant speech delay. He exhibited a ravenous hunger and would eat anything – even to the extent of picking up dirt and putting it in his mouth. With the care and firm boundaries of his adoptive parents, his behaviour settled and speech improved. It took some time for them to be convinced that his difficulties were a manifestation of serious psychological problems that were beyond the reach of the normal strategies that parents might employ to improve a child's behaviour. They were kind and well intentioned, but could not understand the catastrophic nature of the losses that these children had suffered. His older sister had speech and language difficulties, and was given both educational and psychological support, unlike Tony who managed without, until he showed signs of developmental breakdown in early adolescence.

The therapy

Over the course of his six-year treatment, Tony had two therapists. The first therapist saw Tony weekly for two years, from the age of 12 to 14, until she left the clinic. His second therapist saw Tony more intensively, for four sessions a week from the age of 14 until he was 18 years old. This resonated with the experience of his adoption in being 'relinquished' by the first and 'adopted' by the second.

In the first treatment phase, the therapist provided Tony with an experience not just of structure but of a mind that could process emotional experience. His puberty had brought about internal changes which prompted Tony to search for something undefined. It became clear that he wanted to attend therapy in order to understand. By the time his first therapist left, he was developing a capacity to think and to experience the existence of a consistent mind that could keep hold of thoughts and feelings.

The second phase of his treatment was more intensive, with four sessions a week until he reached adulthood. In working through the loss of the first therapist, painful issues relating to his adoption and the separation from his mother surfaced. He began to think about loss, gaps and having no memory. This intensified the importance of searching for his birth mother. Anxieties about leaving home and separating from the second therapist as he moved into adulthood became focused on his internal conflicts about meeting his biological mother which could soon become a reality.

First phase

In the first few sessions, Tony sometimes mumbled quietly to himself, excluding the therapist completely. At times his light blue eyes would look intently at the therapist but seemed quite absent. He could not retain anything the therapist told him: not the time, duration, or day of the session, nor even her name. Gradually, he began to speak more coherently and to recognise the therapist as someone who could be more firmly held in mind. He made a lot of faces and his grimaces looked like expressions of pain which related to the slightest contact of his body with the objects in the room – like brushing the edge of his chair with his leg, or touching the table with his hand. He looked very dishevelled and his school uniform was usually quite dirty. His hands were frequently covered in ink, as he was often busy with a large collection of pens, felt-tips and pencils. He said that he was given them, or that he had stolen or bought them from a friend. They dropped out of his pockets, and he fiddled endlessly with them, unscrewing them and shaking bits out – then forgetting how to put them together, or not seeing where they had fallen, or where he had put some bit or other. He created an atmosphere of chaos and confusion.

Tony seemed to have internalised the experience of a psychotic mother of infancy, who was incapable of providing a continuity of attention towards her child. One might imagine that at times she forgot who the child was, or where he was – that she might not know how to look after him, or what to feed him. Tony had fragments of a mother, and perhaps felt that he only existed in fragments for her. We do not know the exact nature of her psychotic illness, but she was probably not totally absent – it was more likely that she was intermittently available. The father was physically absent for periods of varying length, so there was no regularity or continuity in the child's experience of him. Tony's very existence probably fluctuated in his mother's mind and this would have contributed to a fragmentation of his ego: there was a Tony in pieces. It was as if the erratic and unpredictable presence and absence of the mother created holes in Tony's mind, through which he allowed all thoughts, memories, and feelings to leak out. As a defence, this permitted him to empty his mind of painful experiences, and to disconnect completely from what was going on around him.

For Tony, pain was concrete and physical: that is, psychic pain was felt or not felt at a bodily level. He denied hurting himself, saying that he felt no pain. Yet his grimaces in the sessions revealed another sensibility, much more fragile – so much so that the slightest touch to his skin seemed to elicit manifestations of pain. The real emotional contact with the therapist, which occurred from time to time, also produced something like pain in him, and Tony could only convey this through grimacing.

The other symptomatic behaviour displayed by Tony was to seek various different forms of containment. For instance, he was preoccupied with time. Gradually he began to be able to explore the concept of time in relation to the duration of sessions. He got a watch, with which he played in the sessions, taking it off and putting it back on many times, and fiddling with the strap. Sometimes the watch was stopped, or the strap broke, or sometimes he lost the watch and he found it again. In the sessions, Tony liked to compare the time on his watch and that of his therapist. He was very aware of the beginning and ending of each session, and would tell her – with evident satisfaction – how mistaken she was if the session ended a minute or two before or after he thought it should, according to his watch. Rather than 'controlling' the session and his therapist, this seemed to be Tony's way of trying to use time to organise the chaos in his mind. Internally, he had no sense of rhythm, or of how something could be planned in an orderly sequence that could help him to perform ordinary daily tasks. The very irregular care he had received as a young child seemed to be reflected in his current state of disorganisation.

Another form of containment was to steal and use nappies. He wore them at night and left them, without much shame, behind the bed or in the wardrobe. The nappies were generally dry, occasionally wet, but never soiled. He did not deny using them, although he felt awkward when his parents confronted him. At this stage, it was not possible for him to bring the subject into his therapy.

Tony became more and more conscious of the 'holes' in his mind. However, his tendency for thoughts or memories to escape his mind – in order to avoid the possibility of feeling psychic pain – resulted in his feeling empty, disconnected and unable to think. Yet he still felt a certain amount of curiosity about how things were put together and worked. His habit of dismantling objects could be perceived as a primitive attempt, at a phantasy level, to investigate how the damaged and ill mind of his mother worked – perhaps even to try and repair it, which was inevitably doomed to failure. The nappies evoked an idea of a mother who can hold and contain her child. This gave him the feeling that there was someone or something that could receive what he expelled from his body, and could prevent him from feeling that everything he had inside would spill out. This links with Bion's (1962) idea that the function of the mother is to receive feelings and anxieties that are not yet processed, to be able to contain them and give them back to the child in a mentally digestible form. In this way, Tony sought the early experience of the baby contained by his mother, but he lacked the development to allow him to pass from a concrete to a symbolised experience.

These two symptoms in Tony's behaviour were in opposition to each other. The fragments that Tony scattered around him could be seen as the result of projection of intolerable and fragmented parts of himself and his mind. On the other hand, the use of nappies to seek containment could be linked to a more integrated and whole internal version of a mother and an attempt to recover this. It was as if Tony was trying to recreate in his mind a baby cared for by a mother. Faced by the pressure of puberty and adolescence, Tony was stuck in his regressive practices, which served as defences against disintegration.

Second phase

Tony, now 14, seemed friendly on first meeting his new therapist, efficiently writing down the times of his four sessions in his diary. She soon discovered the extent of his difficulty in organising his thoughts and remembering or holding anything in his mind. He was preoccupied with mending damaged toys cars, scraping and repainting them. He also bit his nails until they bled and talked incessantly about smoking. These early themes of damage, his anxiety about damaging himself and trying to mend things seemed to communicate both a sense of how internally damaged he was and also his feeling of hopelessness and helplessness. There was no sense that anyone could help him to think.

Tony had made a good relationship with his previous therapist. The early work with his second therapist focused on working through this loss. Meeting a new therapist resonated with the experience of his adoption. Jokes about the names of the two therapists, such as 'Valli-Dalley', to link them in his mind helped to bear the emptiness, the gap that had been left. This also stirred up turmoil for him, as he could not wait for his sessions, reflected in his blocking toilets or knocking plant pots out of the window – actions reminiscent of his 'wild' behaviour at the point of adoption. There was a question about whether the new therapist represented his adoptive mother, who cared for him, or his biological mother, who relinquished him.

Early on in these sessions, he talked about being adopted and how he would like to find his real mother and father. He did not know where they were, but thought they lived in Australia. He had only one memory of being in his father's cement lorry with his brother. They pressed some buttons which made the lorry tip up. He laughed, 'luckily it was empty as my father was not there'. The absence of his father made his memory a blank. He could not remember his face.

These partial memories brought to the surface perplexing questions of who he was, what his parents looked like and why they gave him up. He spoke of the painful experience of not remembering them, his longing to meet his biological mother and hatred of his father for abandoning him. 'I just want to see her. I want to know what she looks like as she might be walking down the street outside and I would not know it was her.' He had no mental picture of his mother. The question of why she relinquished him became all the more frightening as he had nothing to hold on to, no organised experience to construct a representation of her. In these preoccupations about his identity, there was a strong sense that the same question applied to his new therapist: who was she – and was she, in his fantasy, his mother?

His habitual smoking, which helped his entry into the adolescent group, was also an important link to both his adoptive and biological mothers. He knew that his biological mother smoked, which helped him to feel connected to her. His adoptive parents did not want him to smoke and he became caught up with the secrecy of not telling them. He craved cigarettes but also wanted to stop smoking. The conflict of being without or giving up something that he needed was just unbearable and created a cycle of craving and anxiety, replaying the deprivation of his infancy. He wanted to impress his therapist with the idea that he could give up, but at the same time was terrified that she would take something from him – that she would become a person who deprived him. 'Giving up' smoking had become synonymous with being given up by his mother, which was now part of his own self-representation.

Powerful themes of stealing and being stolen emerged as he linked his craving to smoke with hunger. He always arrived for his sessions 'starving' and desperate for a cigarette. He continually said that his biological mother would have let him smoke and that his adoptive mother was controlling, mean and intrusive. As his therapist did not accede to his requests to give him food or money for cigarettes, he became furious: in his mind it confirmed the cycle of deprivation, his sense of feeling undeserving, empty and being without. Tony turned to his body for comfort and control, as he had done as an infant, as this helped to satisfy his needs. His therapist felt that she had become like the adoptive mother – depriving him of cigarettes and food, which felt like stealing from him. She wondered whether he held a fantasy that he had been stolen from his mother and linked this with whether he had also felt stolen from his previous therapist. This gap, feeling abandoned and deprived, was continually being reworked in the therapeutic relationship.

His chatter and impulsive excitement turned to sadness as feelings of loneliness and the experience of emptiness, abandonment, hopelessness and helplessness began to emerge. He talked about feeling that his body was different and that he had yellow skin. As his body was changing, he struggled with his self-image as a developing young man and retreated into the sense of being a damaged, castrated, non-sexual child. It was through his obsessive watching of films such as *The Lion King* and *Titanic* – which he talked about at length – that he could begin to build a sense of a more potent male identity. He identified with the predicament of Simba who, like Tony, lost his father at a young age but was able to build up his kingdom and fight off the aggressors. Similarly, the character of Jack in *Titanic* became important for Tony. As the handsome hero in the film, Jack has a love affair with Rose, the heroine, and saves her from drowning. Jack was played by Leonardo di Caprio, and Tony modelled himself on the character and also, in an idealised way, on the actor. He would arrive at his sessions, pretending to be di Caprio, with similar clothes and hair style, experimenting with these different identities.

It was soon after these themes were elaborated in his sessions that the issue of his nappies emerged. Tony responded trancelike, speechless with terror, finding this unbearable to think about. He told the therapist to shut up, as if fending off an intrusive mother. This made her think about his experience of toilet training. Intense loneliness as a toddler without an available mother meant that the hours spent in dirty nappies may have perversely become a source of comfort, a substitute container. The nappies may have become a psychic organiser to keep control of his body, supporting his terrifying emptiness by preventing everything falling out of his mind. Like his smoking, the nappies provided a psychic connection to his biological mother, but had also helped him manage an important point of transition in his development in her absence.

Tony's masculine identifications were changing along with his body. At the beginning of treatment, he repeatedly spoke of a film, *Oliver and Company,* about a young puppy who found an owner who loved him. This seemed to encapsulate his early adoption fantasy. As a young man, he began to fantasise about becoming Judge Dredd, Rambo or James Bond and driving a new car in *Top Gear*. He recounted violent films and videos, as he brought a succession of gruesome fantasies and painful experiences which reverberated with his infantile terrors and archaic fears. These graphic images – of decapitation, blowing people's brains out and aliens who grow inside and then explode – began to speak more of the pressures upon his fragile body schema. How could he hold himself together in the face of his adolescent transition to his male adult self?

These descriptions coincided with the recognition of loss, as he began to realise that he had a sense of an emotional inside. These feelings inside him led, in turn, to an awareness not just that things could be lost, but that they could be taken away. To remain empty helped to avoid this dilemma. When he began treatment, he described his infancy as being like a 'black hole'. As far as he was concerned, his conscious life started just after his fifth birthday, when he was adopted – which he talked about as his first birthday. Five years after starting therapy, just before his seventeenth birthday he imagined being in the womb and felt comforted to be attached, safe and in control. 'This time seventeen years ago I was still inside mum's tummy – and when I was born and saw her face', he said, 'go away you are ugly.' It was unclear at that moment who was talking to whom in this poignant moment of rejection. Longings for his birth mother had been revived by his birthday and once again the theme of nappies returned to his material in sessions. This time, however, the feeling in the room was intense and intimate. In the countertransference, there was a feeling of fusion or umbilical attachment, as if he was now inside the therapist. Nevertheless, Tony was able to stay with thinking and insisted (in relation to the nappies), 'I am trying to give them up'. This theme of relinquishment coincided with his conscious wish for a sexual relationship with a girl he had met. For the first time, he expressed a wish to give up something *for* someone else. That is, this relinquishment was a necessary precursor to the ability to think about another and to form meaningful relationships.

Throughout his treatment, Tony frequently mentioned his wish to contact his biological mother when he was eighteen. As his adulthood approached, he spoke about this less and less. In his struggle to separate from his adoptive parents, he was also trying to loosen infantile ties to his biological mother, in spite of his longing to meet her. In this emotional vacuum he began to be more concerned about his therapist and who she was. Becoming curious coincided with his developing a capacity to be thoughtful, more philosophical and self-reflective. In organising his thoughts, he was also beginning to remember. To have a memory was not so dangerous. It was possible to share a memory or a fantasy with the therapist and to explore possible meanings together. For example, in a jumbled way he spoke about how it would be easier if he were a woman in his computer game – raising questions about his own gender identity and earlier references to being a girl. Perhaps, in his fantasy, he may not have been adopted if he had been a girl. By wearing a nappy did he pretend to be a girl, to control his phallic aggression and keep his penis hidden? The character Mrs Doubtfire came into his mind and it was possible to explore feelings about the man who dressed up as a woman in order to be close to and take care of his children. Confused about the role of his own aggression in driving his father away – as the pre-Oedipal child – the Mrs Doubtfire figure helped Tony to separate out a conscious wish for a father who cared about him from a mother about whom he did not feel so conflicted.

As his adulthood approached, his confusion was expressed through his own terror of growing up, leaving home and his therapy. He said he felt like an infant in a man's body. Lacking an internalised sense of an adult or parent, he felt that he was growing into a sense of nothingness and became preoccupied with death, AIDS and the music of Freddie Mercury. When he thought about his mother, he said, 'she could not cope with me and had to give me away'. Although the experience of the separation and adoption had been like a death for him, the beginning of a resolution to the question about why he had been given up heralded an important development as he moved towards adulthood. With this configuration in his mind, he could begin to reconstruct a self-representation as a wanted child. If his birth mother were dead, then he would not have the conflict of whether to find her and discover this in reality.

From a very early age and lacking an available maternal figure, Tony withdrew into fantasy in order to escape the pain of his psychic reality and to manage his confused fragmented world on his own. As Tony moved out of his need-fulfilling existence towards a capacity for thought and the possibility of relatedness, thinking became gratifying, not just terrifying. As he could understand the difference between being deprived and depriving himself, being neglected and neglecting himself, and that he had a body that needed to be looked after and nurtured, he was not so frightened to move out of his isolation. With an experience of a therapist – someone there for him who could act as a container and modify his projections through thought – he could think about leaving. As an adult, he was now legally entitled to make contact with his biological mother if he wanted to.

Conclusion

At the time that Tony became an adult and his therapy came to an end, he had a job and was in a stable relationship with a girlfriend, with whom he was thinking of living. He could now experience a stable relationship as something that he wanted – but was highly conflicted about leaving home, as he felt that this placed further pressure on him to find his birth mother. To some extent, the intensity of the transference to the therapist was worked through, but the finality of the ending was difficult to comprehend – which is a common experience for adoptive children who, even in adulthood, live with the fantasy of meeting a maternal figure in reality.

A traumatised boy like Tony, who lost his mother and father in a way that must have been incomprehensible to a young child of three, has no way of thinking about what has happened to him. Psychic pain has no other expression but the concrete – that is, in bodily, physical terms: containing what he had suffered was impossible. Tony did not experience himself as having an inside with psychic contents, but rather as being full of holes, through which what was unthinkable and painful could drain out. His physical numbness was a concrete defence, as well as a sign of his despair at not knowing what he felt. Like many deprived children, he repeated his infantile trauma – he invited attack, attacked his own mind and body, took refuge in disintegration and fragmentation – as if to confirm the terrible neglect he suffered in his early years.

Tony's adoptive parents wanted more than anything for him to be normal. Tony, for his part, stayed stuck in an abnormal way of behaving during infancy and latency, so that nobody could forget his past. He did not have the means to think about, understand and digest such a history. He needed someone to take charge of thinking for him. When he reached puberty, the bodily changes, and the feelings associated with them, pushed him to seek something, perhaps not easily defined. It seemed that Tony accepted the idea of therapy – even though for a time he did not seem to know how to use it – because he found that both therapists were interested in the scattered and intolerable mess of fragments of thoughts and feelings he brought, and that they wanted to at least try to describe them. At home and at school the aim was to control and to regulate, which was undoubtedly necessary, and it gave him structure and security. But he also needed someone who could stand the chaos and confusion that he constantly carried with him.

Tony's physical presentation indicated that his body was both the spokesman and the screen that gave us clues to understanding something of his internal world. Thinking and words could only emerge once his original body ego could begin to detach itself from the sensations in the body. At that moment there was the beginning of a body-schema, a symbolic field, and an internal relation with the self, which implies the existence of a more consistent mind that can keep hold of feelings and thoughts. As he developed, we came to see Tony's 'seeking something' as a need to establish an identity – both internally and externally – which is after all one of the cornerstones of the adolescent process.

References

Bion, W. (1962) *Learning from Experience*, London: Heinemann.
Blos, P. (1967) 'The second individuation process of adolescence', *Psychoanalytic Study Child*, 22: 163–85.
Brodzinsky, D., Smith, D. and Brodzinsky, A. (1998) *Children's Adjustment to Adoption*, London: Sage Publications.
Freud, S. (1923) 'The ego and the id', *S. E.*, IXX, London: Hogarth Press.
Laufer, E. (1991) 'Body image, sexuality and the psychotic core', *International Journal of Psychoanalysis*, 72: 63–71.
Laufer, M. (1968) 'The body image: the function of masturbation and adolescence', *Psychoanalytic Study of the Child*, 23: 114–37.
Hodges, J. (1984) 'Two crucial questions: adopted children in psychoanalytic treatment', *Journal of Child Psychotherapy*, 10: 47–56.
Mahler, M. (1963) 'Thoughts about development and individuation', *Psychoanalytic Study of the Child*, 8: 307–24.
Torras de Bea, E. (1991) 'Body schema and identity', *International Journal of Psychoanalysis*, 68: 175–84.

16 Adoption and adolescence

Idealisation and overvalued ideas

Sheila Spensley

Adolescence is, above all, a time for measuring up to the reality of personal existence; the 'facts of life' come into focus and it is a time for passing muster in the world of adult human beings. The whole psychic climate moves inexorably towards the need to engage with reality, internal and external, and it is the degree to which these realities can be faced that will determine how satisfyingly adult life can be experienced. When this crucial adaptation to reality has to include the experience of adoption, the task is all the greater.

Adaptation to external life is set in motion at birth and during the years of infancy, childhood and puberty, balances have to be struck between the self-oriented pleasure-seeking existence appropriate to infancy and the reality of dependency on personal relationships that culminates in altruism. The task, as Freud put it, is the relinquishing of pleasure principle living in favour of reality principle benefits (Freud, 1911).

The processes of growth, as accretions of learning derived from experiences of living and relationships (Bion, 1962), are helped or hindered by the quality of the personal relationships that can be sustained in infancy and childhood. It takes two, mother as well as baby, to achieve a 'psychological birth' (Mahler *et al.*, 1975; Tustin, 1981b) in which a potential for empathy and an ability to envisage a world of other sentient beings emerges, to give depth and meaning to human life. I shall draw on the work of Frances Tustin to examine the consequences for adolescence, when the circumstances surrounding psychological birth – that is, the inception of psychic life in the infant – have put the development of these capacities for relationship and empathy in jeopardy. Tustin introduced the concept of 'premature' psychological birth in relation to the limited social responsiveness and the insensitivities associated with autism, which she attributed to a critical failure of psychic development. Further clinical exploration of this perspective suggests that her concept may usefully contribute to a deeper understanding of these early mental processes and their consequences.

Premature psychological birth

Much of the work of Frances Tustin focused on the consequences of what she termed 'premature' psychological birth, a concept which has facilitated thinking about that transition into psychic life and the capacity to abstract from sensory experience, which is the mark of humanity. Tustin (1982b: 97) contrasted what happens in normal development after birth, where 'the newborn infant is sheltered in what might be called the "womb" of the mother's mind', with what happens in premature psychological birth where 'for any of a large number of possible interacting circumstances, the infant is "catapulted" too soon or too harshly from this essential womb-like state' (Tustin, 1981b: 98). Tustin used the concept of premature psychological birth to illuminate the state of animal isolation associated with autism, but in so doing has also provided a concept which facilitates exploration of other mental phenomena in infancy and in adolescence (Tustin, 1972, 1981a, 1986). In this chapter, I will discuss the way in which poverty of psychic life is the fateful and overriding characteristic of children with early experiences of severe maternal deprivation; children who, in the first years of life, have been driven from pillar to post in search of a 'psychological womb', within which the emotional storms of infancy might be tamed and tolerated.

The experience gap and its consequences

The consequences of missing out on this vital maternal experience are dire, whatever the precipitating factors, and presage trouble for those who subsequently have to try to make up for the deficit. Unlike the physical immaturities accompanying premature birth, which are usually restored by intensive care and nutrition, the deficiencies associated with premature psychological birth remain problematical. This is because poverty of psychic life disables those very capacities for internalisation and learning from experience which are essential to healthy development. For the adolescent who has experienced premature psychological birth there exists instead a deep and intractable state of mind, described by Sydney Klein as an 'impenetrable encapsulation' (Klein, 1980). Klein had discovered this phenomenon among neurotic patients in whom he observed a particular resistance to change resulting from their persistent failure to take in interpretations. It is this state of encapsulation and unreachability (Spensley, 2005) to which I want to draw attention, in relation to the impasses of incomprehension and hopelessness experienced by adoptive parents trying to make sense of an adolescent's apparent indifference and rejection.

Among the cries of desperation, frustration and sheer incredulity from fostering and adoptive parents of adolescents, we hear again and again of the adolescent's ingratitude, lack of appreciation, self-defeating destructiveness, defiance and rejection of help from whatever quarter, whilst a sneering contempt for their own dependency and real neediness is unshakeably maintained. It is puzzling and heartbreaking for eager, well-meaning adoptive parents to find that they cannot *give* a child a good home and be good parents, or rather that their good home and good parenting is not being received as such by the child. Instead, parents and adolescents (and social workers too) can become embroiled in conflicts and frustrations – often ending with qualms on both sides about whether the whole enterprise is really worth the candle. This is a particularly painful experience for those adoptive parents who even come to regret their decision to adopt and are left feeling angry and guilty. Professional interventions usually focus on trying to salvage some family peace and reconciliation in the face of a growing despair about whether the problems can ever be resolved.

Incomprehension

To many parents, it seems inherently nonsensical to go on providing good parenting to a rejecting and contemptuous young person and it is hard for them to believe in the significance and value of their role as parents to their adolescents, in the face of its debasement by them. Incomprehension is the order of the day and the point may be reached where exasperation pushes a parent to react negatively or punitively. No sense can be made of the adolescent's behaviour and the powerful temptation is to give up. That this does not happen is vital and depends on grasping the nature of the experience (and perhaps more importantly, the absence of experience) that may underlie the adolescent's contradictory and incomprehensible behaviour. This is not the same as supporting parents to discover reserves of empathy, tolerance and understanding, such as to enable them to put up with unreasonable behaviour, because it can be attributed to an appalling childhood history. The more pressing need is to help strengthen the judgement and self-confidence of parents, by providing them with a new perspective on the nature of the child's disturbance that has made them feel duped and trapped.

The adolescent's need is for the steady and stable parental world to prevail against their furious efforts to topple it. These adolescents are young people whose mental processes involve evacuating thought and feeling triumph over capacities for taking things in (Rosenfeld, 1987). Their attacking behaviour may be impelled more by an urge to relieve themselves of fears of dependency than by a specific desire to inflict damage on the parent. The distinction is as important as it is hard to detect, but it underlies the contradictions of adolescent behaviour, particularly among those at the renegade and destructive end of the behavioural spectrum. Such individuals figure prominently in that social group now described as 'looked after' children; looked after, that is, by adults other than their birth parents who have failed, for one reason or another, to provide the conditions for psychic containment which they now so conspicuously lack. For these young people, the developmental turmoil characteristically experienced during the adolescent years takes on seismic proportions.

All adolescents engage in a struggle to achieve a sense of self and to become less dependent on adults in the move towards separation from the family, but when the childhood attachments that require to be loosened in adolescence have never been authentically formed, the task is Herculean. Without psychic maturity, separation means danger to the sense of self more than loss of the other. When identity and self-confidence are dependent on taking the other for granted, it feels catastrophic to give it up. These are young people whose experience certainly needs to be understood (Steiner, 1993), but for whom understanding itself feels persecutory and/or incomprehensible.

The resulting communication impasse is one which faces parent and psychotherapist alike. Often the most basic requirements for treatment (Rustin and Quagliata, 2000) are problematical, when assessments reveal that carers or teachers, and not the adolescents themselves, are more likely to have initiated the request for treatment. At the same time, responsibility for supporting the treatment of the adolescent comes as a surprise to the beleaguered parent. It is unexpected and often felt to be burdensome and unwelcome. Whilst the paradigm of family and 'family shape' (Kraemer, 1997) has value and meaning for adoptive parents, in the mind of an adolescent with minimal experience of sharing and of the Oedipal constellation, it may exist only as an ideal, devoid of attachment responsibilities. The situation is familiar in the despairing protests of both parents and psychotherapists, 'I don't think he listens to a word I say!' Little is achieved in sustained attempts to make sense of the adolescent's view of his life: explanation, persuasion or encouragement all fall on deaf ears as the self-made mind resolutely remains a closed shop where blind belief maintains an impregnable fortress. Such individuals are extremely difficult to reach, for the psychotherapist as much as the parent represents the reality of life and love which is so feared that it can only be treated with hatred and contempt – the 'couldn't care less' response. This enshrines the communication difficulty, demonstrating how the scissions occur internally and unconsciously, but also warp the experience of personal relationships.

Daniel

The underlying nature of this communication impasse, all too familiar within family relationships, will now be explored as it is experienced in the relationship between psychotherapist and patient. I am grateful to Sue Davies for her permission to use case material presented to me in supervision. Supervision is often seen as an opportunity to obtain a second opinion on patient material and the therapist's understanding of it. I prefer to think of the supervisory setting as one which allows the combining of two perspectives that magnify the picture of the patient's dilemma, much as the human lens acts to increase magnification of the eye's interior for examination by ophthalmoscope. Like psychotherapy, supervision is a two-person activity and the supervisor has the benefit of the observational 'lens' of the therapist, so that together they can see more than either could see separately. The supervisor's capacity to add understanding is contingent on the degree to which meticulous attention to detail and observational candour imbues the recording of the session. When, as in this case, that level is high, the sharing of the clinical experience in supervision is a very real privilege.

When Daniel arrived for psychotherapy he was 14 years old and 'pissed off'. His adoptive parents, already in couple therapy, were 'at their wits end'. Conflicts at home were dramatic and draining (both parents prone to depressive episodes). But I shall not pursue the family dynamics in the interest of focusing primarily on Daniel's incomprehension regarding his life and his difficulties. Suffice it to say that Daniel was adopted at the age of 10 years by a well-intentioned couple who had two college-aged children of their own. Daniel was six when he was finally taken into local authority care because of concerns about the level of child care available in the home. The children were appearing at school dirty and hungry, and the parents seemed to be entangled in an unsavoury world of sex, criminality, and alcohol abuse. Until the age of six, Daniel's life had been rather nomadic and chaotic, with an incompetent mother who got herself into relationships with violent men. Both of his parents had been in care themselves and seemed to have little notion of how to bring up children. Nothing is known of his father's whereabouts now and his two younger sisters, who have a different father, were adopted when very young. Daniel suffered from maternal neglect and from abuse by an older brother who later had to be removed from their foster-care home, for that reason. Four years later his foster mother also rejected Daniel, against his wishes, in favour of another and less troublesome foster child. Finally, at age 10, he was adopted by hopeful parents who expected to provide what was needed to enable Daniel to make something worthy of his life and to help him follow in the footsteps of their own sons.

After being taken into care, Daniel continued for a time to have contact with his birth mother, for whom his feelings oscillated between affection-seeking and aggressive contempt and the quality of their relationship was causing concern. Contact with mother was ultimately terminated, by permission of the Court, prior to the adoptive placement. Daniel, on the other hand, waits expectantly for his 16th birthday when he thinks he will be reunited with his birth mother, although his ideas about his relationship with her have remained muddled and inconsistent. He clings to one particular anecdote: that his mother has written him a letter which he will only be allowed to read when he is 18. It was reported that this restriction was felt to be prudent and in the child's interests, but periodically, when Daniel is filled with grievance, it provides a ready bone of contention with adults. He idealises his birth mother and believes he would be free of problems if he could go and live with her.

Encounters

The therapist found Daniel to be a lively, intelligent boy, 'a likeable rogue'. He was articulate about his complaints and talked forcefully about how he saw current issues and how the situation could be alleviated. He ridiculed the efforts of his adoptive parents to get him to complete his school assignments and his acerbic criticisms of them and the school could be quite amusing.

It was not long, however, before his therapist began to feel that Daniel was not listening to a word she said, her experience faithfully replicating the experience of his adoptive parents. They would argue, cajole, reward, sanction and at times, were even reduced to threats – all to no avail. In the consulting room, disparagement of his therapist and traducement of her words gave Daniel a feeling of superiority, leaving her feeling inept and absurd. Daniel seemed immune to empathy, unable to take anything to heart, because he thought concretely and saw the answer to all his needs in taking action to change the external situation. Within family relationships, the best he could do was to conform when there were material benefits in it for him which provided immediate, if short-lived, gains. The quality of the discomfiting clinical encounters is encapsulated in the following quotations, plucked from sessions across the one-year period of intensive psychotherapy:

> 'Why do you keep bringing it back to me?'
> 'Yeh, yeh, ... whatever'
> 'Boring, boring, boring, boring, ...' (spoken over the therapist's words)
> 'What me? Nah ... you've got the wrong person.'
> 'She (adoptive mother) would have more chance of getting through a brick wall.'

I think the deepest levels of anxiety are concealed in this inauspicious therapeutic atmosphere and all attempts to understand Daniel's experience of life have to keep this clinical fact at the forefront, not simply as part of the 'total experience' (Joseph, 1985) but as the defining characteristic of the therapeutic relationship. Daniel had plenty to say for himself and it was easy to be seduced or diverted by him into attributing greater meaningfulness to his arguments than they deserved. Daniel did not have *problems*, he had *solutions*; *he was* supremely confident in his explanations and advice. Because the balance of projection/introjection was so heavily weighted on the side of projection, Daniel operated in life as a giver, not a receiver. He was brimful of ideas for surmounting any difficulty, 'he would get a car and just drive wherever he wanted, stress-free: he might join the army, or the police, or become a psychiatrist, which he thought he would be good at'. Reality and work did not feature as stepping stones on the way to achieving his goals, because he had a capacity to divide his mind to accommodate incompatible ideas. He was a master of hair-splitting and in his own terms 'won' any argument (including his own). For example, after failing an exam, he acknowledged that he had not revised, but quickly added that these exams were not really important; next year was the important one – as if he would, by then, have put all to rights, and the present concerns of his adoptive parents were totally misplaced. Alternatively, as quoted above, he would ignore or dismiss with contempt any new idea that did not suit his logic. Daniel did not really attend to his therapist's words although he heard them, very much in the way once described to me by a young woman who said, 'I hear what you are saying, but it doesn't go past my ears' (Spensley, 1995). These are cases where it is important to direct therapeutic attention to the speaker rather than to what is said (Sohn, 2006).

On the subject of adoption, Daniel was opinionated and provocative. He was in no mood to listen to attempts to enlighten or to present another perspective on his narrative, because he was certain there were no two ways about it: he was right, and if the therapist had a different view, she simply hadn't listened properly. In the session, a sense of futility took hold. Daniel was trigger-happy with his list of grievances, leaving the therapist feeling redundant, while, on home territory, he fanned the disappointment of his parents into moral outrage:

'Why did they adopt me if they just want a clone of A and B (his adoptive siblings)? What did they expect? I'm my own person. Had they gone round looking at other children before choosing him? Like going to buy a new house or a new car? ... You can get books with photographs in and you can choose which child you want ... It's awful, like going to Argos to buy a child. What do they look for – to see if a child is going to be a scientist or a writer or going to fit in or be well behaved? If they thought I was going to behave, they got that wrong!'

Daniel also twisted the knife in the wound. He boasted that he called his adoptive parents '*fake*' parents and used his adoptive mother's Christian name when he wanted to hurt them. This usually happened when his parents had said things that made him feel stupid or small. Whilst he seemed to have some sense of regret about going to such lengths to hurt them, his (predictable) answer was that they should not have adopted him: had they fostered him, he would not have been able to say such things! For the therapist, this was a painful picture of family life, but Daniel was miles away from the impact of his words, as he was in relation to his own and his parents' hurt.

The following extracts from the dialogue further demonstrate how deep-rooted anxiety and confusion masquerade as contemptuous argument and in the home this served only to drive Daniel's adoptive parents into a downward spiral of retaliatory sanctions, recrimination and despair. In this session, his therapist feels obliterated and the absence of meaningful contact makes her feel, she says, 'as if the session hadn't happened' (i.e. there had been no session). The mood of this session was confrontational from the start and it remained a power struggle to the end, with Daniel either talking over the therapist, or ostentatiously turning his eyes up to study the ceiling:

> Daniel declared that he was 'sick of it all'; that after nine months, he'd done enough and that he wasn't coming after Christmas, no matter what anyone said. He was only here because his parents had said he had to, not because he wanted to.
> 'I should be out playing with my mates now – that's where I want to be.'

Interpretation of his anxiety about talking to the therapist about himself drew the retort:

> 'Oh, God, of course I'd rather be out with my mates; it's got nothing to do with you.'

His therapist made a number of relevant and appropriate comments to try to engage Daniel in thinking, but he was adamant that he knew what he needed. However, in the midst of his arguments he did also let slip that his parents thought his behaviour had improved since he started to attend psychotherapy. He, of course, knew that his behaviour had changed because he was older and because he had learned to keep his head down and not backchat – and that had nothing to do with coming to psychotherapy! Daniel then went on to talk about all the things he had noticed about the therapist and about others in the clinic with a level of observational detail that came as a surprise. However, there was to be a sting in the tail:

> 'Were there any men doing this job? … I might become a psychiatrist. I might be good at that. It's an easy job, just sitting there, listening.'

His response to an interpretation about his wish to change places, revealed a very different agenda.

> 'Oh no, I wouldn't want to sit in your chair, I'd have a room with a couch, so that people could lie down and go rambling on and then I could go off and have a cup of coffee and they wouldn't even notice.'

Despite the mocking cruelty of the scene conjured up, his therapist was still able to think about Daniel's fears of not being helped or taken seriously by her, but her comments were met with ridicule and incredulity:

> 'What? No of course not, that's a ridiculous idea. As soon as I walk out of this room, I forget about you.'

The ridicule and mockery of psychotherapy conceals not only his fear of needing his therapist but, more importantly, his terror of being reached by her, because this would bring him into contact with the existence of an emotional life which he has contrived to obliterate since infancy. To allow his therapist to exist as 'needed' means the generation of an internalised personal experience of her bringing psychic life into existence; this in turn creates the opportunity of differentiating between internal and external.

The challenge of getting through

In this exchange, the depth of the split in Daniel's experience is prominent and it is as if internal life has been deep frozen. The resulting incomprehension, whilst serving the omnipotent defence, also renders him incapable of taking anything in from the therapist so that this becomes the primary challenge. Daniel is a spectator more than an observer. He watches and wants to copy, not learn. The therapist tries to show him something about himself and occasionally there is some evidence that he does venture to accept a tiny therapeutic morsel. Technically, then, there seem to be two alternatives. First, infinite patience in the hope that these rare moments will eventually coalesce sufficiently in the face of the storm of contempt, to engender some psychic awareness; or secondly, interpretation directed towards his incomprehension, insofar as it results from his contempt of reality and his exclusive focus on a self-made world. He talks boldly and knowingly, feeling one jump ahead of everyone, yet the net result is that he is constantly in trouble. In terms of his own 'logic', his behaviour achieves nothing and it might be helpful to try to interest him in the contradictions in what he asserts – not least because it reduces the risk of his feeling blamed.

In the session described, the idea that the therapist has helped him is energetically ridiculed and dismissed by Daniel. At other times, he goes on talking as if the therapist has said nothing. As most of us would, the therapist continued to consider alternative interpretations which might finally 'hit the spot'. But, as we discovered together, her more pervasive impression was that he was not really listening and that she felt de-skilled and obliterated by him. Instead, she set about trying to find ways around this impasse. As with his parents, her tolerance was pushed to extremes and she found herself exercising great care not to be retaliatory in her exasperation. For example, 'Why have you come then?' (knowing too that he has already answered that question).

Would this boy respond any differently if his inability to listen were to be related to his frustration? Projective procedures rely on the use of the eyes, not the ears, to comprehend the environment, so that Daniel 'knows' more about the minds of others than his own. Some confirmation of this perspective came early in the therapy, when Daniel talked of a wish to visit his birth mother. He said that he wanted to go and look; that he would not necessarily want to speak to her, but felt he really needed to go and have a look, to see what she looked like. He would like to know where she is and what she is doing.

Throughout the therapy, Daniel feels strongly that he is a victim. He believes he does not get what he wants, because people do not understand and instead persist in giving him what *they* think he needs. He argues his corner with great ingenuity but he also sabotages the help and support he is offered. He is deceptive and flouts the rules both at school and at home. He is always in trouble, but his prime concern is how to get away with it, or how to get out of it, and he never loses enthusiasm for pranks and chicanery. He has no wish 'to see ourselves as others see us' (Burns, 1786) but a shift of focus towards clarifying how he appears to see himself might be met with less incomprehension.

The capacity to 'take back projections' which lies at the heart of the therapeutic endeavour, is highly problematical when Daniel is oblivious of any difference between what he believes to be true and what is true. He has difficulty distinguishing between internal and external, doomed to seek solutions in the wrong places because he has so little awareness of the existence of internal space and life. His thinking is concrete; the solutions always reside in changing the environment. Incredulous, he demands, 'Why do you always bring it back to me?' – totally unaware of any relevance in the therapist's words. He lives largely in an illusory world in which he bestows meaning and has no need for learning. Under these circumstances, traditional and perhaps overvalued interpretations of his words which treat him as a listener have to give way to bringing the contradictions of his own statements to the fore in the hope of engendering self-reflection and a psychological birth.

For example, we might consider whether he might be less hostile were his own theories to be given serious attention. He says he should be outside playing with his mates – 'That's where I want to be'. So, he wants to be able to have fun and he would feel much better if he did have fun but he also knows that fun always gets interfered with and he ends up in trouble instead. This allows a possibility for helping him to see that his own well-being is related to the way he behaves and might enable him to give birth to the thought that he contributes to his own unhappiness. It offers him an opportunity to become aware of his own functioning, rather than being asked to take in a well-meaning but, as far as he is concerned, an 'alien' construct. After some attempts to draw his attention to himself in this way, the therapist was also able to bide her time amidst many angry and sarcastic battles of words. Daniel 'bites the hand that feeds' but it would not be useful to tell him that. Eventually, in a session filled with righteous indignation and derisive retorts, he finally ended with two parables which could hardly have presented Daniel's dilemma more excruciatingly, although he was not consciously aware of this.

Parable 1

'A scorpion asked a frog to give him a lift across the water on the frog's back, promising not to sting him. Half-way across, the scorpion stung the frog and both the frog and the scorpion drowned.'

Daniel did not know what to make of this parable but gave another which he thought he did understand.

Parable 2

'Two mice fell into a bowl of milk and were swimming around. One gave up and drowned while the other kept paddling and, eventually, the milk turned to butter and he was able to climb out.'

Daniel thought that this parable was about not giving up.

While the scorpion image provided a useful reference model, its significance had far more meaning for the therapist than for Daniel. She was careful not to interpret, but to wait for any reference to sabotage and wrecking behaviour to come first from him. Tentatively, it did, a few sessions later. Sighing and smiling he began:

'Wow, things are kicking off. I got thrown out twice over the weekend. Thrown out? Me? I ask you. What about that? It's shocking.'

Attempts by the therapist to get a grasp of what had happened were met with 'total over-reaction' as if he were completely innocent and the whole thing had now become a bit of a joke. Quickly, he wrapped his story up with 'Well it's cool now; everything's sorted'.

In the course of this session, the therapist was able to come closer to discovering what had taken place in the family and to Daniel's feeling that he was misunderstood and falsely accused by his adoptive parents. Without interpretation, he started to talk of his perplexity and of how he could not understand what had happened or why, especially since he had been feeling that things were going well and was thinking he was in a good place. With help from the therapist who suggested that he might, surprisingly, find it a struggle to be part of something good, he ventured to talk about whether it might not be better for him to go, since he did hurt his adoptive parents and made them ill. He then turned to the intrinsic adoption dilemma, as he saw it. He said he could not believe that his adoptive parents cared about him:

'My own mother, she didn't care about me', i.e. she hadn't been able to stop him or his sisters from being hurt – 'so why would anyone else care? I'm not even their son, not their flesh and blood.'

At the end of that session, Daniel said that every time things were going well, he messed it up and asked what he could do; how could he stop it? Unfortunately, this session still ended sadly, as Daniel reverted to the dispossessed, victim status he was familiar with and, whistling in the dark, answered his own question:

'It doesn't matter. I'll be alright on my own. I can manage.'

Momentarily glimpsing the scorpion, Daniel found it easier to go back to churning his butter.

Relevance for parents

The close resemblances between the relationship Daniel makes with his psychotherapist and that with his adoptive parents is not surprising and it will be pertinent to consider whether any aspects of the therapist's experience can be used to inform the psychological support that can be offered to adoptive parents. This is not to advocate an extension of psychotherapy, but to consider the implications for adoptive parents when the child's grasp of emotional reality is being both effaced and defaced. It may be possible for the downward spiral of recrimination and reproach to be checked, if parents can come to be more aware of the seriousness of the problem in which they and their child have become embroiled. The difficulties are complex and deep seated, although the level of argument that usually prevails assumes (on both sides) that it should be a simple matter to solve.

Like many other adopted children, Daniel struggled with unrealistic expectations of his new parents. His perception of his needs was distorted by his idealistic notion that no bond other than 'blood ties' can be valid and relied on, and that deeply held conviction underlay his perception of all alternatives. He had not seen his abusive brother for seven years, yet he was convinced that they 'look out for each other' because they are brothers. He clung tenaciously to a belief in reunion with an idealised mother and – grim experience notwithstanding – he lived in hope that all his dreams would then be realised. At times, moments of awareness of reality were observable, when he was able to acknowledge that he was in a good place and that it was better to have a home than to be exposed to the risks of being influenced by drug and gang culture – as he feared his brother might be. Unfortunately, such common-sense moments did not remain intact for long, before resentment and contempt interfered and his moment of better judgment was blown away.

For adoptive parents to begin to understand how severely a child's capacity to experience reality can be obstructed by early deprivation or abuse, makes a significant difference to the tolerance and judgement they are able to exercise in response to rejection and provocation. In order to counter the child's underlying phantasy about the restoration of the birth parents, adoptive parents need to be able to provide benign but firm judgement and support. Often, they too are filled with unrealistic expectations, confident in the power of benevolent loving care to overcome the disappointments, disillusion and bitterness of a child's history. For many children, particularly those adopted late in their childhood, like Daniel, provision of a good experience of stability and support is not in itself enough. Daniel has had a raw deal in his experience of parenting as, it seems, did his birth parents, but he has not simply missed out on something – his mind has been distorted by the experience, so that the very experience of loving support is difficult for him to stomach. It turns bad inside him and he finds himself spoiling a good experience in order to spare himself more fearful pain and guilt. In the absence of the life-giving parenting experience that results in psychological birth, he has developed a hard internal core to his 'self', '*an impenetrable encapsulation*' (Klein, 1980). It means that his thinking is concrete, determined predominantly by external experience in the absence of that connectedness with another human being which promotes a sense of identity and of being valued.

Like many other adolescents, Daniel did not continue in intensive therapy for as long as he needed. His hostility and trickiness did not win much sympathy from the adult world of teachers and parents who saw him as trashing their goodwill and support. For the psychotherapist, there is as much challenge in finding ways to help parents and carers to acquire a deeper understanding of the effects of 'premature psychological birth' which leaves a hard 'impenetrable encapsulation'. They need to see how their very success in providing good loving care may in itself create in the child a backlash of pain which results in their attacking that which is good. Neither parent nor child finds this comprehensible and it is the job of the psychotherapist to help both to appreciate and negotiate this obstacle. It may not be removable but the problem becomes more comprehensible when it can be appreciated that disordered thinking is involved and all that that implies.

Ingratitude is the most difficult and painful reaction for parents to bear, whether or not the child concerned has been adopted. Few find it easy to understand the severity of the emotional disturbance and the complicated mental processes which underlie it. Ruby, a 15-year-old adolescent with severe agoraphobia who could not travel on public transport, lost her symptoms in the course of psychotherapy

(Spensley, 1995). Was she even pleased, let alone grateful? She was extremely angry. Family and friends were delighted with the change that enabled her to go to school in the normal way again. But Ruby told me, 'What's so marvellous about going on a train? Everybody does that!'

This chapter has tried to direct attention to the role of the child psychotherapist in bringing into everyday life something of the knowledge and understanding which has been gained from the clinical setting, to ensure that the paralysing severity of unconscious mental processes is not mistaken for mere cussedness or ingratitude. There is ingratitude, but it is better described as an inability to tolerate feeling grateful. Parents cannot become therapists to their children, but a deeper appreciation of the existence of 'impenetrable encapsulations' may add to the wisdom and the forbearance they can bring to their parenting.

References

Bion, W.R. (1962) *Learning from Experience*, London: Heinemann.

Burns, R. (1786) 'To a louse', in D. Daiches (ed.) *Selected Poems of Robert Burns*, London: André Deutsch.

Freud, S. (1911) 'Formulations on two principles of mental functioning', *S.E.* XII.

Joseph, B. (1985) 'Transference: the total situation', in M. Feldman and E. Bott Spillius (eds) *Psychic Equilibrium and Psychic Change: Selected Papers of Betty Joseph*, London: Karnac.

Klein, S. (1980) 'Autistic phenomena in neurotic states', *International Journal of Psychoanalysis*, 61: 395–402.

Kraemer, S. (1997) 'What narrative?', in R. Papadopoulos and J. Byng-Hall (eds) *Multiple Voices: Narrative in Systemic Family Therapy*, London: Duckworth.

Mahler, M., Pine, F. and Bergman, A. (1975) *The Psychological Birth of the Human Infant: Symbiosis and Individuation*, New York: Basic Books.

Rosenfeld, H. (1987) *Impasse and Interpretation*, London and New York: Tavistock Publications.

Rustin, M. and Quagliata, E. (eds) (2000) *Assessment in Child Psychotherapy*, London: Duckworth.

Sohn (2006) Personal communication.

Spensley, S. (1995) *Francis Tustin*, London: Routledge.

Spensley, S. (2005) 'Classics revisited: Sidney Klein, autistic phenomena in neurotic states', *Journal of British Association of Psychotherapists*, 43: 45–54.

Steiner, J. (1993) *Psychic Retreats*, London: Routledge.

Tustin, F. (1972) *Autism and Childhood Psychosis*, London: Hogarth Press.

Tustin, F. (1981a) 'Psychological birth and psychological catastrophe', in J.S. Grotstein (ed.) *Do I Dare Disturb the Universe?*, London: Maresfield Library.

Tustin, F. (1981b) *Autistic States in Children*, London: Routledge and Kegan Paul.

Tustin, F. (1986) *Autistic Barriers in Neurotic Patients*, London: Karnac.

Further reflections

17   A cautionary tale of adoption

Fictional lives and living fictions

Graham Shulman

the thousand forms of past associations

(Brontë, 1847)

Adoption in one form or another is a recurrent motif in some of the greatest works of western literature through the ages, starting with Sophocles' story of Oedipus. Literature often contains profound psychological truths and observations about the human condition, and this applies no less in relation to adoption. One way of thinking about Emily Brontë's classic novel *Wuthering Heights* is as a cautionary tale of adoption (of course it is far more than just this). The novel dramatically illustrates some of the primitive states of mind and emotional dynamics associated with adoption. Close attention to selected details of *Wuthering Heights* is revealing, and the novel confirms Emily Brontë's rare and extraordinary insight into relationships and the human psyche.

Strangely, while the story is part of popular consciousness it is not common knowledge that the protagonist Heathcliff is an adopted child, though it is an obvious and prominent fact for any reader of the novel. The circumstances of Heathcliff's 'adoption' are of course very different from those of modern planned adoptions. Heathcliff is not *explicitly* taken into the family as a new member of the family – as happens in modern legal adoption – and his introduction into the family is not planned or expected. Nevertheless, many of the emotional dynamics in relation to Heathcliff are an extreme version of dynamics that can occur in formal adoption situations.

Narrative of an informal adoption

The circumstances and story of Heathcliff's 'adoption' are both evocative and instructive. Cathy and Hindley's father Mr Earnshaw goes on a journey from their remote and isolated family home in the moorlands of West Yorkshire to the city of Liverpool. He is away for three days. (The precise reason for his journey is never made clear.) He walks the sixty-mile journey each way. While in Liverpool he sees a boy in the streets, 'starving, and houseless and as good as dumb' (p. 37). Unable to find the child's parents or anyone who knew or claimed him, Earnshaw decides it is better to take the child home at once, 'because he was determined he would not leave it as he found it' (p. 37). He carries the boy home – a feat of physical exertion that leaves him feeling 'flighted to death' and 'never so beaten' (p. 36). He arrives home with his overcoat wrapped in a bundle in his arms, opens his coat to reveal a child inside, and deposits the boy on the floor in a symbolic enactment of a birth. The family crowd round to peer at the 'dirty, ragged, black-haired child; big enough both to walk and talk … [who] only stared round and repeated over and over again some gibberish that nobody could understand' (pp. 36–7).

Earnshaw exhorts his family to 'take it as a gift of God', while adding that it looks 'as if it came from the devil' (p. 36). Mrs Earnshaw was 'ready to fling it out of doors' (p. 37). When Hindley discovers the fiddle which his father had brought him as a present was 'crushed to morsels', he 'blubbered aloud'; and when Cathy finds out that her father, while 'attending on the stranger', has lost the whip he promised her, she 'showed her humour by grinning and spitting at the stupid little thing' (p. 37). The brother and sister 'refused to have it in bed with them' (p. 37), and the nurse Ellen Dean 'put it on the landing of the stairs, hoping it might be gone on the morrow' (p. 37).

The family subsequently christen the boy Heathcliff, this being 'the name of a son who died in childhood' (p. 38). The children's father 'took to Heathcliff strangely', and Heathcliff inexplicably becomes Earnshaw's favourite. Earnshaw's favouritism towards, and idealisation of, Heathcliff remain unshakeable; he irrationally takes Heathcliff's side against his own two children and shows no recognition or acknowledgment of the reality of a deeply unattractive side to Heathcliff's personality and actions – though this contrasts sharply with his fault finding and complaints about Hindley and Cathy.

These selected facts – dispersed in the narrative but gathered together here – are rich in association to some of the primitive emotional experiences and dynamics of adoption. The boy Earnshaw finds is an embodiment of neglect and abandonment, representing in extreme form circumstances common to adopted children, whether or not they have been literally abandoned. Earnshaw feels powerfully impelled to provide for the child and improve the child's lot – feelings that are perhaps universal for adoptive parents. And yet, apart from such feelings, nothing is made explicit about Earnshaw's motivation for his unusual action; we are left almost completely in the dark about the *deeper* emotional undercurrents of Earnshaw's decision to take the child into the family. What is clear is that the task of taking the child home and 'taking the child in' presents an almost impossible challenge; the extraordinary physical feat of carrying the boy home for sixty miles is a powerful metaphor for the sheer *enormity* of the psychological task involved in taking on, and taking in, an abandoned and neglected child.

There is a striking duality in Earnshaw's two contrasting comments about the boy when he introduces him to the family: on the one hand Earnshaw refers to the child as a 'gift of God', and on the other hand he describes the boy looking 'as if it came from the devil'. These two contradictory associations to a neglected and abandoned child who has been brought into the family aptly reflect two contrasting and polarised currents of feeling that can be evoked by the adopted child. First, where a child has been longed for and expected, the adopted child is indeed likely to be felt and appreciated as a 'gift of God' or the equivalent. Second, however, where the child's birth family have become demonised (see Chapter 6), or where an adopted child presents disturbed or – worse – destructive behaviour, or where such behaviour is feared or anticipated, the child can easily become identified with badness – if not actually demonised (not necessarily consciously) in the minds of the adoptive parents.

Who is this stranger?

A recurrent sense of alienation occurs in relation to Heathcliff. Earnshaw's use of 'it' rather than 'him' to refer to the child – who at that point in the story is not yet named and therefore in Earnshaw's eyes without an identity – underscores the denial of the child's selfhood and identity as a separate *person* with a history and life of his own, even if unknown. This persists in the nurse Ellen Dean's use of 'it' to refer to the child in her account of the events which she tells Lockwood many years after they occurred. The boy is only referred to as 'him' *after* the point in the story at which he has been given the name Heathcliff – the name of the son who had died in childhood. In this way he is at first dehumanised – turned into an 'it', an object, in the minds of the family.

This feeling of alienation is reinforced by Earnshaw's description of the boy looking as if he 'came from the devil' and being 'as good as dumb' when he was first found by Earnshaw in the streets of Liverpool. The seemingly innocuous but richly resonant and ambiguous phrase 'as good as dumb' carries the possible meaning that the boy's goodness lies in his dumbness/lack of speech – he is 'as good as he is dumb'. Speech is that by which the self is expressed, and one reading might be that unconsciously the boy is seen as good as long as his self remains unspoken – in effect, another denial of the child's self. This might seem far-fetched, were it not for the fact that Earnshaw almost perversely persists in denying what Heathcliff is really like through his idealised view of him; Earnshaw ignores or denies any badness or wrongdoing in Heathcliff, though there are repeated and glaring instances in the narrative. Ellen Dean describes Heathcliff as 'insensible' and comments that she wondered what her master (Mr Earnshaw) saw to admire in 'the sullen boy who never ... repaid his indulgence by any sign of gratitude' (p. 39).

When Earnshaw first brings him home the boy spoke 'some gibberish that nobody could understand', which he 'repeated over and over again'; this conveys not only a sense of literal foreignness – some have taken the description and circumstances of the boy to hint at him being from Ireland or abroad – but also a more deep-seated psychological sense of 'foreignness', in terms of the boy being a *stranger* to the family who cannot understand him. Furthermore, the boy's repetition, 'over and over again', of words that are incomprehensible to the family is a compelling metaphor for the idea of behaviour that is expressive of the child's identity and past but cannot be communicated or understood, and therefore gets repeated.

This profound sense of alienation is also reflected in Ellen Dean's description of the boy's speech as 'some gibberish': this seems partly to suggest an instinctive primitive response to that which is felt to be 'foreign' and 'strange'. This is not to ignore the obvious powerful feelings of jealousy, rivalry, displacement or intrusion which the situation stirred in Hindley, Catherine and Earnshaw's wife (i.e. as a result of the unexpected introduction of a child into the family home, which is of course not the case in adoption), but simply to add or emphasise another dimension to their feelings which is *related to what is unknown about the child*. It is the psychic significance of this latter feature which is frequently less dwelt on or thought about in adoption: that is, the emotional meaning – whether conscious or otherwise – for adoptive parents and child of the *unknown* in the child.

Heathcliff is on one level the personification of 'otherness': within the details of the story this otherness encompasses his marked *difference* in physical appearance (his dark skin and black eyes and hair), the fact that his origins and history are unknown, and the fact that he is an outsider from the family (and from the village and the area). This psychic experience of otherness, of a most extreme form in relation to Heathcliff in *Wuthering Heights*, is a hallmark of the primitive realm of the emotional experience of adoption.

Narrative gaps and absence of the past

Heathcliff's origins and lineage are a blank – he is in effect a cipher, as some commentators have observed. Heathcliff is a complete outsider (as noted above, there is some suggestion he might even be foreign). But in the novel it is far more than simply a matter of the facts of Heathcliff's past not being known by the other characters. The situation is one in which the fact that Heathcliff *has* a past is in effect *erased in the minds of others*. It is a striking feature of the reactions of the characters to Heathcliff that no-one in the family appears to give a thought to his past or background, with the single exception of the nurse Ellen Dean's passing reflection, in relation to his 'sullen, patient' nature, that he might be 'hardened, perhaps, to ill treatment' (p. 38). In adoption, it is not uncommon for the *emotional significance* of the child's actual history and past experience – whether the 'facts' are known or not – to be downplayed, ignored, forgotten or denied in terms of their possible relevance to the present. This is despite a system in which there is clear recognition of the *idea* that the adopted child's past is relevant.

Holding in mind the existence and emotional significance of the adopted child's past – whatever the exact circumstances that led to adoption – is inherently painful; it is a reminder to the adoptive parents of the fact that the adopted child was born to other parents and has a history of being 'not their child', and it therefore touches on all the underlying painful emotional issues (some of which may be unconscious) linked to becoming adoptive parents. This is a challenging emotional and psychological task which is *of a different order from the ordinary tasks of parenting* (see Chapter 6 for discussion of this theme).

There is a further dimension to this difficulty of holding in mind and engaging with the adopted child's past. Nestor (2003), in her Introduction to *Wuthering*

Heights, astutely observes that Earnshaw 'constructs a version of the perfect son in Heathcliff' (p. xxiii). Nestor discusses what Heathcliff comes to represent in the minds of others, and the psychological process by which this occurs. She identifies Heathcliff's '*lack of personal history*' (my emphasis) as a key factor 'which makes him such a suitable focus for others' projections' (ibid.). Nestor writes: 'Lacking a personal narrative ... Heathcliff becomes a receptacle of other people's fantasies' (ibid.). This process of a child becoming the 'receptacle of other people's fantasies' is of course not unique to adoption; however, limited information about an adopted child, or failure to acknowledge the full emotional significance of the 'facts' of a child's history, readily compounds this process. Moreover, even where some of the 'facts' are known, the child's 'personal narrative' is likely to lack the immediacy, continuity and emotional reality of shared, lived experience in the minds of the adoptive parents.

The longing to be one: psychological boundaries of self and other

Nestor also fascinatingly discusses the nature of the relationship between Cathy and Heathcliff, and her discussion of this seems particularly pertinent to the experience of adoption. Nestor argues that in the relationship between Cathy and Heathcliff, 'the novel both recognises and explicitly appeals to a universal desire in relationship for the perfect Other' (p. xxii) (the ultimate example of which might be the wish for a relationship with God, though Nestor does not make this connection herself). She further suggests that Cathy and Heathcliff's relationship speaks to 'the desire for an impossible symbiosis, for a state of non-differentiation between the self and the Other' (p. xxiv) – a desire which she sees expressed in Cathy's declaration, 'I *am* Heathcliff'. Nestor points out that the 'longing for the "Imaginary" [Lacan] union of completeness is not in itself unique or aberrant' (ibid.). However, in the context of adoption, where an infant or young child has been permanently separated from his or her primary attachment figure – normally mother – the primitive and unconscious longing for 'an impossible symbiosis' and the 'desire in relationship for a perfect Other' *are likely to be powerfully intensified*. These may be felt by the child – consciously or unconsciously – in relation either to the birth mother or the adoptive mother. There are obvious potential links with the well-recognised phenomenon of the adoptive child's idealisation of, or longing for, the birth mother, as well as with problems of separation, individuation, and identity (see Chapters 7 and 16), that can be experienced by adopted children.

Nestor goes on to highlight the connection between the universal desire for fusion and the themes of identity and psychological boundaries. She writes: 'Cathy's desire to incorporate or fuse with the other ... brings her into tension with the boundaries of identity' (p. xxvi). Nestor rightly points out that 'Boundaries ... serve the attempt to regulate psychic space' (p. xxvii), and she discusses the vulnerably of such boundaries as a motif in *Wuthering Heights*. This notion of the vulnerability of psychological boundaries also seems pertinent to adoption. Of course, Cathy is *not* an adopted child, and this precisely underscores the point that these impulses and longings are not in themselves unusual or aberrant, though their intensity and primacy in an individual's psychic life may be. However, it is no coincidence that these impulses and longings in Cathy are felt and expressed in her relationship with a child who is in effect adopted. (It should be remembered that Cathy's intensely close relationship with Heathcliff begins in childhood, when she is six and he is of a similar age.)

Drawing on Nestor's argument – though she does not frame it in terms of adoption – we might hypothesise that in adoption *psychological boundaries of self and other are particularly susceptible to specific vulnerabilities associated with specific psychological dynamics*; and that these may have a disturbing or damaging impact on relationships and the quality of family life – as they clearly do in the lives of the characters in the novel. I would suggest that these specific vulnerabilities and dynamics of adoption are partly unconscious – they are in part linked to primitive emotional and psychological processes that have their roots in infancy – and that the manifestations and implications of them are complex, at times far from obvious, and often far from straightforward to understand or recognise.

Psychic pain, loss and losing the capacity to think

In *Wuthering Heights* we see the intensity of primitive feelings stirred in different family members by the introduction of an unknown child into the family. At the most basic level, the adopted child – who represents a living embodiment of painful loss – may be felt and experienced as creating a *disturbance* to the emotional equilibrium of family life, along similar lines to the idea of a new baby as a 'crisis' for the couple (see Chapter 11). If this 'disturbance' within the family cannot be sufficiently contained, it may have a destructive impact on family life and relationships – as it clearly does in the novel. This will be compounded if the adopted child has significant or severe emotional difficulties.

Conventionally it is the hopeful and positive aspects of a new baby or new child in the family which are the primary focus or emphasis in people's minds, but if the focus on these more positive aspects is to the *exclusion* of being able to acknowledge or think about more negative, uncomfortable or painful aspects (as we see with Earnshaw in *Wuthering Heights*) or if more negative aspects predominate in people's minds (as occurs for instance with Earnshaw's son Hindley), serious problems may ensue and people may lose the capacity to think about or process their emotional experience – either their own or that of others. This is precisely what we witness happening in the events of the novel.

Ellen Dean tells Lockwood that the boy taken into the Earnshaw family was christened with 'the name of a son who died in childhood' (p. 38). This single and *easily passed over or forgotten fact* casts a dramatically different light on the emotional dimension of the story. It brings into the frame the theme of the replacement child (Cain and Cain, 1964; Reid, 2003) and of unprocessed losses and bereavements in an adoptive family. It also suggests one possible psychological explanation for the motivation of Earnshaw in taking the boy into the family –

about which there otherwise remains a peculiar silence in a novel which is all about the psychology and inner worlds of its characters. It is noteworthy that although Ellen Dean mentions the fact of the family's loss of a boy who died in childhood, this fact is being told to an outsider and visitor many years after the family events being recounted. Ellen Dean mentions this in passing, and she appears to make nothing of it herself. Within the narrative of the family story, *there is a complete absence of reference to or mention of this family loss* by the characters themselves – and yet at another level the dead child was obviously still in their minds as evidenced by the very fact that the parents gave the dead child's name to the boy who was taken in.

Heathcliff thus occupies a particular space in the minds of the parents and, as a result, in all likelihood also in the minds of their two children: it is a space that would be suffused with the pain of loss, grief and accompanying feelings. This introduces a whole new level of emotional meaning into the events and relationships in the Earnshaw family: one which it would be difficult to ignore or dismiss in terms of its relevance and significance. It suggests the idea of a source of psychic pain from the past which cannot be thought about, yet continues to exert an influence on the inner lives and relationships of the family – and in particular on their responses to the boy whom they name after the dead son. This might in part explain the seemingly 'over-determined' quality of the various family members' reactions to the boy.

We are probably all familiar with the natural impulse *not* to want to be in touch with or dwell upon what is felt to be acutely painful emotionally, and to find ways of keeping this pain at bay. Shakespeare brilliantly captured the wish to be rid of mental pain that is felt to be unbearable, in the following lines:

> Canst thou not minister to a mind diseas'd,
> Pluck from the memory a rooted sorrow,
> Raze out the written troubles of the brain,
> And with some sweet oblivious antidote
> Cleanse the stuff'd bosom of that perilous stuff
> Which weighs upon the heart?
>
> (Shakespeare, *Macbeth*, Act V, Scene III)

Adoptive children and parents are no exception, and this is likely to be an especially complex dynamic where the adopted child's pain touches on or resonates with that of adoptive parents (again see Chapter 6, and also Chapters 4 and 11), either at a conscious or unconscious level. In adoption too, the wish to 'Raze out the written troubles of the brain' can sometimes take the form of an unconscious wish for an 'antidote' to the 'perilous stuff/Which weighs upon the heart'. One version of such an antidote may be either an idealised child or idealised parents (or displaced versions of these).

In the novel, Heathcliff has clearly lost his parents – whatever his precise circumstances were – just as the Earnshaw family has lost a child. And yet, as noted above, no mention whatsoever is made of either of these losses by any member of the family or by Heathcliff. It is precisely as if the emotional experience of these losses has been 'razed out' of their thinking minds. (The nurse Ellen Dean does later in the story (p. 58) encourage Heathcliff to 'frame high notions' of his birth mother and father, but this is in the context of trying to give Heathcliff some way of coping with the 'oppressions' of Catherine's older brother Hindley, and the meaning of her comments is not primarily about Heathcliff's experience of loss in relation to his birth parents, even if this loss is implicit in what she says.)

In fact, there are various examples of characters in *Wuthering Heights* seeking an 'oblivious antidote' to the pain of loss in relation to family bonds, and taken together these constitute a theme of the novel. This theme is in a minor key foreshadowed in the narrative frame of the novel, from which the reader may infer that Lockwood – to whom Ellen Dean recounts the Earnshaw family story – has taken up lodgings in a remote and isolated moorland setting as an 'oblivious antidote' to a broken heart. Heathcliff appears to serve the psychological function of a 'sweet oblivious antidote' for Earnshaw. Heathcliff in turn seems to obliterate any pain of separation and loss in relation to parental figures by obliterating the parent–child relationship itself, as it might pertain to him: he makes no meaningful emotional attachment to either Mr or Mrs Earnshaw, thus becoming a child who is, emotionally, 'unparentable'. In this context, Heathcliff's symbiotic childhood relationship with Cathy seems on one level to function for him as a substitute for the nurturing relationship between child and primary maternal figure, as well as a substitute channel for his primitive emotional life. Cathy in turn perhaps finds in her early childhood relationship with Heathcliff an 'oblivious antidote' to the evident lack of a close emotional bond with her mother, and to the loss (or absence) of her position as loved daughter in her father's mind (Earnshaw 'took to Heathcliff strangely … petting him up far above Cathy, who was too mischievous and wayward for a favourite' [p. 38]). Hindley's marriage seems little more than an attempt to 'raze out' the pains and 'troubles' of his childhood.

In their drive to 'raze out' the 'rooted sorrows' and 'written troubles' of painful family experiences, these characters lose the capacity to think about their psychic pain in a way that could serve to contain and transform it (Bion, 1962, 1967). As a consequence, their behaviour and relationships are frequently determined by the very pain they strive to escape – that is, *enactment replaces thought*. In such circumstances, misperception easily replaces perception: in the novel we see how characters' perceptions of others are often distorted, shaped more by projection of their own inner fantasies or fictions, or by ascription of aspects of themselves to others. Through the action of the novel we are shown how the lives of the characters are to varying degrees shaped by their fictional versions of other characters. This too is a major theme of the novel, also foreshadowed in the narrative frame in the opening pages: Lockwood, on first meeting the adult Heathcliff – in a rare moment of self-insight – catches himself ascribing his own characteristics to Heathcliff: 'I bestow my own attributes over-liberally on him' (p. 6). (Incidentally, this opening scene also introduces and illustrates the idea of Heathcliff as an easy object of other people's projections.)

Thus, the complex, highly patterned and tightly woven inter-generational family plot of *Wuthering Heights* dramatises the sequelae to a family loss of a child and a subsequent adoption; it shows the destructive effects on the characters' relationships and lives of the 'perilous stuff/Which weighs upon the heart' that is connected to these two focal events but cannot be thought about by those involved. (It is beyond the scope of this chapter to describe how these are elaborated through the novel as a whole.)

Loss, loss of self, rejection and hatred

As described earlier, the ways in which Mrs Earnshaw, Hindley, Catherine and the nurse Ellen Dean treat the new arrival in the family are shockingly unsympathetic and heartless at best, and cruelly rejecting, inhumane or sadistic at worst. Mrs Earnshaw refers to him as a 'gypsy brat' and is 'ready to fling it out of doors'; Cathy at first spits at the boy; both Cathy and her brother Hindley refuse to have him 'even in their room'; Ellen Dean 'put it on the landing of the stairs, hoping it might be gone on the morrow' (p. 37); Hindley 'hated him' from the beginning, and regularly hit him; and Ellen Dean tells Lockwood 'we plagued ... him shamefully' (p. 38). Whatever or whoever the boy was, he was self-evidently in an abject state – above all, he is an incarnation of neglect and abandonment. Earnshaw had found the boy starving and homeless in the streets, and the child's physical condition is also a metaphor for a state of emotional starvation. He appears to be a child without parents, without love, without origins – a child who does not belong, and who has lost all. How is it that a child in this state can evoke such cruel responses? What occurs is not just the absence of empathy or concern for the boy, but also something much more active and chilling. Even though in time Cathy and Heathcliff become soul-mates, Cathy 'never put in a word on his behalf, when she saw him wronged' (ibid.). It is as if something about the boy's condition seems to evoke an instinctual and innate sadistic response or trait in each of the other characters.

I suggest that emotionally, this waif – who has lost everything – *represents at a primitive level a terrifying and unthinkable state of utter rejection and non-belonging, and an accompanying loss of identity and non-being.* Earnshaw himself instinctively reacts sympathetically to the boy when he finds him, but his subsequent idealisation and treatment of him once at home is based on an unthinking erasure of the boy's separate identity and blind non-recognition of his actual character. Earnshaw's fictional version of Heathcliff seems to act as a replacement for any *thought* about the reality of his horrifying experience and inner world, or of his hardened personality. With the exception of Earnshaw, the other characters all respond to Heathcliff with *cruel rejection* of varying intensity and persistence. Such cruel and emotionally violent rejection is most obviously expressed in terms of physical ejection or expulsion; this is reflected in Mrs Earnshaw's impulse to '*fling* it [the boy] out of doors', in Cathy's *spitting* at the boy (my emphasis), in the two siblings shutting him out from their room, and in Ellen Dean putting him out 'on the landing of the stairs'.

Cruel rejection is in fact an emotional leitmotif in the novel, and at its root is hatred: this is not merely the ordinary and more everyday hatred of familial relationships, born of frustration, thwarted wishes, rivalry, jealousy and so on (though these do play a significant part in the story too). Rather, it is a visceral and toxic hatred – for some momentary and passing, for others enduring – born of a deep-seated terror. A keynote of this terror is sounded in the narrator Lockwood's nightmare – again a central theme is announced in the opening of the novel: in the dream, *a 'waif' outside his bedroom window knocks importunately, demands to be let in, grasps his arm and holds on tenaciously*. Within the action of the dream Lockwood is adamant that he will *never* let the waif in; and in his report of the dream he tells the reader, 'Terror made me cruel', and that the girl's grip on him was 'almost maddening me with fear' (p. 25). This terror is linked to a primitive, elemental, life-and-death fear of annihilation – a fear that in Lockwood's dream is associated with rejection and exclusion: the waif says she has been wandering on the moors for twenty years, and importunately demands, 'Let me in – Let me in!'

This is an unconscious terror that has its roots in aspects of pre-verbal infantile experience of the kind discussed earlier in this book (see the introduction to Part III); it is also a terror that is liable to be 'expelled', 'exiled' or 'evacuated' (Bion, 1962) from the mind because it is intolerable, and may unconsciously be projected into others. However, having been 'split off' (Klein, 1946) from the conscious mind and unconsciously projected into or ascribed to another, the risk is always of its violent and dangerous return. Some literary commentators on *Wuthering Heights* have suggested that the waif in Lockwood's nightmare symbolises a disowned, unconscious, terrifying part of Lockwood's mind demanding psychological ownership and a 'home': they draw attention to the story of Lockwood's failed romance in which a woman took confused flight from Lockwood's unconsciously cruel rejecting behaviour. It was this episode that led to Lockwood's retreat to the moorlands – representing a kind of 'psychic retreat' (Steiner, 1993) from the pain of experience and self-knowledge.

Conclusion

Within the main story of *Wuthering Heights*, Heathcliff is a personification of otherness and of the outsider in the family; he becomes a receptacle for violent and hateful projections associated with cruel and painful rejection, with devastating consequences for those in the present and subsequent family generations. Heathcliff is taken into the family as a sequel to the death and loss of a child and is named after that child. The novel thus serves as a cautionary tale of the way in which, in adoption, the wish to erase what is painful from the mind can lead to a situation where an adopted child comes to embody or represent unconsciously that which cannot be thought about or tolerated emotionally, because it is felt to be too painful or difficult to process.

References

Bion, W.R. (1962) *Learning from Experience*, London: Heinemann; also London: Karnac, 1984.

Bion, W.R. (1967) 'A theory of thinking', in *Second Thoughts*, London: Heinemann.

Brontë, E. (1847) *Wuthering Heights*, London: Penguin, 2005.

Cain, A. and Cain, B. (1964) 'On replacing a child', *Journal of the American Academy of Child Psychiatry*, 3: 443–56.

Klein, M. (1946) 'Notes on some schizoid mechanisms', in *Envy and Gratitude and Other Works 1946–1963*, London: Hogarth, 1975; also London: Virago, 1985.

Nestor (2003) 'Introduction', to *Wuthering Heights*, London: Penguin.

Reid, M. (2003) 'Clinical research: the inner world of the mother and her new baby – born in the shadow of death', *Journal of Child Psychotherapy*, 29 (2): 207–26.

Steiner, J. (1993) *Psychic Retreats*, London and New York: Routledge.

Final thoughts

Debbie Hindle and Graham Shulman

> It is only in our intimate relationships where our passions are engaged, that
> we can experience the conflict of emotional meaning which nourishes the
> growth of the mind.
>
> (Meltzer, 1984: 46)

These 'final' thoughts represent not so much a 'conclusion' to what has come
before, but rather ideas which have developed or crystallised in our minds out of
the process of producing the book and our ongoing reflection on its themes.

In approaching the end of this book, we found ourselves coming full circle
to thinking again about the centrality of emotional experience to psychic life,
the significance of truth and a sense of truthfulness in emotional experience,
and the importance of continuity to a sense of self. These stand as cornerstones
in psychic growth and development. Adoption – in which discontinuity and
duality of experience are defining features – can present profound challenges
in these areas of psychic life. Throughout the book we have been struck by
the complexity and multiplicity of emotional experience described, and the
resulting complexity of the psychological task of processing and integrating
such experience.

Continuity of being

Winnicott (1960 [1965]: 47) emphasised the importance of the 'continuity of being',
initially linked to physical and psychological 'holding'. He describes 'holding' in
the first instance as a function fulfilled by maternal care, including the need to take
into account the limited ability of the infant to regulate temperature, sensations,
and primitive anxieties. It includes 'the whole range of care throughout the day
and night ... and follows the minute day-to-day changes belonging to the infant's
growth and development' (Winnicott, 1960 [1965]: 49). With ordinary 'good-
enough mothering', in an almost imperceptible way, the infant's environment
provides this essential experience of 'continuity of existence' and 'continuity of
being'. This gradually becomes internalised by the infant, allowing for tolerance
of separation and the beginnings of a sense of self. Winnicott (1960 [1965]: 70)
stresses that it is the *'continuity* of the human environment, and likewise of

the nonhuman environment, which helps with the integration of the individual personality'.

In ordinary life and development, there are of course many everyday disruptions and impingements that are part of an infant's experience. How the infant reacts to these – including their ability to recover and their repeated experience of recovery – with the help of a carer's sensitivity and empathy, is integral to the development of the sense of a 'continuity of being'.

For children who have suffered trauma, neglect or abuse, their earliest experiences may have been characterised by the lack or failure of such 'holding' and of a 'holding' environment. This is most poignantly described in relation to the experience of trauma:

> Trauma means the breaking of the continuity of the line of an individual's existence. It is only on a continuity of existing that the sense of self, of feeling real, and of being, can eventually be established as a feature of the individual personality.
>
> (Winnicott, 1986: 22)

Infants or children who have experienced massive impingements and disruptions to their continuity of existence and of being may need exceptional 'holding' to begin to re-establish, or perhaps even to establish for the first time, something internally that can begin to provide a holding and containing (Bion, 1962) function.

Winnicott (1962: 60) discusses the way in which repeated disruptions to the 'continuity of going-on-being' can have damaging and potentially crippling consequences for a child's emotional and personality development. He argues that the infant's reaction to impingement is itself a disruption to their 'going-on-being', and that 'If reacting that is disruptive of going-on-being recurs persistently it sets going a pattern of fragmentation of being'. Winnicott (1962: 52) incisively observes that, 'In the extreme case the infant exists only on the basis of a continuity of reactions to impingement and of recoveries from such reactions'. This in turn leads to recurrent states of 'disintegration' involving 'an active production of chaos in defence against … unthinkable or archaic anxiety' (Winnicott, 1962: 61).

The potential void of past emotional experience in adoption

When the ordinary but vitally important continuity of experience and continuity of self is disrupted – as has happened to children who are adopted, either in infancy or in childhood – a whole period of their emotional experience and life becomes disconnected from the family and setting in which it was rooted. The situation is perhaps analogous to the past traumatic experience of refugees which belongs to another time and place, though it may be very much alive and present still in their minds. In reality, for many adopted children there have been multiple disruptions and discontinuities in their lives and care situations. The younger the child was adopted, the less accessible this prior emotional experience is to the child's conscious memory and recall. What happens *internally* to the adopted child's emotional experience and life prior to adoption? How does this prior emotional experience find a new *internal, psychic home* in the child's mind – and in the mind of the adoptive parents – after adoption?

Ordinarily, in birth families, it is the child's ongoing relationship with the parents that provides a psychic 'home' and container (Bion, 1962) – and hence the continuity of experience and of self – for the emotional experience of the baby and of the child at different stages of the child's life and development. The narrative of the child's emotional experience from birth is embedded and held in the minds of the parents, and this is the counterpart and container of the child's internal, subjective experience. For adopted children, it is precisely this container – however inadequate it might have been – which has been lost. That is, the child has lost the external 'holder', and the external reference points and bearings, of his or her past emotional life and attachments.

In such circumstances, the adopted child's pre-verbal emotional experience in infancy, and possibly also later experience prior to adoption, can become an *internal* absence, a gap, or a void in the mind. It may continue to exert a profound influence on the feelings, moods, states of mind and behaviour of the child – as happens with any child – but in the case of the adopted child it is de-coupled from the present and from present attachments. The existence in the mind of something indefinable may be apprehended or sensed, but its shape and meaning are beyond the mental grasp of the individual child alone. Even in the circumstances of open adoption, which usually occurs at a time when the child has a conscious memory of their birth parent(s), there is a discontinuity – and therefore a psychic gap – in the internal experience of 'going-on-being' (Winnicott, 1962) which has its roots in infancy and which is linked to the ongoing day-to-day presence and psychological function of the primary attachment figure.

Here there is a parallel between the profound and sometimes unconscious sense of absence linked to the experience of the lost or never-known birth mother and father – particularly for children adopted in the pre-verbal or the very early verbal stage of development – and *a realm of emotional and psychic experience in the inner world* which belongs to a former life that is 'gone forever' and no longer has a home.

Imprisoned pain and temporal splitting

This domain of emotional experience prior to adoption is inherently difficult to be in touch with and to get to know and understand, but it may also be an area of experience that is actively avoided or mentally kept at a distance by the adopted child. One extremely thoughtful teenager who had been adopted in infancy (not at birth) and sought therapeutic help in mid-adolescence told her therapist in a session that she had 'put up a wall' in her mind in relation to thinking about her earliest life and experience before she was adopted. She had always avoided asking questions and finding out information about the story of what happened to her before her adoption, and was aware of 'not wanting to go there' in terms of thinking about this part of her life. It was understandable to her therapist why this teenager had not wanted to think or find out about this first phase of her life and her adoption as a baby, because whenever the subject came up in sessions the girl's eyes welled with tears and she conveyed a sense of immense, overwhelming and acutely painful sadness which was in complete contrast to what she said she felt about her adoption.

This adopted girl was at one level aware that she was avoiding something, but it was clear to her therapist from their discussions that at another level she was equally unaware of, and out of touch with, the nature and depth of her feelings about the loss of her birth mother and about being adopted as a baby. Cognitively the girl knew she had a life prior to being adopted, but she seemed to be keeping her emotional knowledge of this on the 'other side of the wall' in her mind. It was as if the emotional experience and meaning linked to that period of her life was in her mind split off and kept completely separate from the rest of her feelings and life experience.

We might conceptualise this as *'temporal splitting'* – a form of splitting in which the emotional significance of an entire phase or stage of life is mentally separated off from the rest of one's life and disowned or denied. The potential for this type of internal splitting to occur in adoption is self-evident. It also has obvious links with, and may be unwittingly re-enforced by, the fantasy of the 'forever family' where, as Sprince observes in Chapter 6, 'forever' is sometimes taken to imply both after and before the adoption.

This kind of internal emotional 'splitting off' (Klein, 1946) of a significant phase or stage of life prior to adoption can lead to a state of 'imprisoned' or 'frozen' pain (Symington, 2000) linked to the emotional experience of adoption. Indeed, this is implicit in the description of the teenager mentioned above who had been adopted as a baby. She was clearly aware that she had attempted to 'seal off' an area of emotional experience in her mind associated with her life before her adoption. This suggests the idea of a 'sequestered space' within the mind in which extremely painful feelings can be kept 'locked away', and an accompanying fantasy that such feelings do not exist or have no impact on the self. Inevitably, the 'unlocking' of such 'imprisoned' or 'frozen' pain and its 'transformation' (ibid.) is likely to lead to profound 'psychic turbulence' (Daniel, 2000). For adopted children, psychotherapy can offer a space to get to know and understand these more remote or obscure regions of the inner world that are bound up with their earlier and often pre-verbal lives and therefore with the meaning to them of their adoption.

In contrast, attempting to maintain a state of 'psychic equilibrium' (Joseph, 1989) because of fear or anxiety related to such turbulence can give rise to instability and to serious problems – partly because there is usually felt to be a constant or recurrent threat of eruption of this imprisoned pain, which it is feared will have devastating psychological consequences, and partly because it conflicts with the 'intrinsic need for integration' within the self (Klein, 1955).

Another teenager adopted before she was one year old eloquently described the different parts or phases of her life and aspects of her personality as like 'different pieces of a jigsaw', and this was a source of puzzlement but also tension; her therapist suggested that perhaps she felt as if she was not even sure the different pieces were all from the same jigsaw, and this seemed to strike a chord and to make sense for her of her emotional experience linked to her life history and her adoption. While speaking in a session about how she had felt and thought about her adoption before coming to therapy, and the changes in the way she thought about herself and her adoption as a result of therapy, she said evocatively: 'It feels like someone put a knife into my heart, and it burst open with upset.' This seemed to be related to both the original experience as a baby of the loss of her birth mother, and the experience of thinking and talking about it with the therapist in the present.

'Cracked wide open': the emotional impact of adoption

Barbara Waterman (2003: 34) incisively discusses the emotional and psychological process necessary to overcome a major experience of loss. Waterman writes:

> A willingness to have one's heart cracked wide open is, in my experience, a necessary condition for turning a major loss into an opportunity for transformation.

Waterman makes this point in the context of her theme of the psychological process of becoming an adoptive, foster or stepmother. She compellingly argues (2003: 57–8) that:

> The more a mother – biological, adoptive, step or foster – comes to terms with her own life and losses, the more she will be able to be *cracked wide open* as a mother, capable of loving a child for who she/he is rather than needing the child to fulfil a specific identity in her fantasy life.

Drawing on Waterman's idea of having one's heart 'cracked wide open', we would suggest that this powerful and apt metaphor can also fittingly be applied more specifically to the emotional impact of adoption on adoptive parents and child; indeed, we would argue that a necessary emotional condition of a successful adoption is for adoptive parents and child to be willing and able to have their hearts 'cracked wide open'. Where children have experienced traumatic loss or severe abuse or neglect at an early age if not from birth, this willingness to have one's heart 'cracked wide open' means in reality laying oneself open to potentially massive emotional turmoil and impingement, possibly for years, on a scale that for most is far beyond the nature and intensity of ordinary family emotional life and experience. Such emotional impingement and turmoil is likely to be a major challenge to any ordinary parent, as many of the chapters in this book vividly illustrate; for some adoptive parents and families, this challenge to the limits of what is emotionally bearable, endurable and comprehensible may become a recurrent or chronic strain on, or threat to, day-to-day life, relationships and even psychological well-being – taking them to uncharted areas of emotion or emotional intensity that they are not equipped to deal with – and for a few this challenge will be too great.

For adoptive children, who have in one way or another already experienced this type and level of massive emotional turbulence or impingement from the earliest of ages, their need for emotional containment – and the type of containment needed – require their adoptive parents to be open and receptive to their pain and/ or disturbance, and able to withstand it. These are children who have already had their hearts – and in some cases spirits – broken, at an age at which the children themselves may not even be consciously aware it has happened, and being emotionally open and truthful to these children's emotional pain or disturbance is heart-*breaking*. We would speculate that the degree to which there is a willingness and ability in adoptive parents and child to have their hearts 'cracked wide open' will be one of the key determining factors in the quality, strength and resilience of the new attachment relationships between them.

What is required for these children is not emotional 'first-aid' in the form of ordinary parenting – it is 'intensive care' which may be long-term. Intensive care is of course a specialist activity, requiring a team and special equipment. It is enormously labour and resource intensive. For some adoptive families the 'team' and psychological 'equipment' may be sufficiently provided by extended family, friends and an adoption network; however, for others (some might argue for most) – for a variety or combination of reasons – the emotional intensive care needed may only be adequately provided with substantive additional specialist professional input and support.

Finding a psychic home

A young girl, Amy, aged 6½, who had been adopted aged 3 years, was seen by a child psychotherapist initially for three sessions, with a view to trying to understand the worries her adoptive parents found difficult to describe. Although she was getting on well at home and at school, they felt concerned about what seemed to be her lack of emotional connection to them. In her third session, Amy hesitated before selecting the crayons and beginning to draw. With purpose, she drew a house with four walls, a door and windows. To this, she added a roof. But at this point, she hesitated again and carefully coloured in the roof using three separate colours. She paused to look at it and seemed pleased with her efforts. It was an ordinary enough house, but the therapist wondered out loud about the roof with three colours. The therapist then recollected the fact that Amy had had three families – her birth family, her foster family (to whom she had been very attached) and now her adoptive family, and she ventured to suggest that perhaps the three colours stood for her three families. Amy immediately seemed surprised by the therapist's comments, and perhaps also by what she had drawn. Then a sense of real engagement and delight blossomed as she pointed to each colour and reiterated the names of her birth mother, her foster mother and her adoptive mother in turn.

In this brief encounter, something of her emotional experience of the discontinuity of her life could be acknowledged, but also contained within the shape of the single roof. The drawing of the house seemed to be symbolic of this young girl's deeply unconscious sense of self, and to represent an integration of her experience. For Amy, given her good experiences with her foster parents and her adoptive parents, she was able to bring them together 'under the same roof'. The therapist came to see the house Amy had drawn as representing a *home* – an internal sense of a home which could encompass her different and discontinuous experiences.

It was, however, her engagement with the drawing, facilitated by a mind that could attend to a deeper level of her emotional experience, that enabled her to see and to understand something she had not been able to articulate or to consciously grasp. That is, although she knew she was adopted and remembered her foster parents, she had not emotionally been able to put the pieces of what internally felt like a puzzle together. In this session, and in the brief ongoing work, Amy began to establish a more meaningful and personal sense of continuity.

This child's developing capacity to think and to emotionally process her experiences seemed to be a pivotal point, not only for her, but also for her adoptive parents. At the end of the session described, Amy asked to show her drawing to her parents. In subsequent sessions with them, her drawing of the house/home became the focus for further discussions. Amy had been adopted some years after the parents had lost a child in the late stages of pregnancy. They too had painful and disparate experiences to gather together (see Chapter 12). For them, her drawing resonated with their hopes of being a family – the three colours of the roof representing mother, father and child, the three of them together. For all of them, something of the emotional connectedness that the parents had felt was missing started to develop. A sense of home and of family and a real warmth and understanding began to develop between them.

In adoption, the particular constellation of unconscious forces and dynamics in the child, the parents and the professional system can militate against – and sometimes create formidable obstacles to – knowing and being in touch with the reality and complexity of the adopted child's inner world, and of their emotional pain and experience. We hope to have shown, however, that truthful engagement with and understanding of this reality and complexity – by the adopted child, the adoptive parents and the professional network – is of fundamental importance in the forming of new attachment relationships and in the emotional growth and development of the child. In adoption, the conflicts of emotional meaning are among the most complex and primitive, and we believe that the challenges to facing and meaningfully engaging with these – for all those involved – cannot be overstated, and should not be underestimated. Where the primitive and extremely painful conflicts of emotional meaning in adoption can be acknowledged and faced, it is more possible for them to be processed and worked through; in such circumstances, as the above clinical illustration so beautifully illustrates – the adopted child and the adoptive parents may be helped to integrate the disparate, dispersed and often fragmentary elements of the child's emotional experience and life, and to make a more meaningful pattern out of the pieces of the puzzle that makes up the adopted child's inner world.

References

Bion, W.R. (1962) *Learning from Experience*, London: Heinemann; also London: Karnac, 1984.

Daniel, P. (2000) 'Psychic turbulence', in J. Symington (ed.) *Imprisoned Pain and its Transformation*, London and New York: Karnac.

Joseph, B. (1989) *Psychic Equilibrium and Psychic Change*, London: Routledge.

Klein, M. (1946) 'Notes on some schizoid mechanisms', in *Envy and Gratitude and Other Works 1946–1963*, London: Hogarth, 1975; also London: Virago, 1985.

Klein, M. (1955) 'On identification', in *Envy and Gratitude and Other Works 1946–1963*, London: Hogarth, 1975; also London: Virago, 1985.

Meltzer, D. (1984) *Dream-Life*, Strath Tay: Clunie Press.

Symington, J. (ed.) (2000) *Imprisoned Pain and its Transformation*, London and New York: Karnac.

Waterman, B. (2003) *The Birth of an Adoptive, Foster or Stepmother*, London and New York: Jessica Kingsley.

Winnicott, D.W. (1960) 'The theory of parent–infant relationship', in *The Maturational Processes and the Facilitating Environment*, London: Hogarth Press (1965).

Winnicott, D.W. (1962) 'Providing for the child in health and in crisis,' in *The Maturational Processes and the Facilitating Environment*, London: Hogarth Press (1965).

Winnicott, D.W. (1986) 'The concept of a healthy individual,' in *Home is Where We Start From*, Harmondsworth: Penguin Books.

Index

abandonment, adopted child's fear of 58–60, 85–6, 143–4, 169–71
abdicated caregiving 45–6
abuse and neglect 13–14; and adolescent search for identity (case study) 228, 231; and adoption of traumatised children 99–113; early experiences of (case studies) 57–62, 228, 229–35; entrenched damage 60–2; impact of on early development 44–6, 49–50; intergenerational 141–2; loss, rejection and hatred 261–2; and 'premature' psychological birth 237–9, 248; and primitive states of mind 117–18; psychotherapeutic approach to 62–4; 'stories' of adopted and fostered children compared 52–3, *see also* early development; trauma
activities, in therapy sessions 65–8, 127–8, 129–31, 140–5, 160–3
adaptability, and change 53
adolescence 6, 222–4, *see also* idealisation; identity
adopted children: caregivers' knowledge of 91; case studies of 57–62; early memories of 'being dropped and picked up' 136–46; and emotional impact of adoption 268–9; fear of abandonment 58–60, 85–6, 143–4, 169–71; Heathcliff as adopted child (fictional character) 253–62; idealisation of 182–3; identity and alienation 55–6, 106–7; and maternal experience gap 238–9, 266–8; parenting of traumatised child 92–3; and primitive states of mind 118–19; relationships with psychotherapist 64–8, 125–6, 164–5, 210–11, 247; self-image and image of birth parents 5, 16–17, 77–8; 'stories'

of, compared with fostered children 52–3; transition from foster care 155–7, 160–3; transition to adoptive home 182–3; and trauma 91–2, 95–7, *see also* adolescence; babies; early experience; parent–child relationships
adoption: definition of 3; emotional impact of 268–9; explanation and intervention 32–4; historical periods of 2–4; impact of early experience on adoption outcomes 51–3; as intervention 28–32; as motif in *Wuthering Heights* 253–62; motivations and reasons for 90, 170, 223, 254–5; and Oedipus myth 137–8; pre-adoption assessment 180; process and context of 100–1, 102–4; and secondary stress disorders 94–5
adoption support services 3
adoptive fathers 195, 197, 200–1, 202
adoptive mother: anxieties and relationships 87–8, 198; of deprived and damaged child 58; mother–child relationships, and father-figure 198, 200–1, 202, 204; Oedipal and triangular relationships 212–13, 217–18; pregnancy of 142–5; role of, and adolescent's identity 226; trauma and family history 86–7, *see also* couple psychotherapy; parent–child relationships
adoptive parents: and adolescent search for identity 227, 228; and adopted child's past history 113, 256–7; adoptive family life cycle 12; attachment history of 46–8; confidence, and parenting experience of 99–100, 215–16; and emotional impact of adoption 163, 268–9; family psychotherapy sessions 140–2; impact of child's